Ulster

Conflict and Consent

Ulster
Conflict and Consent

TOM WILSON

Basil Blackwell

First published 1989

Basil Blackwell Ltd
108 Cowley Road, Oxford, OX4 1JF, UK

Basil Blackwell Inc.
432 Park Avenue South, Suite 1503
New York, NY 10016, USA

British Library Cataloguing in Publication Data

Wilson, Tom
   Ulster: conflict and consent.
   1. Northern Ireland. Social conditions.
   I. Title
   941.60824
   ISBN 0–631–16245–3
   ISBN 0–631–17006–5 (Pbk)

Library of Congress Cataloging in Publication Data

Wilson, Tom
   Ulster: conflict and consent.
   p.   cm.
   Bibliography: p.
   Includes index.
   ISBN 0–631–16245–3
   ISBN 0–631–17006–5 (pbk.)
   1. Northern Ireland—Politics and government—1969– . 2. Irish question. I. Wilson, Thomas, 1916– .
DA990.U46U37   1989   88–26743
941.60824—dc19   CIP

Typeset in 9½ on 11 pt Ehrhardt
by Opus, Oxford
Printed in Great Britain by T.J. Press Ltd, Padstow, Cornwall

Contents

Acknowledgements

I am indebted to a number of people who have commented on drafts of the book. Sir Charles Carter has read the draft in full and given me the benefit of his advice, not only on the economic issues but on various political and constitutional matters as well. Dr D. G. Boyce has also read the complete draft and made valuable comments on both the historical chapters and those dealing with more recent political issues. Sir Arthur Knight has given me his views not only on industrial development but on other matters discussed in the text. I am much indebted to Dr John Benn, Canon Eric Elliott and the Rt Hon. Basil MacIvor for their comments on education. I have also had an opportunity to discuss the difficult topic of university development in the 1960s with Dr Arthur Williamson. On recent housing policy, I profited from discussion with members of the Northern Ireland Housing Executive. One of the most difficult chapters to write was that on the religious divide, and I derived much assistance from comments made by Canon Elliott, Dr E. R. R. Gallagher and Fr Brian Lennon, SJ. Dr Benn, as former Commissioner for Complaints, has also been helpful on the difficult issue of discrimination. Professor Kieran Kennedy kept me informed about the work of the Economic and Social Research Institute in Dublin on economic development, North and South, and has also given me information on the social services in the Republic. Dr Paul Compton has let me have his advice on demographic issues and has kindly allowed me to reproduce the map showing sectarian divisions on p. 300. Dr Clifford Jefferson has made available statistics on recent changes in industrial location. The Blackstaff Press has kindly allowed me to reproduce a quotation from the poem 'The Coasters' from *The Selected John Hewitt* (ed. Alan Warner, 1981), in chapter 8.

The book has been in preparation for a number of years and I have derived much benefit from discussions and correspondence with a large number of people in public life, in the media and in the universities. Without presenting a long list of names, I should like to express my gratitude to all of them. I must, however, add a specific reference to the assistance I have received from Mr Gordon Gillespie of the Queen's University who has checked both my historical references and many quotations from more recent political statements. Finally, I must acknowledge the vast amount of patient assistance and valuable criticism I have received from my wife throughout the writing of the book. I must, of course, absolve all those I have mentioned from any responsibility for the views expressed in the book on so many controversial topics.

Tom Wilson
Bristol
November 1988

Introduction

The Ulster problem is widely regarded as unique, incomprehensible and insoluble. It is hardly surprising that this should be so after twenty years of civil unrest and terrorist outrage with no end yet in sight. Moreover the present troubles are only the latest phase in the long history of conflict between nationalists and unionists in Ireland. Shortly after the end of the Great War, Winston Churchill observed in a much-quoted speech in Parliament that: 'The integrity of their quarrel is one of the few institutions that has been unaltered in the cataclysm that has swept the world.' Long after a second great conflict, in a world that has witnessed further changes of immense importance, the integrity of the ancient quarrel seems unimpaired. Various attempts have been made to find an answer but these have seemingly failed. Thus it has become increasingly hard to avoid the conclusion that the problem remains unsolved because it is inherently insoluble.

The basis for this pessimism clearly needs to be further examined and assessed. What is also illuminating is to consider the practical significance of such a pessimistic verdict if it should prove to be unavoidable. What inferences for policy must then be drawn? In particular, how should British attitudes be modified – if modified at all – in the light of such a conclusion? One possible inference is that Britain should withdraw from Ireland and 'bring the troops back home'. If the results of the opinion polls are reliable, there is now a substantial body of opinion in favour of abandoning Ulster, and the apparent hopelessness of continued effort is presumably one of the principal explanations. For it must appear, on the face of it, as though British blood and British treasure have been expended to no avail, and the terrible and quite pointless waste should now be ended. Any suggestion of callousness towards British people in Northern Ireland that may be conveyed by this recommendation is then seemingly dispersed – with a rapid switch from hopeless pessimism to cheerful optimism – by asserting that, if left to themselves in this way, the 'Irish' would soon find an appropriate answer. It is hardly necessary to add that the IRA strongly endorses this opinion, but those Irish nationalists who oppose violence in favour of a constitutional approach are in a more difficult position. For them too the British troops are 'an army of occupation' but they are also well aware of the dangers of a withdrawal. Their plea to Britain has been described by Dr Conor Cruise O'Brien as: 'Please say you're going, but for God's sake stay' – a plea which, as he observes, has the advantage that it 'gives equivocal voice to equivocal aspirations'. If it came to crunch, the Ulster Catholics, for their part, might be at least as apprehensive as the Ulster Protestants about the sequel to withdrawal. At Westminster, no government of any party has so far believed that it would be prudent policy to abandon Ulster to its fate. For it is feared that the civil war only just averted by the intervention of the army in 1968, might then start in earnest with consequences that could not be ignored by the neighbouring island. Indeed, by giving almost unanimous support to the Anglo-Irish Agreement of 1985, the British Parliament has bound itself to retain Northern Ireland as part of the United Kingdom unless a majority of the inhabitants express a desire to depart.

My purpose in referring, at this stage, to these controversial topics is to show how confusion is liable to follow when it is implied that it is only possible to contrast a situation where a 'solution' has been found, with one where no solution has been found. From the point of view of practical policy, the objective must be to adopt whatever measures are most likely to ameliorate the situation, even if a 'solution' – in some ultimate and usually undefined sense – should prove to be elusive. From this standpoint, it is clear that the efforts made during the past twenty years have not been in vain. The worst disaster – that of outright civil war – was averted and there followed a very marked decline in the scale of violence. Moreover, if more has not been achieved, the explanation may be that certain mistakes were made which were not inherent features of the 'Ulster problem' and might have been avoided. So much is what clearly emerges from a common-sense approach, and more relevant questions follow. How much amelioration has to be achieved before, in a deeply imperfect world, a solution will be deemed to have been achieved? What are the obstacles that impede progress, and where does the responsibility for them lie?

Whether soluble or not, the Ulster problem is by no means unique and incomprehensible. There is nothing unique about a conflict between rival national aspirations, and nothing unusual about the complaint that minorities have been or may be, oppressed. It is true that whatever the country where such problems are encountered, there will be marked traces of local colour, but there is no apparent reason why the situation in Ulster should defy understanding to an extent not experienced elsewhere. If, for many observers, a suggestion of incomprehensibility nevertheless persists, the explanation may well be found in the fact that the names of the Christian denominations – 'Catholic' and 'Protestant' – are used in order to identify the protagonists. For the absurdity, as well as the impropriety, of such a conflict seems obvious to people in other nominally Christian countries where, for a variety of historical reasons, there has not been the same correlation between denominational attachment and political loyalty. It is indeed true that the religious factor remains important in Ulster, as in the rest of the island, but it is hard to see how that fact, in itself, can warrant the complaint that the Ulster problem defies understanding.

If an understanding is to be achieved, the first step is to appreciate the importance of certain views about Irish nationality and to recognize that these views are based on misconception. This is the purpose of my first chapter.

There appears to be a strong inclination to accept without question the notion that the people of one island must constitute one nation, but those of two islands cannot possibly do so. What is now termed 'the map-image' has a marked effect on practical attitudes adopted towards Northern Ireland, not only in Ireland itself but in England and the United States of America as well. There is also an unquestioning attachment to the myth of a historic Irish nation, supposed to exist before the English came to Ireland. Irish unity is an entirely proper objective; but its achievement calls for a creative task of new construction, not one of pseudo-antiquarian restoration. Those who wish to pursue that creative task will do so more effectively if unencumbered by false assumption and unsustainable beliefs. Irish nationalist politicians are wont to assert that 'the Irish nation has an indefeasible right to unity'. But national unity is not a question of 'right'. It is a question of tradition, sentiment and common purpose. Although the members of any particular nation may differ widely in their views on many matters, they must, nevertheless, have enough in common to want to belong to the same state and to live under the same central government. A nation, in this sense, needs to be founded on a *consensus*, and that is a far more searching requirement than a ballot-box majority. There is no such consensus among the people who live in the island of Ireland, and they cannot be said to constitute a 'single nation' in any normally recognized sense of the term. To claim that they do so is to ignore 'the integrity of their quarrel' and to suggest, with a disregard for both history and recent experience, that there has been no real disagreement after all about national identity. It is to overlook the fact that Irish nationalists have insisted on complete separation from the United Kingdom and have refused to accept the unity of the two islands. The Ulster unionists, for their part, have sought to maintain that unity – hence their name – and have demonstrated in the most unambiguous way that they do not want to belong to the Irish Republic. Indeed it is hard to see how the two sides in Ireland could have displayed more clearly a divergence of views about the political unity of the island of Ireland on the one hand, and the unity of the British Isles on the other.

In order to understand this conflict of national loyalties, it is necessary to look back over Irish history. History records that Ireland was invaded by the English; but so, of course, were Scotland and Wales. Those two countries have successfully retained a sense of national identity, but have combined it with a sense of British nationality and so remain part of the United Kingdom. In Irish nationalist eyes, however, there is an inescapable conflict between being Irish and being British. How have these differences in attitude come about? Why did Irish nationalism – which became an important force only as late as the second half of the nineteenth century – lead to a demand for complete separation? This is one of the questions to which we shall address attention in the first part of the book.

In writing this historical section, I have been faced with the difficulty that, although I have been deeply interested in Irish history for many years, I am not a professional historian. One possibility would have been to confine myself to a highly summarized record of the main events, but I am inclined to the view that such skeleton accounts convey little meaning except to those readers who are already familiar with the history and do not, therefore, need them. A more extended treatment has seemed appropriate and one that would, moreover, be focused directly on the factors that led to the divergence in national sentiment and loyalty. That focus was desirable, but it entailed a cost, for some important aspects of Irish history have recived little attention. For example, I am conscious of the fact that little is said about the immense cultural achievements of the Protestant Ascendancy.

But it was hard to see how such deficiencies could be avoided without a further substantial addition to the length of the book.

Partition would have provided a neat solution to the conflict of national identities in the island if the population in the six counties that remained withing the United Kingdom had been a homogenous group of Protestant unionists. Admittedly, even with that condition met, the more visionary nationalists would probably have been dissatisfied and would have tried to assert a 'historic' claim to the whole of the island. But they would have had some difficulty in carrying conviction. The real situation was quite different, for a substantial minority of the population of Northern Ireland was Catholic – initially about a third, now close to two-fifths – and Catholics are assumed to be nationalists. The price of self-determination for the Ulster unionists was, therefore, its denial for the Ulster nationalists. Although the border could have been better drawn, there was no other way of drawing it that would have avoided this difficulty.

The impossibility of reconciling the different claims to self-determination has been the core of the Irish problem. It is essentially for this reason that the problem has been judged insoluble.

National self-determination is not, however, the only objective of human endeavour, and the weight accorded to it, in competition with other objectives, may alter over time. Moreover opinions can change, and those who wish to see such a change can take positive action to bring it about. Irish nationalists, for their part, have always maintained that they want a united Irish nation, and the task for them should have been to win over – not score over – the million Protestants in Northern Ireland. We must inquire whether the nature of this constructive task has been clearly perceived, and how it has been approached. This question will be encountered and discussed at various points in the book, and more specifically, in chapter 21.

A similar question must be asked about the attitude of the Protestant or unionist majority in the six northern counties towards the Catholic minority. Did the majority seek to reconcile that minority to its loss of self-determination? The responsibility for dealing with this minority problem was made to rest all the more directly with the Ulster majority because the Government of Ireland Act of 1920 accorded Northern Ireland a large measure of legislative devolution. The outcome was bound to depend upon the willingness of the minority to cooperate with the majority in devolved government, and upon the readiness of the majority to make room for the minority and to welcome its participation.

The future of the northern state was the central issue at every election. For this reason – not as a consequence of electoral malpractices – the Unionists remained in power throughout the whole period of devolved regional government. In such circumstances discrimination in favour of the majority was liable to occur. There was nothing unique or incomprehensible about such favoured treatment. All governments everywhere are disposed 'to look after their own'. But the unfairness of patronage is diluted when there is an alternation of parties in power. Unfortunately in those areas where the same party holds office for long periods, this corrective adjustment does not take place and Ulster, as we have observed, was one of those areas. In Northern Ireland there is the further complication caused by using the names of religious denominations which suggests that discrimination has reflected the bitterness of doctrinal differences. Discrimination, when it occurred, may seem less bizarre – though not, for that reason, defensible – if, from time to time, we substitute 'unionist' and 'nationalist' for 'Protestant' and 'Catholic' respectively.

In the second part of the book, the treatment of the minority in Northern Ireland will be subjected to detailed examination. 'Discrimination' is, of course, an emotive term that will have to be defined. In these chapters, particular attention is given to a number of important areas: recruitment and promotion in both public and private employment; the geographical location of new industries; housing policy; and education in an area where the Churches have insisted on denominational segregation.

In dealing with these topics, the various measures of reform are reviewed, both those taken under the old Unionist regime and those adopted since 1972 when legislative devolution came to an end and was replaced by 'Direct Rule' from Westminster. That year marked a watershed. It is important to stress this point for allegations of discrimination are frequently made in such a way as to leave the vague impression that the Unionist Party is still in power. In fact the responsibility for ensuring that all are treated fairly – in so far as this lies with the competence of government – has rested with Westminster for about seventeen years.

This experiment with legislative devolution in Northern Ireland between 1921 and 1972 has been the only one of its kind in the United Kingdom. The experience thus gained should be relevant in assessing the case for future changes in sub-central government in Great Britain – whether for some form of regional government, which still has its supporters, or for the extensive reform of local government. What is of particular importance is that these lessons from the past should be properly taken into account in considering whether devolution, in one form or another, ought to be restored in Northern Ireland itself.

The responsibilities of the Northern Ireland Parliament, as established in 1920, were very wide, as is explained in the second part of this book. But fiscal autonomy was narrowly constrained, with taxing power limited and expenditure closely supervised by Whitehall both in total and detail. Moreover, less assistance was provided than that given to other poor regions within the UK – a fact that has not usually been observed. Output per head, though higher than in the Republic, was low by British standards, and unemployment was heavy. For these reasons serious difficulties were encountered in providing public services for all citizens of the area, and a distorted impression will be gained if attention is narrowly confined to the treatment of the minority. All were affected by these difficulties and all benefited after the Second World War, largely as a consequence of a long period of world prosperity but partly as a consequence of the expansion of the welfare state and of the development programmes adopted by the Unionist Government in the 1960s in order to improve the infrastructure, extend the training of the labour force and provide various forms of industrial assistance. As it happened, I was associated as consultant with the preparation of two of those programmes and, in writing this part of the book, I have been able to draw, to some extent, upon personal experience.

A large improvement in personal living standards and in the provision of welfare benefits had taken place over the twenty years preceding the revolt of 1968. It is often assumed that revolts occur when conditions are getting worse, but there is plenty of experience from different countries to show that increasing prosperity may also lead to unrest. For the improvements already achieved can have the effect of raising expectations to unattainable heights, and bitter disputes may also arise about the distribution of the rising flow of benefits.

The protests made by the Civil Rights Movement in the late 1960s were soon followed by conflicts between rival mobs, and the small police force was unable to cope. As has been observed, Northern Ireland was moving rapidly towards civil war when the British army was called in – a fact that must not be forgotten. Mob violence gradually declined but a new terrorist campaign had been launched which still continues in the late 1980s. As is explained in Part III, the sequence of events in Northern Ireland may be regarded as a classic example of the evolution of a modern guerilla campaign and there may be lessons here that are sadly relevant elsewhere.

In seeking to restore some form of provincial government in 1973, the British Government proposed an ambitious and unique experiment which came to be known as 'power-sharing'. Unfortunately this term has given rise to serious misunderstanding outside Northern Ireland, and its true meaning requires to be carefully examined and explained. At this stage it must suffice to observe that it did not amount to the simple granting of ordinary political rights – for those had always been provided – but to the institution of proportional representation, not only in elections to a new Assembly but in determining the composition of the Executive as well. What was implied was permanent coalition government. It was not easy to envisage such an arrangement working satisfactorily in Northern Ireland where there was not even a consensus about the existence of the state itself. Thus the conditions that made 'power-sharing' in this sense seem desirable, also made its success less likely. In the event, the new system of government worked surprisingly well during its brief lifetime. It was, however, opposed from the outset by the hard-line Unionists whose popular support, initially limited, was to grow when it became clear that even power-sharing would not bring peace. For the IRA's concern was to seize power, not to share it, and it chose to intensify rather than abandon its terrorist campaign. Moreover an attempt to combine power-sharing with the establishment of a new institutional link with the Republic – a Council of Ireland – aroused widespread suspicion in the unionist majority. The climax was an extremely effective strike which brought the brief experiment to an end in 1974.

Some further attempts were made, over the following decade, to restore devolved government of one kind or another, but two obstacles were encountered: the SDLP, undeterred by the experience of 1974, would accept no arrangement that lacked an 'Irish dimension', and the Unionists, especially the Paisleyite wing, were opposed to sharing power with what was regarded as an essentially nationalist party. Over these years, it was a principle of British policy that all parties should be consulted and no new scheme adopted unless it had general support. After many years of failure, this approach was abandoned and the Anglo-Irish Agreement of 1985 was imposed entirely without consultation. Thus the Ulster people felt themselves severely snubbed, and this treatment was the more keenly resented by the majority because the leader of the Ulster nationalist party – the Social and Democratic Labour Party – had been consulted throughout, not by the British but by the Irish Government.

The Anglo-Irish Agreement can be regarded as an attempt to resolve the conflict of national aspirations. The unionists – the British/Irish – were given an understanding that their position in the UK would be secure unless a majority of the total population of Northern Ireland were to vote for joining the Republic; the minority was provided with a new advocate in the person of the Foreign Minister of the Republic who would defend their views at regular conferences with the Secretary of State for Northern Ireland, and would also symbolize the national sentiment that linked them with the Republic. It has the appearance of being an ingenious arrangement, though scarred from the outset by the manner of its introduction. On closer examination, however, it is apparent that it suffers from serious weakness and from damaging ambiguities in its drafting. These faults are described in chapter 19.

The fact remains that, for good or ill, it has established a framework for future policy which may be modified but is unlikely to be abandoned.

The attitude of people in Great Britain to Ulster has been greatly affected by the strike of 1974 and by the indignant response to the Anglo-Irish Agreement of 1985. On both occasions unionist behaviour appeared rough and unreasonable, and the case for withdrawing from Ireland seemed to have been strengthened. The unionists, for their part, felt that they had been betrayed – even by Mrs Thatcher. It is important to understand why this was so, but also to recognize that disillusionment with Britain has led to no greater feeling of kinship with the Republic. In so far as sentiment has moved away from Britain, the movement has been in the direction of an independent Ulster.

In the last section of the book, I abandon the chronological approach and take up some issues of central importance. The first is the religious divide. The continuing importance of religious differences needs to be assessed with attention directed to the social consequences within Northern Ireland and also to the implications, as perceived by non-Catholics, of becoming members of an Irish Republic where the Roman Catholic Church is still powerful. I then go on to discuss the attitudes of the Churches to violence. Violence has, in fact, been roundly condemned by Church leaders and there has been much more cooperation in dealing with its consequences than may be realized outside the Province. The distinction between 'violence' and the legitimate use of 'force' has been drawn in statements presenting the attitudes of Church leaders, but little attempt has been made to explain this distinction to the general public. On the contrary the distinction has often been blurred in clerical statements about terrorist activity on the one hand and the actions of the security forces on the other. Although ecclesiastical authority must not be exaggerated, even in the case of the Roman Catholic Church in Ireland, a further contribution could very well be made towards the task of combating terrorist violence.

Chapter 21 has the rather mysterious title 'The Republic and its Three Minorities'. The explanation lies in Article 2 of the Constitution of the Republic which asserts a *de iure* claim to the whole of the island. This claim is still maintained and we must assume that it is viewed with respect even by constitutional nationalists.

Thus the Republic has three minority groups. First, there is the Protestant majority in the North. Have successive governments and the leaders of public opinion in the Republic treated these Protestants as fellow citizens who are entitled to consideration and – not least – to protection? The second minority group is the Catholic population in the North, for it would be wrong to assume that they are no different from Catholics living in the Republic as already established. The third minority consists, of course, of the non-Catholics living in the Twenty-Six Counties. Their position has always been a matter of close interest to non-Catholics in the North.

The prolonged terrorist campaign is a cause as well as a symptom of disaffection. For a country can be caught in a vicious circle of violence with killings on one side provoking killings by the other. The action of the security forces can also lead to fresh grievances, even if they behave with the utmost restraint, and at times some of their members may be so goaded that they will fail to do so. It is often said that action against terrorism will not succeed without social and political reform. Many reforms have been carried out, but the IRA has no interest in reforms and, in the areas it dominates, can exert brutal pressure on those who might wish to respond. The need for an intensified anti-terrorist campaign seems apparent, but the difficulty is to determine the form such a campaign should take.

The problems confronting the security forces and the judiciary are described in chapter 22: the border which provides an escape route for the terrorists; the urban bases in areas dominated by them; the proper anxiety to keep to a minimum the infringement of normal civil rights. The Irish Government, for its part, has not succeeded in convincing people in Ulster that it has been conducting a whole-hearted campaign against terrorism.

The controversy about the judiciary, in particular the Diplock Courts in Northern Ireland, is reviewed and a comparison drawn with the powers accorded to the Special Court in the Irish Republic. The difficulty of obtaining convictions even against persons who are well known to be assassins has led to a proposal for internment, in both parts of the island, as in 1955/62. It is hardly necessary to add that this is a highly complex and controversial matter which must be handled with caution. Some possible scenarios can, however, be sketched.

The view that the Ulster problem is insoluble is sometimes qualified by the assertion that it will be solved in time by demographic change. Indeed it is widely believed that, within a few years, the Catholics will outvote the Protestants, and the North will then be absorbed into a united Ireland. On the basis, however, of the recent trends discussed in chapter 23, it will be well into the next century before there will be a Catholic majority of voting age. Indeed there may never be such a majority, for the Catholic birth rate has been falling and may continue to do so. A large change in relative emigration rates might occur which could affect the outcome, one way or the other, but it is reasonable to leave aside the somewhat remote possibility of a Catholic majority in formulating current policy. Moreover a majority, even if achieved, would be too narrow a foundation for national unity. Once more it is necessary to stress that genuine unity must rest on a *consensus*.

Economic conditions on both sides of the border impose a severe constraint on political change. It is essential to abandon the belief that in some undefined – and indeed undefinable – sense, Ireland is an economic unit. Both areas depend upon wider trade connections, and must continue to do so if a tolerable standard of living is to be maintained. There is some obvious scope for cooperation in economic affairs but that has been achieved and could be extended without political unity.

Political unity would raise new economic difficulties. The Republic has what are probably the highest taxes in the EC and is burdened by a vast national debt, two-fifths of it in foreign currency. Union with the Republic would mean, for the North, acceptance of a share of responsibility for that debt in addition to the loss entailed by departure from the British welfare state. For the Protestant majority, cold calculation as well as national sentiment is against Irish unity. Ulster's Catholic minority, for its part, is by no means indifferent to the fact that unity would be purchased only at the cost of heavy losses to themselves. Successive opinion polls have suggested that less than 10 per cent of the *total* population in the North want to leave the United Kingdom. Of course, such expressions of opinion must be treated with caution, but the results have been too consistent to be ignored.

If demography does not open the path to unity and economic conditions impose a barrier to it, does it follow that the conflict between national aspirations will persist indefinitely with the apparent corollary that, for an indefinite period, the Ulster problem will remain unresolved? And, if unresolved, must it be anticipated that the frustration will be so deep and bitter that a reasonable measure of peace and tranquillity will be unattainable? In fact, as is shown in chapters 21 and 23, the desire for Irish unity appears to be much less widespread and far less strong, both in the Republic and among the Ulster minority, than might be supposed from the repeated assertions of nationalist politicians. If those politicians could somehow be induced to recognize that fact and also to accept the full implications of their own assertion that national unity must be based on a genuine consensus of sentiment and purpose, the situation would be transformed.

The final chapter brings together and summarizes the proposed social and political changes that should accompany an intensified drive against terrorism. Of the various political changes required, by far the most important is the need to remove uncertainty about the constitutional position. Northern Ireland has been governed under supposedly provisional arrangements for almost seventeen years and the uncertainty thus perpetuated has been an incentive to the subversives to carry on their campaign and has also done much harm to economic development. It is time to determine, one way or the other, whether devolved government, in some form, is to be restored. What is of much greater importance is to establish clearly and unequivocally the fact that Northern Ireland will remain part of the United Kingdom for an indefinite period ahead. That fact itself is not seriously in doubt but, quite needlessly, it is made to appear so by the British reluctance to make appropriate constitutional adjustments. The nature of these changes is discussed in the final chapter.

In that chapter, it is maintained that if Irish nationalists were to concede that unification must be left to a distant future, they would cut the ground from under the republican militarists and open the way towards reconciliation with the Ulster majority and thus to the ultimate unification they profess to desire. For, if genuine unity is ever to be achieved, the integrity of the ancient quarrel must surely be broken.

PART I
Independence or Unity?

1

Island, State and Nation

'A nation is a group of people bound together by a common error as to their origin and a common hatred of their neighbours.' There is an uncomfortable element of truth in this observation of Arnold Toynbee's. Nationalism has usually been nurtured on myth and has often been given a distinct delineation by suspicion and dislike of others. A nation can thus derive a measure of self-confidence from romantic tradition that cold history may fail to provide, and this nurturing of self-confidence may be particularly important after a long period of rule by another country in which local people have been treated as dependent and inferior. Such has been the common experience, and Ireland has shared in it. But it is also the common experience that unless myths are uprooted or drastically pruned once nationality has been successfully asserted, their effect can only be harmful. The harm may take the familiar forms of over-aggressiveness, of an exaggerated suspicion of other nations and of a reluctance to work together with them for a common good. In the case of Ireland, the damage has been still more extensive, for a too close attachment to myth has fostered attitudes and policies that have proved to be a barrier to the achievement of one of the objectives most dearly prized by Irish nationalists themselves: the union, in a single nation, of all the people who live in the island of Ireland. A belief has been fostered in an ancient all-embracing nationhood, suppressed but never extinguished, that claims the recognition and commands the loyalty of all. What has thus been concealed is the troublesome fact that such unity never existed but is rather something that nationalists have yet to achieve. Mistaken attitudes and self-defeating policies have followed from this erroneous initial assumption in ways that will be described in some of the chapters that follow. The first step, however, must be to examine the myths that have encouraged self-deception and to confirm that they are indeed without foundation. In doing so, we shall be engaged in no mere academic pursuit for these beliefs have had, and continue to have, an important effect in shaping Irish nationalist policies and in influencing the views of many people outside Ireland who concern themselves with Irish affairs.

A quotation will provide a neat summary of the unfounded assumptions on which political attitudes have been based. It is taken from the *Handbook of the Ulster Question* prepared for the government of the Irish Free State in 1925 as a basis for negotiating a change in the Border with Northern Ireland.

Ireland is by natural design a complete geographical entity. This natural design enforced on the political life of Ireland at an early date the idea of national unity, and it is doing violence, not only to nature but to the whole trend of the political life of the island to divorce politically at this late date in her national existence a considerable section of the northern population from the motherland.[1]

We have here a clear official statement of an assertion often made in the past and still repeated today. In the Sinn Fein election manifesto of 1918, it had already been held that the claim to nationhood put forward by this party at that time was 'based on our unbroken tradition of nationhood, on our possession of a distinctive national culture and social order'.[2] The following year de Valera, then the leader of Sinn Fein, told an American audience that Ireland had been 'a nation before Augustine set foot on English soil' and he insisted that: 'The Irish nation is *one* nation not two.'[3] Forty years later Sean Lemass, when Prime Minister, endorsed this view:

It is, indeed, the simple truth that Ireland is one nation, in its history, in its geography and in its people, entitled to have its essential unity expressed in its political institutions . . . Ireland is, by every test, one nation. *It is on that essential unity that we found our case for political integration.*[4]

Of the many other quotations that might be given, the most appropriate is from the Constitution of 1937:

Article 2: The national territory consists of the whole island of Ireland, its islands and the territorial seas.

Article 3: Pending the reintegration of the national territory, and without prejudice to the right of the Parliament and Government established by this Constitution to exercise jurisdiction over the whole of that territory, the laws enacted by that Parliament shall have the like area and extent of application as the laws of Saorstat Eireann [i.e. the Irish Free State] and like extraterritorial effect.

It is these articles that have caused such deep offence to British people in Northern Ireland who are thus deemed to belong to the Irish Republic whether they wish it or not. The offence thus given has done nothing to foster a unity that should be genuine, not pretended, but has, on the contrary, provoked a reaction that only makes the claim itself more unwarranted and more unrealistic. The repeal of Articles 2 and 3 would indeed be a helpful step in fostering goodwill and reconciliation and it may be worthwhile to observe in passing that, apart from the direct affront they convey, these articles can have practical effects that have done nothing for unity. For example the security forces in the Republic are forbidden to hold any direct communication with the British army in Northern Ireland which, given Article 2, is held to be improperly present on national soil. All messages, however urgent, concerning operations against terrorism must therefore be transmitted through the Northern Ireland police who are deemed to be a legitimate force – at least in principle.

While these unilateral assertions remain part of the Republic's constitution, the supporters in the North of the union with Great Britain will naturally be unimpressed by any pledge – such as that given in the Anglo-Irish Agreement of 1985 – that the status of the Six Counties will not be altered without the consent of a majority of the inhabitants. They are well aware that, notwithstanding the

Agreement, any attempt by a Dublin government to achieve the repeal of these Articles – which would require a referendum in the Republic – might well be defeated. When the Agreement was debated in the Dail, the leader of the Opposition (then Charles Haughey) strongly denounced the pledge to the North because, in his view, it implied the recognition of partition and was therefore inconsistent with the Articles quoted above.[5] All this was a repetition of what had already happened in Dublin, in a more dramatic way, in 1974 during the power-sharing experiment in Northern Ireland, as we shall see in chapter 17.

It is important to understand why this attachment to unreal assumptions should be so firmly maintained by Irish nationalists. Indeed it should require no great exercise of the imagination to appreciate something of the bitterness that must have been felt when, after a long and hard struggle, independence from Britain was achieved only at the cost of a divided island. It was an outcome that could and should have been foreseen, but that fact did not make its realization any the less unpleasant. One can also understand the concern felt by Southern Catholics about the fate of the Northern Catholic minority who, it was feared, would be the victims of an Orange tyranny. That, however, was really a different point for it cannot be supposed that, even if this concern has been shown in the event to be without foundation, partition would then have been acceptable to strongly committed Irish nationalists.

The belief that the unity of Ireland is, in some sense, 'natural' is by no means confined to these nationalists. Its truth is also taken to be self-evident by many other people both in Great Britain and abroad. Thus the British Labour Party is already committed to give its support to the ultimate achievement of this unity. In some undefined sense, the political division of the island is regarded as 'artificial', a distortion contrived in the past that ought now to be removed by the absorption of the six Northern counties into the Republic. Presumably there would be a good deal of support outside Ireland for the assertion made in 1984 by the New Ireland Forum that the origin of the modern Irish problem was 'the imposed division of Ireland which created an artificial political majority in the North'.[6] Because British mistakes in the past are believed to have created this state of affairs, some British people appear to have feelings of uneasiness and guilt about the fact that part of the island is still under British rule and defended by British troops. This hesitant posture is an incentive to the IRA terrorists to keep up their pressure in the belief that the British will lose heart and withdraw.

What, then, are the grounds for the proposition that – as a matter of fact, not just as an expression of desire – the island of Ireland comprises a single nation? Why should any sense of nationality be said to embrace the whole island but to be prevented, by a sanitary cordon of salt sea water, from extending beyond its shores, so that the Irish people must therefore stand alone, separate and politically isolated from the people of the neighbouring island of Great Britain? Such questions clearly call for answers, and the answers given may be conveniently grouped under two headings: first, that it is in some sense natural for the people of one island to form one nation; and secondly, that a historical Irish nation of great antiquity has been arbitrarily broken apart and divided into two unnatural parts which should now be reunited. We shall now consider these answers in turn.

THE MAP-IMAGE AND THE NATION

The term 'geographical unit', like the term 'economic unit', is rarely, if ever, defined but it can be used in such a way as to convey an impression of scientific assessment and can win unwarranted respect and support for propositions which, on closer scrutiny, are seen to be vacuous or false. Thus, when it is claimed that Irish political unity is dictated by geography, this claim really amounts, first, to making the undeniable assertion that Ireland is an island and, secondly, to assuming implicitly, and quite wrongly, that there can be only one nation in one island. It should be necessary to do no more than make this reasoning explicit in order to show that it lacks foundation. For there is no natural law which requires that single islands must always correspond to single nations. Yet the assumption, provided it is kept concealed, that there is such a law can often go unchallenged. Sometimes the high-sounding phraseology, of which examples have been given above, may be deliberately favoured because, if not examined too closely, it appears to provide objective scientific support for the nationalist aspiration – which, as an *aspiration*, is of course entirely legitimate. But the acceptance of this strange geographical doctrine may also have been unconsciously acquired from long exposure to what is now described as the 'map-image'.

The effect of map-images in making people uncritically receptive to political conclusions has received a good deal of attention in recent years. To quote from Boulding: 'the shape of the map that symbolises the nation is constantly drilled into the minds of both young and old, both through formal teaching in schools and through constant repetition in newspapers, advertisements, cartoons and so on.'[7] The relevance of this effect to the formation of opinion in Ireland is clear. To quote from Heslinga:

The absolute claim that the Republic makes to Northern Ireland ultimately rests on the assumption that 'Ireland was always regarded as one nation, clearly defined and bounded by the hand of God'. To many Irishmen it is almost a slogan that the Creator has predestined Ireland to be a national and political unit, because it is a 'perfect geographical entity' in the sense of a natural (physical) entity. This belief, a typical instance of confusion between natural features and the Divine will, has many parallels.[8]

It is of interest to note that Heslinga's quotations contained within this passage are from evidence submitted to the Foreign Affairs Committee of the House of Representatives in Washington in 1950, which shows how widely this dubious reasoning has been disseminated. The map-image has also attracted critical attention from Bowman who describes how it has its effect: 'This constant exposure to the map shape is particularly prevalent in Ireland, whose external morphology, being an island, is sharply delineated ... Given that the state [i.e. the Irish Republic] occupies so much a large part of the island, it is scarcely exceptional that the map used is that of Ireland.' He goes on to add that the border between the Republic and Northern Ireland is constantly omitted.[9]

The map-image, in this context, fosters an insularity of national sentiment that extends to the whole of an island but does not extend beyond it. The blue-coloured sea seems to suggest so formidable a barrier to communication that those who live on different sides of the blue must constitute separate nations. The sea may, indeed, be a barrier, but may also – as in Greece – provide a means of communication less difficult than communication by land. In the case of Northern Ireland, it was certainly easier, in past centuries, to cross to Scotland, only a dozen miles away at the closest point, than it was to travel overland for two to three hundred miles across forests, bogs and mountains, in order to reach the south of the island. The association between Ulster and Scotland is very ancient and extends back far beyond the Plantation of the seventeenth century. The trading links were close and there was a substantial movement of people between these areas. The coming of Christianity strengthened this association with Irish missionaries seeking to convert the people in the neighbouring island. 'Through these journeys of monks and itinerant craftsmen a cultural province was defined, that of the 'Dalradian Sea', which linked northern Ireland with western Scotland, not only in religion but in many aspects of secular culture.'[10] Even central Ireland was farther away than Argyll or Ayrshire. Indeed, even today, it is easier to cross from Belfast to Glasgow than to travel from Belfast to Cork. Without labouring the obvious any further, let us conclude by saying that there is no physical law of nature which prescribes that one island shall correspond to one nation, and no law of nature which prevents two islands from being a single nation. Unless other evidence of a quite different kind can be put forward, the partition of the British Isles caused by the establishment of the Irish Free State in 1921 was just as 'artificial' as the partition of Ireland.

It may be in place before moving on to the next topic, to anticipate a closely related issue that will receive some mention in later chapters. This is the difficulty experienced in the past by some Irish nationalists in appreciating at all adequately the importance of trade and commerce across the sea. Thus, until fairly recent times, political nationalism and economic nationalism went together. Moreover a greatly exaggerated emphasis was placed on the importance of having an extensive 'hinterland'. It was then a natural – but faulty – inference that the six counties of Northern Ireland constituted too small an area to be 'economically viable' – another term that is widely used but never defined. As we shall see, important political consequences were to follow from such mistakes.

A HISTORIC IRISH NATION

If geography fails to provide a 'natural' foundation for a united Ireland, can history be made to do so? Is it really true, as de Valera asserted, that Ireland was 'a nation before Augustine set foot on English soil'? In making claims of this kind, as nationalists have frequently done, what meaning is being given to the concept of 'a nation'? Admittedly, it is possible to dispose of any such reasoning as irrelevant, for even if it could be firmly established that there was such a nation something like a thousand years ago, it could not be inferred that a united Ireland was desirable, or feasible, in the late twentieth century. Let us, however, consider the basis of these historical assertions to which, quite clearly, much weight has been attached in modern times and apparently continues to be.

In this context where the emphasis is being placed on 'ancient rights', the Gaels are usually accorded a central place; but they were not the original inhabitants of

Ireland. The shadowy people who came first, perhaps from Scotland, were not Celtic. When at a later stage the Celts began to arrive, they did so in successive waves. In Ulster, the Pretani or Cruthan who may have constituted the second wave, were later overcome by the Ulaid who were defeated in turn by the Gaels in the fifth century AD. The Gaels were only the latest arrivals before the Vikings and the Anglo-Normans. Like the English, the Gaels themselves were invaders, but they appear to have succeeded in establishing their ascendancy over their predecessors with a greater and more lasting thoroughness. Their language, Q Celtic, displaced the older P Celtic and was, in its turn, to be largely replaced much later by English.[11] The seven centuries of English rule in Ireland have often been described as a foreign intrusion, but the Gaels had been in Ulster only about seven centuries before the coming to Ireland of the Anglo-Normans. It may, therefore, seem a little puzzling that one period of seven centuries should be held to establish a right of possession that is valid in perpetuity, but a more recent period of seven centuries conveys no such right.

It is true that the Norman settlement in Ulster was only peripheral and did not endure. Even, however, if we move forward to the seventeenth century when the colonization of Ulster by immigrants from Scotland and England took place, we are dealing with something that occurred three to four centuries ago, and we may reasonably ask how long a people have to be settled in an area before they can claim to be 'natives'. The ancestors of the Ulster Protestants – the Scots-Irish as the Americans call them – were arriving in substantial numbers in Ulster about the time when the *Mayflower* sighted Plymouth Rock. Although these families have been in Ulster far longer than have the families of the vast majority of today's Americans, there are Irish-Americans who regard them as mere interlopers. When de Valera, for his part, compared the Ulster Protestants to 'The robber coming into another man's house, and claiming a room as his',[12] we can only assume that for him the seventeenth century was as yesterday.

We have clearly been drawn into a fantasy world, but it is one with distasteful features. For the sharp distinction between the Gaels and the Planters is basically racist. It is the kind of attitude which, if adopted in England towards the Indian and West Indian immigrants of the post-war years, would lead to a storm of protest. Apart from any moral objection to theories of this sort, their factual foundation is, to say the least of it, insecure. As we have already observed, the Gaelic-speaking people were an amalgam of different waves of immigrants among whom the Gaels themselves were probably in a minority. Subsequently, over the centuries, there has been a vast amount of inter-marriage with the English, Scots, Welsh and with people from Continental Europe. As Estyn Evans has observed: 'A pure race is a nationalist myth; indeed it is now thought that in the evolution of man the mixed breeds were the winners from the start. We [in Ireland] are mongrels and should be proud of it, but the proportions of the various racial elements in the mixture vary from region to region.'[13] He then goes on to examine these regional differences in a way that leaves little surviving trace of the simple Gaelic myth. For example, it turns out that the Aran islanders, long regarded as the purest of pure Gaels, had English Cromwellian soldiers among their ancestors. 'I wish I had known', writes Professor Peter Levi, 'when I was taunted as a Jew by the Irish [Christian] Brothers that the most traditional communities of all Ireland, the Aran islanders, are the offspring of Cromwellian soldiers.'[14]

Like the notion of a pure Gaelic race, the notion of a united Irish nation that existed before the coming of the English is a pleasing fiction. There was no such nation. Gaelic society was tribal and semi-nomadic with no effective central authority. The High Kingship was an imposing title for which the chieftains of the clans might fight but, apart from brief periods under Brian Boru and Edward Bruce respectively, it meant little in political or military terms. A different verdict would, of course, be required if the words 'Gaelic nation' were really a misnomer for Gaelic society and culture. The achievements of the old Gaelic – or, better, the old Celtic – culture are something in which the people of the island, irrespective of creed and political affiliation, can – rather obviously – take pride. This achievement did not, however, rest on political unity. On the contrary: 'The absence of political unity makes the cultural unity of the country all the more remarkable.'[15] As Beckett has observed, it was not until the seventeenth century that Ireland was 'united for the first time under a central administration.'[16] It was the English who established that administration.

When an Anglo-Norman band landed in Ireland in 1169, there were from one to two hundred petty kingdoms in the country, usually engaged in war with each other. It was because he wanted help in a struggle for the title of High King, that the king of Leinster asked Henry II to allow Strongbow and his knights to come to Ireland – with consequences that proved to be lasting. Even so, about four and a half centuries were to elapse before tribal power was finally broken. It was only then that the authority of the state could be gradually extended to the whole of the island. The Tudor monarchs who were responsible for doing so could not, however, be said to be embarking upon a policy of deliberate colonization. Henry VII felt obliged to assert his authority only after a Yorkist revolt. His successor was drawn into a substantial campaign in order to preserve that authority, and then became the first English monarch to assume the title King of Ireland. The descendants of the old Anglo-Norman families – who will be referred to hereafter as the 'Old English' – surrendered their land and received it back as vassals of the king. So did the clan chiefs, although this was later to be a cause of some dispute because these lands had not been held in personal ownership but, under Brehon (Gaelic) law, on behalf of their clans. Even then the authority of the government was not successfully maintained, and Elizabeth was obliged to embark, most reluctantly in view of the cost, upon the subjugation of Ireland as a pre-emptive strike against a possible landing by Spanish forces. It was, however, a war directed against the clans or petty kingdoms, not against a 'historic Irish nation', and the clan leaders were far from united. The manner in which the conquest was achieved was a shameful episode in English history for the forces under the English general, Mountjoy, behaved with the utmost cruelty and ferocity. That, however, is a different point.

It was in Ulster that the last stand was made by Hugh O'Neill. When, after a brilliant defence, he was obliged to surrender, the way was at last opened to establishing the authority of the central state in Ireland. That state was to survive until 1921, but it failed to evolve into a nation state. In the following chapters we shall ask why this was so.

The purpose of the present chapter has been to clear the ground. For it is essential, at the outset, to discard some of the myths and correct some of the misunderstandings that have long marred the presentation of the nationalist case for a united Ireland and continue to do so. This clearing of the ground does not, of course, exclude the possibility that a consensus in favour of a united Ireland may ultimately emerge. Whether or not that is likely to occur is still an open question at this initial stage in our investigation. What should, however, be quite clear to even the most casual observer is the absurdity of pretending that Ireland already consists of a single nation. For it must be understood that national unity requires more than a mere majority vote in its favour. It requires a *consensus*. If such a consensus is to be gradually fostered the old preoccupation with antiquarian mythology must be replaced by a new approach and a willingness, on both sides, to respect the preferences of all those who live in the island of Ireland. Whether much progress can ever be made within the now old-fashioned confines of nationalistic separatism is another question that must, at this stage, remain open.

2

The Emergence of a Unified State without Consensus

'The existing political systems in Ireland have evolved from the 1920 constitutional arrangements by Britain which resulted in the arbitrary division of the country.' This quotation is from the Report of the New Ireland Forum of 1984 in which the main political parties of the Irish Republic had participated together with the Social Democratic Labour Party, the nationalist party from Northern Ireland.[1] This assignment of the responsibility for partition has been made repeatedly over the years with an impatient disregard for the truth. As we shall see in chapter 6, the partition of the island followed from the reluctant acceptance, on the part of the British Government, of the fact that the people of the island were deeply divided. The Forum would have been on stronger ground if they had maintained that the colonization of a large part of Ulster in the seventeenth century had erected, in fact if not in intention, a barrier to the subsequent emergence of a united Irish nation. Admittedly, it would be wrong to predicate the inevitability of partition from that point onwards, for many things could have turned out differently over the intervening centuries. If the Irish had been well treated in the years that followed, the emergent Irish nationalism might have been less hostile to continuing membership of the United Kingdom. What happened in the case of Scotland might have happened in the Irish case as well, and the need to choose between independence and unity might then have been avoided.

THE PLANTATION

As was observed in the previous chapter, the links between Northern Ireland and Scotland were much older than the seventeenth-century Plantation and go back, indeed, to prehistoric times, with a continuous movement of people in both directions across the narrow sea. In Heslinga's words: 'It is frequently said that it was the Scots who made modern Ulster. There is as much reason for saying that it was Ulstermen who made ancient Scotland.'[2] These references to a distant past may seem to have little direct bearing on modern problems but can nevertheless perform a useful purpose as a prophylactic against the assumption made rhetorically by modern Irish nationalists that there is something false, artificial and contrary to tradition and history about any political association between any part of Ireland on the one hand and Great Britain on the other.

The Plantation is therefore to be regarded as one important episode in the long history of this movement of people, but it did introduce some new features. First of all, the settlers were not only people from Scotland but included a large component of English people as well. Secondly, the Scots who came were mostly Lowlanders. It is true that the ancient links between Ulster and Scotland had been with the Lowlands as well as the Highlands. Moreover the Lowlanders themselves were partly of Gaelic stock, derived from early settlers from Ulster. But the settlers who arrived in Northern Ireland in the seventeenth century were then English-speaking and Protestant. Moreover they came in large numbers and took the best land. The legal opening for the Plantation was provided by the flight of the leaders of the two large Ulster clans: Hugh O'Neill (Earl of Tyrone) and Rory O'Donnell (Earl of Tyrconnell). Finally defeated in their long and hard-fought war against the English, they had subsequently been pardoned but, for whatever reason, felt it prudent in 1607 to emigrate. The lands they held as vassals were then deemed to be escheated under English law – that is to say, to have reverted to the Crown. An elaborate plan for a settlement was prepared and carried broadly, though not fully, into effect.[3] The situation at that time was particularly favourable to colonization because Ulster was underpopulated, partly as a consequence of the war that had just ended. Moreover agricultural output could be substantially raised by the introduction of the better methods then being used in Scotland and, still more, England. In the original plan of settlement, as approved by Chichester, who became Lord Lieutenant, it was contemplated that land would first be assigned to the local population and then to the settlers, for there should have been room for both. But the revolt of a petty chieftain which initially achieved a surprising degree of success, caused much concern about the possible threat posed by the Gaelic-speaking population, and a case was made and accepted for pushing them into smaller areas on grounds of security. The bitterness caused by this treatment was bound to be long-lasting – and would have been so even if the newcomers had also been Gaelic-speaking and Catholic.

Two of the six counties planted – rather thinly planted – are now in the Republic of Ireland: Cavan and Donegal. The other four were Armagh, Fermanagh, Tyrone and Londonderry (formerly Coleraine). Two of the counties of modern Northern Ireland where unionism is now particularly strong – Antrim and Down – were almost wholly excluded from the Plantation because they were not part of the escheated territory. A large influx of colonists from Scotland did, however, take place, partly as the result of a deal, privately arranged but sanctioned by the Crown, between two Scottish lairds and a local chieftain. There was also a large inflow on a less organized basis. Indeed there can be no doubt that, even without the Plantation, immigration would have occurred on a still substantial, if smaller, scale as land-hungry Scots moved across from the Lowlands, provided the escheated land had been made available. As it was the inflow was not confined to the early years of the century. Checked by the Civil War in the middle years, it was resumed in the later decades.

Whatever its other consequences, the colonization of Ulster was highly beneficial to the Ulster economy. The clansmen had been mainly concerned with the raising of cattle and had moved with the seasons from one area to another. Their methods of cultivation were primitive. There was then plenty of scope for better farming and the area of useful land could be extended by clearing some of the extensive forests and by draining the swamps. The Plantation also provided for the establishment of about twenty towns, for the Gaels were not town-builders, and there were only a few small settlements, in origin Norman or Viking. (Dublin itself is a Viking foundation.) The support of the London guilds was enlisted and they were responsible, in particular, for making the settlement at Derry – thereafter Londonderry – into a strong walled city.[4]

The new colony was too large to be subsequently expelled and too different to be easily absorbed. Thus, at the very time when Ireland was acquiring the administrative institutions of a unitary state, the prospect of becoming a unitary nation-state became much less likely, though not altogether impossible. The outcome would depend upon the policies and attitudes adopted in the succeeding years, but very favourable circumstances would be required for national unity embracing the whole island to be achieved.

There were now three parties to the critically important religious issue on which so much would depend: the established Church of Ireland, Protestant and Episcopal, of the Ascendancy; the Roman Catholic Church of the Old English as well as of the Gaels; and the Presbyterian Church, of Scottish origin, of the majority of the settlers. The Catholics, for their part, could not accept the Act of Supremacy by which the monarch, not the Pope, was declared to be head of the Church, and the 'Old English' who wished to be loyal to the Crown were placed in a very difficult position. The laws against recusants were tightened under the Stuarts and enforced more firmly with the result that, after years of devious negotiation, the Old English were repulsed and made common cause with the Gaelic chiefs. The critical point was reached when there was a general uprising of the dispossessed in the North in 1641. The Plantation had been only partially successful because there had been an insufficient number of colonists, and the Irish had been taken on as tenants and allowed to settle in what were officially 'Protestant' areas. This had turned out to be a bad 'security risk'.

The explosion which took place put the future of the whole settlement in peril. Massacres occurred in various places as the Irish wreaked their vengeance on the settlers. Accounts of the killings, even if discounted for exaggeration, are grim enough and, as might be expected, contributed to a feeling of insecurity that was to persist long afterwards in the Protestant community. As Stewart has observed of the rising: 'The fear which it inspired survives in the Protestant subconscious as the memory of the Penal Laws or the Famine persists in the Catholic.'[5] The Ulster rebellion was to be followed by the outbreak of civil war in England which was to tear the neighbouring island apart. In Ireland there were soon five different armies in the field, including a Scottish army in Ulster to defend the settlers.

The authority of central government, so recently established, was in a state of collapse until restored with uncompromising firmness by Oliver Cromwell. As our concern, in this chapter, is partly with the origin of the folk memories of today, particular mention must be made of the seige and subsequent sacking of the town of Drogheda. Once again tradition appears to have exaggerated the reality; Beckett has warned that 'there seems no foundation for later stories of indiscriminate slaughter'.[6] But the sacking of Drogheda is still recalled with a bitterness and emphasis not accorded, for some reason, to the prolonged and extensive Elizabethan campaigns which were still more horrible. Perhaps the reason is that association with a particular place brings resentment to a sharper focus. It is also interesting to observe that Cromwell is not one of the great heroes of Ulster tradition. The Presbyterians, like their Scottish brethren, disapproved of the regicide Independents and acknowledged the dead monarch's son as their king long before he was crowned Charles II.

The restoration of order by the Cromwellian forces was followed by a new Plantation which differed from the previous plantation of Ulster in two respects: first, it related to other parts of Ireland, and secondly, it involved a change in the ownership of the landed estates but had little direct effect on the tenant farmers, cottiers or labourers. These estates were transferred in whole or in part from those deemed to be 'delinquent' and were granted mainly to Cromwell's soldiers and to the 'Adventurers' who had helped to finance military expenditure. In 1641, the recusants lost not only much of their land but their role in civic life was severely curtailed and they were, in effect, excluded from parliament. After the Restoration, the dispossessed naturally expected that Charles II would restore the confiscated estates to their previous owners but he felt it prudent to make only some limited changes after which the recusants owned only about one-fifth of the land as compared with three-fifths in 1641.

It was hoped by the Catholics that a different line would be taken by James II but he, too, saw that an attempt to reverse the Cromwellian acts of settlement would be dangerous and initially promised that this would not be done. Many other changes were carried out, however, with great speed and thoroughness by Richard Talbot, Earl of Tyrconnell,[7] who became commander-in-chief and then Lord Lieutenant. Protestants were quickly replaced by Catholics in the army, the judiciary and the corporations, and the Irish parliament became almost entirely Catholic. The whole Protestant position seemed to be in danger and the North was soon in revolt. The landing of William of Orange at Torbay in 1688 and the flight of James were the start of what was to be described by Protestants as their 'great deliverance'. In Ireland James decided that he would, after all, undo the Protestant land settlement, but any possibility of carrying out this resolve was removed by his military defeats at Londonderry, Enniskillen, the Boyne and Aughrim – the battles still celebrated by the Orange Order. For William, the Irish campaign was part of his long struggle against Louis XIV in which his allies, at that time, included the Holy Roman Emperor, the King of Spain and also the Pope. The defeat of the Jacobite forces at the Boyne was celebrated with a *Te Deum* in Rome – a fact which Catholics and Protestants in modern Ireland, by tacit agreement, prefer to ignore.

THE PENAL LAWS

The events of the seventeenth century had scarcely been favourable to the gradual emergence of any sense of national unity, but Ireland was a poor country where the vast majority were fully engaged in the struggle for subsistence and political attitudes were not yet hardened. The tragedy was that in the years that followed, the policies adopted were so harsh. William was no bigot and the Treaty of Limerick, which ended the conflict with the Jacobite forces, appeared to offer some protection for the Catholic population. The history of the eighteenth century would have been very different if the Irish parliament had been prepared to act accordingly. With Catholics excluded from parliament by an act of the same year, that body became aggressively Protestant and much then depended upon the attitude of the king himself. One course of action would have been to abolish the Irish parliament in favour of what, in modern times, is called 'integration' with England under the Westminster parliament. A suggestion to this effect was raised in a state paper of 1690,[8] but to carry it out would have entailed a hard political struggle which would have been a serious embarrassment to William in his Continental wars. The proposal was revived in 1703, supported in the Irish House of Commons but rejected in London. A takeover by Westminster would not, of course, have given the Catholics the protection they needed for the Westminster parliament itself was hostile, but their lot might have been a little better. There would also have been economic consequences for Westminster would not then have been able to impose the same damaging mercantilist restrictions on Irish trade, as were in fact imposed in the new century.

The Penal Laws introduced during William's reign were strengthened still more under Queen Anne. The Catholic landowning class was one of the main victims. Its share of the land had dropped from about one-fifth when James II came to the throne, to about one-seventh by the end of the century, and new restrictions were introduced in order to prevent any ground that had been lost from being regained. A Catholic could neither buy land nor lease it, and any land already owned had to be divided among his sons on his death and thus split up. Various other restrictions relating to property were also imposed. By the end of the eighteenth century, the Catholic share of the land was only about 5 per cent[9]. Although Catholic merchants prospered in Dublin, no career in parliament was possible for a Catholic and no public employment unless he became a Protestant. Nor could he send his sons abroad to be educated. In 1727, the Catholics, already excluded from parliament, were also deprived of the right to vote. With the severely limited franchise of the time, most Catholics were not directly affected, but the scope for influencing parliament, already small, was then removed. It is not surprising that many of the Catholic gentry decided to leave the country. An important consequence, with long-term effects, was to follow. With their upper-class leadership so much weakened, the Catholic population became increasingly dependent for leadership upon the Catholic Church. It is true that the Penal Laws were also directed against the Church itself. One in particular banished bishops and regular clergy and this would ultimately have had the effect of preventing any new secular – i.e. parish – clergy from being ordained. In fact the law was not strictly imposed and was abandoned after a few years, together with some of the other penal restrictions directed specifically against the church. As was to be expected, education was regarded as particularly important and it had been decreed in 1695 that 'no person of the popish religion may teach school or instruct youth'. The 'hedge schools' were a means of evading this restriction which proved hard to enforce effectively and was later allowed to lapse.[10]

The Church, therefore, was far from being extinguished. On the contrary, the importance of its role was increased for the majority of the Irish population. For those ordinary Catholic people, to remain true to their Church entailed serious disabilities, if not persecution, and some, as might be expected, turned to Protestantism. But the fortitude and faithfulness of the vast majority remained unshaken.

The harsh treatment meted out to Catholics must, of course, be seen in its historical context. The persecution of the Huguenots in France was a recent memory. In England James II would have imposed minority Catholic rule on the majority and the fact that, in Ireland, Catholic rule would have been majority rule was ignored by the Protestant Ascendancy. There was a further complication which helps to explain the persistence of the hostility directed against Catholics. This was the recognition by Rome of the Old Pretender as the legitimate king. In one respect the conflict of allegiance did not turn out to be important for there was no stirring of support for the Jacobite cause in 1715 or in 1745. But Catholics were nevertheless faced with a problem that further exposed them to discrimination until the Old Pretender died in 1766 and the Pope at last recognized a Hanoverian, George III, as the legitimate monarch.

It might have been supposed that the Ulster Presbyterians who had so strongly supported the 1688 Revolution would be well treated by the Irish parliament, now a wholly Protestant parliament. The Act of Supremacy which had previously affected them as well as the Catholics, was indeed relaxed, and employment under the state was opened to them for a time. But their position was changed for the worse again by the Penal Laws. A sacramental test was imposed in Anne's reign which excluded them from public employment and required them to leave the important positions in municipal government to which they had attained. As in England, their marriages were not recognized by the established Church which, given the current relationship between Church law and state law, affected rights of inheritance. Like the Catholics, they were required to pay tithes for the benefit of a Church to which they did not belong. Unlike the Catholics, they had at least some compensation in the form of a royal grant (*regium donum*) to the Presbyterian Church, first given by Charles II, renewed by William, removed by Anne and restored by George I. But it was a modest offset to the payment of tithes. (It should be said in favour of James II that he had proposed to have tithes paid to the respective Churches of the tithepayers.[11]) In these circumstances, a substantial number of Ulster Presbyterians decided to emigrate to America where they were to play an important part on the side of the colonies in the War of Independence. Thus there were two waves of emigrants to America: one in the eighteenth century that was almost entirely Protestant, and one in the nineteenth century that was predominantly Catholic. In both cases, the emigrants had little reason to feel any affection for Britain.

Both Catholics and Presbyterians were subjected to harsh civil and political disabilities. Both were obliged to live under a landlord system, even if it was somewhat less harsh in the North.[12] It might be expected that the oppression to which both were subjected would have brought Catholics and Presbyterians together in opposition to the Anglo-Irish Ascendancy which used its power to serve its interests. The fact that this did not happen until the end of the eighteenth century, and then only on a small scale, is an indication of the enduring strength of their mutual hostility.

For our purposes, the main features of the latter part of the eighteenth century can be summarized under four headings: first, the changing constitutional position; secondly, the growth and importance of secret societies in the countryside – forerunners of today's terrorist organizations; thirdly, the United Irishmen; fourthly, the Act of Union of 1800.

CONSTITUTIONAL CHANGE

Ireland had a parliament with powers roughly corresponding to those of a state government in a federation. That is to say its authority did not extend to such matters as the Crown, foreign policy, war and peace. The authority with which its powers were exercised was the issue at dispute. By an old fifteenth-century ruling, the parliament in Dublin was subordinated to the Privy Council and its authority was curtailed further by an act of 1720 which ruled that the Irish parliament was subordinate to the parliament at Westminster.[13] There was a further complication of great importance: the executive, under the Lord Lieutenant, was responsible to Westminster. The Irish parliament had, however, control of money bills and, in this way, could make its influence felt not only upon strictly financial issues.

The restraints imposed on the Irish parliament were much resented by the Protestant Ascendancy and various appeals were made to Ireland's 'right' to self-government. Nothing was achieved, however, until England's military weakness in her struggle with both France and the American colonies in the 1770s led to the formation of an Irish volunteer force for local defence. As a result of the muscle thus acquired, the Irish parliament was freed from its old restrictions in 1782, and could even have its own foreign policy, subject to the consent of the king. But it did not, even then, acquire control of the executive. A freedom from responsibility for its actions was thus implied as well as a restriction of power. There was a moral in all this that was to be underlined on subsequent occasions and was to become part of the republican opinions of a later date: military pressure was necessary to extract concessions from England and could best be applied when England was in difficulties abroad.

Membership of the newly liberated parliament – 'Grattan's Parliament, as it came to be called, after the leader who had done so much to achieve reform – was still restricted to the Protestant Ascendancy. Grattan himself did not wish it to be so and there were other influential figures in support of reform. It is of particular interest to note that at a convention of the Volunteers in Ulster in 1782 a resolution was passed which asserted the right to private judgement in religion and expressed satisfaction at the relaxation of the Penal Laws against Catholics. There was thus an important move, led by members of the Anglican Ascendancy itself, in favour of toleration. There was also powerful opposition to change.

When new legislation was passed in 1792 and 1793 in order to ease the burden on Catholics, an important factor was pressure from Westminster where a Catholic Relief Act had just been passed. All the remaining penal restrictions relating to such matters as education were swept away and the vote was at last restored to Catholics. But, with no accompanying reform of the franchise which, as in England, was very restricted, the increase in Catholic political power was still limited. Nor were

Catholics allowed to sit in parliament. Not surprisingly, disillusion followed. What is of particular interest is that there were friendly relations at this time between Catholics on the one hand and at least a section of the Ulster Protestants on the other.

THE SECRET SOCIETIES

At a lower level in the social scale, developments of a different and more sinister kind were taking place. For the shortage of land caused bitter sectarian competition and physical conflict. The shortage was caused in large measure by the big rise in population from about 2.5 million in 1700 to about 5 million a hundred years later.[14] The fact that the economy was able to sustain so large an increase, even if large numbers were at subsistence level, was, in itself, an indication of the economic development that had taken place. There had also been a large rise in average *per capita* income which may have roughly doubled.[15] As is invariably the case in situations of this kind, no conceivable redistribution would have done so much although that fact did not remove the legitimate sense of grievance at continuing unfairness. The position was, however, becoming more precarious even if the potato had helped to prevent any recurrence of famine after the grim experience of 1740–1. The shortage of land was intensified for the peasants by the increase in the area devoted to grazing, partly under the pressure of normal economic change and also because, rather absurdly, tithes had to be paid on tillage but not on pasture.

Secret agrarian societies were not new but new ones began to be formed: the Defenders, on the Catholic side; the Peep o'Day boys on the Protestant side. Families on each side of the sectarian division were attacked by the society belonging to the other side in order, if possible, to drive them off the land. There were also attacks on landlords and cattle farmers whose fences could be destroyed and their cattle maimed. These organizations corresponded to the paramilitaries of today with atrocities on one side held to be justified by atrocities on the other side. As Edith Johnston has observed: 'This slippery logic has given Irish terrorism a seemingly permanent cloak for action without responsibility.'[16] Those who took part were not always the desperately poor, and some of the worst outrages occurred in relatively prosperous areas.

A battle between the two factions in Armagh in 1795 was followed by the founding of the Orange Society which, after a chequered career, still exists with a large membership as the Loyal Orange Order. Three years later there was an explosion of rural violence which, as it happened, was also the year when the United Irishmen finally embarked upon their heroic, if futile, rebellion.

THE SOCIETY OF UNITED IRISHMEN

The Society of United Irishmen, founded in Belfast in 1791, and quickly extended to other towns, can be regarded as the culmination of the tendency, apparent for some years, for groups of Protestants and Catholics to come together. Its objectives can be grouped under two headings. The first was a programme for parliamentary reform which included manhood suffrage, voting by ballot, biennial parliaments and, of course, Catholic emancipation which would allow Catholics to sit in parliament. It was an ambitious package for the time – forty years before even the first of the Westminster reform bills. As can be seen, it anticipated, in some respects, the demands of the Chartists in the England of the 1840s. There were other organizations in Ireland at the time which supported some of the reforms in this package, including the removal of the remaining disabilities on Catholics, but not always the combination of Catholic emancipation with manhood suffrage. The second part of the Society's policy went very much further and amounted to revolution in the literal sense. Not only was the existing government to be overthrown, but English domination was to be broken. With the assistance of the French, an independent Irish republic would be established which would – presumably – adopt a radical system of democratic government along the lines described. This was the basic objective of its founder, the Dublin Protestant Wolfe Tone, who remains one of the legendary heroes of the republican movement in Ireland.

It may seem astonishing that more than a handful of Protestants should ever have been prepared to support a revolution of this kind – and to do so not just in principle but in arms. One factor was the deep sympathy felt for the American revolution in which Ulster Presbyterians had played so important a part. For some time there had been a particularly lively intellectual movement among Belfast's middle class, which may originally have derived some of its stimulus from the training in speculative thought acquired by Ulster students at the University of Glasgow during the great period of the Scottish Enlightenment. There was a radical side to this intellectual activity in Belfast, and Thomas Paine's *Rights of Man*, reprinted by four newspaper firms, was widely read and admired. When the French Revolution broke out it was greeted with admiring enthusiasm. In view of later history, the following observation by James Beckett should be borne in mind: 'The idea of an "Irish nation", indifferent to religious rivalries, rooted in history, but enlightened by the Revolution, takes its rise in the Belfast of the late eighteenth century.'[17] A republican revolution of this kind had, from the outset, a negligible chance of success, but for a time it could well have been a very serious matter for an England already heavily engaged in France. It must be remembered, in assessing the importance of the threat, that Ireland was not at the time the relatively small country of modern times, for the Irish population was then about half the English. There were several reasons for the failure of the rising in addition to the action taken by government: chance, poor discipline and mismanagement, and also inadequate support from both the Protestants and the Catholic communities. Chance comes first because it was the chance of bad weather that prevented a French fleet from landing in Bantry Bay in 1796 after the British fleet had been successfully evaded. There was subsequent mismanagement in that the rising was too long postponed and, in the meantime, the movement was undermined by treachery and weakened by the arrest of some of its important members. When the action did start its timing was not synchronized in the main areas. The revolt began in Wexford but, with a tragic lack of discipline, turned almost at once into a traditional Catholic pogrom against the local Protestant community. In the North, the rebels, mainly Presbyterians, were also defeated. The Catholics had largely failed to turn up and Presbyterian support came mainly from Belfast and the two eastern counties,

Antrim and Down. Delay had weakened sympathy for the revolt as news of the Terror in France reached Ireland. In all areas, the rising was suppressed with ferocious severity. Thus, when it came to the crunch, the revolt was not, after all, a revolt of 'united' Irishmen, and it is scarcely surprising that it has left behind no traditional memory of a kind that would today help to draw Protestants and Catholics together. Meanwhile, in central Ulster, especially in Armagh, the conflict at the grass-roots continued between the rival jacqueries with the new Orange Society now prominent on the side of the Protestants.

THE 1800 ACT OF UNION

The fourth of the possible paths of change mentioned above was the abolition of the Irish parliament in favour of government from Westminster. As a point of interest in passing, we may observe that this was the course Adam Smith had advocated a quarter of a century before, when he compared the position in Ireland with what it had been in Scotland before the union of the crowns:

By the union with England, the middling and inferior ranks of the people of Scotland gained a compleat deliverance from the power of an aristocracy which had always oppressed them. By a union with Great Britain the greater part of the people of all ranks in Ireland would gain an equally compleat deliverance from a much more oppressive aristocracy; an aristocracy not founded, like that in Scotland, in the natural and respectable distinctions of birth and fortune, but in the most odious of all distinctions, those of religious and political prejudices; distinctions which, more than any other, animate both the insolence of the oppressors and the hatred and indignation of the oppressed, and which commonly render the inhabitants of the same country more hostile to one another than those of different countries ever are. Without a union with Great Britain, the inhabitants of Ireland are not likely for many ages to consider themselves as one people.[18]

To Pitt and Castlereagh, the Act of Union seemed the only way of achieving Catholic emancipation, given the continuing resistance of the majority in the parliament in Dublin. Moreover, emancipation achieved in this way would be very much 'safer' because Irish Catholic members would be in a minority in the larger British House of Commons. What is also of interest is that the Catholic hierarchy at that time favoured union on the assumption that it would be followed by emancipation. For them the revolutionary republicanism of the United Irishmen had no appeal. On the contrary, it was precisely the kind of movement that had proved so dangerous to the Church in France and must be avoided in Ireland. The hierarchy did not, therefore, support the United Irishmen which weakened their already slender chances of success. There were, however, some parish priests who did give their support and the Church, to this extent, was divided. It was a division that was to reappear on various occasions over the next two centuries.

Let us now recapitulate. We began our brief historical review and commentary by recording that the 'ancient Irish nation' is only a cherished myth and by noting that Ireland did not even have the political and administrative machinery of a unified state until this was provided by England. That state was not a nation state but, in those early days, Irish nationalism had not yet emerged as a strong force committed to separation from England. The colonization of Ulster was a complicating factor of critical importance because, thereafter, an unpleasant choice might well have to be made between Irish independence from Britain and Ireland's political unity. The succession of events over the two centuries we have covered did not bode well for the future, but attitudes had not yet hardened and various possibilities were still open. The next phase was to be one of Irish political unity as a part of the United Kingdom. The policy measures then adopted and the response to them were bound to be of critical importance during this new phase when national sentiment was becoming gradually stronger and more widespread throughout the island.

3

Irish Unity within the Union

With the Irish parliament gone and the whole country governed by Westminster, there was a fresh chance for the gradual emergence of an Irish nation. That nation would not admittedly be independent but, like England, Wales and Scotland, would be one of those comprising a United Kingdom to which all belonged. Thus, as part of a larger unity, the Irish people might gradually have acquired a greater sense of unity between themselves or, at least, a greater capacity for mutual tolerance and respect. Speculation along these lines is not as pointless as it may seem. By asking why this development did not occur, we can learn something more about the influences which shaped the current attitudes that are with us today.

By the end of the previous century, a claim for national independence with complete separation from England had indeed been asserted by Wolfe Tone, but there was no reason to suppose that this was the general and ineradicable view of the Catholic population. For the vast majority, the absorbing preoccupation was to continue to survive on the verge of total destitution. To quote from Corish:

No political figure really understood the grievances of the poor. Tone did not grasp them and neither did Grattan. In so far as it was possible to understand these problems, they had little to do with parliamentary reform or with the rights of man. When they spoke of 'liberty' what they had in mind was delivery from tithes and taxes and a relaxation of the burden of rent that would give them a little better grip on the land. There are scant indications that they felt their lot could be bettered by throwing off allegiance to the throne and sufficient indications that they had no real desire to do so.[1]

Of those with more economic security and more education, most were quite prepared to accept the union when it had been carried out, even those who had initially opposed it. Moreover, as we have observed in the previous chapter, those who had supported it included the Catholic bishops who thought it would be better to be ruled from Westminster than by a Dublin parliament under the control of the Protestant Ascendancy. In Beckett's words, there was 'an opportunity to conciliate Irish opinion, and to promote a real, as distinct from a formal, incorporation of Ireland with Great Britain in the United Kingdom'.[2] In the event, that opportunity was not taken.

The main features of the tangled history of the first fifty years of the Union can be conveniently summarized under four headings: Catholic emancipation; the tithe war; the achievements and limitations of a constitutional arrangement broadly similar to what we should now call 'administrative devolution'; and, finally, the famine of the 1840s. Behind these and all the other issues lay questions of basic importance. Was Westminster really prepared to regard Ireland as a full member of the United Kingdom and to treat her accordingly? Would complete integration have the full support of the English people so that, after a time, it would be taken so completely for granted that it would cease to be an issue? For it is an error – and one easily made in view of the doctrinaire assertiveness of a later generation of Irish nationalists – to suppose that the future of the Union depended solely upon the willingness of the Irish to accept it. The welcome they received was bound to affect the attitude they subsequently adopted.

CATHOLIC EMANCIPATION

The right to sit in parliament without taking an oath that was incompatible with Catholic belief should have followed at once after the Act of Union. Pitt had initially intended to put both measures forward at the same time but, unfortunately, did not do so, and when emancipation was subsequently proposed it was bitterly resisted by the King and part of the Government. Pitt's resignation expunged any charge of personal dishonesty but Britain's national dishonour remained. The Catholic bishops had then every reason to feel that they had been betrayed. Although the establishment of the Union was so quickly followed by disillusionment, Catholic emancipation was not turned into a burning political issue until Daniel O'Connell did so in the 1820s. In the end, the disability imposed on Catholics was grudgingly removed only in 1829, and only after a period of intense agitation that threatened violent revolt. There were two morals to be drawn by Irish Catholics which appeared to be further endorsed on later occasions: first, the English were not to be trusted when they made promises about Ireland and, secondly, they would eventuallly concede to physical force, or the threat of physical force, what they had previously denied to fairness and reason.

Emancipation did not, of course, permit the Irish people as a whole to take part in representative government, for the franchise was severely restricted as in the rest of Britain. Indeed emancipation was accompanied by a further restriction with a rise in the county freehold qualification from 40 shillings to 10 pounds which *reduced* the Irish electorate from 100,000 to a mere 14,000.[3] Subsequent extensions of the franchise were needed to make emancipation really effective. O'Connell's next campaign for the repeal of the Union, which was violent in expression if vague in specification, carried the country once more to the verge of revolt, but this time the Government called his bluff – for that was what it turned out to be. Again there was a lesson for future revolutionaries.

The tithe war

There was widespread agitation against the payment of tithes for the benefit of a Church of which only Anglican Protestants – no more than part of the Protestant population at that – were members. In the main, the protest took the form of a refusal to pay but also erupted into many acts of violence, though not on an organized scale. A limited reform of the established Church was carried out but tithes were still imposed and were still paid to the minority Church until its disestablishment in 1871 when the revenue was diverted to the state as a land tax. Over all these years this iniquitous levy was a continuing sore, sapping the strength of the Union.

Administrative devolution

The third of the factors mentioned above was described in modern terms as the effect of 'administrative devolution'. That is to say, the country was not administered directly from Whitehall but had its own executive with a member of the government at its head. As we have seen, the executive before the Act of Union was responsible in a similar way to Westminster, not to the Dublin parliament. The abolition of the Dublin parliament with its control over money bills had affected the behaviour of the executive but, in the perception of the ordinary citizen, little change may have occurred, and the impact on local consciousness of the Act of Union itself may have initially been slight. The old Ascendancy gang were still seen to be there, still running the country. The impact of the change would, no doubt, have been considerably greater if the previous administrative organization had been swept aside and replaced, in a less grand way and at a lower level in the British bureaucratic hierarchy, with what we should now describe as 'regional offices' of the Whitehall departments. To some extent this is what happened, although not immediately. But there was an obvious danger of over-centralization and inconvenience. After all, if administrative devolution is thought appropriate for modern Scotland, it was surely so for nineteenth-century Ireland where the special problems were so much more complicated and when communication with London was so much slower.

Decentralization was required and the future of the Union would inevitably be much affected by the performance of this Dublin executive. To make an adequate assessment of the quality of the administration over the century that followed would require a detailed historical knowledge to which I can lay no claim. It is clear, however, that a number of reforms including the reform of the civil service itself, were carried out in the first three decades of the Union. In the mid-1830s the pace of reform was accelerated under the Whig administration (1835–41). A number of measures with which the name of Under Secretary Thomas Drummond is particularly associated were then implemented.[4] Some important changes were made that would give Catholics a greater share in the administration of the country and in the judiciary. A stipendary magistracy was introduced and a national police force was created. This vigorous Scot was determined to ensure that the country was governed both with fairness and efficiency, and that participation in government would not, in practice, be restricted to Protestants. He took a leading part in curbing the activities of the Orange Order by prohibiting its demonstrations and weakening its influence in law enforcement and administration. Of more doubtful wisdom was the extension to Ireland of the new Poor Law in 1837.

The autonomy permitted by administrative devolution had already been used, in 1831, to introduce a national system of education in Ireland, long before this was done in England. That in itself was an important step but even more was to be attempted. For Lord Stanley, the Chief Secretary, intended that the new schools should be 'integrated', to use the modern term. That is to say, children of all denominations would be educated together. They would work together and play together but would be separated for religious instruction. 'Joint secular and separate religious instruction', to be provided as the various denominations thought fit, was what Stanley proposed.

One can only speculate about the probable effects that might have followed if this policy had been adopted, but there was no real chance of that occurring. All the denominations rejected the proposal. Thus, as the new age of mass education began in Ireland, it assumed from the start the ominous shape of strict religious segregation. The schools were for the most part denominational and were so in the most narrow sense. For there was not only the division between Protestant and Catholic schools but the Protestant schools themselves were further divided between the different Protestant denominations. The result in many areas was a larger number of small schools than was consistent with efficiency, with about two-thirds of all the primary school children attending schools of a single denomination in 1900.[5]

The Conservative administration, with Peel as Chief Secretary, also laid great stress on the need for conciliation and fairness to Catholics if the Union was to be preserved. His enlarged grant to Maynooth, the Catholic seminary, in 1845 was one of his attempts to implement a policy along these lines. His proposal to extend university education by the establishment of three Queen's colleges was, however, to meet strong opposition. The education to be provided was to be secular with provision made for religious teaching and pastoral care by the various denominations. It was a well-intentioned proposal which left no room for any complaint that the new institutions would be used for proseltysing by Protestant churches. But the Catholic Church wanted much more for its young people than protection from Protestantism. It was determined to ensure that they would be protected from the evils of a secular training in 'godless' colleges. Catholic students must therefore have Catholic teachers for not only logic, metaphysics and moral philosophy but also for history and even geology. When the government rejected these conditions, the Church ensured that few Catholics would ever attend such colleges and, in 1854, established its own privately financed Catholic University under John Henry Newman, but with only limited success. O'Connell, for his part, was a strong opponent of secular education. It was at this time that he declared in the journal of his movement that the crucial distinction between Englishmen and Irishmen was 'the distinction created by religion'. It was a remark that had ominous implications for Irish Protestants, especially those in Ulster, and thus for the possibility of creating a united Irish nation on a new basis if – as he was soon to recommend – the

Union with Britain were to be broken.[6] But the whole of O'Connell's political activities had been carried on with no regard to the effect on Protestant feeling in Ulster.

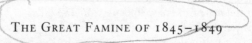

THE GREAT FAMINE OF 1845–1849

The years preceding the famine were marked by agrarian unrest with a rapidly rising population competing for the available land. As in the previous century, the unrest was often violent, with the rural societies fighting each other and attacking landlords and their agents. There was no doubt about the need for reform but it would, at the same time, be unwise to assume that such reform, even if forthcoming, would have prevented famine from occurring when the potato crop failed for several years.[7] The Irish population had roughly doubled over the previous century and had increased by about two-thirds, from five million to over eight million in the first forty years of the new century.[8] The increase would have been checked by hunger still earlier had it not been for the potato which allowed poor families to survive on farms as small as ten acres or even less. It was the potato that was largely responsible for staving off serious famine between the 1740s and the 1820s, and thereafter until the 1840s, but a large part of the rural population, especially in the west, was in a very vulnerable position for a crop failure could be disastrous. Even without a crop failure, so large a rate of growth could not have been sustained for much longer unless indeed there had been very rapid industrialization.

Ireland therefore appeared to provide a textbook example of the overpopulation predicted by Thomas Malthus. His teaching clearly affected the attitude adopted by some of those in authority, in particular in the Treasury. The Government was in fact being forced to consider a situation that is sadly familiar today in parts of the less developed world. Famine relief may help to avert famine, or at least reduce its scale, but is no more than a short-run solution. Can it be sensible to attempt, in a rather futile way, to postpone the inevitable? The answer is, of course, that we do not know for sure what *is* inevitable. Given time, adjustments may be made and the Malthusian situation may not persist indefinitely. The case for famine relief is still stronger in a situation where the immediate cause of the famine is crop failure. For crops of normal yield can be anticipated later and will allow further time for adjustment. In Ireland some evidence can be discerned that an adjustment was already taking place before the famine in the form of emigration and also some decline in the birth rate with a higher age of marriage.[9] The short-term humane response to the situation in Ireland at that time was not, therefore, inconsistant with long-term realism, and the same conclusion may hold in many less developed countries in the modern world. It must be emphasized, however, that this does not imply acceptance of the foolish dogma that over-population can *never* occur! By far the most important modern example is, of course, that of Communist China where Malthusianism, dismissed as a bourgeois fallacy by Chairman Mao, has now become the basis of a severe official policy of family limitation.

When the famine first struck in 1845, the Conservative administration did in fact respond quite quickly by moving successfully for the abolition of the Corn Laws which permitted the free importation of grain and by special relief works in the badly affected areas. No one died of famine when Peel was Prime Minister – 'Orange Peel' as he had been somewhat unfairly called by O'Connell. When, however, the Whigs returned to power in mid-1846, the official measures began to falter. The new Prime Minister (Russell) did not want to concede that it was the responsibility of the state to feed the people. It was held that 'Irish property must pay for Irish poverty' – though this could only be done by state assistance in the first instance with the cost to be recovered later by some special levy on that property. Moreover, the insistence on the property being Irish naturally prompted the question whether this was really a way of trying to shuffle off responsibility for a country that was still not regarded as fully British. It is certainly easier to adopt a stern Malthusian line with regard to a remote area than to one close at hand. Beckett has observed that 'no one could doubt that if a comparable crisis had arisen in England the government would have ensured adequate supplies of food, at whatever cost to the economy; or that an independent government in Ireland would have done the same.'[10] A particularly bitter grievance, remembered in Ireland with anger to this day, was that food was exported from Ireland throughout the crisis. It is rarely observed that, over the same period, imports were five times as large.[11] Moreover, the starving cottiers and labourers lacked the means to buy the food they needed, for these were the classes that suffered most, not the better-off tenant farmers.

In the end, a relief policy was adopted with the result that the enormous figure of about three million people were finally receiving assistance, of a sort, from official sources, in addition to the substantial amount of assistance from private charitable sources.[12] But it came too late to prevent disaster. The exact number of deaths caused directly or indirectly by the famine cannot be determined with precision but is believed to have been 0.8–1 million, or about 10–13 per cent of the population. It is worth recalling that there were famines in other parts of northern Europe about the same time, and there was also a famine, though on a smaller scale, in the Western Highlands of Scotland. There would appear to be scope for further comparative historical research into these events which would allow the famine in Ireland to be seen in a wider perspective – without of course in any way diminishing the tragedy that took place. Moreover, as the Irish disaster is so often attributed to an excessive attachment to *laissez-faire* policies, it is also worth recalling that about ninety years later the USSR had to endure an appalling famine as a consequence of Stalin's agricultural policy – which scholars in Russia are now allowed to discuss. From 4 to 7 million are believed to have died from starvation at that time, and to these must be added the many deaths among those transported to Siberia. This famine occurred not in poor farming areas such as the west of Ireland but in rich farming country that had normally produced a large surplus of grain. With such events in mind, it is clear that a simple ideological explanation of the Irish famine will not suffice.

The fall in the Irish population, as a consequence of the famine, of the heavy emigration that followed it and of the decline of the birth rate, was immense. In 1841 it had stood at 8.2 million; by 1911 it was only 4.4 million. In the north-east, although the rural population density was high and the farms small, the widespread rural textile industry provided some cash income with which to buy food. Even so, the toll was heavy at about 200–250,000 deaths in Ulster as a whole. With about 30 per cent of the Irish population, Ulster had between 20 and 25 per cent of the total deaths. The subsequent fall in population was also somewhat less in Ulster with the result that the population of this area, which had been about 30 per cent of the Irish total before the famine, had risen to 36 per cent in 1911. In Ireland as a whole, the famine was felt more severely in the west and, within the nine-county Province of Ulster, it was the western counties that came off worse. In Belfast the population was soon swollen by refugees from the disaster areas and the eastward movement was to continue as industrialization proceeded. In the second half of the century the Catholic population of the city rose steeply and serious sectarian antagonism began to appear.[13] Belfast was then to lose its earlier reputation for tolerance. It is a reputation that has not yet been regained.

The famine was not followed by a wave of indignant political activity. On the contrary, the political scene in a country numbed by disaster remained quiet. It is true that the Young Ireland Movement, led by William Smith O'Brien, attempted rebellion in 1848, the year of rebellions throughout Europe. It was a small and futile gesture, though a brave one, but it caused some transient ill-will in England against the apparently ungrateful and ever-troublesome Irish. The Irish attitude for generations to come was to be soured by the traditional belief that England was entirely to blame for all the evil that had occurred.

In its first fifty years the Union had not been notably successful. If it were to prove impossible, in the years ahead, to maintain it intact, the implications for Irish unity would also be unpromising, although that was not perceived to be so at the time.

4

Independence or Unity – the Home Rule Phase

The second half of the nineteenth century was dominated by two issues: land reform and Home Rule. The two were, of course, connected. Land reform could be regarded as one of the benefits that would follow from Home Rule, but land reform could also be advocated as one of the most important ways in which Home Rule could be 'killed by kindness'. Both were bound to have important implications for maintaining the unity of the United Kingdom and for strengthening or undermining any sense of unity within the island of Ireland itself. The pressure for land reform could conceivably have brought farmers in Ulster and the rest of Ireland closer together in the pursuit of a common interest and, for a time, there were some indications that this was starting to happen.

LAND REFORM

The intensification of the pressure for land reform may seem a little surprising in view of the steep decline in the population after the famine which, with other things equal, was bound to reduce pressure on the land. Without the fall in numbers, the rural crisis would, rather obviously, have been far more acute. Even with numbers so sharply reduced, there were other factors that sharpened the hunger for land. Landowners were responsible for rates on small-holdings and therefore had an incentive to get rid of small-holders. The farmers, for their part, set their faces against the old practice of subdividing holdings among a number of sons. While these changes in attitudes were gradually taking place, the abolition of the Corn Laws was followed by a shift away from arable towards livestock production, and the competition for land was intensified even in industrializing Ulster. Landlords were therefore in a strong economic position and in the old traditional picture of the period, they exploited that position to the full. For most farmers, the law provided no protection against rack-renting for they had only annual tenancies with no security of tenure and no legal claim to compensation for any improvements they might have carried out on their farms. To have tried to exploit the situation to the full by rack-renting and eviction would, however, have damaged the landlords' position in the long run, for it was obviously in their interest to have reasonably prosperous tenants. Indeed the traditional account of their behaviour seemed to imply, not only the absence of any paternalistic restraints, but also a general neglect of what the pursuit of enlightened self-interest would require. Modern research has shown that – whatever the reason – rents did not, in fact, keep pace with the rising value of output. Between 1851–5 and 1871–5, the rise in rents appears to have been between 20 and 30 per cent whereas output rose in value by about 40 per cent.[1] There were, however, marked differences in the increases demanded between one estate and another even in the same locality, and the comparisons thus invited may have been one of the causes of discontent. Another may have been the erratic and uncertain way in which rents were raised. A steady but smooth increase might have been less of a hardship than less frequent but larger increases. Moreover, even if rents had gone up by much less than prices, they absorbed as much as one-quarter to two-fifths of the farmers' incomes. Over the following years, the agitation for land reform waxed and waned in ways that reflected fairly accurately the changes in agricultural prices and the volume of output.[2]

In the North, tenants had long been in a favourable position as a consequence of the Ulster Custom which gave them security of tenure (if they paid their rents) and carried with it the right to sell tenancies. The annualized proceeds of these sales of tenancies were, in fact, usually far above the corresponding rents.[3] The payment thus received by an outgoing tenant might be partly as a compensation for improvements but would also reflect the fact that rents were well below the level at which the supply of land would be equal to the demand for it. By the middle of the century, it had become apparent that the Ulster Custom might not be respected by the landlords in the future and, in 1850, the Ulster Tenant Rights Society was formed under the leadership of Sharman Crawford, an Ulster-born MP, and with the backing of many of the Presbyterian clergy. For a time the Society joined forces with the Irish Tenant League, founded in the South in the same year. On this particular issue there was at least some suggestion of union between Irishmen.

In the years that followed the famine, there was a gradual acceptance in Britain of the need for Irish land reform but much disagreement about the way in which this could best be done. The Liberals were uneasy about measures that would hamper efficiency by interfering with market pressures and processes. Security of tenure could protect an inefficient farmer by depriving a more efficient one of the land he needed. 'Fair rents' were demanded but what rents were 'fair'? What criterion was to be applied? And if this meant that land was below its free market price, what consequences would follow? The claim to compensation for improvements to be paid to an outgoing tenant was a different matter for this was a property right and efficiency in the market requires that property rights should be respected. So much was recognized by an Act of 1860 and security of tenure – so long as uncontrolled rents were paid – was provided by another Act in 1870. These reforms did not meet the demands and the agitation continued. It must be borne in mind that the English landlords, still so powerful at Westminster, were concerned about possible action at home in response to Irish reforms. The disastrous harvest of 1879 brought matters to a head, with a sharp increase in rural violence all over the country. It was in that year that Michael Davitt founded the Land League in the South.

What is of particular concern to us is that Ulster was by no means immune from these disturbances. Although security of tenure had been given legal form and the continued cooperation with the South in support of tenant rights had come to an end, there were still bitter disputes within the Province itself. The Ulster Custom could be interpreted in different ways. Was it being fully respected? In a year such as 1879, when a new famine was threatened, should rents not be reduced or payment postponed? Different landlords responded in different ways and there was a wave of evictions. Protestant tenants opposed Protestant landlords and violence erupted in central and western Ulster. This was a situation that might be thought conducive to some alliance with the South but the vast majority of the Ulster tenants were wary of being associated with any nationalist movement that sought Home Rule as well as land reform. The Orange Order, initially divided, was swung into action in favour of the more unyielding of the landlords.[4] When reforms came in 1881, the agitation lost most of its force.

There can be little doubt that Gladstone made a serious mistake in rejecting the advice of his colleague John Bright, who advocated a land purchase scheme to buy out the landlords. Instead he opted in 1881 for 'the three Fs' – fair rents, fixity of tenure and freedom to sell the tenancy. Even after an amending act had been passed to help tenants in arrears with rents, the scheme proved unsatisfactory. How would the new tribunals determine what was a 'fair rent'? How often should rents be revised? And so on. If the landlords had been bought out at this stage and the tenant farmers turned into peasant proprietors, the Home Rule movement would have been greatly weakened and there would have been no possibility of agitation of the kind launched in 1886 in defiance of the landlords but with nationalist objectives that went beyond land reform. It is true that peasant proprietorship is not always conducive to efficiency but the Irish landlords, for their part, had, in general, an unimpressive record in estate improvement. In any case land purchase was to come. It started with the Ashbourne Act of 1884 passed under a Conservative government. Gladstone proposed land purchase as well as Home Rule in 1886 but both measures disappeared together. A strengthening of the Ashbourne scheme began at the end of the century but it was not until 1903 that the Wyndham Act really brought the old system to an end. By then Irish nationalism was too strong to be checked by reforms of this kind.

HOME RULE

The movement for Home Rule, founded in 1870 by Isaac Butt – a Protestant and a Conservative MP – had, as its objective, the establishment of devolved government for Ireland which was to be achieved by peaceful constitutional means.[5] A much more radical organization had already been in existence since 1858 which regarded devolution as too limited an objective and constitutional reform as too timid a means to achieve success or to deserve respect. This earlier body was the Fenian Brotherhood, or Irish Republican Brotherhood (IRB), a secret society founded in 1858 with American support that was to become increasingly important in the years ahead. The Fenians were totally opposed to any continuation of English rule. England was the traditional enemy, the source of all ills, as Wolfe Tone had so wildly asserted. The hated English must be driven out by any means that might be effective, including terrorism – to use the modern term. An entirely independent

Irish state would then be established. The Fenians claimed to be able to speak for Ireland because they knew 'what the Irish people really wanted'. As we shall see, the same assertion was made by the leaders of the rebellion of 1916 and, a little later, by de Valera. In reality it was fanciful to suppose that the Irish Catholic community was so wholly dedicated at that time to the cause of militant nationalism as to justify the Fenian claim to be its spokesmen. On the contrary, their aims and, even more, their methods were rejected by the constitutional nationalists and strongly condemned by the Catholic hierarchy. Cardinal Cullen, who had been in Rome at the time of Garibaldi's rebellion of 1848, was a passionate opponent of revolutionary movements of any kind and a supporter of the Union with Britain. It is scarcely necessary to add that the Fenians simply ignored the views of the Ulster Protestants and failed, like their successors in 1916, to perceive that their policies would entail the partition of the island. The Fenian rebellion of 1867 proved to be a sorry failure but its terrorist activities continued. These activities caused a great sense of outrage but also had the effect of drawing attention to Irish affairs. As a result there was a growing feeling that 'something must be done' in order to alleviate the country's grievances – or, in the modern jargon with which we are so familiar, an 'initiative' needed to be taken. The upsurge in agrarian crime, notably in the 1880s, had a similar effect.

In 1880 Parnell became the leader of Butt's Home Rule movement, and its methods took on a sharper edge. Although not himself involved in terrorist activities, as was to be falsely alleged,[6] he was in contact with the Fenians and held that, in their way, they had achieved some success. He also became president of the Land League, and a strong campaign was launched on both fronts. In Westminster, the practice of parliamentary disruption was developed as a fine art, with filibustering performances of extraordinary duration which were possible in those days before the introduction of the parliamentary guillotine. It should be noted that Ireland's parliamentary representation had not been reduced in line with the large fall in population after the famine, and its still larger decline relative to the English population. As a result, the Irish members were all the better placed to determine the balance of power by switching their support from one of the main parties to the other unless their demands were being met.

Gladstone, formerly an opponent of Home Rule, came finally to the conclusion that such a measure was necessary, and a bill to this effect was introduced in 1886 which would have provided a measure of autonomous government for Ireland.[7] This Home Rule bill was bitterly opposed in Great Britain both by the Conservatives and by part of the Liberal Party itself on the ground that it would merely be the first step towards the break-up of the United Kingdom. In Ireland, the opposition of the Protestants was intense and should have conveyed the warning that Home Rule for the whole island might well be unattainable. The reluctance on the part of the nationalists to heed the warning signs was unfortunate, to say the least of it. Subsequently, repeated attempts have been made to explain away this Northern hostility as something deliberately created by the English Conservatives.[8] As evidence it has been customary to quote Randolph Churchill's too well-remembered observation that: 'The Orange card would be the one to play'. By this he meant not that he had himself devised such a card, but that Orange opposition, already powerful, should be used to combat Home Rule for any part of the island.

The ferocity of local opposition was demonstrated in the sectarian riots with which Gladstone's bill was greeted in Belfast, and it might have been supposed that Irish nationalists would then have come to perceive that they were faced with *grass-roots* resistance. Unfortunately they preferred self-deception – and continued to do so a century later. It is true that eight of Ulster's 28 MPs were Liberals – and there might have been more if Parnell had not, for tactical reasons, supported the Tories at the 1885 election. But the whole Liberal Party was soon divided over Home Rule and, in Ulster, was to go into decline for this reason. The reasons for opposition to this measure of devolution may be seen as threefold. First, there was a firm determination not to submit to being governed by a parliament where Catholics would have a permanent majority. Home Rule would mean Rome Rule – and so, in various ways, it has done. Secondly, Home Rule would be only a first step to independence and the break-up of the Union. Thirdly – an objection less widely felt but regarded as important by the business community – was the fear, again well founded, that an independent Dublin parliament would be protectionist and would damage the interests of an area such as Ulster, already so much committed to international trade. What was not clear, under this last heading, was whether the proposed parliament would have the power to control tariffs. Such power is nowadays generally regarded as going beyond devolution and implying a high degree of independence, but contemporary views were less clear. Anyhow if Home Rule were once granted a higher degree of independence might come later and with it protection.

An entirely different view can be taken for it can be held that the Irish would have been satisfied with Home Rule and the United Kingdom would thus have remained intact. Its rejection in 1886, and again in 1893, can therefore be regarded as a disaster which led to the Irish war of independence and ultimately to the establishment of a fully independent Irish republic. In attempting to come to a verdict on this issue one may speculate about the true motives of the main actors. Obviously the Fenians would not have been satisfied, and Parnell's own position was ambiguous. At the dates of the first two bills, there was certainly no general demand for independence in Ireland, but opinions might have hardened. On the other side, allowance must also be made for the influence the Ulster people themselves would have exerted with Ulster members in a Dublin parliament. Obviously there is ample scope for speculation on these issues but a more definite answer can, perhaps, be reached by directing attention to some of the main features of the legislative provisions for Home Rule which, quite apart from the hostile reaction in Ulster, were bound to affect its success. It is now generally agreed that the financial clauses were unsatisfactory.[9] This defect might not, however, have been fatal, for changes could have been made – as happened many years later after Ulster had been given Home Rule (see chapter 9 below). A more persistently disruptive factor, slow-acting but powerful, might have been the disillusionment that would have probably followed when Home Rule failed to bring the social bliss that some expected of it – failed, not necessarily from any defects in the scheme, but because unrealistic expectations had been entertained about what could be achieved by devolution. A natural reaction would then have been to demand still more independence.

There is also another – in this case an almost certain – reason why the Home Rule proposals of 1886, 1893 and 1912 would have been doomed: this was the failure to solve satisfactorily the problem of parliamentary representation in both the

Westminster and the Dublin parliaments. Initially, in 1886, Gladstone proposed
that there should no longer be Irish members at Westminster when Home Rule had
been instituted. After so many years of boredom, uproar and disruption, the
prospect of getting rid of the Irish altogether must, one would suppose, have been
immensely attractive to other members of the House. A less responsible assembly
might, indeed, have passed the measure without delay and with unanimity and
acclaim! In the event this enticing prospect was sacrificed for the sake of
constitutional propriety and national unity. For it was clear that the Irish could not
have their foreign policy and some of their main taxes determined for them by a
parliament in which they were no longer represented. That was not a position that
could have been sustained, as Gladstone himself had to concede. He then
suggested that the Irish might be invited to attend for parliamentary business
relating to non-devolved affairs, but this too was seen to be an unworkable
suggestion that had to be dropped. For the advent of the Irish on such occasions
would have had such an effect on relative party strengths in the House that it could
well have changed the party in power – one government when domestic policy was
under consideration, but a different one when it was foreign policy or defence! So
the 'in-and-out' clause was abandoned in its turn. The Irish were, therefore, to have
dual representation. In their own parliament they could determine policy for
devolved affairs and, in Westminster, they could also exert their influence – often a
decisive influence – in determining how the same issues would be settled for people
in Great Britain. The British people would soon have found such a situation
unendurable. The problem was of critical importance but was still unresolved when
the final instalment of Home Rule legislation for Ireland was introduced in 1920.
The most that had been done had been to reduce the proposed number of Irish
members both in the 1914 and 1920 Acts in order to make the problem that much
less acute. We can conclude, then, with some confidence that all the schemes
proposed for Irish Home Rule would in the end have foundered on this particular
difficulty. It was not merely that Irish nationalists might have decided that any such
scheme was inadequate but that the English, the Scots and the Welsh would have
thought it intolerable. In the event, the only measure of legislative devolution that
came into force was that for Northern Ireland and the difficulty was then rendered
less acute because there were only 13 MPs at Westminster, later lowered to 12.
Even so, the presence of the Ulstermen could be important at times and was
resented accordingly.

What is so remarkable is that this critical lesson from the attempt to devise Home
Rule for Ireland was neglected completely by those responsible for drafting the
legislation of 1978 for the establishment of devolved assemblies in Scotland and
Wales.[10] Indeed it was not even proposed to reduce the number of Westminster
MPs from these countries. Yet the conclusion is clear: devolution cannot be
appropriately accorded to one or two areas in isolation unless these areas are very
small. If it is to work effectively and survive, there must be 'Home Rule All Round' –
to use Joseph Chamberlain's phrase. The case for a federal structure was put
forward again in the years before 1914 by Amery and Oliver but without success. It
could, indeed, be objected then – and in 1978 – that there was no demand for
devolution for the English regions; but it would have been possible to have had an
assembly for England as a whole, as Chamberlain himself had contemplated. If even

this was not thought to be feasible, then devolution for the other large parts of the United Kingdom would not work. Even if only one area were to be selected for devolution – and that a very small one – there could be difficulties when there was a hung parliament at Westminster. In this respect, the situation has not changed since the time of the movement for Home Rule in Ireland.

HOME RULE WITH PARTITION

The demand for Home Rule derived, as the forgoing review implies, from two causes. The first was the belief that Home Rule was necessary if a number of bitter and longstanding grievances were to be removed; the second was the desire for self-government. The defenders of the Union might then meet the first point by removing these grounds for complaint. This was Balfour's policy of 'killing Home Rule with kindness', and a great deal had been done to this end by the early years of the present century. The landlord system, previously reformed, had then been abolished altogether by two important pieces of Conservative legislation, and the Irish farmers now owned their own land. Local government had also been reformed. The parliamentary franchise had been extended, in Ireland as elsewhere. The episcopal Protestant Church had long since been disestablished. A new policy for university education had been adopted. Special measures had been taken to provide assistance in the congested western counties. The new institutions of the welfare state were being gradually introduced at Westminster which were bound, in the end, to swing the fiscal balance in favour of such poor areas as Ireland, although this could not be fully foreseen at the time. Moreover there had been a marked improvement in economic conditions which had roughly trebled *per capita* income over the nineteenth century[11] Social and economic progress did not, however, dispel the demand for self-government. On the contrary, for various reasons this demand was to be strengthened.

One reason, suggested by Garvin, is that young educated Catholics could not in practice find the openings they needed in the administration of the country or in its social life. They belonged to the lower middle class or were the children of farmers or workers. There might be no deliberate discrimination against them but they lacked contacts and were denied entrée. 'In Yeats' classic phrase, many of them indeed possessed great hatred and suffered from little room; little room was accorded them by Irish society or by the Anglo-Irish establishment, and great hatred was commonly the consequence.'[12] It is a familiar feature of many societies. It was to be very apparent in Northern Ireland in the 1960s.

Another factor was the formation by Arthur Griffith in 1898 of a new movement in Ireland: Sinn Fein. As its name implied, it stood for independent action without relying upon support from any Westminster party – Ourselves Alone. When the landslide of 1906 brought the Liberals into power with so large a majority as to allow them to assume office without Irish support, the Government displayed no real interest in making any new attempt to confer Home Rule. Arthur Griffith could then urge all the more convincingly the need for self-reliance. Sinn Fein, later to be so important in its own right, was a goad to action on the part of the constitutional Nationalists, led by John Redmond. The Gaelic revival, with its emphasis on the glories of ancient Irish civilization, caused a further strengthening of nationalist sentiment that made it still more immune to any British policy of 'killing Home Rule with kindness'. Hence the new emphasis on an Irish Ireland: 'Ireland not free only but Gaelic as well; not Gaelic only but free as well.' It was not a slogan to which the Ulster Protestants would be likely to respond, but little attention was paid to them by the enthusiastic nationalists in the South.

Even if a new autonomous Irish regime were to choose to adopt precisely the same measures as those adopted by Westminster, it would be exercising national freedom of choice in doing so and this freedom of action, apart from the merits of the policies followed, was what any committed nationalist must demand. Not that the new policies, in so far as these were anticipated, were in fact to be the same. Irish industries would be protected, the country's great natural resources used to the full, and so on. When such beliefs were strongly held, the preservation of the Union *without* Home Rule was bound to be difficult, and might not be possible *with* Home Rule. What was also bound to be difficult was the preservation of political unity in the island of Ireland.

After the bitter experience of the two previous attempts to introduce Home Rule, it might have been supposed that the case for partition would have received serious attention when Home Rule was once more placed on the political agenda after a new Liberal Government came into power in 1910 with the support of the Irish Nationalist Party. If the nationalist demand for devolution had to be met but the Northern majority, with equal determination, refused to be governed by a Dublin parliament, the need to divide the island became an inescapable inference. This was so, at all events, unless the application of the principle of self-determination to one part of the population was to be accompanied by its denial, backed by force, to the remainder. Even the moderate Redmond who had deceived himself into believing that Ulster's resistance was largely artificial bluff, was to insist that: 'Irish Nationalists can never be assenting parties to the mutilation of the Irish nation.'[13] Indeed his more extreme fellow nationalists would have rejected him if he had said anything else. The Liberals, for their part, also under-estimated the strength of Ulster's opposition. In any case they were dependent upon Nationalist votes if they were to remain in office. Asquith himself was saying the same in July 1912. In his biography of Asquith, Roy Jenkins goes on to say that the Nationalists could have taken no other line: 'For them to have abandoned any part of the country at the first whiff of braggadocio from Craigavon (sic) would have been political suicide.' Only braggadocio? It is a revealing comment.[14]

Thus, when the bill was introduced in 1912, it made no provision for partition. The events that followed were to leave a deep and lasting scar. The Unionists in Northern Ireland made it clear that they would not submit to Home Rule. They would reject the legislation. 'We must be prepared', said their leader, Edward Carson, '. . . the morning Home Rule passes, ourselves to become responsible for the Government of the Protestant province of Ulster.'[15] A defence force was recruited from volunteers with the recruiting sanctioned by magistrates and therefore legal. The Ulster Covenant and Declaration had 471,000 signatories, which ought to have convinced everyone of the strength of the mass opposition to Home Rule. The formation of the Ulster Volunteer Force imposed at least a little discipline and may therefore have slightly reduced civil disorder. The fact remains that this was an act of defiance and it is also true that the Unionists were strongly encouraged to resist by the Conservative Party in Britain.

The obvious solution was to exclude the Ulster counties, or at least some of them, from the Home Rule legislation. A choice had to be made between Home Rule and Irish unity. It should have been clear to all that there was no escape from this conclusion unless there was to be a settlement imposed by brute force. But Nationalists were not prepared to accept the reality of the situation and the Liberal Government which depended upon their support was in a quandary. The Ulster Unionists had begun to realize that the area excluded from Home Rule should not be the whole Province of nine counties for the sectarian balance would then be too close and might soon change in favour of joining the other 23 counties. A smaller six-county 'Ulster' would be more stable. Even more stable would be the four counties proposed by a liberal member, Agar-Robartes. But the Catholic majorities in Tyrone and Fermanagh, the two counties that might have been excluded, were not large. It would have been still more sensible to have recognized that there was no particular significance about county boundaries and to have directed attention to smaller districts which could have been grouped together with a somewhat closer regard to the sectarian distribution of the population.

In March 1914, Asquith tried to defuse the situation by proposing the 'county option' for Ulster by which the Members of Parliament for each county could vote for its exclusion for a period of six years. Redmond was persuaded to agree but Carson rejected what he described as 'sentence of death with a stay of execution for six years.'[16] Meanwhile the danger of conflict grew ominously greater. The year 1913 had seen the formation not only of the Ulster Volunteer Force but also, in Dublin, of both the Citizens Army and the Irish Volunteers. Drilling was going on and arms were being smuggled in. Britain has often been reproached by Irish nationalists for its failure to impose the will of parliament on the rebellious North, although no attempt is usually made to specify what precisely should have been done. The Liberal Government did indeed contemplate a combined naval and army exercise in March 1914 but were foiled when army officers at the Curragh camp accepted the option of resignation rather than service against Ulster. It was certainly a bizarre situation. The Ulster Unionists, for their part, would certainly not have wanted to fire on the King's uniform, and would not have been easily induced to shed the first blood, as it was, apparently, hoped they would do.[17] The Unionists had meanwhile been arranging for the importation of arms on a big scale and these arrived in April.[18] The Irish Volunteers responded with their own gun-running operation in July. Thus, on the eve of the First World War, the country was on the verge of civil war. Meanwhile the Government declined to do what it should have done in these circumstances. It refused to ask the King for a dissolution so that the views of the electorate could be sought, as the Conservatives had proposed.[19]

As things turned out both sides achieved success – of a sort. The Twenty-Six counties got Home Rule, although this did not become effective until the end of the war when it was considered inadequate and was to be superseded, as we shall record, by a much larger measure of independence in the form of Dominion Status in 1921. Six of the Ulster counties managed to keep themselves out of the new southern state but were to be under prolonged attack – and remain so today.

UNIONIST RESISTANCE TO HOME RULE

There can be no doubt that the Unionists inflicted serious damage on their own reputation by their behaviour at this time. For they had defied the authority of Parliament, had begun to establish a provisional government and had built up and had drilled a new armed organization, the Ulster Volunteers. Thus they had set an example to the rebels against authority in the rest of Ireland or indeed anywhere else in the British empire. Their claim to be loyal and law-abiding citizens then seemed hollow and insincere, and was derided by their opponents as only conditional and basically self-seeking. After such behaviour they could not expect the same respect, still less the same affection, from the British nation to which they claimed so loudly to belong. This would, I believe, be a fairly accurate statement of the indictment brought against them. It would, however, be unwise to leave matters there. If real progresss is ever to be made with the solution of the Irish question, it is essential to try to understand the different points of view – including that of Ulster loyalists, although people in Britain now apparently find it much harder to do so than to understand the viewpoint of Irish republicans.

It is important to begin by recognizing that the legislation rejected by the Ulster Unionists was of a rather special kind. It was not legislation about property or taxation or social benefits or any of the other numerous issues that were the normal concern of government. It was legislation about the constitution and, even within this category, it was of a peculiar nature. For it provided for the transfer of the unwilling Northern majority from the jurisdiction of the Westminster parliament to that of a new parliament to be established in Dublin. Admittedly the new legislative assembly would be a subordinate body, but it was clearly understood that Westminster would not interfere in its affairs, and there was, of course, no suggestion that this devolution of authority, once granted, would ever be revoked. On the contrary the somewhat limited measure of autonomy proposed in 1914 could be seen as only the first step. That was how Redmond himself regarded it: 'Admittedly it is a provisional settlement . . . When the time for revision does come we will be entitled to complete power for Ireland over the whole of our financial system.'[20] Ulster could then expect to be harmed by a policy of economic nationalism, and, more generally, the enhanced degree of power over finance would naturally be accompanied by a wide extension of autonomy over other matters.

The Ulster Unionists could still regard themselves as a 'loyal band' whose respect for the Crown was undiminished, although they were unyieldingly opposed to the policy of the political party in power – a party that was proposing to break 'the implicit contract' on which the constitution was based.[21] What they were resisting was an attempt to drive them out of the United Kingdom and place them under the authority of a new regime for which they felt no sympathy. It was one thing to submit to normal legislation and accept the decisions of the Westminster parliament in a law-abiding way, but the Liberal Government was going much too far in claiming that it could expel the Northern majority, determine its subsequent political destiny and at the same time lay claim to loyal obedience. In such circumstances, the formation of a provisional government for Ulster could be regarded as a natural and, indeed, a justifiable response. Let us free ourselves from the 'map-image' discussed in chapter 1 and suppose that the people of one of the regions of Great Britain had been faced with a similar threat. We can safely infer that they would have responded in the same way as the British people in Northern Ireland. How could they or any other people be expected to be 'loyal' to a government that was kicking them out?

There is a further point of some importance. The Ulster Unionists were accused of defying 'the authority of parliament', but it is necessary to ask what was the basis of this authority. There was certainly no approach to consensus at Westminster in favour of Home Rule, as there should have been in dealing with an important constitutional issue of this kind. The Asquith Government could not even command a majority of votes in the House without the support of the small Labour Party and of the Irish Nationalist Party itself. The high moral tone adopted by the Liberals in presenting their proposals was also somewhat out of place. In 1906, when they could assume office without the help of the Nationalists, they had not been much interested in Home Rule. When they came to depend upon their support in 1912, Home Rule for the whole of Ireland became a moral issue and its opponents could be represented as irresponsible anarchists. To Ulster nostrils, there was a Pecksniffian odour about all this that was felt to be somewhat disagreeable.

A strong defence can be presented along these lines of the measures taken in Ulster to set up a provisional government. It is right to emphasize this point because that action was to be so widely condemned as rebellion posing as loyalty. There are, however, two important respects in which Unionist behaviour may be called in question. The first was the gun-running operation in 1914 organized by Colonel Crawford and the arming of the Ulster Volunteers; the second was the attitude adopted by the Unionists towards the Catholic minority in the North.

Could a provisional government have been supported by passive resistance, contemplated in 1893, as an alternative to opposition by force?[22] Is it possible that, when it came to the crunch, such resistance might not have been put down by brute force? At the Curragh army camp, the officers had taken an opportunity offered to them to resign their commissions rather than move against Ulster. It was doubtful whether the army or the navy would really have been prepared to open fire on people whose 'crime' was simply a determination to remain subjects of the King within the United Kingdom. Might it not have been wise, if bold, on Carson's part to have communicated with Crawford *after* the Curragh incident in order to tell him to cancel, or at least postpone, the gun-running?

Montgomery Hyde records how Carson asked Asquith in 1913 what he intended to do when the first 500 Ulstermen were shot down in Belfast: 'Asquith looked alarmed. "My God", he exclaimed, jumping to his feet. "Five hundred. I tell you that if one Ulsterman were shot in such a quarrel it would be a disaster of the first magnitude".'[23] Less direct means of repression might have been found but, whatever the exact method employed, the inconsistency in Liberal policy was undeniable. The Party had decided that it was neither right nor, in practice, feasible to continue to repress the Irish; but they were proposing to do just that in Northern Ireland. Even one of the Nationalist politicians, John Dillon, was to declare that 'You do not put down Irishmen by coercion. You simply embitter them and stiffen their backs.' With sympathetic insight he saw that this warning was true of the Ulster Unionists as well as the Nationalists themselves.[24]

The arming of the Ulster Volunteers would not have been decisive if, nevertheless, an armed conflict with Britain had taken place. It may be objected that the real purpose of the gun-running was to allow the North to protect itself against the South; but Home Rule would not have given the South an army, only control of the police. Subsequently a powerful guerilla offensive might, however, have been mounted, as later experience was to show. Another argument is that only by a show of force could the British Liberals be obliged to take Ulster's resistance seriously. Asquith, himself, had asserted in 1912 – with a fine disregard for the evidence – that 'Ireland is a nation, not two nations, but one nation'. As late as November 1913, Redmond informed him: 'I do not think anything like a rebellious movement can ever take place.'[25] The implication was that Ulster's resistance would be peaceful and could therefore be overcome. It must therefore be admitted that in a situation of this kind, the arming of the Ulster Volunteers provided a more powerful and convincing response than passive resistance.

A heavy cost was incurred by demonstrating Ulster's determination at this stage in this way. The military training in the South of the Irish Volunteers, already in hand, then seemed justified, and the example set in Ulster was to be copied almost at once by running guns into Dublin. Above all, Ulster's reputation was to be permanently damaged by what has come to be described as an act of armed defiance against parliament – a highly question-begging description, it is true, but one that has come to be widely and uncritically accepted.

What has just been said about the possibility of effective resistance without gun-running was necessarily speculative and uncertain. What must now be said, as we move on to the second reason for questioning Unionist behaviour, is not so. As has been stressed, the Irish nationalist movement had been quite insensitive in its attitude to the Ulster Protestants. The Ulster Protestants, in their turn, were to be quite insensitive in their attitude to the Ulster Catholics. The fact that the Ulster minority had also a claim to self-determination was simply ignored. In the circumstances, it was indeed the case that there had to be some losers. The doctrine of self-determination can be pushed to absurd extremes and lead into a hopeless impasse – as experience throughout the world has shown. Compromises are essential and partition was certainly the right alternative. When some such compromise has been reached, however, the winners are clearly under an obligation to treat the losers with fairness and generosity in all other respects – a moral obligation which, if observed, should also make for greater stability. Unfortunately the emphasis placed by the Unionists on 'Protestantism' was as much out of place as the Nationalist emphasis on 'Catholicism'. It is only fair to add that some of the Unionists did not adopt this attitude. Most notably, Carson himself did not. But the Unionist movement in general, closely linked as it was to the Orange Order, was clearly and emphatically Protestant. One can, therefore, well understand the Nationalists' attitude, expressed by Redmond, that 'The rights and interests of the Nationalists of Ulster will not be neglected or betrayed by us.'[26] The fact remained that partition could not be avoided. The questions for the future were whether the Nationalists – both in the North and the South – could bring themselves to concede the need for compromise and accept the division of the island, and whether the Unionists, for their part, would recognize their obligation to treat their minority with fairness and, indeed, with generosity. The prospects, on the eve of the First

World War, were not propitious on either side, and the events of the next eight years were to deepen antagonism and make a tolerable outcome still more difficult to achieve.

5

Independence or Unity –
Towards a Republic

The crisis in Ireland was averted, at least for the time being, by the outbreak of the First World War. It was then decided to postpone the implementation of the 1914 Home Rule Act until hostilities had ceased and a peace treaty had been signed. But the war did more, initially, than provide a reason for postponement; it also brought a new unity between both parts of Ireland on the one hand and Great Britain on the other which might, if all had gone well, have lowered the barrier between the Unionists and the Nationalists within Ireland itself. Any possibility of this kind was to be removed by the events of 1916, but initially the commitment to a new common cause may have seemed a hopeful development. On the part of the Unionists, the strong commitment to the war effort was only what was to be expected. The vast majority of the Ulster Volunteers now offered their services to the army that had so recently been ordered to threaten them. Their rifles were largely surrendered to the authorities. In the rest of Ireland, the response was also overwhelmingly one of support. Redmond at once declared himself on the side of the Allies, as did all the moderate nationalist leaders. There was, however, a split in the Irish Volunteers with a group of more extreme republicans under Eoin MacNeill refusing to support the Allies. Although only about a twentieth in number of the total Volunteer movement, they retained the name, Irish Volunteers, and the majority became the National Volunteers. The importance of the Irish Volunteers was to grow dramatically after 1916.[1]

Irish support for Britain was clearly manifested with about 170,000 men serving in the forces. There appeared then to be a real chance that the division between Unionists and Nationalists might be reduced by their joint involvement in the Allied war effort. But such a possibility was swept away by the republican rising of 1916 and the British blunders that followed. This rising, carried out in legally treacherous, if quite ineffective, collaboration with Germany, was one of the decisive steps towards a partitioned island.

The revolt was organized by the Irish Republican Brotherhood (IRB), with much of the initiative coming from John Devoy in the United States, who was in close touch with the Germans. Sinn Fein, with Griffith as leader, continued to oppose the use of force. The operation was carried out by part of the Irish Volunteers, although their commander, MacNeill, was not informed. When he finally learned what was planned he managed to prevent more than a few small incidents from taking place outside Dublin, but failed to do so in Dublin itself. The Government had been warned that there might be trouble but no forestalling action was taken in time. Roger Casement, who had been attempting to organize the supply of arms and ammunition from Germany, had been captured on 22 April after landing from a German submarine and a German ship carrying arms for the rebels had been sunk. These events appear only to have reassured the authorities instead of serving as a warning.[2] On 24 April 1916 the rebellion began and a number of positions were occupied in Dublin of which the General Post Office was the most important. It was there that Pearse proclaimed the establishment of a republic – to the astonishment of some passers-by. This rising proved to be an event of great importance. It is still celebrated every Easter by republicans, North and South, and the proclamation itself has become a hallowed text. It included the following sentences:

IRISHMEN AND IRISHWOMEN: in the name of God and the dead generations from which she receives her old tradition of nationhood, Ireland, through us, summons her children to her flag and strikes for her freedom . . . We declare the right of the people of Ireland to the ownership of Ireland and to the unfettered control of Irish destinies, to be sovereign and indefeasible . . . Standing on that fundamental right and again asserting it in arms in the face of the world, we hereby proclaim the Irish Republic as a sovereign independent state.

The first point to observe is that Pearse and the other six signatories had no mandate whatsoever from the Irish people to make this proclamation. They were in fact asserting that it was they who knew what the people really wanted. It is an assumption of a kind that was soon to be made on a much larger stage by Lenin and his fellow Bolsheviks and the world was to become familiar with the doctrine that an enlightened minority, however small, 'knows what the people really want'. In Ireland, the same aptitude appears to have come naturally to de Valera, who claimed in 1922 that: 'whenever I wanted to know what the Irish people wanted, I had only to examine my own heart and it told me straight off what the Irish people wanted'.[3] This is what Conor Cruise O'Brien has described as 'cognition through cardiac introspection'.[4] It may be tempting to dismiss as merely absurd such undemocratic arrogance, but experience suggests the need for prudence. The fact that such a claim was *initially* unwarranted did not prevent it from *becoming* effective, as subsequent events in Ireland were to show.

It has been estimated that only about 1600 men and a few women were involved in the rising. The Dublin populace, far from giving it even passive support, were strongly opposed to what appeared so clearly to be an act of folly involving useless slaughter and the destruction of part of the city for no purpose whatsoever. Thus John J. Horgan, a prominent Nationalist, was expressing a view widely held at the time when he wrote:

The only vestige of truth in this rhetoric [i.e. the proclamation of a republic] is the clear implication that the Irish Republican Brotherhood, the whole membership of which could have been comprised in a concert hall, was the mainspring of the whole business. This small body of conspirators by putting nationalism before religion had placed themselves outside the pale of the church. Ireland, which is surely the people of Ireland and not some disembodied figure of speech, had not been consulted at all.[5]

If the presumption of the rebels in claiming to speak for Catholic nationalists could thus be regarded as unwarranted, the pretence that they were speaking for all Irishmen was absurd. The Protestant unionists, who were roughly a quarter of 'the Irish people', had already shown in an uncompromising way their hostility even to Home Rule and were, to say the least of it, bound to oppose to the last ditch their inclusion in an Irish Republic.

There is no reason to suppose that Pearse, for his part, had understood that it would be necessary to coerce this large minority, although that was the logical inference from the Declaration. Nor was he a callous tyrant like Lenin or Hitler. The truth is rather that he failed completely to understand the Ulster problem or to appreciate the significance of what he was doing to Irish unity. This does not alter the fact that the Easter rebellion had driven a great new wedge between the two main groups that inhabited the island. The unionists were not only bound to resist the proposal for an independent Ireland, but to recoil from the treason of which, in their view, the rebels had been guilty. The latter had been collaborating with the German enemy with whom the Ulster Division was soon to be locked in a new and desperate battle on the Somme, and that was something that would not be forgotten. Moreover, the rebels were so narrowly obsessed with their own ideas that they had included in their proclamation, which was to be a founding document of the new republic, a grateful reference to their 'gallant allies in Europe'. These gallant allies were fighting not only against Ulstermen but also against men, mainly Catholics, from all the rest of Ireland. In a remarkable way the rebels combined great personal devotion and courage with a narrowness of vision amounting to naivety. Thus in the lulls of the fighting, Pearse and Plunkett were discussing the possibility of inviting a German princeling to become 'King of Ireland' – not a republic after all – when the Central Powers had won the war.[6]

It is not surprising that the rising was initially so unpopular in Dublin itself. Moreover, the circumstances were not such as to make armed rebellion justifiable from a Catholic theological point of view, and, to make matters worse, the IRB was a secret society which Catholics were forbidden to join. In the event, the rising was condemned by seven Catholic bishops with only one prepared to speak in its defence. But the other twenty-two kept silent and Cardinal Logue made no attempt to ensure that the condemnation would be general.[7] We cannot exclude the possibility that a general condemnation would have followed in time – if the original popular assessment of the action had remained unchanged. But this was not to be so. Within a matter of a few days, public opinion altered in a remarkable way. The rebels ceased to be regarded as criminally irresponsible extremists and became national heroes. An explanation usually given is that the military authorities behaved with undue harshness in executing the leaders. In defence of General Maxwell and his staff it could be said that the leaders of an armed rebellion planned with the help of the enemy in the course of a great war would have been treated in the same way in any other country. Moreover, the number of executions carried out was limited to fifteen – or roughly 1 per cent of those involved – and this at a time when, in all the armies, exhausted and shell-shocked infantrymen were liable to be shot for alleged cowardice in refusing to face the enemy. The fact remains that this was a bad political mistake. If the leaders had been treated as a few unbalanced eccentrics and condemned to moderate prison sentences, their cause might possibly have been discredited. But it was well-established British practice to alternate firmness with weakness – often out of phase with events – and at this point they were, momentarily, in a firm phase. The executions were made all the more offensive to public opinion by the fact that they were spread over nine days, so that, in the words of one commentator, 'it was like watching a stream of blood coming from under a closed door.'[8] Odd though it may seem, popular opinion might not have turned so much in favour of the rebels if they had been tried at once by drumhead court martial and executed without delay, but Maxwell followed the more 'correct' procedure of individual trials. The courage of the condemned men made a deep impression and, indeed, a growing respect for the courage displayed in the operation itself soon replaced the initial indignation provoked by its apparent pointlessness. In Yeats's much quoted words, it seemed that 'a terrible beauty is born'.

The organizers of the revolt had not expected to achieve a military victory and were fully aware from the outset that they would probably lose their lives. Their aim was to rouse the Irish nation. It was Pearse who expressed most clearly that the cause to which his life was dedicated could only be served in this way. He believed that bloodshed was 'a cleansing and a sanctifying thing' and for this reason had welcomed the war in Europe. 'The old heart of the earth needed to be warmed by the red wine of the battlefield.'[9] The son of an Englishman, he was a schoolteacher and a poet. He was a most devout Catholic and Christ's sacrifice appears to have been very much in his mind when he talked of the need for a new sacrifice in order to achieve a rebirth in Ireland. One man might free the Irish people, as one Man had redeemed the world.[10] Anyone who glorified bloodshed in this manner today would be denounced as a fascist or an admirer of Hitler's SS. In fairness, we must recall that many people viewed war differently at the time he was writing. One can think, for example, of the English war poet Rupert Brooke: 'Now God be thanked Who has matched us with His hour'. Thus the fact that Pearse was not alone in his views and the fact that he had had no experience of the reality of war must be taken into account. Yet it remains true that he expressed, in the most extreme form, views which would nowadays be regarded as absurdly wrong-headed and socially dangerous.

How far these views were shared by his comrades, including Tom Clarke and the Marxist James Connolly, may not be altogether clear but, if less inclined to romanticism, they were nevertheless prepared to believe that it was right to sacrifice their lives in order to make a gesture that would have profound repercussions, even if it appeared initially to be a failure. In political terms they were right.

Dr Garret Fitzgerald has reported the way in which his father, Desmond Fitzgerald, reacted to the outbreak of war.[11] Initially the reaction was 'one of jubilation. England would now be beaten and a resurgent Irish nationalism would assert and make effective our claim to real autonomy.' This elation gave way to despair when Redmond pledged Ireland's support for the Allies. 'But more disturbing than the mere statement [by Redmond] was the fact that immediately became apparent that it really represented the views of the majority of the Irish people . . . Our national identity was obliterated not only politically but in our own minds. *The Irish people had recognised themselves as part of Britain*' (my italics).

In a very illuminating passage, Fitzgerald goes on to say:

To those who reacted in this way to the events in Ireland that accompanied the outbreak of the Great War, an armed uprising appeared as the last and only hope of reviving the flickering flame of an apparently almost extinguished national spirit. Even if they had had the foresight to assess accurately the way in which Ireland has since evolved, and even if they had believed that their actions would contribute to a political division of the Irish nation for a period of not less than half a century, perhaps much longer – can we be sure that this would have deterred them from a course of action which they saw as justified in terms of several millennia of Irish history? Might they not have maintained their determination, preferring to pursue what they saw as a last chance of keeping the spirit of Irish nationalism alive, rather than to follow a course which, while it might have been more conducive to the preservation of Irish unity and peace during the twentieth century, might in their judgement have left Ireland united to Britain in aspirations and cultural outlook as well as united politically within its own boundaries?

Fitzgerald contrasts this view with the 'Redmonite' view of recent Irish history. It would be difficult, he says, to resist the thesis that Home Rule would have been granted after the First World War without any armed rebellion, and this would have led subsequently to complete independence. He goes on to report the opinion held by many people that the settlement which might thus have been achieved would have been no more prejudicial to unity than was the settlement in fact achieved. (It would surely have been far less so.)

The repercussions of the rising were profound. Its defeat and the executions that followed were undoubtedly an inspiration to Irish republicanism, and success was ultimately achieved in that the Irish republic they so much desired was established – but only at the cost of the indefinite partition of the island and, in modern times, at the cost of a patriotism debased by fanatics to the level of terrorism. Pearse's 'red line' is now the blood of innocent people of all ages and both sexes, blown to pieces by IRA bombs in public streets, restaurants and bus stations both in Great Britain and Northern Ireland. It would be grossly unfair to suggest that Pearse would have approved of the slaughter of innocent people at Enniskillen in November 1987, but this is what happens in the end when violence is glorified.

The British government helped unwittingly to foster the republican cause, not only by failing to remit the capital sentences but by following this severity with political weakness. Asquith paid an immediate visit to Ireland and, on his return, told the House of Commons that civil society in Ireland was in a state of collapse[12] – which was untrue – and that political action must be urgently taken to deal with the grievances that had led to the revolt. It was reported that some of the condemned men were greatly comforted by news of his statement for this appeared to show that the rising had produced a remarkably swift response.

Negotiations were begun in May, shortly after the rising, with Lloyd George in charge on the British side. He proposed that Home Rule should be accorded immediately but with the six northern counties excluded. Redmond was given to understand that the exclusion would be temporary; Carson that it would be permanent. When the truth was revealed by a Unionist peer (Lord Landsdowne) the negotiations collapsed. The moral for the South was that if you accepted any kind of compromise, you were likely to be cheated. Redmond's position and that of the Nationalist Party suffered accordingly. Lloyd George's next move was a weak attempt at conciliation – the release by the end of 1916 and early 1917 of all those who had been interned or tried and imprisoned. Their number included such extremists as de Valera, who immediately directed all their skill and energy to building up support for the campaign against Britain and to the discrediting of the moderates. From a British point of view, their release at this critical stage was an act of extreme folly, typical of the gyrations of the Government's policy. Thus the politically unwise executions of May 1916 were followed by the setting free, after only a few months in prison, of men who were just as militant as those executed and who had been as much involved in the fighting. (De Valera had escaped the firing squad as an American.) The next step was to summon a Convention of Nationalists and Unionists at which, however, no agreement was reached.[13]

The leadership of Sinn Fein passed from the more moderate Griffith in the autumn of 1917 to de Valera, who also became president of the Volunteers. Thus, within a year of his release, he had achieved a position of great power which boded no good for the preservation of the Union with Britain, or for the preservation of the union of North and South.

The government, for its part, was to make another mistake before the end of the war by introducing a bill to extend conscription to Ireland. This bill, passed in the spring of 1918, was an enabling measure which did not come into force, but it aroused intense resentment. Anti-British feeling was too strong by 1918, and war-weariness everywhere too great. It is noteworthy that the Catholic hierarchy took a very strong line against the measure. After discussions with de Valera and the other political leaders, Cardinal Logue arranged for public meetings to be called in every parish and a special mass to be arranged 'to avert the scourge of conscription'. A statement was to be read which began as follows:

In view especially of the historic relations between the two countries from the very beginning up to this moment, we consider that conscription forced in this way upon Ireland is an oppressive and inhuman law, which the Irish people have a right to resist by every means which are consonant with the law of God.'[14]

This strong concerted action by the hierarchy was in sharp contrast to their divided and hesitant reaction to the Easter rising – an illuminating contrast that cannot have escaped notice in Ulster. The text, drafted for the Cardinal by de Valera himself, could also be taken to mean that conscription should be resisted by force which is, of course, precisely what the republican leaders intended to do. The issue was not, however, put to the test for the war ended before the Act was implemented.

The Khaki Election of 1918 gave Sinn Fein an opportunity to appeal directly to the electorate by putting up their candidates. There was, of course, no question of successful candidates taking their seats at Westminster. They would abstain and assemble in a new national parliament which would be set up as a first step towards taking over the government of the country. In short, the regular election machinery was simply used for their own purposes. When the results were declared, it was seen that the old nationalist parliamentary party, led by Dillon since Redmond's death, had suffered such a heavy reverse that its claim to leadership was destroyed. The election clearly established Sinn Fein in that position with 70 per cent of the seats, much helped by the 'first-past-the-post' method of election. For Sinn Fein had received rather less than half the *votes* cast in Ireland as a whole, or about two-thirds in the twenty-six counties. Even if attention is confined to the South, a two-thirds majority fell well below the *consensus* desirable for constitution-making, as distinct from legislation. Admittedly the validity of the figures must have been somewhat impaired by there being 25 uncontested seats and by intimidation and other malpractices, but there is no way of knowing how a correction for these defects would have affected the size of the majority. It is interesting to observe in passing that, as things turned out, this Sinn Fein majority in votes in the South was roughly the same as that of the Unionists in the Six Counties. It is a similarity that should not be stressed too strongly for the differences between Sinn Fein and other non-Unionist parties in the South were presumably less than those between the Northern Unionists and the Northern Sinn Fein and other Catholic parties. The fact remains that the Dail – which meant effectively Sinn Fein – was not then in a position where it could really claim to speak on constitutional issues for an overwhelming majority in the twenty-six counties, still less in all thirty-two.

As was to be expected, the Dail confirmed the 1916 proclamation of an Irish republic and set up a new government. The official government authorities, for their part, made no immediate attempt to interfere with its activities although it was to be proclaimed illegal and driven underground later in the year. Over the months that followed its inception, the new body gradually extended its power throughout the South in parallel with the waning power of Dublin Castle. It raised a loan, it established its courts and it made its contacts with the local authorities. The Volunteers became the Irish Republican Army, although it took some time to establish effective central control over its activities, not to mention those of the IRB.

A new period of violence was now to begin. On the day the Dail first assembled – 21 January 1919 – the first two policemen were murdered in Tipperary. This was the start of a campaign aimed at the gradual annihilation of the already somewhat demoralized Royal Irish Constabulary. Although the police were armed, their equipment was often poor, and as Patrick Shea, the son of a Catholic police sergeant, has recorded their training in the use of firearms was slight.[15] By the end of 1919, with the RIC greatly weakened, something had to be done. As Townshend explains in his detailed study of the conflict, the army could have been strengthened and could have adapted itself to guerilla warfare. But the Government chose instead to reinforce the police with irregulars – the Black and Tans and the Auxiliaries – whose undisciplined and brutal behaviour was soon to become a further cause of bitter anti-British hatred. There was no unitary command and a serious lack of coordination. To quote Townshend: 'The fundamental problem . . . was that the Government never defined the nature of the Irish conflict, or the respective roles and aims of the police and the military forces.'[16] For our purposes there is no need to recount the events that followed up to the middle of 1921. As usual, many of the victims were not directly engaged in combat. The republican movement, for its part, had made it clear, when formulating its plans to resist conscription, that anyone who was in any way associated with authority was a legitimate target, and it acted accordingly when the struggle commenced in 1919. (This is another tradition that the modern IRA has vigorously maintained.) As we have observed, the British irregular forces acted with great brutality – so much so that their first commanding officer, General Crozier – himself a Unionist – resigned in protest. By the latter part of 1920, Lloyd George was confident that his policy was succeeding, and proclaimed at the Guildhall Banquet in 1920 that 'we have murder by the throat'.

But, as the struggle continued, the moral reaction within Britain against the behaviour of the British forces became increasingly strong.

At last, in 1920, a legislative measure for Home Rule was both passed and implemented. This was the Government of Ireland Act which provided for separate parliaments for the twenty-six counties of the South and the six in the North. In the former, it was an irrelevance. In the North, however, it came into force and was to remain in force until 1972. Its relevance to the immediate context is that, on the occasion of his opening of the new parliament in Belfast in June 1921, King George V made his historic appeal 'to all Irishmen to pause, to stretch out the hand of forbearance and conciliation, to forgive and to forget, and to join in making for the land which they love a new era of peace, contentment and goodwill'. To the adroit Lloyd George, this was an opening that could be used to end an increasingly unpopular conflict, or at least to place the moral responsibility for its continuance squarely on the shoulders of the republican leaders. He therefore proposed a truce. This was accepted and came into force in July. For the Irish guerillas it may have come just in time, for army reinforcements and martial law were beginning to have their effects. After the Treaty had been signed Michael Collins observed to Hamar Greenwood, the Chief Secretary for Ireland, 'You had us dead beat. We could not have lasted another three weeks. We thought you must have gone mad.' Townshend has warned against taking this comment too literally, but one might perhaps speculate about the effect on Ireland's future if Lloyd George had delayed his appeal for a truce and de Valera had been obliged to sue for terms. That, however, is a diversion in which we need not indulge.

6
The Responsibility for Partition

It was ironical that, after a long period of unyielding resistance to Home Rule, Northern Ireland should be the one part of the United Kingdom to be given it. As we have seen, this came about because the British Government was reluctant to admit the inevitability of partition and was, therefore, opposed to the simple exclusion of the North from any scheme for self-government in the rest of Ireland. On the contrary, the two parliaments were to be encouraged to work together through the proposed Council of Ireland and a further devolution of authority at a later stage was contemplated. Partition was to be a temporary phase and the new legislation would lead to Irish unity. As George Boyce has observed, after a detailed study of the contemporary records: 'There is no reason to believe that the British public was insincere in its conviction that north and south would unite at some future date, that Irishmen had no irreconcilable conflict but a community of interests that both sides obstinately refused to recognise.'[1]

The realization of any such hope depended upon the assumption that Home Rule, as then envisaged, would be acceptable to both parts of the country. If it were to be rejected and made unworkable in the South, was there any point in persisting with it in the North alone – the very area where there had been no demand for even this degree of autonomy? It might seem that the answer should have been in the negative, but any such inference was subordinated to the timing of measures which was partly determined by previous commitments. The Home Rule legislation of 1914 was bound to come into force after the signature of the last peace treaty – that with Turkey – unless amended or superseded by new legislation. It is true that, by 1919, the year in which a new Home Rule bill was introduced, it should have required no special insight to see that the degree of autonomy so provided – 'gas and water devolution', as it was sometimes contemptuously called – would not meet the demands of a South dominated by Sinn Fein. A number of observers – including Asquith – warned that the proposed measure was inadequate.[2] But there was another possibility: Sinn Fein might be crushed by strong action and Home Rule might then be acceptable. For there was a general – and understandable – reluctance in Britain to believe that a majority in the South really wanted full independence. On looking back at this period some sixty years later, it may be too easy to take for granted the inevitability of a move towards full independence and also to exaggerate the extent to which such a move should have been obvious at the time. After all, the Government of Ireland Act was being drafted in 1919, only three years after the Dublin rising of 1916 which had then been subjected to strong and widespread condemnation by the vast bulk of the population in Dublin itself. At the very time when the Dail was proclaiming a republic, the Union Jack was flying from houses in the area to welcome the return of soldiers who had fought for the Allied cause. After assessing the strength of popular support for complete separation at that time Tom Garvin concludes that it came to only about a quarter of the population of the island. Another quarter were unionist and about half were only mildly nationalist: 'Few wanted social revolution and few were interested in the Irish language. One could say that this non-moral majority were the true Sinn Feiners; they wished to be left alone by both British and Irish political forces.'[3]

In this situation, a case of a sort could be made for implementing the Home Rule legislation so strongly demanded in the past, though with separate provision for the North in order to meet Unionist opposition. A Home Rule parliament in Ulster as a by-product came to be regarded with some favour by the British Government. A Cabinet committee under the chairmanship of Walter Long concluded that: 'If it [British authority] is retained anywhere in Ireland the opponents of Great Britain will be able to say either that Great Britain is ruling nationalist minorities against their will, or that it is giving active support to Ulster in its refusal to unite with the rest of Ireland.'[4]

As an expression of Westminster's opposition to the integration of the North with the rest of the United Kingdom, these words might have been endorsed in 1985 as well as in 1919 – and by Mrs Thatcher as much as by Walter Long who had also been regarded as friendly to the Unionist case.

The Northern Unionists, for their part, had previously opposed devolution, even if accompanied by partition, for they had no desire for even this degree of separation from Great Britain. Nor is this all. For they were well aware that, in the northern Province where they would be in the majority, they would be accused of oppressing the minority. With full integration, the responsibility would rest with Westminster and the Ulster Unionists could not then be singled out in the same way as a target for vilification. The point was well made by Carson: 'It has been said over and over again, "You want to oppress the Catholic minority; you want to get a Protestant ascendancy there." We have never asked to govern any Catholic. We are perfectly satisfied that all of them, Protestant and Catholic, should be governed by Parliament . . .'[5] The Unionists had, however, come to believe that a Northern parliament might be a valuable safeguard against their being forced into the South. Captain Charles Craig – Sir James Craig's brother – expressed that altered opinion thus: 'an Ulster without a Parliament of its own would not be in nearly as strong a position as one in which a Parliament had been set up.'[6]

It was still necessary to determine the area in the North for which separate provision was to be made and at this point a marked change in attitudes was revealed. The Unionists were now firmly in favour of a six-county area because they perceived that this would provide greater stability, but the Cabinet committee came down in favour of the nine counties of the historic Province because *their* objective was not stability in the sense of a permanently partitioned island.[7] In the nine counties, the sectarian balance could well be too close for lasting exclusion and Irish unity would thus be restored. This was an important indication of the British attitude at that time – with the Conservative, Walter Long, as one of its main exponents. The Ulstermen, for their part, made it clear that their support for the new measure was conditional upon its applying to the smaller six-county area. That part of the Sinn Fein leadership which was prepared to countenance even temporary partition, wanted as small an area as possible to be excluded and were reassured by Lloyd George's promise of a future Boundary Commission which would, they thought, reduce the six counties to four, and four would not be 'economically viable' – whatever that meant. In fact the four would have been stronger economically for being stripped of the poorer western counties as well as more secure politically.

The new Parliament of Northern Ireland was opened by King George V on 7 June, and as we have recorded, the King appealed for forbearance, peace and reconciliation in the Northern Ireland Senate a fortnight later. This speech, prepared with the aid of advice from Smuts, brought to a focus the various pressures for a truce and Lloyd George immediately took the initiative by asking de Valera and Craig to attend a conference. The truce that followed, as we have observed in the previous chapter, came as a great relief to the hard-pressed republican guerillas as well as to the morally self-flagellating British. It was also to bring new dangers to the security of the Ulster majority who were so desperately anxious to remain within the United Kingdom.

De Valera sought at the outset to establish a position as the spokesman for all Ireland, and therefore proposed discussions with Craig as the representative of a minority. Naturally Craig would have none of this and insisted on his right to talk direct to the Prime Minister, notwithstanding Lloyd George's attempt to wheedle him into going to see de Valera. Craig could now claim that Ulster had made what its leaders had regarded as a sacrifice by accepting a measure of Home Rule that a large majority of its people had never sought. The position of the North had, therefore, been settled. It was now for London and Dublin to solve their own problems. In Britain, the Government's approach to these problems had changed. The reluctance to concede dominion status, so clearly felt and firmly expressed only a year before, had now been largely dispelled, and this was what Lloyd George offered to de Valera on 20 July 1921, diluted by certain safeguards and conditions.[8] De Valera refused for: 'the Irish people's belief is that the national destiny can best be realised in political detachment, free from imperialistic entanglements which they believe will involve enterprises out of harmony with the national character.' He went on to say that 'as they would threaten no nation or people, they would in turn be free from aggression themselves' – an astonishing inference in view of Belgium's recent fate. They would be prepared to recommend a treaty of 'free association with the British Commonwealth group'. He then continued:

As regards the question at issue between the political minority and the great majority of the Irish people, that must remain a question for the Irish people themselves to settle. We cannot admit the right of the British Government to mutilate our country, either in its own interest or at the call of any section of our population. We do not contemplate the use of force. If your Government stands aside, we can effect a complete reconciliation. We agree with you 'that no common action can be secured by force'.[9]

Implicit in this statement is the assumption that the Irish people constituted a nation of which the majority in Ulster were a part as much as anyone else. This assumption was still made as though self-evidently valid, notwithstanding the firm and unequivocal way in which that majority had insisted that they belonged to the British nation and were quite determined that they would continue to do so. The assumption that the whole issue could be settled without force if Britain stood aside was also quite unfounded. If faced with that situation, Ulster would have asserted its independence of the Southern state. Kevin O'Higgins once remarked that de Valera 'hates facts like a cat hates water'.[10] It was not an unfair comment but it would be unfair to confine its appliction to de Valera alone in the republican movement – then or now.

In retrospect, the emphasis then placed by Britain on dominion status and by Dublin on republican independence may appear to have been exaggerated, for dominion status has meant virtually complete independence, and the final step to a republic could be taken easily enough if a dominion so desired. Although there was some realization on both sides that this might be the case, there was still a widespread inclination to regard the distinction between republic and dominion as one of immense importance. There was even talk in London of 'dominion Home Rule', an intermediate case which would have permitted Westminster to retain some control over defence and foreign policy. We must, of course, allow for the strong emotions of the time as well as for the practical implications of different possible courses of action. To devoted republicans, such as de Valera, the oath of allegiance to the Crown was intolerable. This distaste had not, apparently, been softened even by the deep concern for Ireland's well-being expressed by the King when addressing the Northern Ireland parliament. To Irish republicans, then as now, it was the symbol that mattered, as much as the substance. To acknowledge the monarchy would be to betray the Irish republic of 1916. The Sinn Fein leaders did not, however, want the negotiations to break down on this issue. It was, of course. very desirable that no such break should occur on *any* issue, for this might lead to a renewal of hostilities and, as they were well aware, this would almost certainly be followed by the defeat of their weary forces. If, however, such a breakdown could not be avoided, the status of the North should be the reason, or should be made to appear so. The British Government, for its part, wanted to avoid precisely this, for they, on their part, were aware that a renewal of the conflict in defence of Ulster would be unpopular.

Up to a point, the two sides were, however, to proceed along the same path. In July, de Valera pointed out to Lloyd George that 'I have made it clear in public statements which reflect the views of the Irish people that Ireland, so far from disregarding the special position of the minority in North East Ulster, would be willing to sanction any measure of local autonomy which they might desire, provided that it were just and were consistent with the unity and integrity of our island.'[11]

The possibility of formulating a solution acceptable to Ulster received a good deal of attention in Dublin. Erskine Childers, in particular, analysed what genuine autonomy would require.[12] He pointed out, fairly enough, that a Home Rule parliament in the North would be subordinate to the national parliament in Dublin which could override its policies and even abolish it altogether. (This was indeed to be the fate of Stormont some fifty years later – at the hands of Westminster.) It might, therefore, be desirable to see whether the Northern parliament could be given a permanent guarantee that its powers would not be changed nor its existence threatened, except with the consent of a majority of its members. What this would have implied would have been federation in the full legal sense, as described by Wheare.[13] The classic example is the USA, where the federal government cannot directly infringe the legal powers of the states. Within their respective spheres, both are sovereign. Childer's sophisticated analysis was only peripheral however to Sinn Fein policy. The British Government, for its part, was attracted by the proposal that Ulster should have Home Rule within a united Irish dominion for this would be a better alternative than a partitioned Ireland with one part independent. In November 1921, shortly before the signing of the Treaty, Lloyd George proposed to Craig that the powers retained by Westminster under the Government of Ireland Act should be transferred to an all-Ireland parliament. To that parliament the North would send its representatives instead of sending them to Westminster. Within the six counties, the provincial legislature would continue to exercise the powers already transferred to it. This proposal – which was to be substantially revived many years later in the Forum discussions of 1984 (chapter 17 below) – was immediately rejected by Craig. We can be sure that, even if the proposal had contained the safeguards suggested by Childers, it would still have been turned down. For the Unionist position had been stated quite clearly and accurately by Craig. If, against the will of the majority of its people, the Province were to be thrust out of the United Kingdom, this majority would want to have the same independence as the South to determine its own future, although they would then use this independence, not to distance Ulster from Britain but, on the contrary, in order to ensure that, in every possible respect, the practical significance of exclusion from the United Kingdom was minimized. It was a firm refusal but a more dignified one than the Paisleyite protests after the announcement of the Anglo-Irish Agreement of 1985.

Even so, the resolve of Ulster's leaders was to be severely tested. For there followed an intense campaign to make them change their minds and fall in with the proposal to accept devolution from Dublin in place of devolution from Westminster.[14] Or, at the very least, they should abandon any claim to the two western counties where the nationalists were in the majority – admittedly by a slight margin. Almost the whole of the national press – even the *Daily Telegraph* and the *Daily Express* – turned its guns on Ulster. With some exceptions – notably Bonar Law – even the Conservative leaders were in favour of a settlement on an all-Ireland basis. There were several reasons for this change of attitude, including extreme weariness with the whole Irish question. Ulster's resistance to Home Rule, so useful in the past when they were trying to preserve the integrity of the whole United Kingdom, was no longer so relevant now that the twenty-six counties had been lost. In the new situation, the aim was rather to build up good relations with the new Dominion which should not be soured by partition. Moreover, the inclusion of Northerners in the Dail should in itself affect in a favourable way the evolution of Free State policy. In the North the effect of pressure from London was a heightened sense of insecurity and suspicion. It is scarcely necessary to add that, in the South, there was no general appreciation of these British efforts to foster Irish unity.

The view is sometimes expressed in Britain, even today, that it was a mistake to give in to the Northern Unionists in 1922. They should simply have been told that they would not be allowed to get away with their bigotry and prejudice and should have been compelled to become part of a united Irish state. Those who take this view should, however, be pressed to say exactly what, in their view, should have been done. Is it their contention that Ulster should have been forced to submit by the use of military force? As we have recalled (chapter 4), the Liberal Government considered doing so in 1914, but encountered strong opposition from the army, and there would certainly have been opposition from the electorate. Should a strong-arm policy have been adopted in 1921/2 and carried through with more resolution? Ulster was in a much weaker position to resist attack from any quarter than in 1914. There was little that the people in the North could have done to defend themselves against military pressure from Britain – even if they had been prepared to fire on British troops. Whether the British troops would have fired on them would however have been highly doubtful. Indeed, the British public would surely have found it hard to stomach the use of force against Ulster in order to conciliate a Dublin government, led by republican zealots, who had conspired with the German enemy, only five and a half years ago, and had engaged in armed rebellion at a time when Britain was fighting for her life. These were also the men who, more recently, had rejected British rule, set up their provisional government and engaged in a bitter guerilla struggle against the security forces. Only a year before, the Prime Minister had made his famous claim: 'We have murder by the throat.' But 'murder' had now become respectable and the Northerners were being urged to depart from the Britain they loved and submit to being ruled by 'murder'. One suspects that a good many British people would have experienced some difficulty in turning somersaults in this way. To have used force as well as persuasion in dealing with Ulster, would have been to go too far – even for Lloyd George.

What is less clear is whether the Provisional Government in Dublin would have thought that the use of force was going too far. As we have seen, de Valera rejected force in his letter to Lloyd George, but he made a number of statements, some of them apparently contradictory. Thus in 1917 he had maintained that 'Ulster must be coerced if she stood in the way' of an Irish republic. He went on to say that Ulster's claim to self-determination was really that of 'the robber coming into another man's house and claiming a room as his' – apparently a reference to the arrival of Protestant settlers in Ulster *three centuries* before. The following year he described the Unionists as 'a rock in the road' and then maintained: 'They must if necessary blast it out of their path.'[15] How much significance should be attached to statements of the latter kind? In August 1921 he told Lloyd George that they did not contemplate the use of force. At a private session of the Dail he expressed his opposition to force on the ground that they lacked the power, and such a policy would not succeed.[16] After all, there was still only a provisional government in Dublin and there was no regular army that could be despatched on a campaign against Ulster. It was, however, still possible to fight the Unionists in the same way as had been used only yesterday against the British forces – by means of a guerilla campaign. This is what, in fact, was done. One of the most astonishing features of the negotiations between the British Government and the Irish Provisional Government is that the truce was not, in practice, made to apply to the North. The IRA could, therefore, carry on with its campaign against Ulster without infringing the truce – and did not fail to do so.

The settlement reached in 1921 was denounced at the time by the republican movement as a betrayal on the part of the more moderate nationalists. In modern times, as the old feud within the Twenty-Six Counties has become less bitter, the political leaders in the Republic have been inclined to concentrate their criticism on Britain. Hence their insistence that it was the British Government that imposed partition on the island at that time, and subsequent British governments have been said to have maintained that division ever since. The evidence contradicts this verdict. The British Government did not impose partition but sought rather to prevent it. Partition did not have to be imposed. In the traditions, sentiments and aspirations of the people of the island, there was already a deep divide to which the Border accorded formal recognition, as was bound to happen when the southern twenty-six counties left the United Kingdom. To Irish nationalists this was a bitter outcome. If Unionists could bring themselves to appreciate just how bitter, that would be an important step towards mutual understanding. But the nationalists themselves cannot expect to achieve a new arrangement, and one more satisfactory from their own point of view, until they emerge from the world of myth and make-believe which they have regarded, for so long a time, as their natural habitat.

PART II
Politics and Policies in Northern Ireland

7

Home Rule in the North –
a Hard Beginning

In 1920 the new regime in Northern Ireland took over responsibility for the various functions delegated to it by the Government of Ireland Act of 1920. Thus it began what would be only a short life if the nationalists were right in supposing that an area as small as six counties – soon to be reduced, so it was assumed, to four by the Boundary Commission – would prove to be not economically viable. In the event, Home Rule in the six Ulster counties was to survive for half a century. As we shall see in a later chapter, its withdrawal in 1972 was not for reasons of economic weakness but was rather the consequence of the particular way in which the Westminster government reacted to civil unrest, rioting and terrorism and to the locus of responsibility for the preservation of law and order. The ending was like the beginning, both marred by violence. It was a hard birth and a hard death.

The difficulties of these early years were to mar the future prospects for devolution in Ulster. It is therefore important to observe the main pattern of events in order to understand more fully the manner in which government evolved in the years that followed. Civil unrest was not the only problem at the outset. There was the obviously difficult task of setting up a new administration for the North which had been ruled from Dublin as part of Ireland as a whole. A Cabinet had to be appointed and new government departments had to be formed. Experienced higher grade civil servants were urgently needed and a substantial number were recruited from the dying civil service in the former capital, some of whom were to continue to occupy important positions in Belfast throughout the inter-war period. Lower rank officials had also to be found and instructed in the ways of government. It was essential that those recruited at all levels should be not only competent but sufficiently loyal to the Northern state to be trustworthy. This was by no means an unduly cautious attitude for it was a well-established fact that the administration in Dublin, even the police intelligence service, had been infiltrated by the IRA.[1]

The many tasks of government had to be carried out by a new and largely inexperienced administration, and this had to be done at a time of continuing and indeed escalating civil war. The security problem confronting the new government may be briefly described. The guerilla campaign of the IRA had, of course, extended to the North, although, as was to be expected, with much less success. As was also to be expected, the Protestant extremists directed their fury against the

Northern Catholics who were suspected of sympathizing with the republican
guerillas and of sheltering them. In 1920 there had been some nasty outbreaks of
sectarian violence. The much weakened police force could not cope and Protestant
vigilante bands were formed to provide protection against the IRA and also to
perform acts of vengeance against members of the Catholic population. In a similar
way, the IRA, viewed as aggressors by the Protestants, could be regarded as
defenders by the Catholics. It was a vicious circle of violence which was to be
repeated half a century later, as we have good cause to know. A particular terrorist
act could provoke a riot or some other form of retaliation such as the expulsion of
Catholic workers from the shipyards which occurred after a policeman had been
murdered at the door of the church he was attending. Sometimes the victims were
chosen for assassination, not because they themselves were in any way involved in
the violence, but because they were held in high regard by their respective
communities and, for this reason, were made to suffer in a cruel game of tit-for-tat
retaliation. The Catholic minority came off the worse and large numbers were
forced to leave their homes. The new Government, for its part, seemed incapable of
restoring order with the limited resources at its disposal.

There should have been an important lesson in these grim events for the
nationalist movement. For this struggle was taking place at the grass-roots, and a
deliberate blindness was required in order to maintain that there was really one
Irish nation artificially divided by British trickery. The sectarian bitterness and
hostility went too deep and was of too long standing for any explanation of that kind
to be remotely plausible.

It was in these circumstances that moves were taken to establish the Ulster
Special Constabulary, and its formation was announced by Dublin Castle in
October 1920. This new body was to reinforce the police, with the A-Specials on
full-time duty for six months, the B-Specials on part-time duty in their own
localities and the C-Specials available for emergencies. Of these, the B-Specials
were to serve until 1970. The recruits for the new force were selected by
magistrates, and its membership was not confined to Protestants as has often been
alleged. What is true is that Catholics had to be screened with particular care and
had also to be exceedingly brave men, for they became targets immediately for IRA
vengeance. In practice, the Specials recruited a few Catholics initially but soon it
was a wholly Protestant force. At the outset they were allowed to act only in
conjunction with the police and could not fire unless instructed to do so; but the
difficulty of manning sufficient patrols with members of the much battered RIC
meant that this ruling had to be relaxed. The very effectiveness of the Specials was
bound to provoke a flood of republican propaganda against them in England and
elsewhere. It was held to be an undisciplined and partisan force that had been let
loose against the Catholic population. Such complaints were predictable. It does not
follow that they were unfounded. In his history of the force published in 1972 after
its disbandment, Hezlet sets aside these charges and gives a cool account of its
organization and activities.[2] A very different impression is conveyed by the bitter
and deeply felt account given shortly afterwards by Farrell.[3] Perhaps the two should
be read together.

Without becoming too deeply involved in so controversial a matter where firm
evidence is so hard to obtain, we may take it for granted that some of the really

serious complaints against the Specials during those early years were justified. It must have been particularly difficult to maintain discipline over small bodies of newly recruited men who were liable to respond to the sectarian bitterness of the time. With arms in their hands, the temptation to pursue the traditional vendetta must have been strong, and it was indeed something of a mercy that atrocities on a much greater scale did not take place. But it must be borne in mind that the alternative, given the policies of the British Government, would have been vigilante bands who would have behaved much worse, and the formation of the Specials had some effect in strengthening discipline. Moreover it must be remembered that the force was required in order to meet the attempt by the IRA to break down opposition to a united Irish republic by the uninhibited use of force against the majority of the inhabitants of the six Northern counties. The responsibility for this situation rested primarily with the political leaders in Dublin but also with the British Government which might have provided the regular police with more support from the army. In negotiating the truce of July 1921 it should have been made clear that it would have to be strictly observed in Ulster as well as elsewhere. The IRA were careful to observe its terms in the South lest hostilities be resumed but felt that they could, with impunity, sustain their campaign in the North. The failure of the British Government to insist upon consistent respect for the truce has received surprisingly little attention. The British authorities, for their part, did take steps to respect the truce in the North as well as in the rest of the country. The Specials themselves were stood down for a time and there was no army activity. The new administration in Dublin took a different line. With the struggle against the British now ended in the Twenty-Six Counties, the full force of the IRA would be deployed in the North with two objectives: first, to provide the Northern Catholics with some needed protection and, secondly, to try to wear down Protestant resistance.

Towards the end of 1921, a very difficult year, responsibility for the preservation of law and order was transferred to the Government of Northern Ireland in accordance with the Government of Ireland Act. Shortly afterwards, the British Government, as a friendly gesture towards the Irish Free State, and with no concern for Northern Ireland, released all the IRA prisoners. For them the struggle in the South was over but its ending only left them free to move into the North where the guerilla movement was thus strongly reinforced. As Buckland has observed: 'From the very start Northern Ireland's interests were subordinated to those of Britain and the need for a settlement in the South.'[4] The months that followed were marked by a bitter struggle in Northern Ireland with police and the Specials at full stretch. The army, of course, was under the control of the British government for this was not a 'transferred' responsibility. Its duty was to defend the whole of the United Kingdom against external attack. Westminster would have been acting only in accordance with what its own legislation implied if it had deployed the army as fully and effectively as possible, especially in the border areas. A cautious policy was followed, however, lest the truce should be put in danger by an attempt to defend Northern Ireland – a cause that would attract little electoral support in England.

In January 1921, the Royal Ulster Constabulary was formed and took over from the old RIC. In April the Northern Ireland Government introduced a Special

Powers Act which replaced the previous Westminster legislation, the Restoration of Order in Ireland Act (ROIRA) of 1920. Under this new Act, orders could be introduced which, as under ROIRA, gave the authorities draconian powers of arrest and detention. This enabling legislation was to be left on the statute book until 1972 – with much damage to Ulster's political reputation – although there were long periods when the more important orders were withdrawn. The Special Powers Act and the B-Specials were to become longstanding grievances of the minority. The RUC was also viewed with some suspicion and resentment. Here again there was one of those vicious circles that are too frequent in Ulster's affairs. Although Craig accepted the recommendation of a committee that a third of the force should be Catholics, it was not easy to recruit Catholics who were at once accused of treachery by their own side. Thus the RUC was to be more predominantly Protestant – and, for that reason, open to criticism. Whatever the truth of the many complaints about the abuse of authority by the various Crown forces, there can be no doubt that the minority felt it was being victimized. Nor can there be any doubt that, as a consequence, the reputation of the Government of Northern Ireland was badly damaged outside the Province.

Craig had two meetings with Michael Collins who was openly prepared to accept responsibility for the IRA campaign.[5] Although a pact was finally drawn up, it failed. Ultimately the activity of the IRA in Northern Ireland was brought to an end, not through such negotiation nor by means of any special assistance from Britain, but by the outbreak of civil war within the Irish Free State itself. For a time, the division between the supporters of the treaty, led by Griffith and Collins, and its opponents, led by Lynch, O'Connor and de Valera, may have had the effect of worsening the position in Ulster. Both sides wanted to sustain their combined guerilla offensive against the North, and Collins, for his part, urged the desirability of combined action in the hope that the breach between the two Catholic factions would be less likely to widen if they were both engaged in the North. For a time this tactic may have helped but the situation in the Free State became tense when the Irregulars – as the forces opposing the treaty and supporting the more extreme republican viewpoint were called – occupied the Four Courts in Dublin in April 1922. Although the provisional government and its supporters won a majority in the election in June, the hostility between the two sides soon flared into open warfare. For the North, this conflict came as a much needed relief. With the IRA split into two factions that were now at each other's throats, tranquility was gradually restored in the North. By the end of the Civil War in the South in May 1923, there was too much war-weariness for the resumption of any new assault against the Protestants. Although there were to be periodic IRA attacks over the next half century, some of them troublesome, these could be contained, and conditions were to remain comparatively peaceful until the beginning of the present crisis in 1968. For the RUC succeeded fairly quickly in crushing the Protestant paramilitaries when the collapse of the IRA offensive allowed them to concentrate their efforts.

The Civil War in the Irish Free State deserves careful attention for reasons of a more lasting kind than the relief it then brought to Ulster. It is important to stress this point because so little appears to be known about this conflict outside Ireland. It is probable indeed that few people are even aware that such a war took place. Yet it ought to serve as a grim warning to those who advocate the withdrawal of British troops from Northern Ireland at the present time and do so on the too facile assumption that the Irish, if thus left to themselves, would be sure to find an acceptable solution to their problems. That is certainly not what happened in 1922–3. The civil war of that period was not one fought between Catholics and Protestants, between the Irish and the pro-British. It was a war fought within the Twenty-Six Counties between two Catholic factions who, only a year before, had been fighting shoulder to shoulder against the British. The conflict was a particularly bitter one, with much loss of life and destruction of property, including part of Ireland's fine architectural heritage. The bitterness of the struggle is illustrated by the fact that Collins himself was assassinated by the Irregulars. On the Republican side, Brugha was to be shot down in action and Childers was to be executed.

The new Government, for its part, was uninhibited in the penalties it inflicted on its prisoners. 'During the last six months of the civil war almost twice as many republican prisoners were executed by the Free State authorities as had been executed by the British during the whole course of the struggle from 1916 to 1921.'[6] Prisoners could be tried by military courts and executed if found in possession of arms and ammunition. What was particularly severe was the official policy of executing important prisoners in reprisal for the assassination of government supporters by the Irregulars. By the end of the conflict, 67 prisoners had been shot as reprisals for actions in which – as they were prisoners – they could not, of course, have taken part. One can readily envisage the horrified reaction there would have been, not only in Ireland but in England and abroad, if the British authorities had behaved in this way, and the outrage that would have been provoked if the hard-pressed Ulster Government had done so.

There appears to be no accurate record of the number of people killed in the course of this civil war but Neeson suggests about 4,000 in total or roughly 300 a month.[7] This estimate is also quoted by Lyons at the end of his account of the conflict. What is puzzling is that both authors accord so little prominence to so high a death rate and content themselves with mere footnote references. Rather more than a footnote would be appropriate even if the number were reduced to 700 as Coogan[8] suggests and Murphy broadly supports.[9] By comparison about 3,000 people have died in the current disturbances in the North which have lasted for twenty years, not just thirteen months. Moreover the struggle in the South was ended only by the imposition of the most draconian measures by the Government and by the excommunication by the Roman Catholic hierarchy of the rebel forces, including de Valera and the other leaders. By comparison the official measures adopted in dealing with terrorism since 1970 have been very mild, but have nevertheless been strongly criticized by the hierarchy. Although the terrorist campaign of the modern IRA is not regarded as a 'just revolt', the possibility of resorting once more to excommunication does not seem to have been seriously considered. Difficult issues are encountered at this point which must be postponed for later discussion in chapter 20.

8

Devolution in Northern Ireland: an Overview, 1920–1972

'The first practical trial of Devolution in the United Kingdom has taken place under conditions that weighted the scales against its success. Yet its achievements are by no means insignificant.'[1] To this fair-minded comment by Nicholas Mansergh we may add the fact that Northern Ireland was not only the first but is still the only British region where government has been devolved. The experience acquired during that half-century under the Home Rule legislation of 1920 should, therefore, be of value and interest in assessing the case for or against devolution in the rest of Great Britain. As was only to be expected, the Royal Commission on the Constitution (Crowther/Kilbrandon) sought evidence on Northern Ireland, but this example has not always been followed.[2] For it would probably be true to say that other investigators have sometimes been so perplexed and discouraged by the special problems confronting government in the area as to conclude that little of relevance to other regions can be inferred from this solitary experiment. A notable exception was the Labour MP, the late Professor John Mackintosh. He conceded that the room for manoeuvre by small countries tied to large neighbours is limited. 'Given that popular demand would insist on no higher taxes and no lower standard of services, the scope for regional variations of policy is small.' He then continued: 'On the other hand, though Northern Ireland never wanted to be forced into Home Rule, it must be accepted that the system has become very popular. Very, very few in the country would wish to give up the experiment now and become a totally integrated part of Britain once again.'[3] Perhaps this was too favourable a verdict. It is certainly one that would have been disputed in Ireland when it was written in 1968, and impending events were soon to shatter the degree of stability achieved at that time. However, this is to anticipate.

THE CONSTITUTION

The Northern Ireland constitution has been described and analysed in a number of authoritative studies and a broad outline will suffice here.[4] The Parliament to which authority was devolved under the 1920 Act consisted of a Governor, acting on behalf of the Sovereign, and two Houses. The House of Commons consisted of 48 members, to be elected by proportional representation. A Senate of 24 was to be appointed by the Commons, with *ex officio* members, the Lord Mayor of Belfast and the Mayor of Londonderry. Although an interesting provision allowed members of one House to attend and speak in the other House, without voting, it was unfortunate that a more imaginative procedure for determining the membership of the Senate had not been devised initially and was not introduced subsequently when it had become clear that the legislation of 1920 would apply only to Northern Ireland where the same party would be in power in the Commons indefinitely.[5] A better organization and less elaborate ceremony might have been more work-manlike. Undoubtedly the ceremony seemed over-elaborate for so small an area, although it must be recalled that the legislation had been designed with the rest of Ireland primarily in mind and it had therefore been thought important to demonstrate that this was meant to be a real parliament with legislative powers which, so it was hoped, would be substantially expanded when the two parliaments, North and South, came together and agreed to constitute the proposed Council of Ireland 'with a view to the eventual establishment of a Parliament for the whole of Ireland.'[6]

The powers of the new parliament were not specified. What were specified were the powers it could not exercise. It could legislate only on matters relating to Northern Ireland and the matters excepted from its authority were those normally exercised by the central government in a federation: foreign policy, peace and war, defence, external trade, exchange rate policy, domestic monetary policy and the like. (These are modern functional terms, not those used in the legislation.) As well as the powers thus 'excepted', were those 'reserved'. The different term was employed because some or all of these reserved powers were to be handed over to a parliament for the island as a whole, if that were to come into being – as the British government hoped it would. These reserved powers were mainly fiscal. The principal taxes were retained in this way by Westminster. The wide range of responsibilities thus left to the Northern Ireland parliament therefore included the preservation of law and order; public health; hospitals; social security and other social benefits; education; roads, railways and internal transport services; agricul-ture, industry and trade; housing; planning; local government. As things turned out, the importance of some of these transferred powers was to expand enormously in the years ahead, in particular those that fell under the broad heading of the welfare state. This could not, of course, have been adequately foreseen when the legislation was being drafted in 1919/20. The legal system, which was similar to that in England, was also a domestic concern. In the event of any dispute over constitutional powers, an appeal could be made to the Privy Council.

A devolved government is subordinate to the legislature from which it has derived its power. In this respect its legal position is quite different from that of the state governments in a true federation like the USA.[7] Even if devolved government were to be established in every region in Britain, this would not turn the country into a federation in the full legal sense, although Bogdanor has suggested that such an arrangement might be conveniently described as 'federal devolution'.[8] The Government of Ireland Act (1920) was quite explicit on this point (Section 75). The decisions of the new assembly could, therefore, be over-ridden at any time by Westminster; but it was recognized that repeated intervention would make devolution pointless and destroy the credibility of any regional government. (As a somewhat cynical postscript we may add that frequent intervention would have deprived Westminster of one of the main attractions of Home Rule – the attraction of getting rid of the Irish.) There was, therefore, a Speaker's Ruling that the policies for which the Government of Northern Ireland was responsible should not be debated at Westminster.[9] It was an understandable attitude but detachment may have been carried too far. For it would have been possible for Westminster to have adopted a procedure that would have allowed it to intervene on some important and potentially explosive issues, such as the local authority franchise and even education, without becoming constantly embroiled. But nothing much was done until too late. Moreover, Westminster's attitude was not consistent, for close Treasury supervision and control were applied when public money was being spent – even when the sums involved were very small. Thus the Northern Ireland Government was not in practice permitted the free hand that might have been inferred from Westminster's restraint in not over-ruling the regional parliament's legislation. In evidence to the Royal Commission on the Constitution I referred to this dubious combination of *laissez-faire* with regard to some matters and detailed control with regard to others. 'This line of thought might be pushed to the point of saying that Stormont has been free from interference in cases where interference might be most justified but has been unduly restrained by financial control in dealing with certain other matters that should be the core of provincial authority.'[10]

The Province was also represented at Westminster by twelve members elected under the same franchise and by the same first-past-the-post method as in Great Britain. The problem of dual representation, discussed in chapter 4, remained. Ulster members could vote on all matters affecting Great Britain including services corresponding to those devolved. As we have recorded, however, Westminster did not debate the internal affairs of Northern Ireland. This was the same unbalanced arrangement as that proposed in earlier Home Rule measures which would not have been permanently acceptable for a larger area with more representation. If, indeed, the Home Rule legislation of 1920 had also come into force in the South, the difficulties created by such an arrangement would soon have been thought intolerable. The only reason why dual representation for Ulster did not lead to collapse was because the number of MPs sent to Westminster was so small. Even so, there were occasions when their presence was critical – and therefore resented by those who encountered effective obstruction or defeat as a consequence. This was one of the respects in which a special feature of Ulster's situation – in this case its small size – proved to be an advantage, not a disadvantage. Devolution for Scotland and Wales, as proposed in 1978/9, would have been a very different matter.

THE BOUNDARY COMMISSION

The authority of the new parliament extended over the six Northern counties but, as we have observed, the boundary was to be reviewed by a tripartite commission. When the commission was established, the Unionist government declined to nominate a representative. 'Not an inch' was Craig's attitude, which was of course strongly supported. It was, however, the wrong attitude. By refusing even to negotiate, the Unionists laid themselves open to the charge of unreasonable obduracy. By failing to recognize that some realignment might actually be helpful to them, they may have made a serious strategic mistake. A local Ulster lawyer was, however, nominated by Westminster to represent them. Eoin MacNeill represented the Irish Free State, and a South African judge was chairman. When it became clear that a large revision would not be contemplated, and that, furthermore, the revision under consideration would take some land from the South even if more would be taken from the North, MacNeill resigned. The status quo was simply preserved. In this way an important opportunity was lost. A substantial transfer of territory could have left the Unionists with an almost impregnable, if smaller, area which might also have been to the advantage of the remaining minority who would then have been living with a more secure and therefore, perhaps, more tolerant majority. It would have strengthened – not weakened – the North economically by removing some of the poorer rural areas. Even without going so far, the border which writhes in and out along the county boundaries, could have been rationalized – and made much more easily defensible. To mention just one example, it would surely have been wholly beneficial to have got rid of the Catholic and fiercely republican salient at Crossmaglen.

The tripartite agreement about the border reached in December 1925 was finally signed 'in a spirit of neighbourly comradeship'. *What this meant was the recognition of partition by the government of the Irish Free State* – one of the occasions on which recognition has been accorded, only to be denied at a later date, or so qualified as to lose much of its meaning. It was scarcely surprising, therefore, that the Ulster Unionists were unimpressed when a Dublin government again recognized the border in signing the Anglo-Irish Agreement in 1985 as though a new concession were being given in each case. In 1925 the agreement was registered with the League of Nations; in 1985, with the United Nations.

GOVERNING WITHOUT CONSENSUS

Of the various conditions that weighted the scales against the success of devolution in Ulster, the most obvious was the lack of a consensus in support of the existence of the new state. It is generally assumed that the Catholic minority who then constituted about a third of the population, were unanimously opposed to the partition of the island and would have greatly preferred to belong to the Irish Free State. This assumption, however valid in 1920–2, did not exclude the possibility that many of them might have been led to modify their views in time by the adoption of sensitive and equitable policies on the part of the successive Unionist governments. The likelihood of their becoming realistically reconciled would also have been strengthened if Dublin had been sufficiently farsighted to avoid thereafter the futility of a clamorous irredentist policy. Unfortunately neither condition was fulfilled. In modern times, however, successive opinion polls have suggested that a substantial majority of Catholics would prefer to remain in the United Kingdom – an issue to be taken up in chapter 21. These polls, if valid, refer in the nature of the case to grass-roots opinion. The minority's leaders were hostile and have continued to be so, with few exceptions. What was of particular importance was the attitude of the Catholic hierarchy which refused to give formal recognition to the provincial government throughout the fifty years of its existence. Although some functional cooperation – in particular in education – was ultimately conceded, at the outset this was not so. Even the obvious need for consultation on practical matters was denied. For example, an invitation to appoint representatives to serve on a committee dealing with educational policy was brusquely rejected by the Catholic hierarchy in 1921. A large number of the Catholic schools throughout the province refused to recognize the new Ministry of Education and even went so far as to reject its pay cheques. Thus for a short time Ulster's Catholic teachers were paid by Dublin until the financial strain became excessive. The local authorities with Nationalist majorities were also in revolt and refused to carry out their duties. According to Lawrence: 'The Ministry of Home Affairs went out of its way to try to establish cordial relations with all local authorities but was obliged to appoint commissioners in place of twenty-one defaulting councils.' This was one of the problems confronted by the Government in attempting to establish its authority in the face of what he describes as 'fanatical opposition'.[11]

As the violent years of the Troubles receded into the past, sectarian attitudes softened, at least a little, and conditions improved; but the events of the early years left an enduring mark on devolution in Ulster. This can be seen very clearly in local government. What was to be done if the authority of the state was not accepted? The difficulty was, of course, exacerbated by the way in which the Border was drawn for a substantial revision would have eased, even if it could not have solved, the problems posed by sectarian demography. But the Border was not changed in 1925 and in any case the Government had already taken action designed to undermine Nationalist power at the local level.

In 1922 proportional representation for local government was abolished in order to strengthen the Unionist position. This was one of the few occasions when a Westminster government challenged the authority of the devolved government, in this case under Section 12 of the Act of 1920; but the challenge was abandoned when Craig threatened to resign.[12] It was an unfortunate precedent. Moreover – then as many years later – Westminster's stance in favour of PR was all the less convincing because no party at Westminster large enough to have any chance of winning power was in favour of the system. It was also deeply discouraging for the Ulster minority who were forced to infer that Westminster was not an effective court of appeal against discrimination. The abolition of PR at the local level was followed by a loss of thirteen councils by the Nationalists and a gain of one. They then held only eleven out of seventy-three.

In local government elections the franchise in Ulster, as in Great Britain, was confined to householders and their spouses which meant that other relatives, lodgers and so on were without the vote. This did *not* mean, as has sometimes been wrongly alleged, that the vote was restricted to those who *owned* their own houses. Naturally both Protestants and Catholics were excluded, with the Catholics affected more in Belfast and Derry according to two sample inquiries.[13] There was also a vote attached to non-residential property, and as a result 1.3 per cent of the electorate had more than one vote. As Whyte has observed: 'On the whole, however, the nature of the local government franchise made only a slight difference to election results.'[14] Unionists gained a little advantage from this local franchise but it would have been sensible from their own point of view to have followed Westminster in 1945 by abolishing the property vote and extending the franchise to all adults. They were not, however, to make even this small gesture to the minority, and the harm done to Unionism in twenty years' time was to be enormous. For this unreformed franchise provided the civil rights movement twenty years later with a powerful slogan: 'One man, One vote'. To people outside the Province this slogan conveyed the false impression that the franchise in all the Northern elections was restricted – and restricted in elections for the provincial parliament and for Westminster as well as in local elections. Even worse, it may well have suggested that Catholics were excluded altogether from parliamentary government by being denied the right to vote. There can be few instances where an act of petty political meanness was to incur such severe retribution.

Much more important was the way in which ward boundaries were drawn. Some departure from exact arithmetical representation is always to be expected but the discrepancy may be deliberately exaggerated in such a way as to favour a particular political party. This practice of gerrymandering is not, of course, peculiar to Northern Ireland. As Barritt and Carter have informed us,[15] the word 'gerrymander' comes from Massachusetts and survives as a memorial to a Governor Elbridge Gerry who was a master of the art. In Ulster the redrawing of the ward boundaries in 1923 helped to compensate for Unionist weakness in some vulnerable areas. In order to assess its importance, the percentage of Nationalist councillors can be compared with the percentage of Catholics in the *adult* population – not the total population for that would include a disproportionate number of Catholic children. It will be observed that a comparison of this kind rests on the assumption that all Catholics voted Nationalist – i.e. in favour of a united Ireland – and all Protestants voted Unionist – i.e. in favour of continued union with Great Britain. The assumption is a fairly reasonable one. Statistics presented by Hewitt[16] for twenty-four areas with Catholic majorities in the adult population show that there was a Protestant majority of councillors in sixteen areas and of Catholics in only nine (1967). There were some marked divergences from proportionality. For example, in Londonderry a Catholic 62 per cent were represented by 40 per cent of the councillors, and in Enniskillen, 49 per cent by 33 per cent. In Downpatrick, on the other hand, a Catholic 69 per cent had 92 per cent of the seats and in Ballycastle 57 per cent had 83 per cent. For the advantage did not always lie with the Unionists.

When all such allowances have been made, the fact remains that local democracy was badly distorted in order to strengthen the Unionists' position. It is true that in the Westminster House of Commons, parties backed by only about a third of the votes have been able to form majority governments as a consequence of the first-past-the-post system; but the disparity in Derry, preserved for so many years, was a greater offence. This was not the way to try to reconcile the minority. Nor was it the way to gain and hold respect outside Ulster – a consideration that appeared to be very rarely taken into account by a Unionist Party that had become so introverted, and thus so different from the party that Carson had once led. It might have been more shrewd – as well as more ethical – to have accepted a larger number of Nationalist controlled councils. If these councils had persisted in the defiant and uncooperative behaviour displayed when the Government of Ireland Act came into force, the fault would clearly have rested on their shoulders, and town commissioners could then have been appointed without the scandal attaching to gerrymandering. And, in the event, the Nationalist councils might not have continued to behave indefinitely in such a way in the face of this threat.

The abolition in 1929 of PR for elections to the Northern Ireland House of Commons was a rather different matter. In this case the aim was not to weaken the Nationalists but to preserve the unity and strength of the Unionist Party in the face of other claims for the Protestant vote. These other claimants were the still small Labour Party and the Independent Unionists who were usually to the Right of the official party. The Unionist ranks must be firmly held both in order to demonstrate that the Border would be maintained, and also to ward against the danger that confusion about the use of second preferences might allow some anti-partitionists to slip into the House. In so far as this last danger was a real one, the Nationalists were denied some small and probably temporary gains. But their position was not in the event made any weaker than it had been, as subsequent elections were to show.

We have referred above to the special features of Ulster politics that hampered this sole British experiment with devolved government. One of the most outstanding of these features was that the same party remained in power throughout the whole of the half-century of the parliament's existence. It would be quite wrong, however, to infer that this dominant position depended upon electoral malpractices. The reason was quite simply that every election was fought on the same issue, the future of the state itself. There could hardly be a more basic one. So long as the state's existence was challenged and the pressure for a united Ireland remained, Protestants would continue to vote with almost complete unanimity for the Unionist party, and were repeatedly successful because the Protestants were about two thirds of the population. No party at Westminster in modern times has ever had anything like such massive support from the electorate. It must be clearly appreciated that Unionist dominance was not achieved by establishing a police state nor even by electoral malpractices. Its support rested on the will of a large majority. To quote the assessment made some years ago by two Quaker investigators: 'Our general conclusion is that in its composition the Northern Ireland Parliament reflects the views of the people [i.e. the majority] with no more distortion than is normally to be found in democratic parliaments. Its real peculiarity is that, being elected mainly on the constitutional issue, it has no alternation of parties in office.'[17]

It is of some importance to observe that the same party is more likely to be returned to power again and again for an indefinite period at the sub-central than at the central level of government. The danger is not new and was clearly described by Madison in the course of the debate about the American constitution.

The smaller the society, the fewer probably will be the distinct parties and interests composing it; the fewer the distinct parties and interests, the more frequently will a majority be found of the same party; and the smaller the number of individuals composing a majority, the smaller the compass within which they are placed, the more easily will they concert and execute their plans of oppression.[18]

Madison's anticipation was to be well vindicated over the years by party politics in some of the American state governments. In Britain, one need only think of Labour domination in local government in Scotland and Wales and of Tory domination of many areas of southern England. So much is commonplace – and in Northern Ireland there was the further powerful consideration that the existence of the region as part of the United Kingdom was at stake.

A party that remains in office for a lengthy period is in danger of losing some of its edge because it is too secure. The Nationalists were the main party in opposition, although they did not accept that official status until 1965 lest, by doing so, they would be recognizing the legitimacy of the constitution. As a permanent opposition, they failed to acquire experience of government and were inclined to accord almost exclusive attention to sectarian issues. Both parties suffered in quality because in this situation politics did not attract as much talent as might have been the case with an alternation of parties in office. To the young Catholic, membership of the House offered a convenient platform for directing propaganda against the ruling party but no prospect of attaining office and acquiring real political power. It might be possible to persuade the government to modify some of its measures a little, as the Nationalist leader, Joseph Devlin, did with regard to education. But that was all. The young Protestant, for his part, was confronted with the fact that, to get adopted for a seat, he would have to join the Orange Order, take part in its parades and commit himself to a doctrinal condemnation of Catholicism as something essentially evil. To many educated middle class Protestants, the price in terms of boredom and embarrassment may have seemed too great to outweigh the modest attractions of being a member of parliament. Moreover, the old men stayed in power too long between the wars, blocking the road to advancement and discouraging independence of thought by their insistence on keeping the ranks firmly closed. Craigavon remained in office until he died in 1940, and was succeeded by Andrews. After a dispute within the Unionist Party, Andrews was succeeded by Brooke (Brookeborough) who remained in office until 1963 when he in turn was succeeded by O'Neill. The Cabinet was then comparatively young and there was a growing suggestion of some change in the political climate. Membership of the Orange Order ceased to be a condition for membership of the Unionist Party, thus reducing a barrier to recruitment. A few of the Unionist MPs were not members and even one or two Catholics chose to join the party and were allowed to do so. But this happened much too late.

It is a familiar complaint that democratic government may be weakened when there is a large 'silent majority' that is too inclined to opt out of politics. In Northern Ireland, the conditions just described were bound to encourage opting out. The middle class, in particular, was inclined to stand aside from regional politics – with the result that the sectarian characteristics became even more marked and enduring. It is not uncommon even today, when so many of the old structures have been swept away, to hear the plaintive observation that political leadership in the Province is so weak because the middle class has simply stood aside, as in John Hewitt's well-known poem, 'The Coasters':

> You coasted along
> to larger houses, gadgets, more machines . . .
> You even had a friend or two of the other sort,
> coasting too: your ways ran parallel.
> Their children and yours seldom met, though,
> being at different schools . . .

You coasted along.
And all the time, though you never noticed,
the old lies festered;
the ignorant became more thoroughly infected;
there were gains, of course;
you never saw any go barefoot.
You coasted along
and the old sores suppurated and spread . . .
You coasted too long.

As was to be expected in the circumstances, the Unionist Party dominated in elections to Westminster, and did not require any electoral malpractices in order to do so.[19] There was, however, a rather special feature of party activity in Northern Ireland which, until recent years, seems to have attracted little attention from historians of the period. This was the fact that, although Northern Ireland was part of the United Kingdom, the British national parties put up no candidates and sought no representation there. The Liberals had lost ground heavily after the Home Rule debacle and the last candidates stood for election in 1929, apart from the University constituency which had a Liberal member in the post-war period. The Conservatives were content to leave matters to their allies in the Conservative and Unionist Party, but the Unionist Party was closed against Catholics because of its association with the Orange Order. What was particularly strange, and surely hard to defend, was that the British Labour Party made no attempt to appeal directly to the electorate in a region so stricken with unemployment and with so many social problems. The separate Northern Ireland Labour Party gained some strength in these conditions in the 1960s but was always rebuffed when it sought amalgamation with the British Labour Party. A serious difficulty was the traditional sympathy of the British Labour Party for Irish nationalism which would have prevented it from winning much support from Protestant workers. (The Northern Ireland Labour Party was unionist.) No one resident in Northern Ireland was even acceptable for membership of either of the two main British parties. This was – and is – an extraordinary state of affairs of which few people in British political life appear to have been aware until it was made the subject of a publicity drive in the 1980s by the Campaign for Equal Citizenship. The Ulster electorate has been criticized for its attachment to 'tribal' political parties but has been denied the opportunity to escape by voting for the main British parties.

With the same party in power for about fifty years, the role of the civil service became even more important in Northern Ireland than is generally the case under representative government. The higher civil servants, many of whom came from Britain, were able to take a wider and less parochial attitude than the Unionist politicians. They were also unlikely to favour sectarian discrimination. More generally they provided the efficient and honest administration which made a large contribution to the welfare of people in Northern Ireland, whatever their needs and political beliefs.

Looking after their own

Any party in power in any representative assembly anywhere is liable to be, at the very least, well disposed towards its supporters. One of the Fianna Fail leaders was very frank about this: 'Of *course* we look after our own.'[20] But the alternation of parties in office may impose a practical, if not a moral, check on such behaviour. It was therefore to be expected that, in Ulster, the Protestants would fare distinctly better than the Catholics – not so much as an expression of theological approval and disapproval, but rather because Protestants were nearly always Unionists and Catholics were not. Unfortunately, this inference of bias appeared to be frankly endorsed by Craigavon when he spoke of 'a Protestant Parliament and a Protestant state'. As with his great opponent de Valera, on certain occasions his reputation was to suffer from his own too memorable remarks. It may therefore be informative to report more fully what he said in the House in 1934 when the following motion was being debated:

That the employment of disloyalists entering Northern Ireland [from the South] is prejudicial, not only to the interests of law and order and the safety of the State, but also to the prior claims of loyal Ulster-born citizens seeking employment.

The Prime Minister then said:

All through this debate the charges made by hon. Members opposite have been grossly exaggerated. Since we took up office we have tried to be absolutely fair towards all the citizens of Northern Ireland. Actually, on an Orange platform, I myself laid down the principle to which I still adhere, that I am Prime Minister not of one section of the community but of all, and that as far as I possibly could I was going to see that fair play was meted out to all classes and creeds without any favour whatever on my part.

'What about your Protestant Parliament?' he was asked. He replied:

The Honourable Member must remember that in the South they boasted of a Catholic State. They still boast of Southern Ireland being a Catholic State. *All I boast of is that we are a Protestant Parliament and a Protestant state.* It would be rather interesting for historians of the future to compare a Catholic State launched in the South with a Protestant State launched in the North and to see which gets on the better and prospers the more. It is most interesting for me at the moment to watch how they are progressing. I am doing my best always to top the bill and to be ahead of the South.[21]

The only part of this speech that was to receive lasting attention was the sentence in italics above. In the full context of this debate, though exceedingly ill-considered, his remarks look slightly less menacing. Thus two recent authors who are by no means supporters of the Unionist party have expressed the opinion: 'When Lord Craigavon . . . spoke of "a Protestant parliament for a Protestant people", he was not so much asserting ascendancy over non-Protestants as claiming the Protestant share' [of the island].[22]

So much may be conceded. What is also clear is that he missed a magnificent opportunity to confirm and develop what he meant by saying that he was 'Prime Minister not of one section of the community but of all'. They might boast of a Catholic state in the South, but – he could have said – the Northern Ireland

Parliament must not, and would not, be a Protestant Parliament for a Protestant people. Thus a contrast with the South could have been sharply drawn. It is true that the Protestant ultras would have grumbled but Craigavon was in an unassailable position. The tragedy of his career as Prime Minister was that he failed to use the strength of this position in order to create the more liberal society which he himself on occasions claimed to desire. There are various possible explanations ranging from deliberate political dishonesty to the muddle-headed inconsistency of an ageing man who was really losing interest in the affairs of the Province. Whatever the true explanation, the outcome was disastrous.[23]

In 1933 Sir Basil Brooke – who was to become one of Craigavon's successors as Prime Minister – made a speech that could only be regarded as a plea for sectarian discrimination in employment. What he said on that occasion has never been forgotten and continues to be quoted as a clear indication of the kind of oppressive regime said to have been established by the Unionists in Northern Ireland.

There was a great number of Protestants and Orangemen who employed Roman Catholics. He [Brooke] felt he could speak freely on this subject as he had not a Roman Catholic about his own place. . . . He would appeal to loyalists therefore, wherever possible, to employ good Protestant lads and lassies.[24]

It is true that there was an influx of Catholics from the Irish Free State which caused concern in the sensitive border areas. For the flow of migrants was always *to the North* where Catholics were allegedly treated so harshly. It is also true that their higher birth rate was seen to be a threat. We may assume that Brooke, for his part, was concerned *not with religious conviction but with loyalty to the state*, and there had been some instances of disloyalty and many of non-cooperation. But it was both unjust and a counsel of despair to correlate disloyalty so completely with Catholicism: 'Ninety per cent of the Roman Catholics in Ireland politically were disloyal and disruptive.' If this were indeed the case the possibility of establishing a stable society in Ulster was, to say the least of it, remote. To write off more than a third of the population in this way was improperly cynical behaviour on the part of a person who later became Prime Minister.

Moreover there were other Protestant extremists who were repeatedly taking the same harsh line. The minority had every reason to feel affronted and threatened. Fortunately it need not be assumed that discrimination on so monstrous a scale did in fact take place. Clearly it did not, but some quite indefensible discrimination did, nevertheless, occur. That is one of the questions to which we must direct close attention in the chapters that follow, but meanwhile there is a point of some importance to be made. Any incitement to discriminate should have called forth a sharp reminder from the British Government or the Privy Council that discrimination in public policy and public appointments was not permitted by the legislation under which they held public office – the Government of Ireland Act of 1920.

THE LIMITS OF POWER

So far we have been concerned with the deep political divisions in Northern Ireland and the responses to them. Let us now turn to issues of a broader nature. By Irish standards Ulster had been a prosperous province with much more industry and a higher standard of living. By British standards, however, it was a poor area with low output per head and the social capital for which the new government became responsible was seriously defective. Moreover, devolution came into force on the eve of the severe post-war depression and even during the partial recovery of the twenties, the old 'basic' industries were to remain depressed. It has been estimated that, in 1924, 60 per cent of the industrial labour force was in declining industries in Ulster as compared with 40 per cent in Great Britain. The new government was therefore faced from the outset with an exceedingly difficult situation. The desperate need for more jobs in total and a faster expansion of total output tended to be obscured by the clamourous debate about the fairness or unfairness of the share-out.

In this situation any regional government was liable to be blamed for what it could not achieve. First of all there were the fiscal constraints to be described in detail in the next chapter. Even, however, if the fiscal arrangements had been fairer to Ulster and even if more flexibility had been permitted, the power of the new government to influence the course of events was bound to be narrowly restricted. The province's great export industries were badly affected by the appreciation of the pound and that was determined in Britain – determined, as it happened, for the Irish Free State as well as for Ulster, given the policy then followed in Dublin. Although responsibility for industry had been devolved to the parliament of Northern Ireland, and that body could and did approve special industrial grants in the 1930s, their efficacy was bound to be limited when there was so much slack in the world economy.

It is true that more might have been done in one or two limited respects. Perhaps the best example was afforded by the local authorities who were responsible for providing assistance to the unemployed when they had reached the end of the period covered by unemployment insurance which was relatively generous by the standards of the time. (It may be observed that when insurance claims have been exhausted, the responsibility is still local in a number of countries, for example France and the USA in the 1980s.) In 1933 there was a quite remarkable occurrence, for Protestant and Catholic workers united in a protest. For a brief period, the traditional animosities were suppressed and the Ulster proletariat began to behave like the proletariat in Great Britain. The meagre allowances provided in particular by the Belfast Corporation could have been increased if rates had not been kept at a low level by Great Britain standards. To this extent the protest against government within the Province was justified. It was also reasonable to protest against the provincial government for supporting the local authorities instead of putting pressure on them to raise rates in order to assist those in desperate need. But government could be held to be only marginally responsible for the high level of unemployment itself which had its causes in national policies and in worldwide conditions. Nor was the government responsible for failing to supply assistance from its own resources for the unemployed who had exhausted their insurance. For it was explicitly prohibited by the Colwyn agreement, as described in the next chapter, from providing any service of a kind not provided by Westminster for Great Britain. When, however, Westminster did take action to help unemployed people in Great Britain by introducing the national means-tested unemployment assistance scheme in 1934, Craig pressed strongly and successfully for the financial support required to make similar provision possible in Northern Ireland. Indeed, it was one of the cornerstones of his policy that social cash benefits should be the same in Northern Ireland as in the rest of the United Kingdom.

In the chapters that follow some of the main fields of public policy will be discussed and an attempt made to assess the successes and failures of the fifty years of Unionist rule. That rule came to an end in 1972 under conditions to be described in the third part of the book. Without anticipating what is said in those later chapters in Part III, we can note that Northern Ireland has subsequently been under 'Direct Rule' from Westminster. Apart from a brief spell in 1974 there has been no provincial assembly with control of the executive, which has been in the charge of successive Secretaries of State who have been members of Westminster governments. Moreover, local government has been shorn of much of its former responsibilities. The year 1972 is, therefore, a watershed which will be reached and passed in the remaining chapters in this part of the book. In each case – for example, in dealing with housing policy – we shall begin with the measures adopted under the Unionist regime and the consequences that followed. We shall then go on to review the further changes that have occurred under 'Direct Rule' in order to carry the account forward to the latter part of the 1980s.

9

Fiscal Constraints and the Subvention

In the previous chapter it has been observed that, in attempting to assess the performance of devolved government in Northern Ireland, account must be taken of the constraints imposed by financial stringency. Some explanation and elaboration of this remark is now clearly required. Every government everywhere is constrained by limited finance. If anything of substance was being said about Northern Ireland, the stringency must, for some reason, have been inhibiting in some special way. That is to say, the financial conditions imposed by the legislation or by the manner in which it was applied, may have placed Northern Ireland at some disadvantage as compared with other regions in the United Kingdom. That, on the face of it, may seem a surprising suggestion, for it is widely believed that Northern Ireland has been heavily subsidized at the cost of taxpayers elsewhere in the United Kingdom. Indeed, the subvention is sometimes denounced with extravagant rhetoric. 'Ulster', it has been said, 'is bleeding the British taxpayer dry.' Although less than 1 per cent of total British national public expenditure, or under two-fifths of 1 per cent of GNP can scarcely be said to entail 'bleeding dry', the fact remains that the subvention came to about £1.5 billion in 1987, an immense sum for one small region of 1½ million citizens. The fiscal treatment accorded to Northern Ireland has, in fact, changed very markedly. Over much the greater part of its half century of legislative devolution, the Province was treated *less* favourably than comparable regions in Great Britain. It was only on the eve of its dissolution that the Stormont government began to receive more equitable treatment and, even then, there was a substantial backlog, especially in deficient social capital, that had yet to be made good. The large size of the present subvention can be partly accounted for in this way.

The first step must be to try to clarify some of the concepts used in this debate. If the objectives of devolved government are to be achieved, there must, rather obviously, be appropriate fiscal arrangements. It is usually regarded as a primary objective that the regional government should have some freedom in interpreting local preferences about what should be spent, out of any given amount of revenue, on one public service rather than another. For example, a government may think it right to spend rather more on education and less on health than is being spent elsewhere. Or it may want to introduce new policies not yet generally adopted and to finance them by cutting back on old ones. It does not follow that autonomy in expenditure must be matched by sufficient autonomy in taxing power to allow a regional government – or, for that matter, a local authority – to finance its programmes from its own resources. That is not so. The central government could retain complete control of taxation but provide each sub-central government with a block grant which the latter might then be allowed to spend as they choose. This was the model embodied in the legislation of 1978 for establishing devolved governments in Scotland and Wales. Apart from local rates, there would have been no independent source of tax revenue in those countries. Block grants are of course a familiar feature of local government finance and, in recent years, have also been made available to the respective Secretaries of State for Scotland, Wales and Northern Ireland. Freedom to tax is not, therefore, an essential condition for freedom to spend. Admittedly, this freedom to spend may be more complete in an area that can pay for its own expenditure from its own resources, for Whitehall may attach strings, so that the block grant does not really convey as much freedom of choice as, in principle, it ought to do. Local government in Britain has certainly been constrained in this way, but it is possible that there would nowadays be fewer strings attached to the finance made available to a region on which legislative devolution had been conferred by parliament.

There is a further and quite different reason for the devolution of some taxing power. Without such power, a sub-central government will be unable to alter the amount of revenue at its disposal. It will simply have to take what it is given, even if it is free to spend that amount as it pleases. Yet in some areas there may be a preference for somewhat higher taxation in order to finance more expensive programmes, in others a preference for lower taxes and lower expenditure. In order to allow such preferences to be expressed, nothing like complete fiscal self-sufficiency would be required because, in practice, the variations in the scale of preferred expenditure between different areas will be limited, but some scope for choosing the level of taxation would be appropriate.

There is another quite formidable objection to fiscal self-sufficiency. If each area had to finance its own expenditure fully from its own resources, either public expenditure per head would be lower relative to needs in the poorer areas than in the richer areas, or taxation would have to be much higher. For there would then be no provision for redistribution between one area and another. The case for redistribution has, however, been generally accepted not only in Britain but in other countries as well. The question then is how far such redistribution should be carried, and the answer is that, in most countries, it is now carried a long way. The basic principle of full-scale redistribution may be summarized by saying that taxes paid at the average national rates should entitle an area to public expenditure on the average national scale when allowance has been made for any differences in the cost of providing each service between one area and another, and any differences in needs. If taxes are lower, expenditure should be correspondingly lower. Higher expenditure at above-average rates would be permitted but would require higher taxation in the region concerned. This is the principle that came to be known as 'parity' in the course of financial negotiations between London and Belfast. It is a familiar principle, much discussed though with different terminology, in the more widely ranging literature on 'fiscal federalism'.[1]

Within Great Britain, very large inter-regional transfers take place but these are the *implicit* consequence of policies about taxation and expenditure that are applied to the country as a whole without there being any attempt to relate regional expenditure to regional tax payments – except in the case of local authority rates. Let us take, for example, what is by far the largest item in national expenditure: the sum disbursed as cash transfers, i.e. pensions, unemployment pay, child benefit, etc. The amount paid under these headings to people in, say, the Northern Region of England, does not depend at all upon what people in that area are currently paying in taxation and national insurance contributions. Their payments go into the national pool and the expenditure comes out of that pool. There are not even any official statistical estimates of either expenditure or taxation in each of the English regions. There are estimates of expenditure alone for England as a whole and for Scotland and Wales, and we shall have occasion later to refer to these figures and compare them with expenditure in Northern Ireland; but, even for these countries, there are no corresponding official estimates for their contributions to taxation. It is only in the case of Northern Ireland that the full accounts are estimated and published. It is only in this case that the fiscal transfer is officially calculated. This is what has happened since 1921 as a consequence of the particular fiscal package that went with the old Home Rule legislation. In 1978, however, the package proposed for Scotland and Wales was different, for there was no declared intention to estimate the contributions to revenue of these two countries which could then be set against their expenditure in order to permit the explicit calculation of their respective subventions.[2] Northern Ireland has therefore been placed from the outset in a particularly invidious position. Let us now turn to a closer consideration of that position.[3]

RESPONSIBILITIES AND RESOURCES

The Parliament of Northern Ireland was given some small taxes which initially contributed about 11 per cent of revenue. This proportion was to decline and, in 1972, would have disappeared with Direct Rule but for the co-incidental take-over of local government and local rates. Much the greater part of the taxation paid by people or firms in the Province was always derived from taxes 'reserved' by Westminster and levied in Ulster at the same rates as elsewhere in the United Kingdom: that is to say, all taxes on income and all indirect taxes on commodities. The estimated proceeds of these taxes in Northern Ireland were naturally credited to the Province and this allocation of revenue should not, of course, be regarded as a subvention. Initially it was never contemplated that there would be any subvention. On the contrary, Ulster was expected to make a contribution of a specified amount to such common national costs as defence and the national debt – the Imperial Contribution, as it was called. This payment had the first claim on net revenue. Only the residue would then be available for domestic expenditure on the devolved services.

These devolved services were wide-ranging. Under the Home Rule legislation of 1920, Westminster retained responsibility for the functions usually performed by federal governments, notably foreign policy, defence, currency and the exchange rate, foreign trade policies and the national debt. The provincial parliament was thus left with the responsibility for providing or supervising Ulster's domestic services, including education, the health services, social security, law and order, railways, roads and road transport, agriculture and industry. The list was open-ended and as new obligations were assumed by Westminster, or existing obligations expanded, it was only natural that the Northern Ireland government should seek to do the same.

The Government of Northern Ireland was therefore faced initially with several formidable problems. As well as those posed by the financing of social benefits, there was an inheritance of inferior public services in Ireland. To quote from Lawrence: 'Every informed person in Ireland, north and south, knew that public services were worse than in England.'[4] He goes on to record that: 'between 1906 and 1920 one official inquiry after another had advocated radical reforms to eliminate the dirt, disease, ill health, poverty, illiteracy and maladministration which for one reason or another were the heritage of British rule.' The term 'leeway' came to be applied to these relative deficiencies and it was not an easy task to make good this leeway, or even to prevent it from getting greater. For it would be necessary also to keep pace with any further advances in Great Britain, if people in Northern Ireland were to have the full benefit of their common British citizenship. To do so and, at the same time, to contribute an Imperial Contribution fixed in amount for three years, soon proved to be impossible.

This contribution had been increased in real terms by the fall in prices when the post-war boom came to an end. Moreover, Ulster's basic industries were hard-hit by the slump and the incomplete recovery that followed. The restoration of the gold standard at the pre-war parity was bound to be harmful, and this was national policy over which the Ulster parliament had no control. With incomes depressed and heavy unemployment, total revenue, including that derived from devolved taxes – initially one-tenth of the total – had fallen by roughly one-third by 1924/5, while expenditure had risen, notably on unemployment benefits. Some change was necessary and was carried out in 1923 when, on the recommendation of an advisory committee (the Colwyn Committee), the Imperial Contribution was made the residual, subject to the condition that it must not become 'negative' – that is to say, must not turn into a subvention. Great care was to be taken to ensure that the residual would not be 'too much' reduced by 'excessive' domestic expenditure, and the restraints imposed to this end deserve attention if the record of Unionist government is to be fairly appraised.

The Government of Northern Ireland was not to be allowed to spend public money on any service that did not exist in Great Britain. Nor could it spend on a superior scale on any service. Thus the scope for using the devolved powers was strictly limited. Independent action would be possible only with regard to matters that did not involve public money. For example, property law or the law relating to divorce could be different. To take an example of greater political significance, so could the law relating to local government elections.

Expenditure in the year 1924 was to be taken as a bench mark. Thereafter *per capita* expenditure in Ulster could rise at the same rate as in Great Britain. This was a welcome concession but a limited one, for the making good of leeway in certain public services required expansion at *more* than national average rates. The Colwyn

Committee, for their part, preferred a quite different emphasis and recommended that account should be taken of 'any lower general level of prices, of wages or of standards of comfort or social amenity which may exist in Northern Ireland as compared with Great Britain'.[5] This statement could only imply that leeway need not be made good in so far as it reflected the fact that Ulster people were accustomed to lower 'standards of comfort and social amenity'.

The financing of social benefits continued to present difficulties which became acute during the depression of the early 1930s. The burden could, of course, have been reduced by providing benefits at lower rates than in Great Britain. Indeed, apart from budgetary pressures, a case could have been made for doing so on the ground that rates of benefit appropriate for Great Britain would be 'too high' for a region where income per head was almost 50 per cent lower.[6] For benefits that were high relative to potential earnings would create a deep 'unemployment trap' and, however strong the work ethic, it was unreasonable to expect people to seek work that would give little reward and might even involve lower incomes for themselves and their families. Migration might also be reduced by high benefits. Any saving thus achieved by reducing benefits could have been spent on training schemes, housing subsidies, assistance to expanding industry, or whatever. But Craig was quite determined that social benefits must be paid at the national rates. To adopt a lower standard would be to accept a lower status for British citizens in Northern Ireland. Moreover, it could not be assumed that any money saved by cutting benefits would be available for other purposes, for that would depend upon the response by the Treasury. The outcome might simply be lower total expenditure and a higher Imperial Contribution. Worse still, the acceptance of lower social benefits might be regarded as an admission that lower levels of social expenditure were appropriate and quite acceptable across the board – as the Colwyn Committee had suggested. Craig therefore felt obliged to warn that:

The screw will be put on and we will be told that of our own initiative we refused to give the same benefits to people living in our area afforded to those [in Britain] . . . and that as we had adopted that attitude there was no necessity for our financial affairs to be so adjusted that we could live pari pasu with the English and the Scotch in other directions.[7]

The prudent policy was one of 'step by step' and there was the further advantage from a Unionist point of view that the harmonization of policies would demonstrate that Ulster was, indeed, still part of the United Kingdom. After all, the Ulster majority had never sought Home Rule and did not set out with any particular desire to pursue different social and economic policies, as the Scots might do if they were to have legislative devolution.

It is necessary to recall these features of the situation if Ulster's experience of devolution in the past is being used to throw some light on what effect devolution might have if adopted in other regions – or, if it were to be restored, in very changed circumstances, in Northern Ireland. It is true that the rigid Colwyn controls were not strictly applied and some trade-off between different services came to be permitted. The fact remains that expenditure was controlled, item by item, throughout the period of Home Rule in Ulster. Sums as small as £50,000 required Treasury consent, even after the Second World War.[8] With expenditure so tightly controlled and with little power to tax, the scope for independent action was narrowly constrained with two consequences. First it meant that, for good or ill, Northern Ireland was bound to follow Westminster in so far as public business required public money. The Province is sometimes described by English commentators as a place that is quite radically different in virtually all respects, not only in those where sectarianism is the central issue. Ulster, it is implied, followed a divergent course under Unionist government. This was not so. Over much the greater part of public policy, Ulster followed Westminster very closely – and could not do otherwise. Secondly, the narrow scope for autonomous action had the natural consequence that the business transacted by the provincial parliament attracted less public interest. Lawrence has gone so far as to say that: 'The one thing that might have stimulated all citizens to lift their eyes to Stormont – local taxation on the grand scale – was wanting.'[9]

Such taxing power would certainly have had that effect, although it is fair to add that, even without it, greater freedom to spend from a block grant would also have been a stimulus. But a grant of this kind was not to be forthcoming until 1973 and by then the Northern Ireland Parliament had been replaced by Direct Rule. For most of its history, Unionist governments had been preoccupied with the problem of obtaining equitable treatment from London even within the constraints imposed.

As we have observed, the financing of social security benefits proved to be particularly troublesome. As things turned out it was a great pity that the responsibility for providing these cash transfers had ever been devolved. It is interesting to note in passing that in the Home Rule Act of 1914 this responsibility was to be retained by Westminster.[10] Moreover when legislation was being prepared in 1978 for the establishment of new assemblies in Scotland and Wales, it was never contemplated.

It has long been taken for granted that the cost of unemployment benefits should be a national obligation. It would have been thought absurd to suggest that an area such as Merseyside or Clydeside should have to meet the cost from its own local resources. This, however, is what was initially expected of Northern Ireland, although there was no reason why Ulster should be treated differently from the rest of the United Kingdom. Moreover the government of Northern Ireland was made responsible for providing state pensions, although it is hard to think of a comparable instance elsewhere in the developed western world. Even in the USA, the federal government has assumed responsibility for basic old age and disability pensions. Account must, of course, be taken of the fact that when the Home Rule legislation was being drafted in 1919, the welfare state was still in its infancy and the implications of moving the burden of providing all the cash benefits away from the centre could not be adequately appreciated. That it was to prove a very serious burden can be appreciated when it is observed that these social benefits accounted for one-third of the total expenditure of the Northern Ireland government in 1923/4, and about one-half in 1938/9. The social insurance contributions paid by employers and employees were not, of course, an adequate offset on the credit side in a depressed region where the government was, moreover, obliged to accept responsibility for non-contributory benefits as well as contributory ones.

The heavy unemployment of the 1920s threatened the solvency of the unemployment insurance fund and an amalgamation with the Great Britain fund was the rather obvious solution. Westminster was not prepared to take this step but agreed, in 1924, to guarantee three-quarters of any excess expenditure attributable to adverse employment conditions in Northern Ireland. It was not until 1948 that the resources of the two insurance funds were, in effect, pooled but with the formal distinction between them still retained. In 1936, support was also extended to means-tested unemployment assistance introduced two years before, and in 1948 Westminster agreed to cover 80 per cent of any extra expenditure incurred on means-tested benefits, on family allowances, non-contributory pensions and the health service. To this extent the welfare state was underwritten, provided tax rates and contributions were the same and provided any extra expenditure reflected only differences in 'need'.

This devolution of responsibility for cash social security benefits had two consequences. First, the burden was disproportionate, as compared with those carried by poor areas in Great Britain. Secondly, assistance from London was extracted only after negotiation and bargaining and was represented as a 'concession', although it was no more than the natural corollary of membership of the United Kingdom. As a result it was all the harder to fight for assistance with any other item of expenditure.

In 1936, the Chancellor of the Exchequer (Simon) made a statement that affected the whole financial position of the Province and amounted to the acceptance of what has been described above as the principle of 'parity'. If there were to be a deficit not caused by extravagance, 'means should be found to make good this deficit in such a way as to ensure that Northern Ireland should be in a financial position to continue to enjoy the same social services as we have in Great Britain'.[11] It may be of interest to note in passing that the same principle of fiscal redistribution between the states was accepted explicitly at about the same time in Australia (1936) and Canada (1940).

The *net* contribution for national purposes, i.e. the Imperial Contribution *less* any assistance conceded to Northern Ireland, had dropped to a small figure during the depression, and by the late 1930s was negative to the extent of a few hundred thousand pounds a year.[12] Under wartime conditions, the net payment became very substantially positive once more. The war also brought a change in attitudes to social affairs throughout the United Kingdom which found expression in various plans for the post-war period. This change was bound to be reflected in public finance, and for Northern Ireland one consequence was the suggestion in 1941 by the Chancellor (Kingsley Wood) that Ulster's grave deficiencies in social capital might be made good.[13] After the war, the Northern Ireland government continued to move forward step-by-step with Great Britain, and the welfare state was enlarged on a similar substantial scale. In 1954 the wider interpretation of parity suggested by Kingsley Wood in order to include provision for capital deficiencies was endorsed, together with a recognition that more expenditure might be justified by Northern Ireland's geographical position. The catching up – for example in housing – was bound to take time, even if it had been started immediately, but another twenty years were to elapse before the official estimates of expenditure per head for regional purposes began to exceed even the average for England and thus to suggest that Ulster's backlog would gradually be made good.

The official statistics available for the post-war period show that expenditure even at the end of the 1950s, long after parity had been accepted in principle, was

TABLE 9.1   Identifiable public expenditure per head

	1959/60	1962/3	1964/5	1965/6	1968/9	1969/70	1982/3	1985/6
England	100	100	100	100	100	100	100	100
Scotland	105	118	116	114	128	131	127	126
Wales	95	99	117	114	117	116	111	111
Northern Ireland	88	92	102	108	114	118	147	149

Sources: The estimates for 1959/60 and 1962/3 are taken from the Treasury's *Needs Assessment* (1979) and relate to the six main programmes to be devolved to Scotland and Wales under the proposals set out in the White Paper, *Our Changing Democracy*, Cmnd 6348, 1975. The figures for subsequent years relate to a somewhat different range of services. These are taken from the *Report of the Royal Commission on the Constitution 1969–72*, vol. 1, p. 178 and from *HC Debates*, 28 October 1987, cols 896–904.

well below the corresponding figure for England. This was so notwithstanding the fact that, in a poor area with heavy unemployment, one would normally expect a higher level of *per capita* expenditure. It was only towards the end of the 1960s that Northern Ireland drew ahead of England but still remained behind Scotland until the mid-1970s, as is shown in table 9.1. Thereafter expenditure has stayed at a level of 41–9 per cent above the average English figure with Scotland also left behind.

These figures exclude such common national items as expenditure on defence, the national debt and so on, and there must, somewhere, be a sufficient excess of regional revenue over 'regionally relevant' expenditure in order to pay for them. Unfortunately the available statistics for the various regions of the United Kingdom do not permit a calculation of net loss or gain, but the Royal Commission on the Constitution felt it was possible to describe the situation as follows:

There is no official information on the subject, but we believe that a geographical breakdown of revenue and expenditure would show large surpluses of revenue over expenditure in the South East and West Midland regions of England, and deficits in Northern Ireland, Wales, Scotland and probably all the other English regions. Some of the deficits would be substantial – areas with low tax revenues also tend to require highest public expenditure.[14]

The initial assumption that Northern Ireland should pay for all public expenditure within the region and also make a net contribution to those common costs – an 'Imperial Contribution' – could not have been carried out without imposing a burden on the citizens of this poor area that would have been out of all proportion as compared with what other British regions were bearing. It was not surprising that the *net* contribution became negative – a subvention. That was the common experience except in the most prosperous areas. In short, inter-regional transfers are a consequence of a progressive structure of taxation and expenditure which favours the lower income groups but, in Ulster's case, the transfers have been explicit. That, as we have observed, has been the essential difference. The amount of the subvention received by Northern Ireland in more recent times is shown for selected years in table 9.2.

TABLE 9.2   Northern Ireland Exchequer Subvention: million pounds

1968/9	74	(28.8)	1980/1	1090	(99.0)
1970/1	88	(29.4)	1982/3	1149	(87.0)
1972/3	181	(51.0)	1984/5	1489	(102.3)
1974/5	389	(89.4)	1985/6	1536	(100.0)
1976/7	620	(97.7)	1986/7	1630	(100.1)
1978/9	848	(105.3)	1987/8	1569	(94.1)

Index in parentheses; 1985 prices = 100

Sources: HC Debates, 14 December 1984, col.610; Annual Statements, House of Lords Official Report; Department of Finance, Northern Ireland

The official procedures for calculating expenditure and thus the subvention were analysed and criticized by the Northern Ireland Economic Council for 1980/1 and for 1985/6.[15] It was pointed out that, in both years, the statistics for expenditure were unduly inflated relative to those for Great Britain as a consequence of certain differences in administrative arrangements which affect what is deemed to be public expenditure. If put on a statistically comparable basis, the difference between expenditure *per capita* in the two areas in 1985/6 would be reduced and the subvention would come down to about £1360 million. The subvention is also swollen by the need for higher expenditure on law and order. If it were possible to bring this item down to something like the English *per capita* rate, the subvention would fall to about £1.1 billion.[16]

Even before the Second World War, when the Imperial Contribution was being offset in varying amounts by receipts under the social security arrangements, Ulster's apparent financial weakness was seized upon by Irish nationalists as evidence that the Province was not economically 'viable' because it was not 'an economic unit' – those undefinable terms that have caused so much confusion in Ireland over the years. It was then inferred that, if only Britain would stop paying these subsidies, Northern Ireland would be obliged to abandon its resistance to unity with the South. Thus the British government had the solution to partition in its own hands if only it cared to use it.[17] There was no attempt to explain why, deprived of British help, the North would then choose to join the Irish Free State, a still poorer country to whose needs Ulster would presumably be required to make a net contribution. A good deal of confusion could have been avoided – and could still be avoided – if persons who use the word 'viable' were to try to explain what conditions are envisaged when an area is deemed to be 'non-viable'. Presumably not outright starvation. Would it mean a lower standard of living than its inhabitants would accept if some political change – unspecified – were to offer them the prospect of a higher standard of living? If so, 'viability' becomes a question of degree – surely the wrong use of the word. In this sense, Northern Ireland was just as 'viable' as the Irish Free State. If the Twenty-Six Counties could 'survive economically', so could the Six. In fact Ulster kept rather ahead of the Republic over the trend, as measured by output per head.

After about half a century of negotiation, Ulster began to receive, under Direct Rule, the fiscal support which any other area with the same needs and resources would be entitled to receive from membership of the United Kingdom. By this time, public expenditure relative to gross domestic product had expanded enormously and the tax structure had also changed. Whereas in the late 1960s Ulster's subvention came to only about 5–10 per cent of total expenditure by the Northern Ireland government, that proportion has now increased to about a third, or the equivalent of more than one-fifth of personal income before tax – if the subvention is taken at its official level without any of the adjustments suggested by the Economic Council. It is true that there is probably some offset – which should be noted by British critics – in that the propensity to save is high in Ulster and there may well be a net flow of investible funds to Great Britain. (No official estimates are available.)

The receipt of a large subvention of this kind may not in the long run be an unalloyed benefit. For the long-run effect is almost bound to be the fostering of a psychology of dependence. There is then a tendency to take the benefits for granted and to claim a standard of living that has not been earned. Here, of course, we are really touching upon the great debate about the appropriate scale and structure of the welfare state into which we cannot enter. But it is right to observe that both the benefits and the disadvantages of the welfare state may be felt in a particularly concentrated way in such less prosperous areas as Ulster or Merseyside or the Scottish Highlands – or, for that matter, in the poorer states, such as Newfoundland, within the great federations.

The Republic, after a couple of decades of vigorous growth, has also become heavily dependent upon external assistance – but as a borrower. What economic consequences are likely to follow and what are the probable political implications? These are questions that are likely to be of basic importance in the future.

10

Economic Progress and Strategies for Development

The twenty years following the partition of Ireland were economically difficult ones, both North and South. As might be expected, the main explanation was the state of the world economy and, in particular, the state of the British economy to which both parts of Ireland were so closely linked. With tariffs of little importance initially, a fixed exchange rate and no impediment to the movement of capital and labour, the institution of the Border could have little effect – although the 'map-image' may mislead by giving the impression that the island's economy had been split into two isolated parts. The tariff barrier raised by de Valera in 1932 was damaging to cross-border trade but, for both areas, trade outside Ireland was in any case much more important than trade within. The great export industries of the North – shipbuilding, engineering and linen – were in difficulties and the structural change so badly needed was hard to achieve. As in the South, agriculture suffered from the world depression in that industry. The conditions that prevailed after the Second World War were very different. In the later period, output grew for about three decades at historically high rates throughout most of the developed Western world, unemployment was low, cyclical instability was slight and the obstacles to world trade were much reduced. For both parts of Ireland, therefore, this was a period of opportunity.

The response in the Republic was twofold. The strategy adopted in 1958, which had been largely devised by T. K. Whitaker at the Department of Finance, involved some changes that were more liberal and some that were more interventionist. This strategy was more liberal in that it prescribed the steady dismantling of the protective barrier raised by de Valera in 1932, with a high degree of self-sufficiency as his objective even if the cost were a lower standard of living. A new outward-looking attitude was adopted and was accompanied by rising living standards, more employment and less emigration. The Anglo-Irish Trade Agreement of 1965 was an important landmark; membership of the EEC in 1973 was another. At the same time, policy became more interventionist in that a programme for economic development, requiring active participation by the state, was launched for the years 1959–63. One of the forms this intervention took was the offer of fiscal concessions and subsidies to foreign firms. A development agency was established and a forum for the discussion of industrial policy was set up. In the

event, the poor economic performance of the 1950s, when GNP rose at only 1.7 per
cent a year, was followed by a period of growth at a very respectable 4.4 per cent a year
during the 1960s.[1]

In Northern Ireland, there had, of course, been no tariff barriers to trade with
Great Britain, still much the most important market and source of imports for both
parts of Ireland. Moreover Northern Ireland shared automatically in the effects of
more freedom for world trade to which British policy contributed. Some assistance
with industrial investment had already been provided in the 1930s, and an active
policy of industrial promotion, backed by investment grants, was adopted after the
war, as the need to accelerate industrial change became increasingly apparent with
the ending of the reconstruction period. A Northern Ireland Development Council,
established in 1955 'to promote new industries and to reduce unemployment', set out
vigorously to modify the industrial structure. Thus a broadly similar domestic policy
was adopted in both parts of Ireland, but somewhat earlier in the North. Over the
1950s GDP rose in Ulster at a respectable 2.6 per cent and a substantially higher
average figure of 3.7 per cent was to be achieved in the 1960s. During these twenty
years both Ulster and the Republic had rather faster growth rates than the United
Kingdom as a whole, although some foreign countries were moving ahead much
more rapidly. Unemployment was heavy by the standards of the time. Was there a
case for further official action? If so, what form should it take? Questions such as these
received much close attention at Stormont in the early 1960s.

Ulster's economy had been the subject of a detailed and scholarly investigation
carried out, at the request of the Government, by K. S. Isles and Norman Cuthbert
and published in 1957.[2] It was a pioneering effort, one of the first of a large number of
works on regional economics that were to appear in the years that followed.
Subsequently the various policy measures had been assessed by a joint Whitehall/
Stormont committee under the chairmanship of Sir Robert Hall, later Lord
Roberthall.[3] Their report was received with some public disapproval because – in
addition to many other things – it presented the case for migration from Ulster. This
particular remedy, which was also unpopular in Scotland, was liable to meet with
special disapproval in Ulster where migration might affect the sectarian balance –
which did not, in the event, prevent large numbers from voting with their feet. The
Hall Report was followed by one on physical planning by the distinguished Edinburgh
architect, Sir Robert Matthew.[4] The next move was announced by the Prime
Minister, Captain Terence O'Neill, in October 1963 when he said that a committee
had been set up to prepare 'a comprehensive Plan bringing together foreseen
developments in different sectors, examining our performance and indicating
directions in which progress might be made.'[5] I was invited to act as consultant, which
I did on a part-time basis with the invaluable assistance of my old friend and former
colleague John Parkinson, then Professor of Applied Economics at the Queen's
University. It was understood that this plan would be issued as a statement of official
policy and we worked throughout with the objective of achieving, in so far as this was
possible, a package of agreed proposals, for an agreed document was less likely to be
shelved and forgotten, the too familiar fate of committee reports. In the end, however,
the Government expressed some reservations and the plan was published as the
expression of the consultant's personal opinions, accompanied by an official note of
qualified agreement. Thus the report came to be known as the 'Wilson Plan'.

It covered the years 1965–70, and was followed by another development programme for the years 1970–5, with Sir Robert Matthew, John Parkinson and myself as consultants.[6] Meanwhile the civil rights movement had begun to gather momentum and the disturbances described in chapter 15 were undermining the stability that was so crucial to economic development. A vicious circle could then be foreseen with the violent expression of discontent leading to a further worsening of economic conditions, and that in turn leading to intensified discontent and further disturbances. Both the British government and the Stormont government were determined to prevent this from happening. Action by the security forces must be accompanied by social and political reform and by whatever measures could be devised to strengthen the economy. To this end, the existing policies should be assessed and, if necessary, strengthened. A new review body with Sir Alec Cairncross, Sir Charles Villiers and Mr Darwin Templeton as members, reported in 1971.[7] As well as a continuing series of progress reports, another large survey together with further recommendations was prepared by a group of officials and published in 1976 – the Quigley Report.[8] Moreover, the reconstructed advisory body, the Economic Council, under the Chairmanship of Sir Charles Carter, acquired its own executive and, over the years, has presented the results of its studies of the provincial economy as a whole and of its various industrial sectors. In 1987, a new official document, *Pathfinder*, was published which set out the views of the Department of Economic Development about the right approach to be followed in dealing with Northern Ireland's economic problems.

DEVOLUTION AND REGIONAL DEVELOPMENT

From this experience of regional development policies on which so much work has been done, what lessons can be drawn that may be of service in determining future policies? Broadly speaking, was the right line followed? On more specific issues, were the right choices made, for example with regard to the financial grants provided to industry? Some of the conclusions reached should be applicable both to regions with a measure of self-government and to those without, but it is also necessary to ask whether, in the light of experience, devolution is likely to help or to hinder. The case for restoring devolution has, of course, been debated almost continuously since the old parliament was prorogued in 1972, but the discussion has been mainly concerned with the manner in which power might be shared between the political parties and with the 'Irish dimension' – that is to say, relations with the Republic. Surprisingly little attention appears to have been given to a consideration of what a new assembly might in fact attempt to do. What would be the *purpose* of devolution? In the present context of economic policy, what could be achieved by devolution that could not be achieved as well without it? These are, after all, questions of central importance. The answer to them must depend partly upon the responsibilities to be accorded to any assembly. Although the full range of these powers need not coincide precisely with those delegated to the old Northern Ireland parliament, it is realistic to assume that among them would be much the same responsibilities for economic affairs, in particular for industry and labour, with which we are concerned in the present chapter.

The term 'devolution' is commonly used to mean the particular form of devolution that provides for a representative assembly, and it has been employed in this way in the sentences above. But 'Direct Rule' from Whitehall, as it has been practised since 1972, has also taken the form of devolution in a different sense – that is to say, 'administrative devolution'. For there have been a Secretary of State and government departments that are separate organizations and not merely regional branches of Whitehall departments. (In these respects – though not in some others – the arrangements have been similar to those in Scotland.) The policies adopted, though now based on legislation at Westminster, have been by no means identical with those adopted in England. These variations have not, however, reflected the preferences expressed through a local representative assembly, as the shorthand use of the word 'devolution' usually implies. The comparison is then between administrative devolution and representative devolution.

There can be no doubt that Ulster benefited, as compared with other parts of the United Kingdom, from the shortening of the chain of command under the old Stormont regime. The Ministry of Commerce had the authority to make agreements with firms that was at that time denied to the regional controllers in Great Britain, whose powers were very limited with every large commitment handled at headquarters in London. Many months might elapse before a definite answer would be received by a firm that wanted to know what assistance it would receive if it decided to establish itself or to expand in a particular location. There were no such delays in Ulster. Moreover, when the close cooperation of other Northern Ireland departments was required, these departments were on the spot and, once again, decisions could be taken quickly. The administrative advantages were important in regional development policy. But it does not follow that, in order to achieve them, a regional parliament or assembly was necessary. Subsequently there were to be large changes in administrative practice in Great Britain with much more decentralization, especially in Scotland and Wales. As we have observed, the Secretaries of State in those countries, and also in Northern Ireland after direct rule was introduced, were given block grants which implied more freedom in spending public money than had ever been accorded to the Parliament of Northern Ireland. In modern Scotland, the administrative freedom in carrying out policies seems as great as it ever was in Northern Ireland in the days of Home Rule, and the assistance of other Scottish departments can be easily and quickly obtained when it is required. In Northern Ireland itself, Direct Rule has not meant the sacrifice of these administrative advantages. If then a representative assembly were to be established once more, its effect in this field of policy might not be on administrative speed and efficiency but, possibly, on the choice of policies themselves. Again there would not be much likelihood of large changes in dealing with assistance to industry, although there are related fields where, at least in principle, some new and autonomous lines might be pursued. Labour-market policy is, perhaps, the most interesting. There would, of course, be some further widening of scope if a new independent assembly were to be given substantially more control over taxation than was accorded to the old parliament. How, in practice, the scope thus afforded would be used is another matter. Would the provincial electorate sanction less expenditure on other social projects in order, say, to provide firms operating in Ulster with a rebate of corporation tax on reinvested profits – on the assumption that the administrative difficulties could be solved? Would they fully appreciate the risks entailed in too much long-term dependence upon public expenditure? Or would they take a short-term view?

PLANS AND STRATEGIES

When our work on a development programme started in the mid-1960s, 'economic planning' was very much in vogue in Britain. That ambiguous term was then taken to mean 'indicative planning' after the model that appeared to have been used with some success at the national level in France.[9] What this implied was the preparation of a phased programme for total output and its constituents. Each important industry was to have its plan for production and investment for a number of years ahead. It was hoped that in this way the more important decisions would be better coordinated, and balanced growth assured. It was then often assumed that a regional authority could also prepare a plan of this kind for its own region – as a smaller scale replica of the national plan. But this was an error. Such planning must be centralized. Programmes for output and investment cannot be prepared and implemented for one region in isolation. It would have been merely foolish for the Unionist government – or for a government of any other political complexion – to have pretended that it could produce an operational plan for, say, shipbuilding, or for the artificial fibre factories, except as *part* of a national plan. This was so in the 1960s and it will also be true in the 1990s. False hopes were fostered then, and may be fostered again, by confusing the preparation of *statistical forecasts* with an *operational* plan which – if the words have any meaning – must imply a commitment on the part of all the leading actors in industry, in the trade unions and in government, to behave in the ways agreed and set out in the plan. It is true that if a central plan is fully elaborated, these decisions will have a spatial dimension, but the regional plans will be an aspect of the national plan, not something determined independently of it. Russian experience has shown quite clearly that the full-scale planning of industrial output and investment requires centralization – with all the disadvantages that entails. The French, for their part, had some limited success in giving their indicative planning a regional dimension, but this was as an extension of central decision-making, not as an exercise in local autonomy. In Britain there were two short-lived exercises in national indicative planning in the 1960s[10] but neither had a regional dimension. Moreover both proved to be essentially exercises in statistical forecasting rather than operational planning in the full sense of the term.

An indicative plan for the Republic of Ireland seemed a more feasible undertaking than it was for Northern Ireland, which was only one region of the United Kingdom. The Republic's Second Programme, 1964–70 prepared by Professor Louden Ryan and his team, had this form, although I do not know how far the statistics were backed by commitments to behave in appropriate ways on the part of those responsible for making the main decisions in both the public and the private sectors. A strong rise in total output did, indeed, take place, but the more detailed aspects of the plan were not implemented and were later abandoned. The scope for sectoral planning is clearly very limited in small nations. For that matter, the scope for it proved to be limited even in large nations, and the French themselves were to abandon 'indicative planning' as it became increasingly clear that the First Plan – the Monnet Plan – had owed much of its success to special circumstances. In some East European countries, in China and now in the USSR itself, there has been a movement away from planning in favour of a greater use of markets. It should hardly be necessary to add that the alternative need not be complete *laissez-faire*. There is a whole range of possibilities and from them must be chosen the package that seems most appropriate.

There are two reasons why these points are still worth making. The first is that the old Unionist Government of the 1960s was criticized for failing to produce a 'real plan' which would have meant a programme for output and investment in the principal industries, and this failure was attributed – wrongly – to ideological bias. For it was not so much a question of ideology as of recognizing the facts of the situation. Secondly, with the swing of intellectual fashion, planning may come back into favour, perhaps under a different name. Old illusions may then have a new day. That would be a regrettable diversion of effort. A regional *strategy* for devolved government is indeed required; but it must be given a different interpretation.

The twin objectives of a regional strategy are a higher rate of improvement in the standard of living and a higher level of employment. Such a strategy should therefore include a number of mutually consistent measures designed to create an environment capable of sustaining the expansion required. Public investment is needed for improving the infrastructure and should be planned for a few years ahead. Although revisions will be required, the preparation of a plan is feasible in this case in a way in which it is not feasible for industrial investment for two main reasons: first, the government has more control over the implementation of the decisions reached and, secondly, the greater part of the output will be acquired by the government itself, instead of being sold on an uncertain market. The preparation of such a plan forces the authorities to weigh up the various possibilities and make deliberate choices – an obvious point, it may seem, but it was only in the 1960s that official procedures were developed in Whitehall to take account of it.[11] In Ulster a start was made in the development plan for 1965–70, with 'leeway' very much in our minds. The process of drawing up a plan for public investment has the further merit of helping to break down the departmental exclusiveness that can develop even in a small administration such as that at Stormont.

Labour surplus areas such as Northern Ireland used to benefit from the general shortage of labour then prevalent throughout the developed world, but more trained workers were required including some highly skilled key workers, in order to take advantage of the situation. Obviously much of the training would have to be 'on the job', but government training centres could provide useful preliminary training and these were greatly expanded. Moreover, under a special arrangement with the training boards, firms with appropriate facilities agreed to take on apprentices well in excess of their own requirements – a scheme suggested by Swedish practice but then unique in the United Kingdom. Thus over the five years 1964–9 a useful start was made with a doubling of the number of school-leavers who were given the opportunity of an apprenticeship. Subsequently, a number of more ambitious new schemes were to be adopted. With heavy unemployment in so many countries, a labour surplus no longer has the same attraction for expanding firms, which underlines the need to be as competitive as possible in the quality of labour that is available. Unfortunately, even today, the British position in this respect is disappointing by comparison with that of some other countries, and a partial explanation is to be found in the inadequacies of the education and training provided and, not least perhaps, in the failure to relate the two in the manner long followed in Germany.[12] This is not the place to try to discuss the changes in education and training policies that have been carried out and proposed, but it is relevant in the present context to observe that the devolution of authority should allow an area like Northern Ireland to move ahead and take a somewhat independent line if this should seem to be appropriate. Even administrative devolution should permit some autonomy and with legislative devolution there could be more scope for following a bolder and rather more independent line, provided revenue was available in the form of a block grant – as explained in the previous chapter – and provided, also, that the electorate was prepared to accept lower expenditure under other headings.

ASSISTANCE TO INDUSTRY

Although the full-scale planning of regional industrial investment would not be feasible – even if it were desirable – there are ways in which investment decisions can be substantially influenced both with the objective of fostering the development of firms already in a region and in order to attract newcomers. The methods available for doing so have been much debated and it will be sufficient to summarize the main points with the case of Northern Ireland in mind, both in the earlier period of Unionist rule and then, since 1972, under Direct Rule from Westminster. Investment grants and loans together with government factories at subsidized rents have been the principal means employed. Although the Ulster administration has always had its own inducements on offer, these have been subject to Treasury control. It is right that there should be such central control in this case, if only in order to prevent different authorities from competing rather meaninglessly, from the national viewpoint, in the bribes they offer – as happens in the USA. The EEC now imposes its own restrictions as well, with the aim of preventing unfair competition within the Common Market – an appropriate objective although the precise regulations imposed may not always be the most appropriate. In the Republic, one of the more effective bribes was exemption from tax on that part of profits estimated to have been earned on exports. Devolution conferred no such control over profits tax, and Ulster suffered from a form of fiscal competition the Unionist government could not match. Moreover, if the UK government had tried to legislate for a similar tax concession on export profits in Ulster or the development areas, it would have been prevented at once from doing so under GATT (the General Agreement on Tariffs and Trade), for small countries can get away with more, at least for a time, than large countries. Even the Republic has subsequently been obliged to end this explicit discrimination in favour of exports but has a general profits tax concession. More recently, an attempt has been made by Westminster to provide a matching concession for Ulster but the measure appears to have proved disappointing.

The main emphasis in Northern Ireland, as elsewhere in Britain, has been on direct public assistance with the cost of investment, and it has often been objected that capitalistic methods have been fostered in a labour-surplus area. Capital intensive projects may, however, have offsetting advantages, such as a higher ratio of male employees which will be desirable when – given other labour-market conditions – there is a particularly severe shortage of jobs for men. Moreover, in subsidizing investment rather than general labour costs, there is at least some presumption that changes will be made in products or processes and this is to be preferred to a hand-out which would simply meet running costs with no improvement in performance achieved. The fact remains that an unconditional grant can merely provide an unnecessary subsidy to firms for doing what they would have done anyway, with little effect on employment or efficiency. It is helpful to place some limit on the amount of capital assistance per job, as used to be done with development assistance though not with the basic capital grants, now abolished in Ulster. The test could then be the number of new jobs that were to be provided but might, in special circumstances, be extended to old jobs maintained.

It may be objected that, in the past, attention was concentrated on manufacturing industry to an extent that has now ceased to be appropriate, for it seems apparent that manufacturing output will continue to expand throughout the developed world with little or no increase in the number of jobs. Is it not therefore necessary to look to the service industries for jobs and to shape development policy accordingly? In reply it may be pointed out that behind any apparent stability in total manufacturing employment, there will always be a great deal of change, with some industries expanding and others contracting. An active development policy for manufacturing industry will still be needed if Northern Ireland is to earn a share of the expansion and thus avoid a further net contraction. Moreover, although little net increase in manufacturing employment can be expected unless output rises at well over 3 per cent a year, manufacturing production will remain crucially important for the balance of payments and as a source of the rising incomes on which the expansion of the private service industries will be based. What must also be anticipated, however, is a continuing change in the composition of manufacturing investment with, in many cases, less relative emphasis on fixed capital and more on software and on the training of the labour force. Official policies will need to reflect developments of this kind.

Apart from the old debate about the more or the less capitalistic methods of production, there is a more basic dilemma that has to be faced at this point. From a wider point of view, a case for assisting less developed regions can be made on the ground that, if support is provided for a time, the region will later be able to stand on its own feet – the 'infant industry' argument. But the assistance should not be maintained indefinitely and, while it is being provided, should be of a kind that will foster the changes required. Naturally it is an argument that makes a stronger appeal to those who pay than to those who receive, but even the recipients can ignore this point only at their own peril in the longer term. There is, however, a different argument to the effect that, in view of Ulster's remoteness and the social and political problems of the region, there is a case for indefinitely prolonged subsidization. It can be further maintained that to withdraw or severely limit assistance would provoke still more social and political unrest with consequences that might be more costly than the industrial subsidies. How, then, can industrial and labour-market policies be devised that will be sufficiently selective to take account of both considerations? Can even permanent assistance be provided in a form that does not simply provide management and labour with a comfortable featherbed? It is with problems of this kind that the Pathfinder Report of 1987, mentioned above, is concerned.

The effectiveness of a development strategy will naturally depend upon promotional effort as well as upon the subsidies on offer. It is hardly necessary to say that the Unionist Government was well aware of this and the Ministry of Commerce followed an active policy both in Britain and in the USA.[13] It was felt, however, that it would be better to have a separate organization for promotion more like the Scottish Development Agency and the Irish Development Agency in the Republic. What finally emerged under Direct Rule was the present Industrial Development Board. From time to time, comparisons have been made between the performance of different agencies, in particular between those based in Glasgow, Belfast and Dublin respectively. For example, in recent years, how quickly has the importance of the Far East been recognized? What attempts have been made to establish links with people of Ulster descent in the USA and Canada? And so on. These illustrations may help to show that the important questions may not be associated in any very close and inescapable way with the form of government, whether devolved or not devolved.

The Unionist government was criticized in the 1960s, in particular by the Northern Ireland Labour Party, for its reluctance to set up a development corporation. As consultants, we naturally took up this point and tried to find evidence of a deficiency in finance. As we had anticipated, this was not easy. In Ulster, as in Scotland, few managers of small firms would admit that they were short of finance, presumably because they thought this would reflect on their credit-worthiness – although they often said they knew of other nameless firms that were so. The bankers for their part would always insist that no credit-worthy firm was ever denied finance. Moreover, they had their own finance house which we visited in the small Dickensian premises where it seemed to lead an untroubled existence. But what was meant by credit-worthiness? What about equity capital? Would it be supplied? Or, if offered, accepted? We felt sure that something more was needed and there was a further chance to press the case when the Government set up a committee of investigation into banking.[14] Other pressures were to be brought to bear and the final outcome was the establishment of the Local Enterprise Development Unit (LEDU) in 1972. Subsequently, in the most difficult circumstances, it was to prove more successful than anyone had any initial right to expect.

How selective should development policy be? The question arises both in promotional activity and also in awarding financial assistance, whether to newcomers or to existing firms. There is always likely to be some selectivity in order to ensure that, if only in broad terms, the special interests of the area are receiving attention. An important example in Northern Ireland is the desirability of attracting firms that would employ a high proportion of men, especially for the Londonderry area where male unemployment has been so much heavier than female. It was in this connection that a senior official replied as follows to an American industrialist who asked him about departmental policy with regard to the employment of Protestants and Catholics: 'In this Ministry, we are interested only in sex, not in religion.'

The proponents of selectivity have sometimes attacked a development policy that encourages the establishment of branch factories on the ground that branches are liable to be closed down during a recession. In fact branch factories survived recessions fairly well for many years but did indeed succumb in large numbers when the severe contraction of manufacturing industry began after the second oil crisis. I think everyone was aware of their vulnerability but there was also a general belief, later to be so rudely shattered, that slumps of any real severity would be avoided by Keynesian measures. Moreover it would be wrong to imply that there was a simple choice in development policy between branches and headquarters and that the wrong choice was made. If the branch factories had been rejected, there would have been little to take their place, either in Northern Ireland or in the Republic, and a period of prosperity on anything like the same scale would not have been achieved. Capital grants and other forms of assistance were always available to indigenous firms but there was too little entrepreneurship to provide sufficient expansion. In the case of both local firms and newcomers, there was a case for giving special assistance to encourage the establishment and expansion of research and development departments. It may be that the Northern Ireland Government was rather slow for a time in taking up recommendations to that effect. There was also a need to foster links between industry and the universities which was not recognized as soon or as fully as it might have been – a deficiency now made good.

The case for selectivity is sometimes expressed in much bolder terms. The development agency must 'spot the winners' – which is at least a welcome change from the older policy of providing special help for the losers, such as the British shipbuilding industry. But many people in many places are engaged in this game of identifying the winning firms, which does not make it easy. Nor is it clear why any official with this remarkable capacity should prefer to work for a pittance in his bureaucratic spotting office instead of going out and making a fortune. On a more serious plane, it may be proposed that an attempt should be made at least to identify the growth industries of tomorrow, if not the growth firms, as a basis for an industrial strategy. Once more there are many participants in the game. The great Japanese companies have a deliberate strategy of this kind which they have, of course, pursued with notable success. There is always the danger that the forecasters all over the world will come down in favour of the same kind of product and over-production will then result – as in the case of micro-chips. Moreover, for a small area such as Ulster, even the finer industrial classifications are not fine enough. Within the huge total of textile manufacturing there may be new products that could well be developed in Ulster.

At the opposite extreme among the policy-makers are proponents of a more detached policy. In their view, the inducements should be available for all firms that seem to be reasonably viable and it should be left entirely to management to decide what lines of production can best be followed. The locus of responsibility is then clear and officials are not trying to do the work of other people. A more selective policy can certainly put the officials in a difficult position. If they try to live down their old reputation for excessive caution, they will be accused of wasting public money should things go wrong. Here was an attractive project – a pioneering factory to make a new type of car in an area of Belfast with a high proportion of unemployed Catholic workers. What could have been better? But it turned into the De Lorean disaster. In reply it might be pointed out that managers as well as officials are fallible, and their knowledge of even currently available facts may be limited – even apart from guesses about an uncertain future. Some useful assistance and guidance can be provided – for example with marketing – without an official commitment to supposedly winning lines. Small firms in particular can benefit from guidance and advice which can be given in a way that does not shift the final responsibility. The basic question is still how far it is sensible for a development agency to pursue a selective policy, but we need not discuss it further in the present context.

This chapter began by drawing attention to the importance of external factors in determining the level of activity in Ulster. These external factors continued to be favourable over the trend – though with some short-term setbacks – up to the end of the period of Home Rule and it is appropriate to record the position reached at that stage in economic development. Although times had been good and an active policy had been followed, it had proved difficult to achieve any large increase in employment. It is true that the target set in the first development plan for new jobs in manufacturing was virtually achieved with 28,000 as against the 30,000 hoped for. But this was a gross increase and there were offsetting declines elsewhere. The net effect for the labour force as a whole was only a slight increase. No doubt the improvement would have been somewhat larger had it not been for the financial crisis in Britain leading to devaluation in 1966, but the fact remains that the outcome was somewhat discouraging. This was also so in the Republic. In both parts of the island there was little change in employment over the decade of the 1960s. By the early 1980s there had been a slight gain in the Republic but it was not retained. It is right to recall these facts in order to appreciate the difficulty of the task confronting those responsible for policy in the 1990s.

It is true that, by the late 1980s, the general economic recovery had caused some reduction in unemployment even in Northern Ireland. Moreover labour, especially skilled labour, had become scarce once more in southern England, and it was possible to anticipate a revival of interest in regional problems and policies. The completion of the European market in 1992 and subsequent years should provide a further stimulus. There is also another important factor that is bound to bring about large changes in labour markets. This is the impending decline in the juvenile intake and the rise in the proportion of elderly people, not only in Great Britain but throughout much of the developed world. Unemployment should then be reduced in both parts of Ireland. It does not follow that there will be any corresponding rise in domestic employment, for emigration may well continue to be the more important factor in both areas. Some increase in the number of jobs at home ought, however, to be attainable. As a labour surplus area, Northen Ireland might again become attractive to industry, especially if the labour force had a good basic training. But the full scope for expansion can hardly be realized while the IRA sustains its destructive campaign and – perhaps even more important – for so long as constitutional uncertainty is allowed to remain.

11

Industrial Location and Discrimination

Unemployment among the Catholics in Northern Ireland is very much higher than it is among the Protestants. The 1971 Census of Population revealed that the rate for Catholics was about 2.5 times the rate for Protestants, and the evidence suggests that this ratio had not changed much even by the end of the 1980s after almost two decades of Direct Rule from Westminster. The contrast is startlingly large and its persistence has been a proper cause for concern. Of the several possible causes, one might clearly be the location of industry and this will be the subject of the present chapter. The other possible causes will be discussed in the next chapter.

In the discussion of the locational factor, it has been customary to divide the Province into East and West. Although such a division is bound to be somewhat arbitrary, any reasonable drawing of the boundary will show a higher proportion of Catholics in the West than in the East. When it is also observed that unemployment is higher in the West, the location of industry and its corresponding effect on the demand for labour, would appear to provide one explanation of the heavier unemployment among Catholics in the Province as a whole. Unfortunately this inference has been drawn in a rather too facile way. Although the proportion of Catholics to Protestants is higher in the West, it does not follow that the majority of the Catholic population is in the West, for that area is less populous than the East. In fact, less than two-fifths of the Catholic population was in the 'West' at the time of the 1971 census.[1] Moreover, although the percentage unemployed was higher in the West, roughly two-thirds of the total number out of work over the period 1951–81 were in the East.[2] These are important points, but the possibility of an official locational policy pursued to the disadvantage of the West cannot, of course, be excluded without further investigation.

GROWTH CENTRE POLICY

As was to be expected, the Unionist Government was charged with discrimination of this kind by Nationalist politicians in the 1960s and this charge has been repeated subsequently on many occasions. The Government, it was said, did not want the Western areas to share fully in any improvement in economic prosperity. For a high rate of unemployment would stimulate a high rate of emigration and any tendency for the relative size of the Catholic population to be raised by its higher birth rate could thus be offset. Broadly speaking, this is what happened. It may be that even with *positive* discrimination strongly in favour of Catholics, it would still have happened, although on a reduced scale, in view of the various disadvantages with which Catholics had to cope. Whether discrimination *against* Catholics was a major factor is another matter. It is held to be so in the Report of the New Ireland Forum: 'They [the Northern Catholics] were deprived of the means of social and economic development.'[3] That forum, as will be explained in Chapter 17, consisted of representatives of all the main parties in the Republic and of the SDLP. Clearly its alleged objective of seeking reconciliation with the North was not regarded as a reason for avoiding harshly rhetorical accusations. There can be no doubt that the complaint about a sectarian location policy has come to be regarded as valid, not only by Catholic politicians in Ireland, but by many persons in England and America who are concerned about the Ulster problem. In particular the assertion that Derry was deliberately done down has come to be accepted as a firmly established proposition that now calls for no presentation of evidence.

In trying to form a reasonable judgement, it is essential to begin by recognizing that industrial location is one of the many matters that are only partially under government control even when an active promotional policy has been adopted. As Peter Neary has observed there is often a tendency to 'exaggerate our ability to control our own destiny'.[4] One of the penalties of adopting a dirigiste policy is that government may then be expected to perform what may be beyond its power, and sinister explanations may be advanced when it fails to do so. From this there follows the further penalty that all those who expect to benefit will attribute any disappointment to incompetence or – in the Ulster case – to downright malice on the part of the authorities. Yet only a little reflection is required to appreciate that the Ulster Government, like any other government in a similar situation, could exercise only quite limited control over the locational choices of incoming firms and, with intense competition from other development areas, too much insistence on particular locations within the Province would have led to industry being lost altogether.

In introducing the measures proposed in the first development plan, we observed that: 'It can be a salutary exercise to try to view Northern Ireland through the eyes of an English or foreign industrialist . . . There is no disguising the fact that Ulster seems a discouragingly remote area on the very fringe of Europe.'[5] Even if locational decisions were being made by central planners in a Soviet Britain, they might well ask themselves whether it would be in the national interest to site new projects quite so far afield. It is scarcely surprising that it was hard to induce industry on the scale required, to come to *any* part of Ulster; it would have been foolish to suppose that firms could be forced, willy-nilly, to go to the more remote districts in a remote region. The more accessible East was likely to be favoured, and a good deal of development would have to occur in that area before a corresponding interest would be shown in the West. There were similar pressures in the Republic.

Financial inducements had been offered to industry since the end of the 1930s, but it was in 1963 that the Government also adopted a more active locational policy which, because it was more active and more explicitly presented, aroused suspicions as to the true objectives it was meant to serve. This was the Matthew Plan[6] mentioned in the previous chapter. Unfortunately the Brookeborough Government had made a serious mistake in asking Sir Robert Matthew to prepare a physical plan for the Belfast region, large though it was, instead of the whole of the Province. Nationalist hostility was to be expected, although Matthew himself recommended that planning should be extended to the rest of Ulster.

Matthew proposed that the growth of the Belfast urban area – as distinct from the Belfast region – should be limited by a stopline. This was very much what some of the Stormont officials wanted, partly because there had been a long battle between the development department and Belfast Corporation – a battle that lost nothing in bitterness because both were under Unionist control. (A similar conflict could have been anticipated in Scotland if an Assembly had been established in Edinburgh in 1979 that would have had to cope with the Strathclyde local government area containing about half of the Scottish population.) It does not seem to have been adequately appreciated by nationalist critics that this stopline was intended to divert some industry to other areas, including the West. Their failure to do so could be partly explained by the emphasis given in the report, and still more in public departmental statements, to the proposal to establish a 'new city' between the towns of Lurgan and Portadown. It was indeed sensible on planning grounds to encourage these two growing towns to expand along the few miles that separated them, but a new city was a rather grand proposal that was liable to draw fire. Nationalist opinion was hostile. This was another plot to do down the West, although the new city – shortly to be called 'Craigavon' with typical Unionist insensitivity – was in *central* Ulster, and with a population to be drawn partly from Belfast 'overspill', it could be expected to *reduce* the Eastern dominance and, in various ways, be favourable to development in the West.

The Government had already accepted Matthew's recommendations when work began on the economic plan for 1964–70. The locational aspects of the economic plan were also to be subjected to attacks that were to be long sustained. Thus about twenty years later one of the New Ireland Forum reports was to complain that: 'In 1964 the Wilson Plan designated most of the growth areas for the North also in the East.' Its authors went on to complain about 'an uneven distribution of unemployment and housing in the North, whereby the nationalist section of the community has done less well than the unionist section'.[7]

In preparing the economic plan, we endorsed the proposal to have growth centres and extended its application beyond the Belfast region. In doing so, we were asking for trouble, although that was not so obvious at the time. For a growth-centre policy must favour some areas rather than others, and it is a well-established law of public affairs that the indignation of the losers will be far stronger than the gratitude of the gainers. It was not contemplated that any town or area would lose but we believed that some areas were more likely to sustain expansion than others, and provision should be made accordingly in the planning of infrastructure. For potentiality as well as need ought to be taken into account in planning investment! Perhaps this approach could, however, have been adopted quietly without any formal statement of growth-centre policy and without the controversy that would follow. The contrast in approaches was to be illustrated shortly afterwards in Scandinavia. The Norwegian Government, greatly influenced by an EFTA (European Free Trade

Area) working party, came out in favour of growth centres in the mid 1960s, and lost the next election – partly for this reason. The Swedish Government astutely denied that they had any such policy, although they did in fact favour the expansion of well-located towns of a reasonable size. In dealing with Northern Ireland at that time, it would have been impossible for the economic plan to have been prepared without any explicit reference to growth centres for that would have implied that the Matthew Plan was simply being forgotten. Without going so far it might, perhaps, have been possible to take some of the (unintentional) sting out of Matthew's proposals by doing more than we did to emphasize the scope for expansion in the various 'key' centres and other county towns – as was, in effect, to be done in a later report.[8] The fact remained that, as economic consultants, we too believed there to be a case for growth centres which should be explicitly presented. We included Derry as one of those centres.

It was necessary to reject the idea that any town, however small its size or however unsuitable its location, had a 'natural right' to development.[9] The percentage unemployed was, in itself, a poor guide. First it was a percentage of the number insured, not of the total workforce, an important point in some places such as Strabane. Secondly, the absolute number available for work might be very small. Mobility was necessary. This had to be said, although always an unpopular thing to say – in Scotland as well as Northern Ireland – even if nothing more was entailed than movement within a reasonable travel-to-work area. In practice, various things had to be done to improve this mobility.

Northern Ireland was in fierce competition for industry with other areas and had to demonstrate that new firms could be accommodated and would find the facilities they required. Thus one of the main reasons for advocating a growth-centre policy was to assist in *industrial promotion*. A policy of this kind had already been adopted in Great Britain. In France, in particular, its merits had been heavily stressed and officially endorsed. We might lose out if we stood aside from all this. In Scotland, for example, there were four new towns seeking to attract industry, all of which were expected at that time to have populations nearly as large as Derry's, and even one – it was then hoped – that would be almost twice as large.

There were undoubted advantages in size: a pool of skilled labour on which to draw, enough labour of all kinds to permit economies of scale and provide scope for future expansion, training centres, technical colleges and perhaps also some management schools, other firms that would be suppliers of ancillary equipment, and a variety of other back-up services, if required. There would also be economies of scale in transport and – an important point – more of the urban amenities that managerial staff might demand. To quote from a Fair Employment Agency Report: 'There has been a clear tendency for the largest projects to locate according to economic criteria – near to transport facilities and the largest centres of population – so that Antrim/Carrickfergus/Larne, Londonderry and Ballymena/Ballymoney have been the major recipients of the large multinational firms.'[10]

We had before us the fact that, of the jobs promoted since 1945, 56 per cent had been in firms employing 500 or more, only 17 per cent in firms employing under 200. It is true that even this 17 per cent meant that the smaller towns too could accommodate additional industrial development, and there was never any question of their being left out in the cold. It must be emphasized that industrial development grants were available *everywhere* with no discrimination in favour of growth centres. Growth centre policy related to infrastructure, *not* to the assistance given to industry. If some firms wanted to go to the smaller towns, this expression of managerial judgement would not be penalized. There was, it is true, a difference in the scale on which assistance was provided, but the difference was *not* between growth centres and the other towns. The difference was that larger grants were available to firms locating themselves in the West of the Province – *anywhere in the West*. If large new establishments were to be attracted to the Province, an expansion in infrastructure in the larger towns would be required. There would also, of course, be improvements in infrastructure elsewhere, but not on so large a scale. Other rival development areas in Great Britain and Continental Europe were stressing what growth centres had to offer in their promotional drives, and it would not have been prudent for Northern Ireland to reject the idea. We thought it would be distinctly helpful to be able to say that, although Ulster was so remote, it had some well-developed and well-located centres where modern industries could be established and would find the room and the facilities needed for subsequent expansion. This was one of the ways in which Ulster could try to demonstrate that it was capable of being competitive.

THE VERDICT ON LOCATION POLICY

The changes in industrial location that did in fact take place have been investigated in the report for 1949–81 prepared by Bradley, Hewitt and Jefferson for the Northern Ireland Fair Employment Agency. The striking results of their inquiry – which have received much too little attention – may be briefly summarized. As was to be expected, the East was more successful than the West in attracting large projects, although Londonderry did rather better than the Belfast urban area, even in this respect. Allowance must, of course, be made for differences in population between different areas and this is done by dividing the additional employment achieved in assisted projects by the population of the area concerned. (The unit mainly used is the area of the Employment Services Offices, or ESOs.) Thus a 'location index' can be constructed and if it comes to unity for a particular area, this means that the assisted employment is in exact proportion to population. When these areas are grouped into an 'Eastern' bloc and a 'Western' bloc, it appears that the East, with 70.5 per cent of the population, got 72.3 per cent of the sponsored employment, so that the location index is 1.03. For the West, the index is less favourable, but only slightly so, at 0.93. The Belfast urban area did poorly with an index of only 0.71. Londonderry, by contrast, did much better with an index of 1.93. The data was also analysed in terms of Protestant or Catholic majorities in the population. A majority is taken to mean 54 per cent or more on average over the years 1949–81. A further distinction is that between areas where the Catholic representation or the Protestant representation is in excess of their respective provincial averages. The results are summarized in table 11.1.

There was only a negligible difference between Catholic majority and Protestant majority areas over the period as a whole. But the Catholic areas did better and the Protestant areas did worse in the sub-period 1964–81 than in the first sub-period,

TABLE 11.1 Employment location ratios

	1949–81	1949–63	1964–81
Areas with Roman Catholic majorities	1.03	0.74	1.30
Areas with non-Roman Catholic majorities	1.02	1.13	0.80
Areas with Roman Catholic representation equal to or above the provincial average	1.13	0.77	1.24
Areas with non-Roman Catholic representation equal to or above the provincial average	0.95	1.10	0.90

although it was in the mid- and late-1960s that an active location policy was being followed by government, allegedly with discriminatory intent. A similar conclusion follows for areas with the Catholic representation above the provincial average.

Catholic families have more children than Protestant families and it would therefore be better to use the statistics for the working population rather than for the total population. Unfortunately this can be done with a sectarian division only for the census year, 1971. For that year the authors conclude that 'the geographical distribution of Government sponsored employment in the Province has not conferred any particular advantage on different religious groups.'[11]

A different approach is to relate employment in sponsored projects to the average number unemployed in order to obtain a different location ratio. Some may be inclined to maintain that this is the really important test for the assisted employment 'ought' to have been distributed according to 'need', as measured by unemployment. This is a view that can, of course, be disputed on the ground that some locations cannot realistically be expected to achieve the same percentages of employment as others, and some mobility is required. Indeed, it would be rather strange if there were to be no dispersion around the average figure for unemployment, given the obstacles to mobility and the failure of wages to reflect at all adequately the differences between the different areas in the supply of labour relative to demand. This particular location ratio must also be viewed with caution but is nevertheless clearly illuminating.

Of the twenty ESO areas, five in the West attracted shares of sponsored employment that were larger than their respective shares of the unemployment. That is to say, their location ratios in this sense were above unity. Two in the West were on the borderline: Londonderry (1.03) and Coleraine (1.0). Belfast did badly. With 34 per cent of the unemployment it got only one-fifth of the sponsored employment. Some areas did very well, notably the Antrim–Carrickfergus–Larne area. It must be borne in mind that one large new factory can make a vast difference to an area with a fairly small population, and the location of these factories would depend upon a variety of considerations over which government would have only limited control. Whatever the complex of factors at work, the location of the sponsored employment was by no means closely correlated with the average unemployment levels over the period as a whole.

Was Londonderry victimized?

Let us now turn to the particular case of Londonderry which was allegedly the victim of discrimination. With a total population of almost 70,000 and one that was rising, and with 4500 unemployed in the mid-1960s, there was clearly scope for accommodating a substantial amount of industrial expansion. The task of promoting the needed jobs was made more difficult by the fact that three-quarters of the unemployed were male and much of the mobile industry employed a high proportion of females. Moreover, to be effective, the potential labour force needed to be trained. A fine government training centre was in fact established and technical education was also improved. An existing industrial estate was expanded and a second estate was begun. A firm of consultants (James Munce Partnership) was appointed to prepare a physical plan which was published in 1968. Early in 1969 a Development Corporation was set up to expedite its implementation. A new bridge was built. The harbour was improved. There had been a severe setback in 1967 when an electrical factory had suddenly closed, but by early 1971, 3900 new jobs had been promoted, over two-thirds of them male, and unemployment had been pulled down from 20 per cent to 11 per cent.

In preparing the development programme for 1970–5, Matthew, Parkinson and myself, now much more conscious than we had previously been of Derry's paranoia, laid particular stress on the need to treat this city as a centre for accelerated growth. We also felt it appropriate to say, with regard to the West as a whole: 'Although we are not in a position to comment on what may have happened in earlier periods, the main facts about the period since 1964 do not support the view that the West has not received its fair share of public investment.'[12]

What must be conceded is that the section on Londonderry in the first planning document (1965–70) was far too short and failed to bring out with sufficient emphasis the measures that were being proposed. In part the explanation was that we did not then know as much about Londonderry as about the places included in Matthew's report. That was why we recommended that a physical plan for the development of the city should be prepared. Even so, this section was weakly drafted and for that I must accept responsibility. Yet it is doubtful whether any different presentation of policy would have done much to still the complaints. The Economic Council – an advisory body consisting of industrialists, trade union officials, civil servants and independent members – visited Londonderry in 1965 and spelt out in greater detail what needed to be done. There were Catholic trade unionists on this body who were well aware that there was no plot to deny the city the industrial development it needed. For that matter the people of Derry could see for themselves that important steps had been taken before the Civil Rights Association embarked on its protest march in October 1968. It might indeed have been urged that the process of change should be further accelerated but that would have been a different matter from claiming that no change had been either made or contemplated. The FEA study to which I have referred shows that Londonderry had been one of the most successful areas.

The authors of that report conclude that: 'In general the analysis shows that, judged on the basis of population shares, areas of the Province with Roman Catholic majorities have attracted the same proportion of assisted employment as have areas with non-Roman Catholic majorities in the period 1949–81.'[13] They go on to say: 'Judged on the basis of our analysis of the distribution of projects and employment in relation to population there would seem to be no grounds to question the fairness of industrial development policy on the basis of religion.'[14] To this we may add that, according to all their tests, Londonderry did comparatively well. Indeed the statistics do not reveal the full extent of the improvement for several firms were interested in a Londonderry location on the eve of the political disturbances of October 1968. Of these one at least was expected to come and even one large factory would have made an important difference when unemployment, though high in percentage terms, amounted to only about 2500 men. The ratio of share of sponsored employment to share of unemployment, quoted above, would then have become markedly more favourable. I can recall a senior civil servant saying with satisfaction that the solution of the Londonderry problem was at last in sight. The widely held belief that Londonderry was the victim of sectarian discrimination in industrial promotion cannot be sustained.

THE GENERAL RECESSION

As the disturbances became more violent and widespread, industrial development naturally suffered, and the Ulster economy received a further blow when the nationwide slump in manufacturing after 1979 meant the closing down of branch factories. Some of the areas that had formerly been so prosperous were then severely affected, especially small areas such as the town and district of Antrim where so much of the former prosperity had been derived from a single large factory. Thus the total number unemployed in Antrim rose by something like tenfold between 1971 and 1987. It is necessary to use the qualifying words 'something like' because, in Ulster as in the rest of the United Kingdom, the basis of the unemployment figures had changed from numbers registered to numbers claiming benefit. There is a further difficulty in that it is no longer possible to assess the unemployment percentage by ESO areas as previously recorded in this chapter. These changes in the statistical bases are a nuisance but a reasonably satisfactory impression can nevertheless be obtained of the magnitude of the changes that have taken place. This can be done by comparing the statistics for the percentage unemployed in the travel-to-work areas in 1971 and 1987, as is done in table 11.2, with the travel-to-work areas for 1971 adjusted to correspond to the official practice in 1987.[15] As has been observed, the unemployment percentages for these two dates are not strictly comparable but the changes in unemployment are so large as to allow us to assume that the orders of magnitude are broadly correct. Moreover this change in the statistical base should not greatly affect the ranking of the various districts at each of the two dates. Inspection of the figures shows that this ranking has not been greatly altered, but that does not tell the whole story. If the different areas are grouped once more into two categories – East and West – it can be calculated (from absolute figures not given in table 11.2) that, of the total number of males officially assessed as unemployed

 36.6 per cent were in the West in 1971;
 28.1 per cent were in the West in 1987.

TABLE 11.2   Percentage of males unemployed in Northern Ireland by region

		June 1971	June 1987
East:			
Ballymena	(25.9)	5.6	17.8
Belfast	(27.3)	7.4	22.5
Coleraine	(23.9)	10.6	29.6
Craigavon	(39.1)	7.4	23.8
Newry	(71.4)	16.7	36.8
West:			
Cookstown	(49.2)	10.5	35.0
Dungannon	(52.3)	21.0	30.8
Enniskillen	(52.5)	15.0	29.8
Londonderry	(64.3)	14.7	37.0
Magherafelt	(54.7)	9.2	34.7
Omagh	(62.1)	12.2	27.5
Strabane	(56.9)	19.9	43.6

Figures in brackets are the percentage of Catholics in the total population in
1971.
Travel-to-work areas are according to the 1987 classification of districts with the
1971 districts grouped accordingly.

The deterioration in the relative position of the East can also be shown by taking
the percentage unemployed in the East as 100 for both 1971 and 1987. The
corresponding figure for the West in 1971 was 217 but in 1987 only 143. Thus
unemployment was more than twice as high in the West as in the East on the earlier
date, but less than half as much again in 1987. The misery had increased
everywhere but – if that was any consolation – it had been somewhat more evenly
spread.

12

Discrimination, Social Structure and Unemployment

One of the oldest and most bitter complaints of the Catholic minority in Northern Ireland is that they have been the victims of sectarian discrimination in employment. Bias in recruitment has long been blamed for the relatively high rate of Catholic unemployment and bias in the workplace is held to be the explanation of the relatively low number of Catholics in senior positions in both the public and the private sectors. In its persistence, this complaint differs from that about discrimination in the allocation of public authority houses which has gradually subsided and ceased to be important. The changing situation with regard to housing is reviewed in chapter 13 and, at this stage, it must suffice to offer some broad explanations of the fact that one grievance has remained but the other has not. First there is the simple but obviously important fact that the supply of houses has been brought much more closely into line with demand, at the prevailing level of rents, whereas, by contrast, the jobs available, at the prevailing levels of wages, have declined. The second and more speculative explanation is that discrimination in employment may be harder to identify and remove than discrimination in housing.

It is true that there has been some narrowing of the rate of male unemployment among Catholics as compared with the rate among Protestants. For whatever reason, the ratio declined from 2.62 to 1 in the census year of 1971, to 2.44 in 1981, the next census year, and to 2.36 in 1983–5 according to the Continuous Household Survey.[1] Moreover, this improvement occurred at a time when total unemployment was sharply increasing. The fact remains that unemployment continues to be very much higher among Catholics and has become the most important of the sectarian social issues. Under the old Unionist regime, discrimination was regarded by nationalist politicians as the main explanation and was believed to be deliberately practised both as a means of rewarding faithful Unionist supporters and as a means of imposing pressure that should cause more Catholics to emigrate. But that regime came to an end as long ago as 1972, and it cannot plausibly be maintained that, with direct rule from Westminster, both Conservative and Labour governments have sanctioned deliberate discrimination against the Catholics. If, none the less, the gap between the two unemployment rates continues to be large, can it be inferred that the good intentions of successive Secretaries of State have been foiled by incorrigible employers in the private sector and by recruitment boards in the public sector? Or does the continuity in the unemployment differential perhaps suggest that it may have other important causes apart altogether from discrimination – causes that may also have been operative when the Unionists were in power?

What is clearly required at the outset is a definition of discrimination. The word conveys a strong sense of moral disapprobation. To discriminate is to act unfairly. Equity requires that persons who are alike *in all relevant respects* should be treated alike. The treatment of different persons may differ and, on grounds of equity, *should* differ, but only when they are not alike 'in all relevant respects'. The problem, as one moves from abstract principle to practical application, is to determine what are 'relevant respects' and then to assess how much *weight* should be attached to any relevant differences.

The area of controversy with which we are concerned is the treatment accorded to people who are distinguished by the names of their respective religious denominations: Protestant and Catholic respectively. Can it possibly be held that religious affiliation is a 'relevant' difference? One's immediate reaction may be to reject that possibility out of hand and to assert that ability and capacity for work must be randomly distributed with no presumption in favour of one religious sect as compared with another. But the need for caution becomes apparent when one recalls that two of the founding fathers of the social sciences took a different view: Max Weber and R. H. Tawney. For they laid great stress on the importance of the Protestant work ethic, especially in Calvinist communities. This view has, of course, been challenged. It would certainly be hard to maintain that English Protestants are better workers than English Catholics. But we are concerned here with *Irish* Catholics and with their cultural heritage of which religion has been one of several components. It must be admitted that, at least in the past, immigrant Irish workers were not accorded as much respect in the USA as were Germans or Scandinavians – or Scots-Irish. The same was probably true in England as well. Indeed the spokesmen of Irish nationalism have themselves given unwitting support to the view that Protestants are better workers by drawing a sharp line between Gaels and Settlers. Many splendid qualities have been attributed to the Gaels but the traditional list does not, I think, include any special capacity for work in office or in factory.

We are dealing here with *perceptions* which may, of course, be false. I must confess that, for my own part, I am inclined to view with deep scepticism any such characterization of ethnic or national groups, at least when one is dealing with the different components of a local community. Admittedly it would be foolish to carry such scepticism to the point of denying any role for cultural factors in explaining the differences between, say, Japanese and British workers; but it is much less plausible to postulate important differences between people living together in so small an area as Northern Ireland who are exposed to much the same – largely secular – influences. Moreover the Protestant work ethic, there as elsewhere, has had its edge somewhat blunted over the years by the trade unions. Nevertheless it has been the case, and may still be the case, that some employers *believe* Protestant workers to be better at the job and more reliable than Catholics. Moreover, with schools strictly segregated on religious lines, a preference for Protestants may reflect a belief that Protestant schools produce better trained pupils – as they have done and may still do in such relevant fields as mathematics and science. This, of course, is really a different issue from the work ethic but the two are likely to be intertwined in perception.

There is the further complication which must be repeatedly stressed that 'Catholic' in Ulster conveys an assumption about political as much as religious convictions. Catholics are perceived to be nationalists who are prepared to give, at best, grudging and provisional support for a Northern Ireland that is separated from the rest of the island. Some will be strong republicans and therefore poor security risks, but it may be hard to identify them. Others may be subjected to pressure from fanatics and may, understandably, give in. Information may be leaked in ways that are dangerous or at least embarrassing. Even apart from the security question, Catholics may not be thought to be so fully committed to performing conscientious work in a state of which they disapprove. That is to say, loyalty may be regarded as a relevant consideration even in peaceful conditions, and could be thought crucially important by employers in particularly vulnerable positions when the IRA is conducting an all-out campaign. Religious affiliation, easily determined in Northern Ireland, could then be used as a crude method of security screening in order to exclude possible IRA sympathizers or persons who, though not sympathetic, might be intimidated into providing the terrorists with helpful information. It is hardly necessary to add that, if screening of this kind is used, it is bound to be grossly unfair to many individual Catholics. In short this is one of the ways in which terrorism can aggravate an already difficult social situation. Again the perceptions may often be false, and the evidence required to establish the truth, wherever it lies, will not be easy to obtain.

If it should be the case that members of the Protestant tribe were, as a rule, better workers than members of the Catholic tribe, then it would not be inequitable to favour them. To say this is *not* to 'justify' discrimination. It is to *deny* that discrimination, defined as inequitable treatment, would then be taking place. But the danger of improper bias creeping in, where so much depends upon subjective perceptions, must obviously be stressed.

The normal procedure in empirical work is to use as a bench-mark the proportion of Catholics in the relevant population group and to compare this with the number employed, say, in local government or the civil service. It is, of course, important to choose the appropriate category of the population for the particular calculation in hand. Sometimes this may be persons of working age; sometimes those with particular qualifications; and so on. If there is a marked divergence, there is then a *prima facie* case for investigation – though not, at this preliminary stage, for condemnatory assumption.

We shall start, in the next section, with a review of differences in class structure and educational attainment. Such differences will be reflected in standards of living, status in the community and susceptibility to unemployment. The section that follows will take up the highly topical and controversial question of differences in rates of male unemployment between Catholics and Protestants. The third section will review some of the main facts about recruitment and promotion. The final section will deal with the measures already taken and those about to be taken in order to prevent discrimination.

CLASS STRUCTURE AND EDUCATIONAL ATTAINMENT

Various estimates have been made of the occupational class structure of the
Catholic and Protestant populations respectively but it will be sufficient to present
those that emerge from an analysis of the 1971 census by E. A. Aunger.[2] His figures
show that 14 per cent of the economically active men and women were in the top
professional and managerial groups with 15 per cent for the Protestants and 12 per
cent for the Catholics. For men alone the figure is again 14 per cent in this class,
but there is now a wider contrast, with 16 per cent for Protestant men and 9 per cent
for Catholics. At the other end of the class structure, 44 per cent of men and women
were in the semi-skilled and unskilled groups, with 52 per cent of the Catholics and
40 per cent of the Protestants. For men alone, the corresponding figures were 44
per cent for the total and 56 and 40 per cent for Catholics and Protestants
respectively. The Catholic population may therefore be described as predominantly
semi-skilled and unskilled, but this statement by itself, although correct, could leave
an exaggerated impression, for 48 per cent were in the higher social classes, or 44
per cent in the case of men alone. The modal Catholic male was unskilled manual
(31 per cent) and the modal Protestant male was skilled manual (27 per cent).

The year 1971 to which these figures relate is one of particular interest because
this was the last year of Unionist government at Stormont. The class structure thus
depicted is what had emerged after fifty years of devolution. Whatever the reasons,
the Protestant class structure was 'higher' – in this conventional sense – than the
Catholic; but it would clearly be wrong to talk about 'class domination' and it would
be an extravagant misuse of language to suggest that, in this sense, there were 'two
nations'. All this information was readily available when the authors of the New
Ireland Forum Report asserted that: 'They [the Northern Catholics] were deprived
of the means of social and economic development.'[3]

The authors of that Report might also have noted that, as Richard Rose had
pointed out, 'there are more poor Protestants than poor Catholics, given the larger
Protestant population' and might have recalled, with advantage, his conclusion: 'In
aggregate, the limited income difference between the two communities is evidence
that the political conflict in Northern Ireland is not between rich and poor religious
groups.'[4]

An analysis of educational statistics[5] shows, again for 1971, that the proportion of
Catholics with A Levels was only about 2.5 per cent less than their share of the
population aged 18–69. Their position in this respect was weaker than that for the
Presbyterians but slightly better than that for members of the Church of Ireland.
The relative Catholic position was nearly as good for higher qualifications as for A
Levels. Catholics were, however, much less likely to have qualifications in scientific
and craft subjects than were Protestants, presumably because the Catholic schools,
largely under clerical control, choose to lay less emphasis on these subjects.
Moreover the teaching of Irish must leave less time for other subjects. These
differences could have implications for employment.

At the other end of the scale a substantial proportion – roughly two-thirds in
1971 and two-fifths in 1975 – left school with no qualifications. There were
proportionately more Catholics in this group than their population share.

It is important to bear in mind that these studies relate to the qualifications of children leaving schools in recent years. But a large proportion of the population of working age were educated at a time when the superiority of non-Catholic schools as compared with Catholic schools may have been a good deal more marked than is the case today.

THE INCIDENCE OF UNEMPLOYMENT

Differences in class and in educational attainment may help to explain the differences in unemployment rates. Unskilled manual workers are more insecure than skilled workers and the proportion of unskilled Catholics is twice that of unskilled Protestants. Some industries are also more vulnerable than others. Over a fifth of the Catholic labour force is in the construction industry, which can be subject to severe instability. Protestants have a proportionately larger share of jobs in the more stable public utilities. The previous patterns of relative industrial instability, based on earlier experience, have, however, been shattered by the contraction in employment throughout manufacturing industry, in particular since 1979, a contraction that has been intensified in the case of branch plants.

One of the most striking differences between Catholics and Protestants is in size of family. The 1971 census showed that the average number of children born alive to Catholic women was 3.64; to non-Catholics, 2.37. The average for the two communities was 2.72. It has been estimated that the corresponding figures for 1983 were 3.24, 2.29 and 2.66.[6] A decline had therefore taken place, even in the Catholic case, but the contrast with the average Protestant family remained large. These figures relate to marriages of all durations. For families that have lasted for twenty years or more, the family size was substantially greater with 5.31 for Catholics, 3.04 for Protestants and 3.55 for Northern Ireland as a whole in 1971. The larger number of children obviously imposes an additional financial burden on Catholic families, increases their demand for house room and makes it more difficult to prolong the period of education. A large family is also much more likely to be caught in the 'unemployment trap'. That is to say the additional reward for working as compared with being on benefit will decline with the size of family. Obviously the critical point will depend partly upon the potential earning power of the unemployed, and experience in Great Britain has suggested that in the case of the unemployed, these earnings will be substantially below the national average. For a family of three children the additional spending power to be acquired by taking a job at two-thirds average earnings would be barely 20 per cent in Great Britain where earnings are higher than in Ulster.

In 1971, 45 per cent of Catholic families had three or more dependent children as compared with under 20 per cent of Protestant families. Almost 30 per cent of the Catholic families had four or more dependent children as against 8 per cent of Protestant families, and about 10 per cent had six or more, as compared with only a tiny proportion of Protestant families. As Compton has shown,[7] there was a clear correlation in 1971 between number of dependent children and unemployment percentage. Two points can, therefore, be made with some confidence. First, the unemployment trap may be one of the factors responsible for the higher rates of unemployment that have persisted over the years in Northern Ireland as a whole as compared with Great Britain. Secondly, the unemployment trap is clearly more important for Catholic families than for Protestant families and as Paul Doherty, another investigator, has concluded, this fact 'may help account for some of the link between unemployment and Catholic religious affiliation.'[8]

To say this is *not* to imply that Catholics are 'spongers' – to use the term unwisely applied to the Ulster people by Harold Wilson in 1974. The point is quite simply that a person cannot reasonably be expected to prefer employment to unemployment if the gain to his family is small.

An attempt has been made by Paul Compton to assess the extent to which this last factor and two other factors may account for the relatively high rate of Catholic unemployment. The other two are social class and geographical location.[9] The calculation is made for the census year 1971 and relates to male heads of households. For them the Catholic unemployment rate, at 15.7 per cent, was as much as three times the Protestant rate of 5.2 per cent. The calculation entails a statistical adjustment or 'standardization'. Thus the effect of social class structure can be separately assessed by comparing the actual rate of Catholic unemployment with what that rate would have been if, with everything else unchanged, the Catholics had had the same class structure as the Protestants. The unemployment percentage for Catholics, as calculated in this way, is 12.2 as compared with the actual percentage of 15.7, which suggests that over a fifth of the Catholic unemployment reflected class structure. The corrected ratio of Catholic male unemployment to Protestant drops from 3.02 to 2.35. A similar calculation is carried out for the difference in the number of dependent children. If Catholic families were as small as Protestant families, Catholic unemployment might be 8 per cent lower at 14.4 per cent, and the ratio brought down to 2.77. In the same way an adjustment can be made for location, which brings the Catholic unemployment percentage down to 12.9 and the ratio to 2.5. The combined effect of these three factors can then be assessed. If, in 1971, Catholics had had the same class structure, the same number of dependents and the same geographical location, then the rate of Catholic male unemployment would have been 9.8 per cent, with almost three-fifths of the difference explained in these three ways and the ratio pulled down to 1.9 – an appreciably lower differential but still a substantial one. It must be emphasized, of course, that these statistical adjustments would hold only if the changes specified did not lead to a variety of other changes in the economy or did not encounter obstacles of one kind or another. The implicit assumption is that other things are unchanged. As illustrative calculations, however, the estimates assist in appreciating the relative importance of the different factors. Barritt and Carter have suggested that it is the *combination* of a number of disadvantages that may have a crippling effect on employment prospects.[10] To live in a relatively poor area with high unemployment, to belong to a low social class and to have had an inferior education may, for a young person of average ability, constitute an almost insuperable barrier to getting a job, except in a market where there is a serious labour shortage. A 'critical level of disadvantage' has, so to speak, been reached.

There is another important factor: the size of the juvenile intake, which consists of roughly twice as many young Catholics as young Protestants, relative to the size of their respective population groups. This in itself is bound to cause heavier

Catholic unemployment, as Compton rightly stresses. For it not to happen, recruitment would have to be biased heavily in favour of the young Catholics at the expense of the young Protestants. It is also true that a more flexible wage-structure would result in a wider gap between juvenile and adult pay, and total juvenile unemployment could then be reduced. This point has, of course, been made often enough in the wider context of comparisons between Britain and Germany, but it also deserves emphasis in the Ulster context as well.

A good deal of detailed research work has also been carried out by other investigators into different aspects of the labour market with particular regard to the disadvantaged sectors of the population and to the possibility of sectarian discrimination as a cause. Many of these investigations have been performed by or on behalf of the Fair Employment Agency, which was established in 1976 (see the section on public policy below). The topics covered have been attitudes to work, educational qualifications and religious affiliation, higher education and religion, the transition from work to school, segregation and its effects.[11] The general conclusion reached by two of those involved is as follows:

Most of the current evidence seems to suggest that the amount of religious discrimination, in terms of individually motivated behaviour, in employment, is relatively small. However, such a conclusion on discrimination could be deceptive in significant ways. . . . Current patterns of exclusion and disadvantage can be the result of past discrimination sustained by contemporary practices and behaviour which are not overtly discriminatory.[12]

When the Standing Advisory Commission on Human Rights (SACHR) decided in 1985 to review the whole question of discrimination and the measures adopted for its prevention, there was a substantial amount of work on which to draw. The Commission decided to sponsor a further inquiry by engaging the services of a research team from the Policy Studies Institute in London. One of the topics to which this team addressed its attention was the one just discussed, that is differences in rates of employment.[13] The new report by David Smith proved to be tendentious and was criticized by other scholars on various grounds: the unsuitability of the source material for some of the purposes to which it was put, the statistical techniques involved and the somewhat sweeping nature of the final conclusion.[14] We need not review this controversy in any detail, but we cannot simply leave it on one side, as merely of academic interest. The PSI investigation is of special political importance because it was commissioned by SACHR and publicized accordingly. It should be enough, however, to draw attention to the main features of the debate in order to illustrate the difficulties and uncertainties.

Smith, in his turn, tries to assess the extent to which the different unemployment rates over the years 1983–5 can be explained by six possible causes: socio-economic group, area of residence, age, number of dependent children, academic qualifications and the type of industry to which the unemployed family belongs. None seems to account for more than a small part of the differential. This estimate may seem, at first glance, not so greatly different from Compton's, but Compton's calculations based on three variables are illustrative, not exhaustive. Smith, however, claims that he has taken account of all possible explanations apart from discrimination against Catholics. The results of a multiple regression analysis are then recorded which suggest that the unexplained residual is still large: 'For a man with a typical set of circumstances (a skilled manual worker aged 25–44 with two children, having no qualifications) the predicted rate of unemployment is nearly twice as high for a Catholic as for a Protestant within most travel to work areas.'[15] Smith then makes a rash claim and draws a faulty inference. The claim is that: 'It might be argued that factors not included explain some of the difference but *the model does include all of the factors that are known to be important determinants of unemployment*. We therefore conclude that after allowing for all the factors that are known to be relevant and important, religion is a major determinant of the rate of unemployment.'[16] In a subsequent article he is still more explicit: 'A large part of the difference in rates of unemployment cannot be explained except on the assumption that Protestants have a better chance of finding a job than Catholics with the same relevant characteristics and qualifications. This is equivalent to saying there is substantial discrimination in recruitment.'[17]

There may indeed be discrimination, but, clearly, there are quite serious errors in this approach. First, Smith's claim that he has allowed for all other possible explanations is untrue. One important omission is the fact that much the greater part of the civil security forces – including guards employed in shops and factories – consists of Protestants. This is not itself a consequence of religious discrimination but of the reluctance of Catholics to join the police, and of the complicated security situation where, in view of hidden allegiances and intimidation, Catholics are regarded as a greater risk when employed as guards in shops, offices and factories. About 25–30,000 men and women appear to be employed in this way. Another factor completely ignored is the 'black economy'. It is possible, though *not* certain, that relatively more of the Catholic unemployed are 'doing the double'. The scope for doing so varies between industries[18] and it is well known that the construction industry lends itself more easily to such practices than, say, the public utility industries. It may therefore be a relevant point that 22 per cent of the Catholic labour force is in the construction industry as compared with 11 per cent of the Protestant labour force. Moreover, in the border counties, some of the Ulster 'unemployed' are said to have jobs in the Republic and, if so, they will be virtually all Catholic. A very important factor may be the immense difficulty in checking claims and preventing fraud in areas dominated by the IRA, such as West Belfast. Clearly, Smith was rash in claiming to have covered everything. The relatively large inflow of Catholic juveniles into the labour market was a further cause of higher Catholic unemployment – a point mentioned above. To this Smith attaches no special importance on the ground, apparently, that it will have been taken into account in assessing the effect of differences in age structure. This is to miss the point that a larger proportion of Catholics have to be placed in employment every year and more will move up into the higher age brackets without having found employment.

It is to be expected that all investigations will end with an unexplained residual. But it is quite improper, as Charles Carter has observed, to use the term 'discrimination' as though it meant 'any residual difference observed between two communities when selected plausible causes of that difference have been eliminated.'[19] Not only may there be some quantifiable causes that have been overlooked but there are others that cannot be *directly* quantified. Unfortunately the unwarranted assertion made on the basis of the PSI investigation may lead to greater suspicion and ill-will in a community which already has a more than adequate quota of both.

RECRUITMENT AND PROMOTION IN PUBLIC EMPLOYMENT

The foregoing discussion was concerned with statistical attempts to assess the importance of some of the various factors that may contribute to the very much higher rate of unemployment among Catholics. In the present section attention will be directed to the questions of recruitment and promotion which, of course, also have implications for differences in the standard of living and for the distribution of power in the community. We shall start with the public sector. In this section, it might be illuminating to substitute 'unionist' for 'Protestant' and 'nationalist' for 'Catholic', but I shall retain the sectarian terms in order to preserve strict conformity with the statistical sources.

In the course of a long review of the evidence about discrimination, John Whyte observes of the public services, central and local, that: 'If all grades are lumped together, there appears to be little if any under-representation of Catholics.' He goes on to add that: 'However, the moment one distinguishes lower grades from higher ones marked discrepancies appear.'[20] It was indeed the case that few Catholics held senior positions in the Stormont civil service. This was shown very clearly to have been so in 1927 and in 1959 in a statistical inquiry carried out by Barritt and Carter.[21] In the former year only one of the six permanent secretaries was a Catholic, in the latter year none. There was one Catholic in the second and assistant secretary grades in 1927 and there were two in 1959. If all civil servants of the rank of staff officer and upwards are taken together, 94 per cent were Protestants in both years. It would be unreasonable to compare these figures with the proportion of Catholics in the total Ulster population, for Catholics have relatively large numbers of children, or even with their proportion of the gainfully employed population, for a smaller fraction of the Catholics was qualified. Barritt and Carter take as a reasonable bench-mark the Protestant proportion of the grammar school population, which was about 75 per cent in 1959. The Protestant 'excess' is thus reduced but is still substantial. A further allowance should, however, be made for the fact that part of the assistant principal grade was recruited through the UK Civil Service Commission and included graduates from Great Britain. The pattern of nominal religious affiliation could therefore be affected. Although historical statistics are not readily available, the position in 1987 with regard to the General Service group may serve to illustrate the consequences.[22] Only 12.1 per cent of the upper staff (senior principals and above) were Ulster Catholic, but 8.9 per cent, of unspecified religion, were educated outside Ulster and religion was unknown for a further 1 per cent. As more of the lower grades are included, the proportion of officers not educated in Ulster declines, as one would expect. The wider field of recruitment must clearly be taken into account when attention is directed to the composition of university teaching staff. Universities recruit from all over the world – and would be open to the most severe censure if they did not do so. It would, therefore, be absurd to suppose that the proportion of Catholics, Protestants and others on the university teaching staff should correspond to the local proportions in Northern Ireland. That would be parochialism gone mad.

To return to the civil service: the heavy preponderance of Protestants when all allowances have been made, clearly calls for explanation. The main reason for the small Catholic entry to the administrative grade through the UK Civil Service Commissioners appears to have been the very small number of Catholic applicants, not sectarian discrimination. For this small entry there could be two reasons. First, young Catholics and their family or other advisers could not be expected to view with much enthusiasm a lifetime in the service of a political system of which they did not approve. Social disapproval would also be incurred from fellow Catholics. The position was described as follows by a distinguished Catholic civil servant who became permanent secretary in the Ministry of Education:

Catholics in the Northern Ireland Civil Service in those [pre-war] days were few. Because of the hard times through which many had lived and from which they had emerged as losers the Northern Catholics were not disposed to claim anything from what they regarded as a hostile government; in any case, they believed that worthwhile employment under the Unionist administration was available only to Unionists and friends of Unionists. It was my experience that some Catholics, and especially those in Belfast where, I had been told, the Bishop advised them against seeking Government employment, looked with suspicion on Catholic civil servants.[23]

The likelihood of promotion through the various grades may also have appeared discouraging. Any such pessimistic anticipations would certainly have been strengthened by the vehemence with which some of the ultras in the Unionist camp demanded that no Catholics should ever be given any government employment. Thus there was created another vicious circle of suspicion and resentment. It is useless to speculate on the extent – if any – to which promotion boards did, in fact, display sectarian bias in the old pre-war Stormont. But it is hard to believe that there was any discrimination at all in its final phase.

There is, of course, no precise way of checking, but it may be in place to record that a number of retired senior civil servants, all of them English, whom I have questioned have assured me in the most firm and unequivocal way that they had never encountered sectarian bias in many years of service on promotion boards. They would feel justified, for their part, in resenting any suggestion that they would have connived at such practices. There were, however, two areas of appointment which, by general admission, were not open to Catholics. One was the Ministry of Home Affairs, the other in the private offices of the ministers. In both cases the reason was that some Catholics might be bad security risks and a blanket ban was preferable to suspicion and surveillance. Moreover some Catholics might not have wished to serve in a minister's private office. It may also be observed that lack of experience in a private office could be a disadvantage but clearly not a serious one as can be seen from individual careers.

In its final phase, especially in the last decade of its life, Stormont began to take positive steps to improve the sectarian balance. One of the methods used was to arrange for senior officials to visit Catholic schools willing to receive them, in order to give career talks. Partly as a consequence, perhaps, and also no doubt because the abolition of self-government in favour of direct rule increased confidence, Catholic applications have risen. Although their performance in tests remained in general rather below the level reached by Protestants sufficient numbers reached a satisfactory level to allow a large rise in appointments.[24] For males, the percentage of Catholics fluctuated around an average of about 20 per cent of the intake in

1968–70, and then rose to 46 per cent in Stormont's last year and went on to increase to over half in 1977. There has also been an increase in the Catholic proportion of the female intake, from just over one-third to over one-half. Since then the proportion of Catholics has slightly *exceeded* the proportion of Protestants year by year. Thus the Catholics have obtained more than a proportionate share of appointments. In the service as a whole, the average age of Catholics is naturally younger. Only 12 per cent are over 50 as compared with 22 per cent of the Protestants and the senior grades will be predominantly Protestant for some years to come. An important change has, however, begun, although it will take time to work itself out.[25]

The membership of public boards was almost exclusively Protestant under the Unionist regime. Partly this was an 'old boy' network and partly it may have reflected deliberate sectarian discrimination. It was certainly unwise as well as unfair. What we do not know is how willingly senior members of the minority would have cooperated, but the ball should have been put firmly in their court. Appointments to the judiciary raised much more difficult questions. Nearly all the judges were Protestants, which was most unfortunate. Was it avoidable? In 1936, the Government revealed that it had offered a County Court judgeship to every Catholic KC in Northern Ireland. Any who accepted were regarded as traitors by the Catholic community.[26] As was so often the case, the difficulty was partly caused by the refusal of the minority to recognize the legitimacy of the state and to cooperate in making it work efficiently.

There can be no question that discrimination occurred in local government. Admittedly about a third of the total number of employees were Catholic but they were over-represented in the lower grades, in particular that of manual labourers. The Cameron Commission was quite firm on this point: 'We are satisfied that all these Unionist controlled councils have used and use their power to make appointments in a way which benefited Protestants.'[27] They go on to give examples of the extent to which Catholics were under-represented in the top posts. Even when the classification was enlarged to include clerical and technical employees, the Catholics were given a poor showing. In Londonderry, they had only about 30 per cent of these posts, although 62 per cent of the adult population was Catholic. In Dungannon, there were no Catholics at all in these grades. In Fermanagh, where there was a small Catholic majority in the population, even the bus drivers were 75 per cent Protestant. Up to a point, a preponderance of Protestants could be explained by a deliberate policy of preferring ex-servicemen, but I am not aware of any quantitative assessment of this factor. It is also right to add that Catholics discriminated against Protestants when their control of a local council gave them the chance to do so, as in Newry.

'We think that the situation which exists in local government will be more readily understood by American than by British readers.' This observation by Barritt and Carter[28] is one that should, in all fairness, be considered by Americans before they attribute a peculiar form of wickedness to the Ulster community. The expression 'pork barrel' is surely of American origin. Barritt and Carter are, however, much too charitable about Britain. There is plenty of bias in local government in a number of areas although the bias may be on political rather than religious grounds – or rather on what, in Ulster, are seen to be religious grounds. Of course it would be totally wrong to excuse unfair practices in Ulster because there were unfair practices elsewhere, but some consistency in applying standards would be beneficial, as well as more honest. For, in the general appraisal of their record, the Ulster majority has itself become the victim of 'discrimination' – guilty unless proved innocent and with any evidence in support of innocence often viewed with a sceptical eye. In the long run this cannot be the way to achieve a better understanding and the healing of old wounds.[29]

DISCRIMINATION AND THE PROFIT MOTIVE

The position with regard to private employment is more difficult to assess. Whyte refers to Aunger's analysis, discussed above, which shows that Catholics were somewhat lower in the social scale, as conventionally determined. This, however, is to restate the problem, not to provide an answer to it. Moreover, in this context language must be used with care. When it is said that some group or class, whether in Ulster or anywhere else, is 'disadvantaged' or 'underprivileged', there is an implication that some other group or class has deliberately placed them at this disadvantage or deprived them of privileges. That may indeed be what has happened, but the evidence needs to be presented. The Policy Studies Institute report, already quoted above, contains the following example of the use of emotive language: 'Catholics are somehow *channelled* into disadvantaged sectors of the labour market. Apart from discrimination or unequal opportunities, no adequate explanation of how they are *confined* within such sectors has yet emerged.'[30] But the verbs, to which I have added italics, are active verbs. Who are those who have been responsible for this action? What means were employed? What evidence can be adduced in support of charges thus implied?

Anyone who has lived in Northern Ireland will be well aware of the fact that many employers preferred to employ persons with the same religious – or, better, the same tribal – affiliation as themselves. Some made no bones about it. Others were more discreet. Quantified assessment is virtually impossible, but some revealing examples are given by Barritt and Carter.[31] They draw attention to the fact that even when the proportion of Catholics employed by a firm was as high as the proportion of Catholics in the total population in that particular travel-to-work area, the Catholics might still hold few positions of responsibility. Protestants would also be at a disadvantage in 'Catholic firms' but there were fewer of them – in itself a fact of some significance.

If businessmen behaved in this way, what were their motives in doing so? It used to be an old complaint of the Left that 'market forces are blind' but, in modern times, it can be appreciated that 'blindness' is often a merit. 'The market is colour-blind' and when market forces operate freely a black skin will be no handicap. With its colour blindness the market must also fail to detect any difference between 'orange' and 'green'. Private firms which must operate in the market, are therefore in a different position from government offices. When politicians are in power they may be able to pass over some more able employees in favour of the less able who belong to the right party or tribe, and any loss of efficiency that results can be laid on the broad shoulders of the taxpayer. But a private firm must cover its costs in a competitive world and try to earn a profit. When therefore it is said that private firms discriminated against Catholics, should this allegation be taken to mean that more suitable Catholics were turned away when appointments were being made, or better Catholics were passed over for promotion, even though the firm's efficiency was damaged as a result and profits reduced? It is possible that some employers with particularly strong religious or political views were prepared to make the sacrifice implied. But there may, in fact, have been no sacrifice for there may have been no ascertainable difference in the suitability of different candidates with different religious affiliations. No gain or loss could be expected from employing a Protestant, and the choice could then be determined by the prejudices of those making the appointment. In large firms the decision would not of course be made by top management and there might be more prejudice lower down the hierarchy than at the top where there might, indeed, be none at all. A sustained bias towards Protestants would mean that more of them would acquire training and experience, and a subsequent attempt to correct the denominational disproportion would then take time – probably a lot of time. There can be no doubt that there was sectarian or political bias in some important private firms in the past, though not in all, and the consequences persist even after deliberate discrimination has ceased.

An element of sectarian bias may be introduced even without deliberate intent by recruitment through an informal network used for convenience or to help one's friends or simply from habit. Whatever the merits or defects of that form of recruitment in a normal labour market, it may result in what can be described as 'thoughtless discrimination' in a society where informal contacts are limited by informal sectarian segregation. The appointment of John rather than Sean need not reflect a conscious act of sectarian discrimination but that will be small comfort to Sean. There is, however, the other possibility. In preferring Protestants to Catholics, many employers may well have *believed* that, apart altogether from satisfying any religious or political preference, they were likely, as a rule, to be employing the most efficient workers. Thus we return to the points discussed in the first section with all the practical difficulties these entail.

PUBLIC POLICY

Although it is scarcely possible to assess the amount of deliberate discrimination or of 'thoughtless discrimination', various public measures may be adopted both as safeguards and as remedies. In its final phase, the Unionist government established a Ministry of Community Relations, a Community Relations Commission, a Parliamentary Commission and a Commission for Complaints. The first three were to disappear in later years as their duties were taken over by other bodies. In the event, surprisingly few complaints about discrimination were submitted and very few could be upheld. In 1973, under Direct Rule, a new advisory body was established: the Standing Committee on Human Rights. A new working party under the direction of William van Straubenzee was appointed and, on its recommendation, the Fair Employment Agency was established in 1974 with powers to investigate and to issue directions which are enforceable at law. A Declaration of Principle and

Intent was prepared and, since 1982, tenders for public contracts have been accepted only from firms on whose behalf this document had been signed. A guide to effective action was published by the Department of Economic Development in 1987. Further legislation was forecast by another government committee in 1987 and proposals were put forward in some detail in the following year. It seems right to record these measures in order to dispel any false assumption that the government has been indifferent to the situation. It received a further strong stimulus to action when that uncompromising Irish republican, the late Sean MacBride, launched a crusade in the USA to persuade public authorities, private firms with interests in Northern Ireland and such financial institutions as pension funds to impose sanctions, directly or indirectly, unless action against discrimination was adopted along specified lines – the MacBride Principles.

An attempt to obtain more detailed and up-to-date information about discrimination by means of a survey was carried out by Gerald Chambers for the Standing Advisory Commission on Human Rights.[32] One of the conclusions suggested by the answers received was that the measures already adopted had caused no great change in employment policies. The difficulty then was to know how to interpret answers to this effect. Was there really little change or was it rather that managers were afraid to admit to changes lest the admission be interpreted as a confession of past misdemeanours? What did emerge with greater clarity was the fact that few firms monitored the sectarian composition of their labour forces and the vast majority followed a policy of letting things 'find their own level'.[33] Few attempted to achieve 'a balanced workforce'. All the familiar methods of recruitment were employed, but with much recourse to informal methods, even at the larger workplaces.

Government action against discrimination

The proposals for new additional legislation against discrimination, put forward by the Government in 1988, were far-reaching.[33] Not merely must discrimination be avoided, there must be an active policy of promoting equality of opportunity. All employers with more than ten employees – twenty-five initially – will be required to monitor the religious composition of their workforces and to submit annual returns. Failure to do so will be a *criminal* offence, and will also entail exclusion from government contracts. The Fair Employment Agency is to be expanded and strengthened. A new tribunal is to be established which will hear individual complaints, and the FEA will provide the complainants with financial assistance. How, it may be asked, will the firms themselves obtain the needed information about the religion of their employees? The answer is that, with a segregated educational system, the name of an applicant's school is all that is required. Any significant extension of integrated education would naturally reduce the reliability of this indicator but the Government, notwithstanding its endorsement of integration, clearly does not expect any such extension will occur.

This is a particularly difficult area of public policy, whether the discrimination is on religious, political or racial grounds. For the problem is by no means confined to Northern Ireland. It is not easy to devise effective means of action. Nor is it easy to ensure that the action taken, even when effective in achieving the immediate objective, will not entail other harmful social or economic consequences. If the dangers are to be minimized, it is important that all concerned should be clear about what is meant by 'discrimination' and clear about the aims that are to be pursued.

The term discrimination is strongly emotive and implies moral disapprobation. It is wrong, therefore, to use that term when, for example, certain applicants for employment are rejected on genuine grounds of security.[35] To repeat, in slightly different words, the definition introduced earlier in this chapter: no discrimination will have occurred if, when all *relevant* considerations are taken into account, the successful candidate is more appropriate for the work in question. A difficulty is caused by the fact that a candidate's suitability may depend partly upon a subjective assessment of his personality – especially for higher level employment. Any official tribunal would have to be reasonably sure of its grounds before setting aside the judgement of an employer, especially a private employer responsible for paying the wage or salary involved. But bad cases of discrimination – and there have been some bad cases in the past – could surely be identified. To uphold the principle of no discrimination would then be a way of ensuring equality of opportunity. It would be a different matter if the emphasis were to be on a 'balanced' labour force. For what is meant by 'sectarian balance'? As we have already seen, various interpretations are possible. The criterion may be the sectarian composition of the total population; or of the working population; or of that part of the working population that has relevant qualifications; or of the labour force in a particular area. The choice of local area within which 'balance' is to be established is bound to be an immensely complicated and contentious matter. But there is no presumption that a labour force deemed to be 'balanced' by any one of these criteria would be appropriate to the needs of a particular employer. Any attempt to impose sectarian quotas could be disastrous. Equality of opportunity is one thing; a balanced labour force is quite another. The pursuit of the former objective, however successful, need not lead to 'balance' – whatever that means. The meaning remains discouragingly elusive. One can only hope that the term will not be an addition to the vocabulary of confusion which already contains such terms as 'hinterland', 'economically viable' and 'economic unit'.

There has been no explicit suggestion that Protestant workers should be sacked to make room for Catholic workers, which would be illegal. The change desired is to be achieved gradually by altering the sectarian composition of the workers recruited as a consequence of constant movement within the labour force. It is estimated that the average worker changes employment every three years, which would seem to permit a gradual but substantial change in the composition of the total workforce, even when some allowance is made for the fact that there are bound to be complications caused by location and the need for particular skills. It must be recognized, however, that a reduction in Catholic unemployment will be matched by an increase in Protestant unemployment unless there should be a sufficient rise in employment and net migration to cause a decline in the total number out of work. The whole process of adjustment would be very much easier in an expanding economy.[36] By comparison, a zero-sum game is hard to play and it can be dangerous. Unfortunately the prospects for expansion are not encouraging, even in scenarios that embody relatively favourable assumptions. How are these prospects likely to be affected by the adoption of the policy itself? If its effect is at least to stave off some American sanctions that might otherwise be imposed on American firms in Ulster, some deterioration may be prevented even if there is no positive improvement. Moreover, in so far as it is true that discrimination prevents the best person from getting the job, there may be a marginal improvement in the quality of the labour force. In this connection more open methods of recruitment should be helpful with more jobs advertised and more recourse to job centres. For informal methods, though adequate enough at times, narrow the field of recruitment and may be inefficient as well as unfair. On the debit side is the underlining of the sectarian division which the policy implies. For this might easily lead to sectarian friction on the shopfloor on a scale that has so far been avoided – thanks in no small measure to the efforts of the trade unions. The elaborate methods now proposed for the submission of individual complaints could also be a cause of trouble to management for everyone with a grouse may feel encouraged to bring it forward.

Indeed if one looks at the Government's proposals as a whole, with the appeals tribunal, the compulsory monitoring of religious discrimination and the threat of criminal prosecution, one can hardly resist the conclusion that their introduction may add to the Province's locational disadvantages and may be a deterrent to any incoming firms in the future. For consider the prospect before any board of directors that is considering an Ulster location together with a number of other possible locations within the European Community. On the debit side is Ulster's remoteness which means that little may be known about the area initially, apart from the accounts of terrorist outrages purveyed by the media. On a slightly closer inspection, the apparent instability of the constitutional position is likely to be a further, and perhaps an even more serious, deterrent. On the positive side, as some offset to the disadvantages, the region has good harbours, good air services, good internal transport and financial inducements that are better than those available in some other areas, if not in all. It also has an official administration that is quickly responsive to special needs. But the availability of manpower, once an important attraction, is no longer so with unemployment now heavy in many other places as well. Moreover the labour position in Ulster is overshadowed by sectarian problems to which the new policies against discrimination have now directed a probing searchlight. Could it be prudent to become involved in a situation of this kind which is so hard to comprehend? Could it be sensible to forgo the normal managerial prerogative of engaging whatever labour seemed appropriate in order to conform to some new set of rules which would entail all the burden of registration and the compilation of returns showing the religious affiliation of the workforce? The board of directors, in the course of its investigations, could be expected to note the special provision for appeals by individuals who had alleged discrimination, with their legal costs met from public funds. How much managerial time and effort would be diverted to dealing with such matters at the expense of the proper duties of management? There would even be a risk of being prosecuted for a criminal offence if management stumbled away from the narrowly defined path across this minefield. How then could it possibly be right to become involved in so much hassle and to incur so much risk when there were various other locations where these somewhat bizarre disadvantages could be avoided?

The task of the Industrial Development Agency is scarcely likely to be made any easier by complications of this kind. It should, therefore, be put in a position to explain that the basic objective of the legislation is to ensure that appointments *are* based on merit, unwarped by discrimination, and are made from a wide field of potential recruits, not from a limited number selected through personal connections. The managerial prerogative need not be over-ridden, and the fearful anticipations reflected in the preceding paragraph should therefore be without foundation. It must also be hoped that the FEA, for its part, will discipline its own activities in order to protect industrial management from undue harassment. As has been stressed already, the whole task of ensuring reasonable fairness in the labour market would be vastly easier if expansion on a substantial scale were taking place, for it will be very much more difficult if Sean's gain can be achieved only at John's loss. It would be particularly unfortunate if the new policy itself were to have the unintended consequence of impeding such a general expansion.

So far the emphasis has been on obtaining employment and achieving subsequent promotion, but the scope for self-employment must not be ignored. In both the USA and the UK a good deal of emphasis has been placed in recent years on the contribution that can be made by small firms. In Northern Ireland, special financial assistance as well as regional grants have long been available, together with advice, when required, on marketing, product development and the like. This assistance is, of course, fully available to Catholics as well as Protestants, to nationalists as well as to unionists. Greater prosperity for all might be achieved if some of the energy so readily expended on political agitation of one kind or another were to be diverted into creative entrepreneurial effort in Northern Ireland's industry.

13

The Housing Shortage and Discrimination

Housing policy was one of the most sensitive political issues during the latter part of the Stormont regime. Its critics maintained that the local authorities under Unionist control discriminated in the most unscrupulous way against Catholic families. By contrast, the Protestant families were said to be favoured without regard to respective needs and were always moved to the front of the queue, sometimes as a reward for particular political services but more generally as a reward for simply being Protestants. It was something of a tragedy that these complaints were brushed aside by the Unionist leadership. Even when Terence O'Neill became Prime Minister, no action was taken to meet, or even indeed to investigate, complaints of this kind which thus became central issues in the civil rights campaign. It was, in fact, an organized protest against the allegedly unfair treatment of a particular Catholic family in Caledon, Co. Tyrone, in 1968, that preceded the new upsurge of unrest in Northern Ireland which, some twenty years later, has not yet come to an end.

That discrimination occurred is not in doubt. Nor can it be denied that the provincial government should have intervened some years before it finally did so and should have insisted upon procedures for the allocation of houses that would have provided some kind of safeguard. But it is also necessary to assess the *scale* on which these abuses occurred and to identify their *location*. For some bad and much publicized cases did not necessarily mean that the Catholic population as a whole was receiving substantially less than its fair share, as judged by some agreed criterion of 'fairness'. Of course it is possible that the weightier charge can also be substantiated, but more than fragmentary evidence is required for that purpose. It is also necessary to ask whether local authorities under Catholic control discriminated against Protestants. These points have to be made at the outset because the charge of discrimination directed against Unionist policy has been repeated so often and with such total assurance that its validity now appears to be widely accepted without question, as though it had been so fully substantiated as to have made any further presentation of the evidence no longer necessary. Indeed, if one may judge from the remarks sometimes made about conditions in Ulster even in the mid-1980s, it is apparently believed that discrimination in housing *still* takes place. If this were indeed the case, the responsibility would rest, not with the Unionists who have long since been unseated, but with the Secretaries of State who have been members of successive Westminster governments, both Conservative and Labour.

The purpose of the present chapter is to review the changing features of the housing situation, to analyse the problems that have been encountered and to assess the significance of the new measures carried out in the last years of Unionist rule and thereafter. At the outset there are two different aspects of the housing situation that need to be distinguished, although they are also intertwined in various ways. They are (i) a shortage of 'decent housing' affecting the welfare of working-class families, both Protestant and Catholic; (ii) discrimination in the allocation of an inadequate supply in favour of the Protestants and to the disadvantage of the Catholics.

THE HOUSING SHORTAGE

Let us start with the first of these points. It was indeed the case that the housing position was poor between the wars when Northern Ireland did not make the same advances as those made in England and Wales. This relative decline implied the loss of a previously favourable position. A very large increase in the stock of working-class houses had been carried out by private industry in the last quarter of the nineteenth century and these houses, if small, were better provided with amenities than many of those across the Irish Sea. Unlike some English cities, Belfast had few houses in 1916 that lacked running water and flush toilets. In 1885 the Royal Commission on housing conditions had placed Belfast and Londonderry among the best cities in the country for working-class housing.[1] But a favourable relative position can be maintained only if the housing stock continues to be expanded and improved as old houses deteriorate, standards rise and the number of families to be accommodated increases.

Northern Ireland did not share fully in the housing boom of the 1930s. Over the whole inter-war period, only 50,000 houses were built, or 41 per thousand of population as compared with 100 per thousand in England and Wales. Part of the explanation lay quite simply in the fact that this was the poorest region in Great Britain with productivity below the average and high unemployment. Moreover, as explained in chapter 9, these disadvantages were not offset by a net fiscal transfer in favour of Northern Ireland on the same scale, relative to needs, as those received by the poorer areas in Great Britain. In England and Wales, about a quarter of the new houses built between 1918 and 1938 were put up by local authorities and let at subsidized rents; in Ulster it was less than a fifth. This fifth included farm labourers' cottages for which generous assistance was indeed made available by Stormont but was not fully taken up by the local authorities, especially in the west of the Province. A new Housing Act passed in 1931 achieved little. As Calvert, an expert on housing policy, was to explain: 'while making statutory provision regarding slum clearance, [it] did not provide any grant from government to local authorities. The money wasn't available and the Act was a dead letter.'[2] Money was, however, provided as subsidies for small houses built for owner-occupation, and it may be asked whether the funds could not have been put to better use in subsidizing local authority houses. There may have been some slight bias here in favour of owner-occupation, but it was also the case that public money used in this way as a supplement to private money could be expected to have a larger effect on the total supply of dwellings and on employment in the building industry than would public funds used to cover the full cost of house building. The supply of privately owned houses to rent was already being affected by rent restriction, introduced in 1915.[3] The destruction of the private rented sector, which was to be such a powerful factor in urban decay, not only in Ulster but throughout so much of the world, was already under way.

In spite of all these difficulties, made worse by faulty policies that were not peculiar to Ulster, the housing stock rose by about a seventh between the wars. Moreover, the comparison of building in England and Wales quoted above is too unfavourable, for account needs to be taken of the fact that Ulster's population remained almost stationary between the wars whereas, in England and Wales, there was a rise of 17 per cent. The marriage rate was also lower in Ulster, and there was less internal migration. About a sixth of the Ulster population moved to new homes during the inter-war period. The number of persons per room was higher than in England and Wales, partly because of the higher proportion of large families, especially large Catholic families. There had, however, been some improvement even by this criterion and the position was rather better than in Scotland.[4]

The first housing survey was held in 1943 and the report published in the following year suggested that 200,000 houses were needed to meet deficiencies which had been much aggravated by wartime bombing and by the diversion of resources to the war effort. Even this figure made no provision for future increases in the population and there was also a large backlog of repairs. The official response was the Housing Act of 1945 which provided, for the first time, for a large expansion of subsidized local authority housing. Unfortunately this extension of the welfare state, well intentioned though it was, opened the door to discrimination in the allocation of houses. Thereafter the danger of discrimination was real although partly offset by another measure taken at the same time: the establishment of the first region-wide public authority housing organization in the United Kingdom. This was the Northern Ireland Housing Trust which was to play an important role over the next quarter century. It was run by a board appointed by the provincial government and, as far as I am aware, no suggestion was ever made that it operated in a sectarian manner. It was there to make good deficiencies in the supply of houses wherever these might occur, sometimes with effects that could be harmful to industrial development. Admittedly the houses it built were of a slightly higher standard than those provided in general by the local authorities and were, to this extent, less suitable for lower income Catholics.

The building record between the end of the war and the end of the 1960s, when social discontent finally exploded, may be briefly summarized. By the beginning of 1965, almost 122,000 houses had been built, or about 6000 a year. Of these, 77,500 were built by the public authorities with the Housing Trust contributing nearly two-fifths. There were still, however, very large deficiencies and the case for further accelerating the pace of building seemed strong. Not only was there a crude statistical shortage of houses relatively to households, but part of the housing stock was defective with one in seven deemed unfit and incapable of repair and a further one-fifth also unfit though capable of being repaired. In the first development plan[5] we therefore recommended a target of 64,000 for the next five years and this was in fact achieved. By 1968 the annual rate of building had reached 12,000 and it would have been hard to do more in view of administrative problems and a shortage of some building craftsmen. (The building unions had been less cooperative than the engineering unions and more opposed to dilution.) Indeed the Housing Trust and the local authorities deserved much credit for achieving as much as they did. When the plan period had come to an end at the start of 1970, 178,000 houses had been built since 1945, of which two-thirds had been put up by the public authorities.[6] By that date, roughly 40 per cent of the housing stock was post-war. The figure of 200,000 suggested in the housing survey of 1944 had almost been met. It is fair to say that house-building on this scale deserved more attention than it received at the time. Indeed, it received little or no attention from the civil rights protesters, or from some of the commentators in the British media who seemed content to follow their example.

In the second development plan, we suggested that 75,000 houses might be built over the five years 1970–5, and the number actually achieved was 67,000. Over the following nine years, 1976–85, another 87,000 were built, and it then appeared that, although there were still some shortages of particular types of housing or shortages in some particular areas, there was no longer any general housing shortage throughout the Province.[7] An important milestone in social improvement had then been passed although there was still a vast amount to be done, as we shall see later, in order to improve housing standards. There was a further consequence. With the supply of housing roughly equal to the demand for it, the scope for discrimination in the allocation of public authority housing had been greatly reduced. In the circumstances of the time this was not, in practice, such an important change for, as is explained below, there was no reason to suppose that the only remaining public housing authority – the Northern Ireland Housing Executive – would have wanted to discriminate anyway. The fact remains that scarcity is one of the conditions for discrimination to take place.

SUBSIDIZED RENTS, WAITING LISTS AND DISCRIMINATION

If the word 'scarcity' is not to be used in a loose confusing way, it must now be defined as a prelude to turning to the allegations of discrimination under the Unionist regime. Scarcity cannot be defined without reference to price. When it is said that there was a scarcity of housing at some particular time, this can only mean that demand was in excess of supply at the given level of rents. In a free market, the excess demand would have been eliminated by a rise in rents, and there would have been no scope for allocating houses in a discriminatory manner. We have noted that 'the market is colour-blind'. It is also indifferent to political allegiance or religious belief. But expenditure on the free market will naturally reflect inequality in the distribution of income, and the aim in subsidizing the rents of public authority housing has, of course, been to reduce inequality in the distribution of real personal disposable income. There has also been a secondary objective – that of achieving greater equality in housing conditions. This second objective has been challenged by the school of thought which holds that the right course is to use taxation and cash benefits in order to redistribute cash incomes which people should then be free to spend as they choose. It may be objected, however, that people could not always be relied upon to spend their incomes in the 'right way' – 'right', that is to say, in the judgement of the legislator or social reformer. In short, an element of paternalism is said – or, more often, is implicitly assumed – to be required.

There is indeed an element of paternalism about subsidies for particular kinds of expenditure. Even so, the acceptance of some element of paternalism need not necessarily lead to subsidized rents, for it would be possible to give people housing allowances on a means-tested basis that would allow them to pay higher unsubsidized rents. Indeed it has often been maintained that it would be better to subsidize people in need rather than bricks and mortar. We are touching here upon a large and controversial topic which raises value judgements as well as a variety of administrative issues and lies well beyond the scope of this book. Although these are matters we cannot pursue further so much had to be said in order to bring out an important point: it was the extension of the welfare state in the form of subsidized rents that set the scene for discrimination in Northern Ireland as elsewhere in Britain – a melancholy example of how a policy with a humane objective can have undesirable side effects, unless great care is exercised in carrying it into effect.

When housing is scarce at the subsidized ruling price, those who allocate the supply may clearly be in a powerful position, and can reward their friends, political supporters or co-religionists if they choose to do so, unless some means has been devised of monitoring and controlling their behaviour. There were no such means in Ulster until the very end of the period of Unionist rule at Stormont and, at the local level, sectarian discrimination could therefore take place. That it did in fact take place is not in doubt, but it does not seem to have been as generally resented even by minority groups as might have been expected. To quote from the Cameron Report:

In the matter of local authority housing there has frequently been what is called a 'gentleman's agreement' among members of certain local authorities that houses in Catholic wards would be allocated to Catholics by Catholic Councillors, and conversely in Protestant wards. Such practices at one time were accepted by almost all shades of opinion as representing a compromise way of life, but it is clear from the evidence we have heard that they are now increasingly felt to be open to objection as operating unjustly and tending to perpetuate rather than to heal and eliminate sectarian divisions.[8]

The Cameron Commission directed particular attention to four areas that had been the scene – at that time – of the main disturbances: Londonderry, Armagh, Newry and Dungannon, and found ample evidence that discrimination had been practised. There were some particularly striking cases. The one that was to achieve so much attention was the Caledon affair of January 1968, which became the *cause célèbre* of the Civil Rights Movement. A house in that area had been occupied by a family of Catholic squatters who came from another area, and had been denied accommodation by the local council's housing management. The latter had, however, allocated a house to a single Protestant girl, a local resident with local connections. When the Catholic parents and their children were evicted, it appeared to be a bad instance of discrimination. It seemed abundantly clear that a Catholic family had been driven out while the much less pressing needs of a Protestant spinster had been met. Austin Currie, a nationalist MP, then organized a squat and subsequently a civil rights march.[9]

The Unionist Government refused to take up these complaints as it should have done by arranging immediately for a close and impartial investigation to be carried out. Both on grounds of social responsibility and enlightened self-interest it was clearly essential to avoid a situation where the complainants would feel that they had no proper court of appeal and must simply take to the streets. Unfortunately Currie's protests were dismissed by the Minister concerned. Even as late as August 1969 – after the Cameron Commission of Inquiry had been at work for some time and on the very eve of the events that were to lead to the deployment of the British army on the streets of Ulster – Faulkner himself, then Minister of Development, was to dismiss a civil rights delegation with the assurance that he had every confidence in Dungannon County Council. Whether or not that confidence was really justified, this was not the way to deal with the situation.

How typical was this case taken up by Currie? That is a proper question although it is one to which a group of indignant demonstrators could not be expected to give prolonged and detailed attention. Yet Currie, himself, may have provided a kind of answer when he observed: 'If I waited a thousand years, I'd never get a better case than this one.'[10]

That there were many other cases of discrimination cannot be doubted. What is necessary, however, is to move beyond the individual cases in order to obtain a reasonably reliable general impression. The Cameron Commission came to the following conclusion with regard even to the four particularly difficult areas with which it was concerned:

Thus the total numbers (of houses) allocated were in rough correspondence to the proportion of Protestants and Catholics in the community . . . The principal criterion however in such cases was not actual need but maintenance of the current political preponderance in that local government area. (para. 140)

These, it should be added, were areas where the preservation of British rule had been challenged from time to time and the Unionists were inclined to take a hard line. John Whyte has concluded that: 'The allegations that I have come across concern without exception areas west of the Bann.'[11] To this may be added the judgement of a former chairman of the Northern Ireland Housing Executive, Charles Brett, who had been a leading member of the Northern Ireland Labour Party: 'It is my view that the majority of councils did not consciously or deliberately engage in any kind of discrimination; but a minority did so, and thereby discredited the whole.'[12]

If this conclusion is valid, its effect is to destroy a familiar line of reasoning that may be presented in syllogistic form as follows:

> All councils discriminated.
> There were more Protestant than Catholic councils.
> Therefore Catholics suffered more from discrimination.

If, however, all councils did *not* discriminate the argument collapses and no verdict can be reached in this particular way.

An empirical assessment of the effects of discrimination under the Unionist regime was carried out by an American political scientist, Richard Rose.[13] He found no evidence of systematic discrimination, although there were more Protestant councils than Catholic councils.

The greatest bias appears to favour Catholics in that small part of the population living in local authorities controlled by Catholic Councillors. . . . . Systematic discrimination cannot be found when patterns are examined in each of the six counties and two boroughs, all controlled by Unionists. In five of the eight instances, a larger proportion of Catholics than Protestants were living as subsidized tenants. . . . the survey found that in four of the eight areas studied – Belfast, Derry City, Armagh and Tyrone – a majority of respondents in public housing were in fact Catholics.

One might, of course, expect that more Catholics would have wanted to live in public authority houses because their incomes were on average lower. It is therefore desirable to refine the analysis by introducing income groups. Even when this is done, it turns out that, in all but one income group, *the proportion of Catholics in subsidized housing was higher than the proportion of Protestants*. Rose also notes, however, that a higher proportion of the Catholics who moved into new houses had been slum dwellers, a fact that must be taken into account in assessing *net* increases in the supply of accommodation made available to Catholics and Protestants respectively.

Rose went on to observe: 'But from a civil rights point of view, each individual case of discrimination is a matter of protest.' Indeed it is. To the best of my knowledge the Civil Rights Movement never took up the case of Protestant families against Catholic councils. If it had done so it would have vindicated its claim to be concerned only with civil rights, not with sectarian politics. The whole atmosphere would then have been different.

In 1970 the Stormont Government appointed a Commissioner of Complaints, and it might have been expected that a large number of complaints about discrimination in housing would have been brought before him. Housing did indeed feature frequently but the complaints referred to a miscellaneous variety of administrative issues. There was only one case in which discrimination was alleged. If discrimination had been as blatant and as widespread as persistent republican propaganda has led so many people in Britain and the Irish Republic to believe, it is inconceivable that only a single case would have been brought before him. The Commissioner concludes: 'It is to be regretted that there should be grounds for even one such finding, but it is clear that the results of two years' work investigating complaints about housing allocations provide very little evidence of discrimination by housing authorities.'[14]

When we were preparing the development plans in the mid and late 1960s, we had no information to hand about the extent of discrimination. With the benefit of hindsight, I now feel that we should have pressed the Government to have a survey organized by an independent and experienced team of investigators. This would have been particularly appropriate at the time of the second plan (1970–5). Although we failed to do so, we became much concerned about the complaints of discrimination. We felt strongly that public money provided in order to carry out recommendations for which we were responsible must be used fairly by the local authorities. It is necessary to add at once that we had no reason to suppose that there was a systematic bias in its use. On that issue we had to remain open-minded in the absence of evidence, but there had undoubtedly been bad individual cases. Moreover, it was necessary that justice should not only be done, but should be seen to be done. Some reform in the administrative machinery seemed the appropriate response. A points system for applicants was one answer. The councils could retain their responsibility for housing but would be required to allocate it with regard to an appropriate allocation of points. This solution had strong supporters at the time but something more might be required, and a more ambitious reform did indeed suggest itself. There was one body that had never been accused of an inclination to discriminate. This was the Northern Ireland Housing Trust, whose work extended to the Province as a whole. So why not transfer full responsibility to that body? Essentially, this was what we recommended[15] and, in the event, what happened was broadly along this line, although the central housing authority was reorganized and given a different name under newly introduced management: the Northern Ireland Housing Executive. The Northern Ireland Committee of the Irish Congress of Trade Unions was taking the same line, although we were not, I think, aware of this at the time.

This proposal was open to criticism on the ground that a province-wide housing executive would be too large and cumbersome.[16] In fact, the Housing Executive as initially established was, indeed, too tightly centralized and had to be reorganized some time later, but this was an initial error and one that might have been avoided. After all, Northern Ireland is only the size of a large English county. The essential point was to shift the responsibility from the elected local authorities to a new body under the elected provincial government, and this new body could have been given a decentralized administrative structure from the outset. Even if there had been some genuinely unavoidable administrative loss from eliminating the local councils, the political gain might have offset any such loss.

CONTINUING PROGRESS WITH HOUSING

We did not, I think, expect that houses would be built at a faster rate than could be achieved by the local authorities and the old Housing Trust together. That was not the point of the proposal. There were, it is true, some critics of previous housing achievements and even of the new official target; but for them the sky was, apparently, the limit. In the event, the rate of building reached its peak in 1971, and thereafter, under the Housing Executive, was on average to be well *below* the old record.[17] The explanation lay partly in the transitional difficulties of setting up the new body, and also in the disruption caused by rioting and by terrorism. In more recent years, the Housing Executive has been fortunate in being given relative protection from the full scale of the economy drive in Great Britain. The need to improve the quality of the housing stock was the principal reason. Although so many houses had been built, the proportion deemed to be unfit in 1974 was 20 per cent as compared with only 7 per cent in England and Wales. Even in 1979, the year of the Treasury's *Needs Assessment Survey* the proportion was still 14 per cent.[18] The case for relatively higher *per capita* expenditure was accepted and a sharp increase of almost a quarter in the volume of real expenditure did, in fact, take place between 1981–2 and 1984–5.[19] (It is only fair to add that, of this rise in expenditure, about three-fifths was matched by higher rents in real terms and by house sales.)

The Northern Ireland Housing Executive was confronted from the outset with two particularly difficult problems: first the increase in civil strife, particularly marked in the early 1970s, and the interference of the paramilitary organizations; secondly, the resentment that had been aroused by a previous policy of urban renewal carried out in the draconian style of the 1960s.

The first of these problems was particularly difficult. At a time of bitter social strife, contractors had to deploy teams of workers that consisted of both Protestants and Catholics because, by tradition, some trades were practised by one sect and some by the other. One part of the team would therefore be at risk in Catholic areas, the other in Protestant areas. This was a situation the terrorists could exploit by extracting protection money. Moreover, in 1975, a civil service investigation found inadequate financial accountability within the Housing Executive's own organization and this was confirmed by a further investigation which revealed that funds were being obtained by the paramilitaries. A reorganization had then to be carried out in 1979/80. This was not all. In the areas largely under their control, the terrorists began to assert their authority still further by allocating houses, and it could be exceedingly dangerous to go against them. There was a tragic irony about this development. The proximate cause of the civil unrest had been indignation at alleged unfairness in housing allocations, but the outcome in these areas was allocation by the gunmen. The cause of justice had scarcely been advanced.

The second problem was the bitterness caused by the way in which urban renewal had been carried out.[20] There is no reason to suppose that the urban planners were worse in this respect in Northern Ireland than in, say, Birmingham or Glasgow, but the effect was deplorable and much resented. Thus in areas such as the Shankill the old sense of a village community was brutally obliterated and families displaced from their old houses were forced into modern apartments which they often disliked intensely. The problem was further complicated by the determination of both Protestant and Catholic communities to protect their territorial boundaries. It may be worth noting in passing that the Divis block of flats which has received some publicity was not designed by a Unionist council as a modern ghetto within which Catholics could be immurred. It was intended to meet the demand of the local parish priest, supported by (Lord) Fitt, who was anxious to ensure that his flock would not be scattered. It is a requirement that has still to be kept in mind in replacing hideous structures of this kind, but it can now be met by new designs for high density, low-rise accommodation.

In Ulster, as elsewhere, there was a reaction against the demolition of the older houses, often much loved whether or not they lacked 'one or more basic amenity', and their replacement by apartments in concrete blocks or towers. The reaction resulted, first, in a new concern with renovation and a good deal of ingenuity was displayed in improving existing dwellings. But the scope for doing so was limited, the cost considerable and the reconstructed environment not always pleasing. The second stage, again as elsewhere, has been the construction of brick-built terraced houses which are usually well designed and well sited. It is not too much to claim that Northern Ireland has now acquired some of the most attractive working-class housing in Britain. In Belfast the rehabilitation of the inner city as a residential area has thus progressed, although there is still a vast amount to be done.[21]

The Housing Executive owns roughly a third of the housing stock and the danger of an overbearing abuse of power is obvious. Fortunately the lessons of the preceding period have not been forgotten and the Executive claims that it takes pains to consult the views of local people rather than impose change upon them from the heights of a paternalistic bureaucracy. There has also been an active encouragement of new building by private housing associations, with the support of the building societies. A large number of publicly owned houses have been sold to the tenants. It is perhaps conceivable that, by trying in these ways to take the community with them, the Executive has been able to impose some check on the interference of the paramilitary organizations in housing matters, but this is no more than speculation. The Executive has at all events maintained its own preference for houses built around courtyards,[22] which are said to have social advantages – though houses built in straight streets are more convenient for the high-speed getaway cars of the terrorists!

These are encouraging developments in an environment where encouragement is needed. On the negative side is the almost complete segregation of the Catholic from the Protestant working class in the larger towns. I can recall how in early 1969 one of the senior civil servants expressed his relief and satisfaction because sectarian strife had so far been absent from those areas where the two groups were mixed. Alas, this immunity was not to last, and the mixed communities, apart from middle class suburbs, were not to survive. Catholics and Protestants now live apart to a far greater extent than was the case before the agitation for social reform began.[23] People believe they are safer thus, and segregation suits the convenience of the terrorists.

Complaints about discrimination in their old form have ceased, but the Executive has to observe closely the boundaries between the areas occupied by the two groups respectively and must take care not to do anything that could be described as an invasion of territory. It has not succeeded completely in avoiding offence on this score and there have also been complaints about differences in the quality of housing, the state of repair and so on. It remains true, however, that housing is no longer the bitter sectarian issue it used to be, partly because the shortage of houses, given the level of rents, is no longer acute.

14

Education – Development within
a Segregated System

Schooling in Ireland, both North and South, is segregated. Catholic children go to Catholic schools, Protestant children to Protestant schools. Admittedly there are some exceptions. Technical – now further – education has never been segregated in this way, perhaps partly because the danger of doctrinal deviation has been thought to be less serious in this case. Moreover, a number of factory schools established in an earlier age by the owners for the benefit of their employees were always inter-denominational. In Ulster, as we shall see, there have also been some new departures from segregation in recent years, although these are still only marginal. A much more important qualification relates to the meaning of the term 'Protestant schools'. The emphasis given to explicit religious instruction in these schools may in some cases be slight and confined to so small a part of the school week that the schools might best be described as non-Catholic. For others the best description may be 'Church-related' – not Church-run. It can be assumed, of course, that there are differences in emphasis with religion more stressed in some non-Catholic schools than in others. At one extreme, the religious emphasis is presumably strong in those Protestant schools, still very few in number and privately financed, that have been founded by Paisley's Free Presbyterian Church. These schools may be compared to the more strongly ideological schools run – but not privately financed – by some London boroughs. If these extremes are set aside in both cases, the non-Catholic schools in Ulster may be regarded as similar to English schools in their treatment of religion, although generalization may obscure much diversity in both cases. The Catholic schools are held to be fundamentally different, with the whole of their work suffused with Catholic teaching. 'To the Catholic parent', says Monseignor Ryan, 'the non-denominational school is almost as great an absurdity as the non-denominational family.'[1] To quote from *The Catholic School*, published in Rome in 1977: 'In the daily life of the school the pupils should learn that they are called to be living witnesses to God's love for men by the way they act and that they are part of that salvation history which has Christ, the Saviour of the world, as its goal.'[2] What this stress on Catholic teaching means in practice for the instruction on many subjects given during the school week may not be altogether clear to the outside observer, but it can be appreciated that the presence of priests and members of religious orders and the sacred pictures, statues and symbols are believed to have effects that go beyond explicit instruction.

The consequence of segregation in schooling is that young people in Ulster may rarely meet those on the other side of the sectarian divide until they go on to higher education or to work. This lack of contact is particularly likely to occur when Protestants and Catholics live in different areas, as they have often done and, since the troubles began, now do so to a still greater extent. They can then grow up almost as foreigners. But that is not all. For the approach to education and the emphasis laid upon particular issues may be different in important respects notwithstanding a common curriculum. The children who have been to non-Catholic schools will have received a substantially secular education, tinged in varying degree with Protestant teaching. They will also have acquired from their schools an interest in Britain and in Britain's historical role in world affairs similar to that acquired by English children, although the confident British nationalism of an earlier age has been somewhat dimmed. The children from Catholic schools not only will have received rather more religious education, but their sympathy for Irish nationalism will have been greatly fortified, and they may tend to regard Britain as a foreign country that differs from other foreign countries only in being more malign.[3] It is therefore reasonable to infer that segregated schooling has contributed greatly over the years to the deep division within the community and still helps to perpetuate that division. Indeed, it is hard to see how any other inference could be drawn. Although attempts have been made to remedy the situation, and are still being made, the success achieved so far has been slight. This outcome is scarcely surprising when deep religious issues as well as nationalistic loyalties have been involved. In order to appreciate these difficulties, it is necessary to look back and observe how the current position has been reached.

INTEGRATION AND SEGREGATION

When the Unionist Government took over in 1920, it became responsible for an educational service that was both segregated and backward. As with housing, the inherited social capital was poor, notwithstanding the fact that the national education system was older in Ireland than in England. There was a requirement for new or improved buildings and other facilities, including books and equipment. The number of trained teachers was seriously inadequate. Even by contemporary English standards, the educational system was in need of improvement but in this, as in other fields, the effect of the financial constraint was severe. These difficulties were compounded by segregation. It was not only that Protestant and Catholic children went to different schools, but the main Protestant denominations ran their own separate schools where it was at all possible to do so. The penalty was a loss of economies of scale. Denominational schools were not, of course, peculiar to Ireland and similar difficulties were encountered in other parts of the United Kingdom. Ireland, however, was particularly affected, as is illustrated by the fact that Ireland as a whole had two and a half times as many schools as Scotland with its somewhat larger population. Expenditure per pupil was high for the service provided. At the grammar school level, there were some old foundations but there was a wide diversity in their standards of service.[4] It is with this poor initial position in mind that the subsequent performance of devolved government in the north of the island must be assessed. Moreover, it is within a context of financial stringency that complaints about Unionist sectarian discrimination have to be judged.

In order to devise a satisfactory new policy, cooperation with all the religious denominations was highly desirable but was not forthcoming from the Catholic Church in the early 1920s. The hierarchy chose to reject an invitation to appoint representatives to serve on a committee of inquiry or even to submit evidence. (This was, of course, an example of the nationalist policy designed to deny recognition to the Six Counties and even to make them ungovernable which has been described in chapter 6.) The new Northern Ireland Ministry of Education pressed ahead, however, and a bold measure that could have ended segregated schooling was introduced in the Northern Ireland Parliament in 1923 – a parliament that was still being boycotted by the Ulster Catholics. The failure of this legislation deserves attention for difficulties of a similar kind, though perhaps less acute, would confront any reforming administration today.

Under the legislation of 1923, the counties and county boroughs were made responsible for providing public elementary schools which could be newly established or schools transferred from the existing managers – in practice, the Churches. Children from all denominations would attend these schools and have the same teaching from the same teachers on all subjects, apart from religious instruction. Provision was, however, to be made for religious instruction along denominational lines outside school hours and it was also anticipated that religion and ethics would receive attention in a non-denominational way within school hours. 'In framing the bill', said the Minister, Lord Londonderry, 'I was particularly anxious to give full opportunity to the churches for denominational instruction . . . I therefore decided to grant the use of school buildings to the representatives of all the denominations, outside school hours, during which children are required to attend compulsorily.' But this would not be all: 'I never had any doubt in my mind that each regional committee would prescribe in the curriculum a certain length of time every day, or its equivalent in the week, during which teachers would impart to the children the lessons of Christian teaching and the moral principles to which we all subscribe.'[5] The education committee could not insist upon teachers belonging to any religious denomination and could not require them to give religious instruction.

These were the main features of the central proposal but there would be no compulsion to accept it. It would be possible simply to opt for the continuation of existing arrangements with the schools remaining under strictly denominational control, but it would then be necessary to meet all capital expenditure[6] and half of the running costs from private sources, *apart from the heavy item of teachers' salaries which were in all cases to be met by the state.* There was also a third possibility which offered a compromise. In this third case – which came to be known as 'four and two' – the management committee would consist of four persons appointed by the Church concerned and two by the local education authority. Schools would then be eligible for assistance with repairs and general upkeep. Denominational education could therefore be retained at a financial cost by choosing the second or the third option. The cost of non-denominational education would, however, be fully met from the public authorities.

To a detached observer, Londonderry's proposal for non-denominational schools may seem reasonable and enlightened. But the legislation of 1923 was to encounter intense opposition from all the religious denominations – Protestant as well as Catholic – and this proved decisive, as it had been to the fate of Stanley's somewhat similar proposal almost a century before (see chapter 3 above). If 'joint secular and separate religious instruction' had been accepted in the 1830s, Irish history might well have been different but, as we have seen, it was rejected. This failure in the past might have been a warning to any reformers in the 1920s, but it could be claimed that, after so many social and political changes, it was right to make another attempt. But this was not all. It was not only a question of needed reform. It was also a matter of statutory obligation that had to be observed, whether or not Craig and his colleagues were genuinely committed to reform along non-sectarian lines. For it was laid down in the Government of Ireland Act that the Parliament of Northern Ireland should not 'establish or endow any religion' or act in such a way as to 'affect prejudicially the right of any child to attend a school receiving public money without attending the religious instruction of that school'.[7]

The opposition of all the Churches to the new legislation was, however, intense.[8] This was secular education. The Ministry was proposing to establish 'godless schools'. On these points, all denominations were agreed and the Minister may have made a mistake in suggesting that religious instruction should be outside, not inside, normal school hours. Even so, it would have been more accurate, perhaps, to say that the schools proposed would have been too ecumenical rather than too secular. Apart from the question of religious instruction, all denominations viewed with extreme distaste the proposal that they should abandon control over their schools. In particular, all were concerned about the danger that their children might be taught by persons from the other side of the religious divide. The Catholic hierarchy, for their part, firmly rejected the invitation to allow any of their schools to be transferred to the public authorities and even rejected the 'four and two' compromise described above, although one might have supposed that this formula would have given them all the protection they needed, even with regard to the appointment of teachers. They were, however, apprehensive about the future behaviour of councils under Unionist control – as were the leaders of the Protestant Churches about councils that might come under nationalist control. If the schools had been surrendered, their property would have gone and they would be in a very weak position if, in the event, the new regime was found to be intolerable.

A substantial number of Protestant schools accepted this compromise formula, 'four and two', but a powerful campaign was successfully mounted by the Protestant Churches and the Orange Order for the revision of the proposal for public authority schools in a way that would both relieve the Protestant Churches of financial responsibility and yet meet their demand for basic Biblical teaching and for a strong say in management. This objective was achieved by means of amending legislation in 1925 and 1930. On the first of the occasions Craig himself, as Prime Minister, pushed the changes through parliament in the absence of the Minister of Education, Lord Londonderry. Thus he submitted to clerical demands, although his position in the Northern Ireland parliament was so strong at that time that he could have resisted. If he had chosen to do so he could have claimed that the Government of Ireland Act in effect precluded religious instruction as part of the compulsory curriculum in state financed schools.

In the event, as a result of the changes finally embodied in the Act of 1930, basic Bible instruction became an integral part of the curriculum and all teachers, even in schools fully financed from public funds, could be obliged to provide such instruction. Was such teaching 'sectarian'? That was a moot point. Craig insisted that it need not be. He told the authorities of the Catholic Church that they could prepare a teaching programme that would cover 'the great and simple structure of our common Christianity.'[8] But, from a Catholic viewpoint, Bible teaching could be misleading and dangerous without the authoritative interpretation of the Catholic Church. Given the basic Catholic position, Bible teaching was Protestant. Craig's assurance that Catholic children need be taught only by Catholic teachers did not convince. This was so although, in the management committees of the schools transferred to the public authorities (and of new schools provided by them to replace former Church schools) half the membership would consist of representatives of former managers which would mean, in effect, Church representatives. One-quarter would be parents and one-quarter representatives of the local education committee. The clergy, with the support of lay members of their Churches and parents of pupils, would therefore continue to dominate the management of schools under public control and thus in practice to influence very strongly the appointment of teachers to those schools. But the clergy may have feared the influence of *any* representation of Unionist-dominated local authorities and may even have had reservations about accepting a situation where they would depend crucially upon the support of Catholic lay members.

When these changes had been completed in 1930 Craig claimed[9] that the schools had been made 'safe for Protestant children' – an unfortunate utterance politically, and one that was not strictly accurate. Under the original legislation of 1923, the Protestant children would have been safe if their Churches had opted for retaining the purely voluntary status of their schools, as the Catholic Church had done, or had even opted for the 'four and two' compromise.

The 1930 legislation did, however, improve the position of the voluntary – predominantly Catholic – schools by providing them with grants for 50 per cent of building costs and loans for the remainder. The cost of 'independence' was therefore substantially reduced, but by no means abolished. Teachers' pay – by far the largest item in costs – was already being provided. Those teachers who were members of religious orders were entitled to pay on the same scale as ordinary lay teachers, but their pay was covenanted to the school authorities and was thus made available for general purposes.

As has been observed, there were constitutional reasons for the choice of policy in 1923 and the changes subsequently made were of doubtful legality under the 1920 Government of Ireland Act. The Home Office in London made it clear that it would refer the matter to the Judicial Committee of the Privy Council if requested to do so by a sufficient body of opinion in Ulster.[10] If the Catholics had protested, Whitehall would have been obliged to intervene, but they did not do so. The reason would seem to be clear. The financing of the *transferred* schools might have been declared unconstitutional because their administration was, substantially, under clerical control, but the financial assistance given to the *Catholic* schools could also have been deemed to be improper, for these schools were *entirely* under clerical control without any representation of the public authorities even in a minority position with a watching brief. The Privy Council might even have insisted that a model along the lines of the 1923 Act was required by the Government of Ireland Act of 1920. That prospect would have been even more horrifying to Catholics than to Protestants.

After the war, the educational system was revised again and a new Act was passed in 1947[11], which was really a modified version of the 1944 Butler Act for England and Wales. Again there was to be 'undenominational religious instructions based upon the Holy Scriptures.'12 This satisfied the Protestants but not the Catholics, who did not change their attitude. The financial assistance they received for capital expenditure was, however, raised to 65 per cent. The Protestant position had been weakened in principle when the Attorney General (MacDermott) ruled in 1945 that the legislation of 1930 by which teachers could be required to give religious instruction in county schools (i.e. transferred schools and those newly established by the education authorities) was *ultra vires*. This offending provision – which had not been of much practical importance – was removed in 1947. But the Protestant position had also been strengthened by giving the Churches the right of representation on the management committees of new county schools. The legislation was thus a balancing act, and a fair one.

The situation was changed again in 1968 when schools in the 'four and two' category were given a substantial advantage over independent or 'voluntary' schools. The Catholic hierarchy now decided that this intermediate category was safe enough to be acceptable. They were thus able to obtain 80 per cent grants towards building costs, later raised to 85 per cent, with the added and very substantial benefit of complete relief from maintenance costs and the cost of equipment. Thereafter the four and two schools were called 'maintained schools'. One suspects that a decisive factor in determining the hierarchy's decision was the right, accorded by the 1968 legislation, to withdraw from the scheme at any time with full use of their property on repayment of the grant. Over the next ten years nearly all Catholic schools were moved into this category. It is particularly interesting that this change in the control of Catholic schools, involving for the first time minority public authority representation in management, had been planned before the disturbances began in 1968 but was then implemented during an unprecedented period of prolonged violence. It was an important change from which the Catholic minority benefited, but it received no attention from the Civil Rights Movement.

The position of the Catholics was therefore further improved with no restriction imposed on their freedom to impart religious instruction and appoint teachers. The social cost was the preservation of the division between Catholic children and non-Catholic children. *Within* the non-Catholic sector, the fragmentation of the earlier period was, however, to be virtually ended. That is to say, this sector was no longer divided between schools run by the Church of Ireland, the Presbyterian Church and the Methodists. To this extent, segregation between Protestant denominations had gone, no doubt with a large improvement in efficiency. But the main division between Catholic and non-Catholic schools persists to this day.

FINANCIAL SUPPORT FOR CATHOLIC SCHOOLS

In the light of these facts about educational policy in Ulster, would it be reasonable to assert that the minority was unfairly treated? Unfair treatment was certainly anticipated by the Catholic hierarchy before devolved government was established in the Province. Indeed, the fear of sectarian oppression in this field was one of the reasons for the strong reaction against partition on the part of some of the Catholic bishops. If autonomy for the Twenty-Six Counties could be obtained only at the cost of Unionist domination in the Six Counties, might it not be better to remain within the United Kingdom, subject to Westminster? The answer given to that question by the Catholic Bishop of Derry in 1917 was a sorrowful affirmative. But, in the event, Ulster did have Home Rule and the much feared oppression in educational policy did not follow. It may be objected that the Catholics were subjected to discrimination, if not to oppression, in that they did not receive the same financial assistance although, as we have seen, the disadvantage was in expenditure on buildings and, under this heading, was reduced by stages to 15 per cent and, in 1988, was totally removed. It is only fair to add that Catholic children could have attended the county schools and the fear on the part of the hierarchy that they would then be attending schools that lacked the special Catholic character was scarcely justified. As far back as 1930, the Unionist Government had explained that Catholic schools could be transferred without being changed in character. Undenominational religious instruction would have been required but there was nothing to prevent its being supplemented by an indefinite amount of denominational instruction. It is unlikely that there would have been any interference with clerical control over the appointment of teachers. Indeed Craig had promised that there would not be. Even if the hierarchy did not trust his pledge, they could have safeguarded their position by opting for the 'four and two' compromise. It seems a pity that they were not even prepared to experiment with a few schools in order to test the proposals.

This situation, however, was by no means unique to Ulster. It is true that in Scotland Catholic schools are fully supported, but in the USA, Catholic schools receive no assistance at all and are therefore much worse off than they ever were under Unionist rule in Ulster. In England, assistance for denominational schools has been forthcoming but this assistance has been on a somewhat smaller scale. Nor is this all, for the Catholic schools in England have not been fully 'independent', as were the Catholic schools in Ulster prior to the settlement of 1968. To quote from a White Paper of 1967:

Voluntary school authorities have over a long period made representations that the burden of their contribution to the system of public education has proved to be much higher than was contemplated in 1947, and have asked for further assistance from public funds. The Government accepts that the cost of providing education has become increasingly heavy. On the other hand it has also had to take into account that, whereas in England and Wales a measure of public representation on the bodies responsible for the management or government of voluntary schools has long been a pre-requisite for the recognition of such schools, in Northern Ireland most grants under the Act of 1947 have not been subject to that requirement. Since 1947 Ministers of Education have on numerous occasions made it clear that increased assistance from public funds could not be contemplated for schools on which a public authority had not at least minority representation.[12]

That was the crux. The Catholic hierarchy wanted full financial assistance but rejected even minority representation for the public authorities, although it could reasonably be held that, in such conditions, no claim to any financial assistance could really be justified. A similar problem arose with regard to the Mater Infirmorum, Belfast's large Catholic hospital. It was not just a question of Unionist prejudice; it was a question of proper administrative procedure. As soon as the Catholic Church agreed to official representation on school boards – 'four and two' – then, as we have seen, the financial assistance provided from the public authorities, already substantial, was further increased.

It may be of interest to note in passing the position in the Republic where the state provides seven-eighths of building costs and only 80 per cent of current costs in primary schools. In voluntary secondary schools, the major part of teachers' salaries are paid and there are grants to assist with other costs. The assistance thus provided is still well below that provided in Northern Ireland.

An important change took place in 1972, when responsibility for education in Northern Ireland was transferred from local government to regional government and important responsibilities were then transferred to Education and Library Boards consisting of nominated members. On some of the boards there is a majority of Catholic members and these boards are responsible for the appointment of teachers in schools where the pupils are Protestants. In the Catholic schools, however, the teachers are appointed by Church-dominated committees. It is now the Protestants who feel, in some areas, that their children are at risk – wrongly, perhaps, but certainly strongly.

THE SECONDARY LEVEL

Grammar school education has also been divided along sectarian lines and continues to be so, although some small breaches have been made in recent years. There has been, however, this difference that complaints about unfair treatment at the grammar school level have been less common. There were other problems that were formidable enough. Although Ulster had a number of very good grammar schools in 1921, the provision of secondary education was well behind what was available in England and Wales or, of course, in Scotland. The transition from elementary to secondary schooling took place rather too late (at 12–13 rather than 11 years of age), there were few scholarships and teachers were in the main poorly paid. Academic standards, if sometimes high, were marred by excessive dispersion and the facilities available in the schools were, with some exceptions, rather meagre. Although substantial progress was made between the wars, resources were not available on a sufficient scale to make up the 'leeway' between the Ulster schools and those in Great Britain. In Ulster the legislation of 1947 marked a very important advance, for 'step-by-step' now permitted Stormont to move ahead and, as we have observed in chapter 8, more allowance came to be made for deficiencies inherited from the past. Grammar school education now became universally available for qualified pupils, and the route to university education was opened up with far-reaching implications.

The management of existing grammar schools could opt to belong to one of two categories with some difference in financial assistance and some corresponding variation in independence of management and in the obligation to accept successful 11-plus pupils from primary schools. It is of interest to observe that the subsequent division of schools between these two categories did not follow denominational lines, for a number both of Catholic and non-Catholic grammar schools preferred greater autonomy at some loss of support with capital expenditure – a loss subsequently reduced from 35 to 20 per cent of the capital outlay.

In attempting to make an assessment of educational policy in Northern Ireland, a distinction must be drawn, as in the provision of other public services, between an improvement in general standards from which all have benefited and a change in the denominational share-out. Under the first heading, the progress made under the old Unionist regime can only be described as immense. To quote from R. J. Lawrence's assessment published in 1965: 'From the present writer's standpoint it seems that the Government's long-term policy has been resplendently successful.'[13] A similar judgement was made some ten years later by two Protestant authors, one of them the headmaster of a large grammar school, neither of them inclined to be uncritical of Stormont's record in other fields: 'The government in the North had no need to apologise for its education system in 1969. It was comparable with any other in the United Kingdom, and was arguably superior to anything in the Republic.'[14] Admittedly the Catholic spokesmen have been more sparing in their praise of Unionist government – partly, perhaps, on the ground that no good thing can come out of Galilee. But educational policy has not been one of the main targets for criticism in modern times.

Academic standards are high, with Northern Ireland now ahead of England and Wales in both A and O Level achievements and, within England, rivalled only by the South East region. This change in relative positions since the bleak days when devolved Unionist government began, can fairly be described as revolutionary. It is true that in Northern Ireland, selectivity remains. Some may find in this fact an explanation of the high relative performance at A and O Levels; others may not. This is one controversy into which, in this controversial book, I do not propose to enter, but there is an important fact to be recorded which is clearly relevant. The selection test is far less fearsome and less harmfully restrictive because accommodation is available at the grammar school level for over a quarter of the primary school population. In England, the proportion had been only about one-tenth. Unfortunately, the statistics also show that a higher proportion of Ulster children leave school without qualifications, and this suggests a fault that should be remedied.

High marks can be awarded for the high standards achieved and also for the more generous treatment, especially since 1947, of the voluntary schools. The fact remains that education is segregated. The coming of power-sharing in 1973 brought new hope and the power-sharing executive came down in favour of integration in its manifesto. The Minister of Education (MacIvor) made a start. In 1974 he put forward the interesting suggestion that there might be 'shared schools' which would not be 'secular' but rather schools 'in which the two groups of churches would be equally involved.'[15] The General Assembly of the Presbyterian Church passed a resolution in favour of integrated education: 'since education is a preparation for life, and since children have got to live together in mixed communities, they should therefore learn together.'[16] The leaders of the Church of Ireland had also expressed their sympathy. Others were hostile. The Catholics for their part were resolutely opposed. Thus Bishop Philbin claimed that: 'Short of banning religion completely, there is no greater injury that could be done to Catholicism than by interference with the character and identity of our schools.'[17] On the face of it, this may seem a somewhat extravagant assertion – although scarcely one that was unexpected – but it was disappointing that some of the SDLP members should have responded with coolness in the Assembly, although the Minister of Education was, of course, a member of a *power-sharing* executive. When that executive collapsed and Direct Rule was resumed, the British Government dropped shared education like a hot brick.

Some progress was made, however, without government leadership. First of all, some Roman Catholics sent their children to Protestant grammar schools, in face of strong episcopal disapproval. This practice has continued. (For example, almost a tenth of the pupils are now Catholics at the Methodist College – not a theological institution in spite of its name.) Secondly, a group of parents called 'All Children Together' was formed and as a result of their efforts a new school was created in 1981 on the 'shared' basis described above, called Lagan College. Although the Protestant Churches were cautious in their approach to this experiment, chaplains were appointed with their approval. But the Catholic hierarchy has forbidden priests to serve as chaplains. About 45 per cent of the 400 pupils are Protestant, about 40 per cent Catholic, and the remainder 'non-denominational'. Official recognition was accorded in 1986 and financial support followed on the same scale as that provided to 'voluntary' schools. Some other schools along similar lines have been established or planned. Progress has therefore been made, but it has been disappointingly small, especially in view of the public support for integration reflected in the *Belfast Telegraph* polls as long ago as 1967 and 1968. About 64 per cent of all adults and 65 per cent of young people then favoured integration. Among the Catholics the percentage was still higher at 69 per cent.[18] Subsequently a number of polls have been held with support never falling below 60 per cent, although only about 30 per cent have expressed their willingness to send their *own* children to an integrated school. The results of research work carried out by the Harbisons and published in 1980 provided support for the view that the traditional antagonisms would be reduced if children from different denominations were brought together for even a limited period.[19] Admittedly any general move towards integration would encounter serious practical difficulties, especially in Belfast where working-class Protestants and working-class Catholics live in different areas, and school busing on a large scale would therefore be required. To a lesser extent, the same difficulty would be encountered in some other places, in particular in Derry, but should not be a serious obstacle throughout a substantial part of the Province. The real difficulties in those areas as elsewhere are, of course, political and clerical, and these will not be easily eroded. When, however, a group of parents have demonstrated their desire for an integrated school, official support has been forthcoming. For the Government's attitude has changed and sympathy has been expressed in the statement of policy of April 1988.

This new official pronouncement was wide-ranging. It extended to the whole field of school education and higher education and included proposals for syllabus reform. On the financial side, assistance with capital costs has been held at 85 per cent for voluntary schools. With current costs fully covered, this means that Catholic schools are almost fully funded by the state. It is a point that might be noted by American critics of British policy in Northern Ireland for, in the USA, no assistance of any kind would be forthcoming. It is also of some interest that these schools will still be under Catholic control. The non-Catholic schools, by contrast, are under Education and Library Boards with their Education Committees. Both, in the Western Area, are now strongly Catholic, and also have Sinn Fein members – as has the Western Health and Social Services Board. British ministers will have no dealings with Sinn Fein on the ground that it is the publicity agency of the IRA, but the unfortunate non-Catholic schools must deal with Sinn Fein board members. Discrimination can operate both ways in Northern Ireland.

There is also to be an innovation in the form of grant-maintained schools. As in England and Wales, these grant-maintained schools will be corporate bodies, fully financed by direct payments from the central government, but run with a high degree of autonomy by boards of governors on which parents would have a larger representation than on the boards of existing controlled or voluntary schools. These schools would be of two types, integrated and non-integrated, and would not have to be newly created institutions. In the case of an existing school, a request for the new status could be initiated by a majority on the board of an existing school or by a request from at least 20 per cent of parents. This latter proposal should ease the path towards integration in those cases where a desire for integration has been expressed. One of the difficulties in the past has been the problem of raising enough private finance to establish and maintain a new school for a number of years in which its viability will have to be demonstrated before a request for official support can be sustained. If, however, existing schools can acquire the status of grant-maintained these initial costs will not have to be incurred. Moreover, even if the school is completely new, the clear indication of government support for integration will be an encouragement and the financial risk incurred by private persons or institutions will be reduced when it is known that official support will, in due course, be fully forthcoming once viability has been established.

Neither the proposed increase in the power of parents nor the blessing given to integrated education can be expected to commend the new proposals to Catholic clerics. The Protestant response may also be somewhat muted.

Integration would already have been possible at a different but very important level – that of teacher training. As well as the long-term contribution to greater social unity that might thus have been achieved, there was a case for some pooling of resources as the number of teachers in training declined. In 1980, a high-level committee made the more modest recommendation that the two existing Catholic training colleges should combine and share the same *site* as the Protestants, but without amalgamation.[20] Even this degree of proximity met with vehement Catholic opposition and the Secretary of State gave in. The two Catholic training colleges, one for men and one for women, were brought together – in itself a departure from tradition – but the denominational division remains. Continuing opposition from the Catholic Church is only to be expected, for the hierarchy is determined to maintain a tight grip on the training of teachers for their segregated schools. From a more liberal viewpoint, integration at this particular point in the educational structure would seem particularly desirable. Moreover, there was a practical case for immediate integration whereas, for practical reasons, the integration of the schools themselves could proceed only slowly, even if the will were there. From this point of view, a promising opportunity was lost. Denominationalism, unchallenged by Whitehall under Direct Rule, carried the day.

THE DISPUTE OVER UNIVERSITY EDUCATION

Let us now turn attention to what has proved, in recent years, to be the most controversial issue – university education. The 1908 settlement had not given the Northern Catholics the sectarian university that the hierarchy would have preferred, but it seems to have been accepted that, in Ulster, this was a lost cause. At all events no attempt was made by the Catholic bishops to stop Catholics from attending the Queen's University, a modern secular university administered on the same lines as the English civic universities, although the teaching was influenced for many years by the curriculum of the ancient Scottish universities. There was indeed a concession in that courses in scholastic philosophy were provided for Catholic students but, in all other respects, education at the university level was integrated and non-sectarian. No serious problems seem to have arisen as a consequence. For this very reason, it may seem surprising that there should have been such a row over university education in the 1960s and 1970s with echoes that can still be heard today. The row was not, however, over university teaching but over the choice of site for a new institution to be established in the expansionary sixties after the Robbins Report on Higher Education.

The desired expansion could have been achieved by increasing the size of Queen's, which was not a large university. Space could have been found easily enough by clearing away some houses in the streets at the back of the main building, as was soon to be done over extensive areas of the city by the urban planners often for less desirable purposes. Or a satellite campus could have been established in the Belfast region. In these circumstances, the government appointed an advisory committee under the chairmanship of the late Sir John Lockwood, Master of Birkbeck College.[21] In due course this body recommended that a university should be established, and it then went on to identify what it considered to be an appropriate site, although this delicate task had not been required of it in its terms of reference. Belfast was ruled out. In part the explanation was the apparent lack of interest in expansion at Queen's University itself. There were, then, two places that came naturally to mind: Derry and Armagh. The former was Ulster's second city. Moreover, there was already a small university institution in Derry – Magee College – and a good deal of currency appears to have been given to the view that this would be a suitable nucleus. Naturally it could also be claimed that the siting of a university in Derry would be of great benefit to the cultural and social life of the north-west, where a stimulus of some kind was clearly desirable. Armagh, another possibility, was also an ancient city and was the ecclesiastical capital of Ireland for both the Catholic and the Protestant episcopalian churches. It was closer to Belfast which could be both an advantage and a disadvantage – an advantage in that it would be possible to share some facilities with Queen's, a disadvantage in that its choice would not convey the same vote of confidence in the north-west. Another possibility was the new town, Craigavon, which was near to Armagh. The committee, however, recommended neither of these places and came down strongly in favour of the small town of Coleraine. Their choice caused much surprise everywhere and much indignation in Derry. It was denounced as evidence of sectarian bias against Derry where two-thirds of the population was Catholic. Thus the siting of the new university became one of the new grievances of the minority during this period of reform.

At that time, I was engaged in the preparation of the development plan but did not, of course, attend any of the meetings of the Lockwood Committee and saw none of its papers. It was arranged, however, for Sir John and myself to meet after the committee had reached its conclusions. It had never seemed at all likely that he would be influenced by the sectarian prejudice that Ulster noses, sometimes too readily, claim to be able to detect, and after the meeting I was quite sure of this. It is also my recollection that he took the position, firmly adopted in the report itself, that the choice of site must be determined by the best interest of the university itself, which must not be sacrificed to any other consideration such as a desire to help one town rather than another. He had clearly been unimpressed by the case for Derry, although that case had been vigorously and ably presented by a group consisting of both Catholics and Protestants. There were, however, some other leading citizens who had been quite hostile. This disagreement did not seem to him to promise a happy environment. By contrast, the Coleraine team was thought to have been united, if not altogether impressive, in its presentation of its case. In assessing the case for Derry, the committee had not been inclined to accord much weight to the existing preparatory liberal arts college there, founded for the instruction of candidates for the Presbyterian Ministry, to which I have referred. Notwithstanding the valiant efforts over the years of some of its teaching staff, Magee was still very small with only about 300 students who were spending some time in Derry before going on to Trinity College, Dublin for the completion of their degree courses. The site of the college was restricted but a new one could have been used for what would really have been a green-field university.

Lockwood believed it would be particularly appropriate if the new university were to specialize in the life sciences and in this area it should be further strengthened by Queen's and the Ministry of Agriculture agreeing to having all the teaching courses in agriculture and all agricultural research concentrated in Coleraine. There was good farm land in the area. An experimental farm would be acquired, and so on. (Comparable facilities would, in fact, have been available at either Derry or Armagh.) In fact, of course, the Ministry of Agriculture had no intention of moving away from Queen's. This development, to which Lockwood attached so much importance, never occurred. I do not recollect that Lockwood, for his part, placed much weight on the Treasury view that Coleraine had the advantage of being close to two seaside resorts with boarding houses where students might live out of the holiday season, with a saving of public money on the erection of hostels. Of the many arguments advanced during the controversy this was surely the least weighty.

If the case for choosing Coleraine was unimpressive, it could at least be urged that there did not seem to be any decisive *academic* objections to this choice. But the *political* reaction proved to be very hostile indeed. From that point of view, the government undoubtedly made a mistake in accepting the Lockwood recommendation on this main issue, even if they tried to soften a little the blow to Derry by rejecting the committee's advice to close down Magee College. Indeed, this rejection of Derry's claims became a bitter grievance – and one that is not yet forgotten[22]. It is for this reason that it has seemed appropriate to go into some detail here in recounting these events. Matters were made even worse politically by the poor drafting of the Lockwood report where the reasons for their favouring Coleraine rather than Derry were not presented. As a final – and quite gratuitous – snub to Derry, the report went on to say that if a *third* university should ever prove to be necessary, Armagh might be an appropriate place. In this context, there was no reference at all to Derry. It is scarcely surprising that the committee was accused of acting as the tool of a Unionist Government that wanted to do down the predominantly Catholic city of Derry. I do not believe for a moment that Lockwood would have submitted to any such instructions from the Unionist leaders, as he was alleged to have done. What is, however, beyond question is that the whole affair was grossly mishandled.

In the 1970s as things turned out, life was easier at the new university because it was situated in the relatively peaceful Coleraine area and not in Derry. For example, the effect of those disturbances on life in Derry was described in the Guardian in May 1974 in an article entitled 'Tumbledown Derry' with the following caption: 'In the last three years more than 5200 houses have been either destroyed or badly damaged; 124 business premises, mainly offices and shops, have also been destroyed and 1809 damaged.' It is true that the rioters and the terrorists might have spared the new university but it would have been very hard, to say the least of it, to recruit and retain academic staff and to attract the same number of students from outside Ulster who came to Coleraine. These difficulties might not, of course, have been permanent, but would have been serious for a time.

To say so is, however, to take it for granted that these disturbances would have occurred anyway, wherever the university had been sited. It can be maintained that the rejection of Derry was what finally convinced even the moderate nationalists that they need not expect fair play from any Unionist government, not even one led by Terence O'Neill. If the Lockwood Committee had come down in favour of Derry, or if the Government had rejected this locational advice which it had not initially requested, things might, it is suggested, have been different. The satisfaction that Derry people would have derived from being chosen could have been important and all the activity attending its establishment would have provided a diversion. If even Armagh had been chosen, there would probably have been less bitterness. All this, however, is speculation and a strong case could be advanced for saying that the disturbances would have occurred anyway.

The Government was soon to lay itself open to criticism on educational grounds – as distinct from the political issues with which we have just been concerned. For it did not subsequently follow a policy consistent with the consolidation of the new university at Coleraine in that it allowed the new Ulster College, which had been established on the advice of the Lockwood Committee, to develop a wide range of degree-earning courses. This institution established at Jordanstown – only a few miles from Queen's – became Ulster's only polytechnic and then set about turning itself into a *de facto* university as fast as its vigorous leadership could contrive. At this stage there was not much the Government could have done to prevent such a development.

If there was to be any such development, it might have been as a satellite campus to Queen's. Instead the new institution became a rival to both Queen's and Coleraine. Views may differ as to whether Ulster really needed two universities, but it would be hard to maintain that there was any conceivable need for three. The consequence in the late 1980s has been the amalgamation of the widely separated colleges at Coleraine, Jordanstown, Derry (Magee) and Belfast (the College of Art) to form the University of Ulster. It is an untidy outcome. Even more important was the opportunity that had been missed. What the Province needed was a high level college of technology and, at a lower level, the extension and improvement of technical education which should have been linked to training schemes. The Ulster economy, which has few assets apart from its manpower, was likely to suffer as a consequence of these deficiencies.

It would be unfair to end this chapter on a critical note without referring to the large extension of official training schemes that has occurred in recent years. Moreover it would be quite wrong to prejudge or ignore the new educational proposals in 1988. These developments may warrant a more cheerful appraisal. There is another factor that does not do so. This is the need for a substantial industrial base where those emerging from the educational and training establishments could acquire the experience and the further training that are essential and where they might also find permanent employment without having to emigrate. What is then required is an exercise in phasing, for a trained labour force is needed to attract industry, and more industry is needed to provide the final training. It is a difficult exercise but one that need not be regarded as insoluble provided an end can be put to the terrorist activity which is so serious an impediment to industrial expansion.

PART III
Revolt, Reform and the Search for a Constitutional Solution

15
From Civil Rights to Civil Strife

The revolt, already simmering, began in earnest in October 1968. The civil rights demonstration of that date was to be followed by growing unrest and increasingly violent disturbances which brought the Province to the verge of civil war. It may seem natural to assume that this revolt occurred as an understandable reaction to prolonged oppression with the minority deprived of employment, denied new housing and condemned to live in bitter poverty by a government that was committed to ruthless discrimination in favour of the Protestant majority. In fact the previous twenty years had been marked by historically strong economic development from which the whole community had benefited. Average disposable income per head had more than doubled, after correction for changes in prices and taxes. The social benefits provided in cash had risen more than in line with net earnings. Unemployment, at about 6 per cent for the Province as a whole, was low and of this roughly half represented the frictional unemployment that occurs as people change jobs in a dynamic economy. About 165,000 new houses had been built since the end of the war. The health service had been developed on lines similar to the NHS in Britain and the vast improvement in medical facilities together with other favourable factors were reflected in greatly improved health statistics. Educational services had been much enlarged and improved at all levels, and training facilities had been much expanded after the adoption of the first development plan. The financial assistance which had opened the path to higher education for children of the lower income groups had been reflected in a marked rise in the proportion of Catholic students at the Queen's University from which some of the young nationalist political leaders themselves had benefited. Moreover relations between the Government and the Catholic minority had shown a marked improvement in recent years. So had relations between the heads of government in Northern Ireland and the Republic, as was shown by the meetings between O'Neill and Lemass.

These meetings were all the more appropriate because the Governments of the two areas had collaborated successfully in the defeat of the IRA between 1956 and 1962. Lemass, moreover, was to show a pragmatic attitude towards partition and had even attempted to have the offending Articles 2 and 3 of the Constitution revised in 1967. O'Neill for his part made the great mistake of arranging the initial meeting without consulting his Cabinet, for nothing in the end could be gained without the support of a majority of his colleagues. He also failed to refer to the agreement of 1925, which provided for such meetings – and also accorded recognition to Northern Ireland. As was to be expected, the Paisleyites made a great fuss about the meeting with the usual wild talk of treachery and O'Neill had deprived himself by his tactics of some of the support that might otherwise have been forthcoming from more moderate Unionists. Nevertheless, from the viewpoint of the minority in the North, the meeting could be regarded as a welcome improvement in relations.

There is, of course, nothing peculiar – nothing queer and 'Irish' – about a revolt that has been preceded by a bettering of conditions. The year 1968 was, after all, marked by unrest throughout Western Europe and North America although preceded by a period of strong economic development, rising living standards and very low levels of unemployment. Of the various possible explanations the one most frequently given is, perhaps, that associated with Alexis de Tocqueville who observed about the years preceding the French Revolution: 'Yet the fact remains that the country did grow richer and living conditions improved throughout the land . . . It is a singular fact that this steadily improving prosperity, far from tranquilising the population, everywhere promoted a spirit of unrest.'[1] Rising anticipations, inspired by the advances already made, outpace what can possibly be achieved and the disillusionment that follows may be more powerful than any feeling of appreciation for the gains that have been attained.

We have here an important part of the explanation, but only part. For people are interested not only in the improvement of their own standards of living, but in accompanying changes in the relative positions of different groups. The debate about 'poverty' revolves around these issues. If the 'poverty level' suggested by Beveridge in 1942 were still thought to be the appropriate bench-mark, then it could be said that, apart from some special cases requiring special treatment, poverty in Britain had long since been abolished. But it is a different matter if poverty is given a relative dimension so that the poverty level is raised in line with rising average income. If a strictly relativist approach is adopted, the numbers 'in poverty' can be reduced only by reducing inequality. There is no need to become involved here in this general debate[2] but it must be stressed that, in Northern Ireland, the relativist criterion was given a sharper edge by the sectarian divide. What is clear is that the minority *believed* itself to be relatively deprived – or, to be more accurate, its vocal leaders maintained that this was the case. A relative improvement was therefore demanded.

The primary objective of the policies adopted at Stormont had been to foster rising output and employment and thus a rising prosperity from which all would benefit. There can be no doubt that this was basically the right approach. It has been demonstrated time and again that redistribution, however drastic, could do far less to assist the lower income groups than will be done over a number of years by rising output. The arithmetic is irrefutable whether one is dealing with Ulster or England or any other country one may care to choose. No conceivable redistribution carried out in 1948 could have achieved the doubling of real earnings that occurred over the following twenty years. To say this is not, however, to imply that relative standards are unimportant. On the contrary, people everywhere are concerned not only with increases in their own standard of living but also with the increases achieved by other people. 'Conservatives' rightly stress the far greater quantitative significance of raising output but may place too little weight on relativities; 'socialists' are right in insisting that distribution is important but then tend to exaggerate the extent to which redistribution alone could improve the standard of living of the poor. Both approaches are proper but the second one – the relativist approach – has the appeal of being the more enlivening. A policy designed to foster growth needs to be based on a careful and painstaking investigation of all kinds of issues that many people regard as boring. Given time, massive gains will be achieved, but patience is required. It is more exciting to assume that we are playing a zero-sum game where my gains will be your losses. It has often been said that British people are predisposed to this zero-sum game to a far greater extent than, for example, the Americans, the Germans and the Japanese. There can be little doubt that many people in Northern Ireland find it absorbing, and this may have been particularly true of nationalist and republican politicians. If so, the explanation may lie not only in temperament and tradition but also in the effect of their prolonged exclusion – and self-exclusion – from positions where they could have exercised practical and constructive responsibility for measures designed to bring about a general rise in prosperity.

Another reason why rising living standards did not prevent revolt was the fact that some of the grievances most acutely felt were political. First, there was the bitter complaint about the way in which, in the west of the Province, the Unionists continued to control the local councils by means of gerrymandering and a limited franchise. It is true that the reform of local government boundaries had been under consideration for some time but even the latest proposals were still only on the drawing board in 1968. Any redrawing of ward boundaries was bound to be a highly controversial matter and a lot of time might elapse before a sufficient measure of agreement could be reached. It would, however, have been quite possible to have taken reform in two stages and to have started by changing the franchise so as to provide 'one man, one vote'. This would have been a shrewd move – and a just one – but it was not made. The second political factor – and much the more important – was Irish nationalism. To the devoted nationalist, no improvement in conditions in the North, however far-reaching, could compensate for partition. The moderates could press for reforms and even attach real importance to them, but the more extreme would prefer to use the grievances of the minority as a way of perpetuating instability and to ignore or depreciate any reforms that might make partition more endurable. For the civil rights movement was a coalition.

Some of the founders of that movement, the Northern Ireland Civil Rights Association (NICRA), were intent on achieving reform within Northern Ireland. The controversy about partition had gone on for a long time and a stalemate had been reached. In their view, it was better to accept this fact, even if it were regarded as an unpleasant fact, and to try to make Northern Ireland a better place to live in. Indeed the civil rights association initially included a few Young Unionists.[3] There was, however, another side to the movement for, even in the early days, a more extreme republican element was also present with the Wolfe Tone Society well represented on the committee. Some leading members of the IRA were also associated with it, though not dominant.[4] The moderate civil rights reformers would have been well-advised to have avoided completely any such association with members of the republican movement for this association immediately gave rise to the suspicion on the part of Unionists – and also on the part of the police – that the movement was merely a stalking-horse for republican subversion. There was one other way in which NICRA could have dispelled suspicion and even won support for its objectives from the more reasonable Protestants. It could have taken up the cause of some Protestants who appeared to be the victims of discrimination at the hands of Catholic councils instead of confining attention to complaints about discrimination against Catholics by Unionist councils. One such case, properly publicized, would have transformed the movement's standing in Protestant eyes. For it would have demonstrated that the movement's concern was essentially with civil rights, not with sectarianism so disguised.

THE TROUBLES BEGIN

The NICRA demonstration in Derry in October 1968 was the start of the long sequence of events that is not yet at an end. The movement was, of course, fully entitled to hold demonstrations if it wished, and there were good grounds for saying that a public protest was fully justified in view of the cavalier way in which Unionist ministers had dismissed complaints about discrimination in local authority housing allocations. There ought to have been a government investigation of housing complaints in the west of the Province but, as this had been denied, there was some case for taking to the streets. The police could, however, impose a ban or restrict the route to be followed by a procession if there was any serious danger of violent confrontation with another section of the community. That was the reason given for the official restriction imposed on the NICRA march of 5 October 1968. It was at this point that the role of the extreme Marxist–republican element proved decisive within a movement whose members at that stage were, for the most part, far more moderate. The organization of a demonstration along a provocatively chosen route was carried out by the extremists in the face of opposition from NICRA headquarters and from such leaders of the Derry Catholic community as John Hume and James Doherty. The march proceeded in defiance of the law and the police over-reacted by launching a baton charge against a peaceful, though illegal, procession. As they vigorously wielded their batons before the television cameras, the police appeared to be providing clear confirmation of the old – but false – assertion that Northern Ireland was a fascist state. Eamonn McCann, the leading Marxist organizer, had good cause to be satisfied for he had achieved his objective, which had been 'to provoke the police into over reaction and thus spark off mass reaction against the authorities.'[5]

Apart from the wider political consequences, these events could seriously harm economic development unless corrective action were taken without delay. This was the unpleasant fact that impressed itself so strongly upon the three economic consultants then engaged in the preparation of the second development pro-gramme. Although much in favour of encouraging local enterprise, we had always recognized that heavy reliance must also be placed upon attracting industrial investment from outside the Province. At this point the political situation could be a decisive factor. Ulster had a poor reputation for political instability but there had been some improvement in recent years. It was, then, of the utmost importance to prevent widespread disturbances which would create a vicious circle of political unrest and economic decline. Back in Scotland, I felt so strongly about this that I wrote to Prime Minister O'Neill and urged the need for the immediate establishment of a committee of inquiry into events in Derry. To have done so would not have been to prejudice the case against the police. From a distance no one could be quite sure about what had happened, but there was, to say the least of it, a *prima facie* reason for an investigation by an impartial body. Unfortunately a serious mistake had been made in appointing William Craig as Minister of Home Affairs with responsibility for the police – who, it may be recalled, were a provincial, not a local, body. Craig declared immediately that there would be no inquiry, and O'Neill would have been obliged to sack him if he had come down in favour of having one. He did not then do so. He was forced to get rid of Craig only two months later but, by then, a critical point had been passed.

For reasons that I cannot explain, two related but separate issues had become harmfully intertwined. First there was the need to appoint a committee of inquiry in order to establish, as a matter of urgency, what had happened in Derry and to make whatever disciplinary or organizational recommendations seemed to it appropriate. The second was the desirability of having an objective investigation into the grievances about civil rights which had led to the demonstration and to some earlier protests. This second exercise was bound to take time but there was no reason why the first inquiry – the inquiry into the particular events of that day in Derry – should not have been carried out separately, and without delay. In the event the Government reached no decision until January 1969, when a commission under the chairmanship of a Scottish judge, Lord Cameron, was appointed and charged with reporting both on the violent incidents – which had by then multiplied – and on their underlying causes. This was a large task and their report did not appear until September 1969, eleven months after the Derry demonstration.[6] Meanwhile a great deal had occurred.

The Government did, in fact, move quite quickly to announce a number of reforms in November 1968: a scheme for the fair allocation of houses; the appointment of a Parliamentary Commissioner for Complaints; the replacement of Londonderry Corporation with a Development Commission; the implementation of the Plan for Londonderry recommended in the first development plan; local government reform which would now include the abolition of the business vote; the withdrawal, as soon as possible, of any orders under the Special Powers Act.[7] These were important steps but were not taken in such a way as to have any very impressive effect. As economic consultants we felt that more should be done, and on 7 January 1969 we submitted a joint statement to ministers in which we said: 'It is a commonplace that political activity is an important factor in contributing to economic development. We would therefore respectfully urge that further reform is needed or a definite commitment that such reform will be adopted as a matter of urgency'.[8] We received no reply and, in the circumstances, expected none. In order to prevent any possible misunderstanding, I must stress that our own position was peripheral. We were not, of course, involved in any of the discussions of political issues and, indeed, had very little contact with ministers during this period when we were completing our report.

The opponents of reform could argue that concessions made from a position of weakness in response to threats would do nothing to conciliate but would only lead to fresh demands. This was a powerful and valid objection as far as it went, but there had been many years when reforms could have been made from that desirable 'position of strength', but had not in fact been made. The Unionist regime, so skilfully attacked for so many years by republican critics and so feebly defended, had now been sullied again in a way that appeared to confirm all that had been said about its being an oppressive tyranny. To reject an inquiry into police activity in Derry and also to refuse any reforms in other directions would be to destroy what little respect was still retained outside Ulster's own frontiers. Craig seems to have been prepared to accept the consequences of complete intransigence, and his advocacy of UDI could be said to follow. If so ill-considered a step were to be avoided – and there was only very limited support for it in the Protestant community – then reforms were clearly essential. This was so notwithstanding de Tocqueville's warning: 'experience teaches us that, generally speaking, the most perilous moment for a bad government is one when it seeks to mend its ways.'[9] Although the Stormont regime was far from being 'bad' by Bourbon standards, its position was perilous enough, but the danger could not be avoided by digging in and refusing any further changes. With strong, skilful leadership and a united team, appropriate reforms might have been made without losing control; but these conditions were lacking. What was particularly unfortunate was the longstanding hostility between O'Neill and Faulkner which reminded one of the similar hostility between Herbert Morrison and Ernest Bevin in the post-war Labour Cabinet. Its effect was to give a disastrous impression of a weak and divided government that would respond only to violent domestic demonstrations or to external pressure from Whitehall.

The events in Derry were followed by further disturbances in some other towns and a particular reference may be made to events in Armagh on 30 November 1968. On that occasion Paisley and an associate, Bunting, organized a counter-demonstration in order to block the path of a civil rights demonstration which had received official sanction. The 'Loyalists' were armed with a variety of offensive weapons, some of which were confiscated, but the police were in insufficient strength to clear the route for the demonstration or to provide adequate protection. Their handling of the affair on this occasion was, however, to be commended with some slight qualification by the subsequent commission of inquiry.[10] Paisley and Bunting were charged by the police with unlawful assembly and served short prison sentences.

A detailed examination of these complicated and confusing events has been presented in the reports of two official committees of inquiry – under Lord Cameron and Lord Scarman respectively – and, with varying emphasis and accuracy, in many non-official accounts. Without becoming involved in such detail, one can observe some of the principal issues that emerged and some of the principal responses. The reform programme did not lead to pacification. It is true that some of the civil rights leaders began to withdraw their support from further demonstrations, partly because some important gains had already been achieved and partly, no doubt, because demonstrations were leading to confrontations and to civil strife of a kind they had no wish to see. An important test was the behaviour of Catholic voters in the election called by O'Neill in February. The apparently monolithic Unionist party had begun to disintegrate with remarkable speed and the O'Neill candidates were challenged by Craig and the more hardline faction. In the event, O'Neill and his supporters won a victory for moderation but by too narrow a majority to be convincing. Their support came almost entirely from moderate Protestants and the outcome could have been very different if they had also received more support at the polls from moderate Catholics.[11] To the more extreme members of the Catholic community, the reforms were not so much inadequate as irrelevant, for their aim was to overthrow the regime. Strong republican views, often combined with Marxist ideology, could be content with nothing less. Thus the People's Democracy, which was far to the left of some of the original civil rights supporters, set out on a march to Derry on 4 January 1969 which was to have far-reaching consequences and – given the basic Trotskyite premises – was to prove successful. The ambush of the marchers by a gang of stone-throwing Protestant hooligans at Burntollet has now become part of the saga of republican politics. The marchers complained that they did not have full police protection, although they had some – and were, after all, looking for trouble. It was also alleged that their assailants included some B-Specials in civilian clothes. There was a fresh eruption of violence in Derry at the same time in which a number of policemen behaved with ill-disciplined violence in a way that was to have lasting consequences.

THE SPREAD OF COMMUNAL CONFLICT

The agitation for reform was thus leading to a new phase of bitter sectarian conflict along traditional lines. That was painfully obvious but it was an uncongenial conclusion for part of the republican movement, in particular for its Marxist element, who had regarded the civil rights movement as a step towards the achievement of a united Ireland which would also be a workers' republic. For this to be realized, however, the Protestant working class would have to be won over. So much appears to have been dimly perceived, but no remotely plausible strategy directed to that end had ever been evolved. It was an end that was scarcely likely to be achieved by claiming that social and economic benefits had to be differently shared out in what was assumed to be a zero-sum game, and by complaining that the Protestant workers had been getting too large a share with too many houses and too many jobs. Nor was it easy to see how the vicious street conflicts between sectarian gangs could be expected to foster the solidarity of the proletariat. From the start the demonstrations had rather the effect of *widening* still more the already wide sectarian divide. It was one outcome that should have been entirely predictable from the outset, but was, apparently, not understood. Although Marxist-republican agitators displayed considerable tactical skill, their strategy for achieving a united workers' republic failed to touch reality at any point.

The long and tragic history of sectarian conflict gave every reason to anticipate a Protestant backlash, and the situation had been made still more dangerous by the emergence of Ian Paisley as the leader of the ultra-conservative theological wing who, even before the eruption caused by the civil rights demonstration, had been organizing opposition to O'Neill's still modest policies. Paisley's demogogic authority, which was to grow over the years, was much strengthened by television programmes which gave him an amount of publicity never accorded, then or subsequently, to moderate unionists.

As we have observed, one of the features of the republican movement that deserves emphasis is its reluctance to admit the strength of popular anti-republican sentiment in Ulster. This sentiment is particularly strong at the grass-roots. To recognize so disagreeable a fact would, however, entail the recognition that a united Irish republic must remain an unrealistic dream for an indefinite future. Perhaps it has been partly for this reason that so much more attention has been devoted to the alleged misdeeds of the police, and later of the army, than to the violence of Protestant mobs or even to the brutality of the Protestant paramilitary organizations. The treatment accorded to the attack on the People's Democracy marchers at Burntollet may serve as an example. Both in the Stormont parliament and in a long flood of publications thereafter, attention was concentrated on the alleged presence among the stone-throwing crowd of a number of off-duty B-Specials. There was good ground for complaint if such persons had taken part in the attack and it was entirely proper that the matter should be raised.[12] That is not in question. But it is also true that, as a result, attention was diverted from the central and unpleasant fact that the left-wing republican demonstration, far from arousing sympathy among 'the workers and peasants' of the Protestant community, had encountered fierce resistance. Burntollet was, of course, only one example of what was to happen again and again. For there was no question of a united proletariat, just as there was no question of a union of all Irishmen. The ancient cleavage not only remained; it had been widened and deepened.

It would be unfair, however, to leave the matter there. For the fact remains that further reforms were needed and those already implemented or promised had been largely in response to the civil rights movement. No doubt O'Neill would in any case have tried to proceed along this path, but the pace would have been very much slower. Thus there was a valid need for a civil rights movement but, as I have observed, it should have been one that concerned itself with the rights of Protestants as well as Catholics and one that refused to admit extreme republicans or to ally itself in any way with members of the IRA or even of the Wolfe Tone Society. As it was, NICRA from the start contained dangerous elements and from this there largely followed the succession of disasters that led to the brink of civil war.

Throughout this period, our work as economic consultants continued, now overcast by heavy political shadows. It was clear that the prospect of economic development was being seriously damaged, although no one then anticipated a prolonged period of unrest, stretching ahead for twenty years. Order, it was believed, would soon be restored, and the development programme should help to remove, or at least reduce, some of the grievances. Thus a further ambitious programme of public investment was worked out, including a heavy building programme (see chapter 12) which would help to improve the quality of life, even if the pace of industrial development could not be so well sustained as a consequence of the disturbances.

THE VERGE OF CIVIL WAR

As it happened, I was in Derry in July 1969 on the eve of the Apprentice Boys parade which was to be followed by such dramatic events. With hindsight, it seems clear that the Government should have banned it, but it would be quite unfair to accuse the Minister of Home Affairs of Orange bias. On the contrary, Sir Robert Porter was one of the strongest advocates of reform in the Cabinet and his moderation and good sense – coupled then with the moderation and good sense of John Hume – prevented even greater disasters from occurring over those months. At that time there was quite a strong feeling among some of the Derry people themselves that the traditional parade should go on, so that the city could demonstrate the recovery of its previous sectarian tolerance. As the Scarman Tribunal was to record: 'No public figure in Londonderry, not even Mr. John Hume, advised him [the Minister] that the parade should be banned. The Minister was also convinced of the sincere wish of the . . . leaders to keep the peace, and their ability, by means of stewards, to do so.'[13] It was, however, a risky gamble. As Stephen McGonagle, a leading trade unionist and nationalist, drove my wife and myself through the Bogside and the Creggan housing estate, the tension in those areas was apparent. For a disturbance earlier in the year had been followed by a police raid that was carried out with quite excessive violence which contributed to the death, from a heart attack, of a well-known Bogside citizen. In the aftermath the RUC had in effect ceased to police these areas. As we drove slowly through there were small groups of men standing about, not with the relaxed resignation of the unemployed, but with an air of waiting and expectancy. Although we were not aware of this at the time, large numbers of petrol bombs were presumably being made in some of the houses we passed and piles of stones were being accumulated. We can still recall how an elderly lady called out to us: 'Mind you, we want no trouble here.'

If trouble came, however, the local people had a plan for resistance. They were determined not to be invaded again by a police force which, as recent experience showed, contained ill-disciplined members. In the event, on 12 August, the parade was held and it passed off peacefully enough; but at its conclusion gangs of young Bogsiders launched an attack on the police which was to lead to far-reaching changes in Northern Ireland.

The police were soon to be locked in a struggle with the Bogsiders which they could not win but from which, partly perhaps as a consequence of a tactical error, they could not withdraw. For two days and nights they withstood a hail of petrol bombs and stones. Although the hostile mob could have been quickly dispersed by gunfire, these armed policemen did not use their guns, a display of discipline that should not be ignored. By 14 August, they were exhausted and the army took over.

Meanwhile there had been sympathetic riots in other areas, in particular in Belfast, initially organized in order to ease the pressure on the Bogside. What then became apparent was that Northern Ireland, for so long denounced as a police state, had far too few police. The total force of the RUC was 3200 for the whole Province. By comparison, the police in London could, on occasion, deploy three times as many men in order to control a demonstration in Trafalgar Square.[14] No police were sent from Great Britain to support the RUC and the Labour Government made it clear that the army would not be forthcoming so long as Stormont had not made full use of all the resources at its disposal.[15] What was required by the Wilson Government was the mobilization of the B-Specials – total strength 8500 – but this caused much anger and consternation in the Catholic population.

As was to be expected there were to be complaints about bias on the part of the RUC and about the unjustified use of firearms in Belfast in August 1969. These were to be the subject of a detailed investigation by the Scarman Tribunal. There is no convenient way of summarizing the mass of evidence it considered but it may be recorded that, in total, ten people were killed, eight of them Catholics and two Protestants. All but two died from gunshot wounds. The need to investigate complaints against the police and the Specials was demonstrated once more, but complaints of this kind must not be allowed to conceal the fact that the real struggle in Belfast had been between Protestant and Catholic civilians – in the main, between the Protestant proletariat and the Catholic proletariat. The RUC was attempting to separate the warring factions and to keep them apart. The army was, of course, to do the same later on – 'Pig in the Middle', to quote the title of a book about its role in the struggle.[16] The point may seem so obvious as to need no emphasis, but this is not so. For it must be recalled once more that the republican movement is wedded to the myth of a united Irish nation, artificially divided by the British imperialists with their 'army of occupation'. The Irish, if left to themselves, would somehow resolve their differences – or so it is maintained. It is hard to understand how this view, also adopted by the 'Troops Out' movement in Great Britain, can be held in such firm defiance of experience – including, in modern times, the experience of 1969–70. For there can be no serious doubt that, had it not been for intervention, first by the police and then by the army, the violence would have continued to escalate to full-scale civil war with the Catholic population being driven out of Belfast and the Protestants driven out of some western areas, including perhaps the city of Derry itself. Although some twenty years have elapsed since these events took place, that lesson still holds true.

The belief that the RUC as a whole behaved during this period with partisan unfairness and gross brutality has come to be widely accepted. It is, therefore, well to recall the conclusions reached by the two official committees of investigation under Lord Cameron and Lord Scarman respectively – neither of whom could possibly be accused of undue bias in favour of the Unionist regime. Both found occasion to criticize the police. As we have seen, there had been an excessive use of violence against the NICRA march in October 1968, and there were subsequent incidents, including the police raid on the Bogside in January 1969 and again in April.

In July of that year, the police were held by the Scarman Committee to have been 'seriously at fault' in a number of respects. There was also said to have been inadequate supervision of the B-Specials in some places. The police failed to do as much as should have been done to prevent Catholic houses from being burnt in two streets in particular, or to sustain their protection of the Catholics in Belfast during a final interim period of some hours before the arrival of the army. It is also true that both commissions had strong praise for the police. Thus the Cameron Commission: 'In the majority of cases we find that the police acted with commendable discipline and restraint under very great strain and provocation from various quarters.' And again: 'Although this unfortunate and temporary breakdown of discipline was limited in extent [4–5 January in Derry] its effect in rousing passions and inspiring hostility towards the police was regrettably great, and obscures the restraint, under conditions of great strain, then displayed by the large majority of the police concerned.'[17] While the Scarman Committee's report observed: 'The criticisms we have made should not, however, be allowed to obscure the fact that, overall, the RUC struggled manfully to do their duty in a situation which they could not control. Their courage, as casualties and long hours of stress and strain took their toll, was beyond praise.'[18]

16

Westminster and the Security Problem

The deployment of the army in 1969 prevented civil war in Northern Ireland. This is a fact that calls for repeated emphasis in order to counteract the assertion so often made and so often uncritically accepted, that the Irish would readily resolve their differences if left to themselves. The evidence is very much to the contrary. The Ulster people, in particular the Catholic minority, had good reason to welcome the arrival of the soldiers who established a peace line between the warring factions in Belfast and, elsewhere, held them apart. After a period of comparative peace, a fresh upsurge of violence occurred in the early 1970s, with the paramilitaries on both sides taking a heavy toll. As has usually been the case in sectarian conflict in Northern Ireland, the Catholics came off the worse, and had particular reason to be grateful for the presence of the 'British army of occupation' as some of their leaders continue to call it. The events of 1969 had shown very clearly that the police force was too small and was inadequately equipped for its task, and its effectiveness had been further weakened by the charges of bias directed against it. Another peace-keeping force was clearly essential if anarchy was to be averted, and the army had to meet that need. Although the plea of the 'Troops Out' movement must, therefore, be firmly rejected, it must also be recognized that, after the arrival of the troops, new difficulties were encountered in determining security policy and in its implementation. The Unionist Government was still responsible for law and order but was obviously no longer in sole command. The sharing of authority was a possible source of difficulty for both Whitehall and Stormont.

A number of matters had then to be dealt with, some of them involving general political questions as well as security matters and most of them inter-related. These matters may be summarized as follows:

1 The decision was taken not to suspend the Northern Ireland Parliament after the troops had been deployed. This may have been a serious mistake.
2 A highly dangerous situation was the continued existence of 'no-go' areas where law and order were not maintained in the normal way. It was decided, however, not to assert the authority of the law for the time being.
3 Initially there was an understandable but exaggerated belief on the part of Westminster in the contribution to peace that could be made, in the

circumstances of the time, by social and political reform. This inspired some false optimism.

4 The belief, long retained by leading British politicians, that a settlement might be negotiated with the terrorists was based on a fundamental misunderstanding of their attitude and the meetings that took place only made matters worse.

5 The attempt had to be made by the security forces to restore law and order but their efforts could have the unpleasant consequence of creating new grievances. These new grievances might offset whatever had been gained by social and political reform.

DEVOLUTION RETAINED

The first of these decisions – to retain the provincial parliament – was contrary to the assumption that the calling in of the troops would amount to an implicit confession of failure to govern which must lead to its suspension or complete abolition. It is true that the army had been used in support of the civil power in the early 1920s and in the mid-1930s without this being regarded as inconsistent with legislative devolution, and the same attitude was adopted, at least for a time, after the crisis of 1969. By then, the Stormont Government had, however, lost much of its credibility. A large number of reforms had been carried through, and the programme of reform was endorsed by both Westminster and Stormont in the Downing Street Declaration of August 1969. But these reforms were introduced too late and could scarcely be expected to impress when Stormont had come to be regarded as essentially a Westminster puppet regime. Thus its leaders lost respect among their own supporters, especially the hardliners, and did so without earning any appreciation from the Catholic minority. It might be objected that the continuing role of the Unionist Government was, in reality, a good deal more than that of a puppet regime and that, furthermore, English ministers – ill-informed, susceptible to the more dishonest republican protestations and unjustifiably suspicious of the Ulster civil service – might have made still greater mistakes with no local ministers at hand to advise and restrain. Native guides may be very useful, although it is only fair to add that the newcomers could sometimes display more sensitivity to local conditions than the old hands. An example is recorded by James (now Lord) Callaghan, the Labour Home Secretary with special responsibility for Northern Ireland, who insisted – to the surprise of the Unionist ministers – on informing Cardinal Conway about a joint communique on proposed reforms just before it was issued at the end of August 1969.[1] It is a small example but it illustrates the difference of approach.

Although some case could be made for a joint operation by Westminster and Stormont, at least in the short run, devolution was bound to appear increasingly unreal with UK ministers and civil servants so closely involved. What was particularly unfortunate was the harm done to moderate unionism by the discrediting of its leadership. London was appealing to 'the centre' but was also undermining the 'centre's' authority. Devolution had become a sham and its retention was an evasion of the disagreeable fact that London, for a time at least, would have to take charge. Paradoxically, if devolution was thought to be desirable, its future would have been better safeguarded by its temporary suspension, and subsequent restoration after various changes had been made in a quite explicit way by Westminster.

There was, however, another and more promising possibility. The Northern Ireland Parliament could have been abolished and at the same time it could have been made clear that there would be no question of restoring it or instituting any comparable legislative assembly in its place. For an indefinite period, Northern Ireland would be governed in the same way as Scotland with a Secretary of State and a bureaucracy in order to cope with whatever modifications in legislation and administration might be required by local conditions. Legislation that related to Northern Ireland would be dealt with at Westminster in the same way as Scottish legislation and there would be a Grand Committee composed of members of both Houses to review Ulster affairs. At the same time, the British political parties would open their membership to Ulster people who are, after all, British subjects. In these ways the constitutional position would have been clearly defined.

The adoption of a policy of this kind would, of course, have met with some protests in Ulster, but neither the Protestants nor the Catholics were in a strong position to object at a time when the British forces were saving them from civil war. The Republic might well have expressed its discontent but it had too clearly demonstrated its impotence for it to carry much weight even with the Ulster Catholics. Britain could, of course, have explained that a 'loyalty poll' would be held every ten years or so but it could also have been pointed out that, even if demographic change were in the end to give the republican side a majority in the North, there was no prospect whatsoever of that occurring for several decades – and it might never occur at all.

The great advantage of such a course would have been political stability.[2] It would have been firmly established that Ulster was part of Britain and would remain so unless, in some doubtful and distant future, a majority of her people opted decisively for change. That would have been the central fact to which all the policies of other parties and organizations would have had to accommodate. Had this firm line been taken, Northern Ireland – and Great Britain as well – would have been spared a great deal of misery over the succeeding years. By contrast, the line actually adopted was an invitation to continued disruption. For it was made clear to all that British politicians did not wish to become any more involved in Ulster affairs than could possibly be avoided and would withdraw as soon as the balance of practical advantage tipped a little in that direction. The future terrorists were encouraged to add their weight to the scales. It must be recalled that the IRA was weak and poorly organized in 1969, before the Provisionals had come into being. Moreover, the ordinary Ulster people had seen the edge of an abyss. At this point, Britain had a magnificent opportunity to restore stability and then to proceed with social reform; but the main British parties preferred to delude themselves with the belief that they could somehow limit their commitment to Northern Ireland. This half-hearted policy of not wanting to stay without feeling able to go has prolonged the unrest. Constitutional instability of this kind can only inhibit any satisfactory political developments and hamper economic development as well as providing a clear incentive to continuing terrorist activity.

NO-GO AREAS

The second problem was that of the continued existence of no-go areas. The failure to resolve it satisfactorily was to have the most serious consequences which are still present twenty years later (see chapter 22). As Rose has maintained, a state that does not attempt to fulfil its basic obligation to maintain law and order in part of its territory has to that extent lost the claim to be a 'state'.[3] The problem is not, of course, peculiar to Ulster. It could become a feature of some of the English cities with large racial minorities, though mercifully the problem is still on a much smaller scale than in Ulster. When a community has suffered from civil unrest, there will always be a temptation to hold back from any further confrontations that might give rise to new grievances. But there is then a very real danger that a local mafia will gain control and it can be difficult to challenge its authority at a later date. Thus an attempt to break a drug ring that has been established in some weakly policed area may be met with a race riot and a new confrontation that leaves another legacy of racial grievances. Clearly no-go areas should not be tolerated, but one does not need to be an expert in these matters to appreciate something of the difficulty of bringing them to an end. In Ulster, as we have seen, the problem had been made particularly difficult by the fact that there were too few policemen and by the further complication that the bad and biased behaviour of a few of its members had been made to discredit the force as a whole. Even before the crisis that led to the deployment of the army in mid-1969,[4] there were nationalist areas that had not been properly policed for a considerable period, and the RUC was in no state by then to do that job effectively. Policing was not the right job for the army, but a strong army presence could have been established immediately and subsequently maintained in areas such as the Bogside, until a strengthened and reformed police force could be brought back to do its proper job. To have taken a firmer line in 1969 would no doubt have meant more friction for a time, but it must be repeated that the Provisional IRA had not then been formed and the resistance to authority would have been far less than at any later date. By holding back, the authorities gave the terrorists an opportunity to establish their bases and to dig themselves in.[5]

The consequences of allowing them to do so may not, even now, have been adequately appreciated in Great Britain. Thus, from time to time, the political leaders have appealed to the ordinary people 'to repudiate the men of violence' without explaining how this could be done. The terrorists, both republican and loyalist, do not come asking for assistance, cap in hand, and do not go away, quiet and crestfallen, if aid is refused them. The following statement by a Catholic priest who was lamenting the violence in his parish gives a better impression of what happens: 'No one stands up to the Provos; they don't want their sons beaten up. I remember one man who wouldn't give up his car. They put his arms against a wall and broke them with hurley sticks. He thought it better than having his knees shot off.'[6] In short, no individual or small group can be expected to resist in isolation. Action on a wider scale is required and was forthcoming for a time in the Peace Movement led by Mrs Mairead Corrigan and Mrs Betty Williams in 1976, but the effect was not lasting.

It would be foolish to ignore the fact of coercion, but it would also be a mistake to infer that the local Catholic communities provided the IRA with the bases it needed only because they were bullied into doing so. For the IRA was also viewed as a defence force which, for all its faults, was the only one on which any reliance could be placed by people who felt themselves threatened by hostile Protestant mobs and Protestant murder gangs but denied, as they thought, the protection of unbiased security forces.

To return to the late 1960s and early 1970s. There was, indeed, a way in which the Stormont Government could have exerted harsh but probably effective pressure on the no-go areas. For it could have ruled that where the police could not go, the social security benefits would not go. 'Free Derry' had been proclaimed and the proclamation of independence could have been taken to mean that any right to social benefits had been voluntarily abandoned. In some other countries, that grim inference might have been followed. It is certainly hard to believe that, in such circumstances, the flow of benefits would have been maintained in Soviet Russia. But there is no evidence of which I am aware that such a response was ever even considered by the Unionist Government at Stormont. On the contrary, it was a matter of pride in the social security department that pensions, unemployment pay, sickness benefit and so on would be unfailingly provided. As it happened, the threat to the supply of benefits to the Catholic areas came, not from the Unionist Government, but from the IRA itself. A number of social security offices were burned down in Belfast, Londonderry, Omagh, Strabane, Newry and Magherafelt – some more than once. The courageous officials had to go about their business, often in the face of brutal threats to their own safety. This was surely one of the more remarkable features of the period in Northern Ireland which has been almost wholly neglected. Far from withdrawing benefits as a sanction directed against the no-go areas, the Unionist Government and, later, the British Government maintained their supply in face of IRA attacks which lasted for a period of about five years – without receiving any acknowledgement from the nationalist politicians.

The no-go areas provided opportune scope for the Provisional IRA, formed as a breakaway movement in December 1969. The old movement, as we have observed, had become increasingly Marxist and its leaders had repudiated terrorism, if not in principle at least as inappropriate in the circumstances. As a consequence, the IRA had been in a position to play only a marginal role during the recent disturbances and had failed to behave as 'protector' of the Catholic population. The existing leadership was then repudiated by a group of such hard men as MacStiofan, O'Bradaigh, O'Connail and Cahill who adopted a title – the Provisional IRA – which referred back to the Provisional Government proclaimed in Dublin in 1916. The rump of the old body – the Official IRA or the 'Stickies' – was to continue to decline in importance although it could show, notably in the bombing of Aldershot in 1972, that its repudiation of violence had been no more than a temporary affair. For both branches, however, and also for the Irish National Liberation Army (INLA) – a later Trotskyite splinter group that broke away from the Officials in 1974 – there were now two kinds of base area from which their attacks could be launched and to which they could withdraw. These were, first, the border counties of the Irish Republic and, secondly, the no-go areas within Northern Ireland itself. It is scarcely surprising that, in these conditions, the 'Ulster Problem' has been hard to solve.

The initial decision to tolerate no-go areas was made while the Unionist Government was still in power and responsible for security. It was not a decision of which its leaders may have approved, but they could not, or would not, press their view in face of the caution urged by Whitehall.

PEACE THROUGH REFORMS

The third point mentioned above was the tendency to exaggerate the effectiveness of social and economic reform as a means of ending civil unrest of the kind experienced in Northern Ireland at this time. The issue is a particularly difficult one and is still important after almost twenty years. Nor is its relevance confined to Northern Ireland.

Social and political reform as a way of preventing social disorder is one thing; it is another matter when terrorist activity has begun. If a number of reforms had been carried out in the mid-1960s the subsequent course of events might have been very different. That did not happen and, as we have seen, the Civil Rights Movement, formed in protest, later changed its emphasis with the republican component, always present, taking over control. Even those supporters of a politically united island who repudiated the use of force could now glimpse some hope of making progress and, in such circumstances, no good nationalist would allow himself to be put off with any package of reforms within the existing regime. It would, however, continue to be good political tactics to give full publicity to old grievances and also to ignore whatever steps had been taken to remove those grievances. For it would never be politically right to admit that any substantial improvements had been made in the lot of the minority. This could be a clever way of playing the cards, although Callaghan, for his part, was not impressed and referred in Parliament to the 'concentration on the imagined and real grievances at times to the complete exclusion of the measures of progress which are being made in this country'.[7] There were, however, many others in Britain who lacked his insight. As for the committed republicans, reforms were at best merely a tiresome irrelevance, at worst a distraction that might weaken support in the real struggle for power.

An interesting example of a failure to understand the nature of an urban guerilla struggle was provided by the Hunt Committee on the reform of the police. The committee envisaged in its report that there might be a resumption of attacks on police stations and customs posts and on the members of the security forces – that is to say, there might be another campaign run on old-fashioned 1955 lines. But even this might not happen: 'It should not be inferred, from this assessment of the possible threat from terrorism, that terrorist attacks are likely.'[8] The committee then went on to recommend the disarming of the police – at the very time when the paramilitary forces were gaining strength and preparing for their offensive. The recommendation was carried out but did not endure. The abolition of the B-Specials, also on the advice of the committee, was bitterly resented by many of the Protestant population, but it would have been hard to retain a force that included no Catholics and was held, not always unfairly, to have been biased. Its successor, the Ulster Defence Regiment (UDR), is part of the army and is used mainly at security checkpoints. At the outset, some Catholics volunteered but, faced with the brutal displeasure of the IRA, they resigned. Predictably, the new force has been accused of the gravest crimes by republican sympathizers. Again the possibility cannot be excluded that some of the officially unverified complaints directed against the UDR may be both valid and serious, but it must also be recognized that republican propagandists have never allowed themselves to be seriously inhibited by any regard for the evidence. What must not be left out of account is the extent to which members of the Regiment have themselves become victims. By mid-1988, 177 of these volunteers had been killed, four-fifths murdered when off duty, some in their homes with their families. They are 'soft targets' of the kind liked by the IRA, for they carry arms only when on duty.

The Downing Street Declaration of August 1969 had set out a number of fields where reforms should be carried out, and in August 1971 the Unionist Government published *A Record of Constructive Change* which described the impressive number of measures that had already been implemented.[9] But there is no reason to suppose that the record thus presented had much effect on the course of events. The two factions could still engage in vicious rioting with gunmen on both sides. A number of soldiers had already been killed, including two young boys who were not even on duty. A reform programme, however far-reaching, would show its effects only slowly and could not have much bearing on the immediate critical situation.

INTERNMENT OR DETENTION

The fourth of the points made above was that, as old grievances were progressively met, new ones were unintentionally created by the security forces themselves in their attempt to restore law and order. The army's raid of July 1970 into the Lower Falls, a Catholic area, was to provide a classic example. It began with a search for arms in a single house. Heavy rioting then followed and grenades and petrol bombs were thrown. The army had to choose between retreat and moving in with sufficient force to assert its authority. The second alternative was chosen, CS gas was used, a curfew imposed and a house-to-house search for arms begun. A quantity of guns and ammunition were discovered but at the cost of house-to-house searches which were unavoidably rough as the soldiers invaded the privacy of private families, terrified children with their presence and proceeded to tear homes apart in their search for hidden weapons – searches which in most cases were bound to be unsuccessful. In such a situation, it is virtually impossible to restore order without new hurt to someone. It is not impossible to break out of this vicious circle, or to start to do so, as subsequent experience was to demonstrate. But skill, time and patience are required.

A new and important grievance was created when the Unionist Government in the face of some opposition from the General Officer Commanding (Tuzo) decided in August 1971 that internment should be introduced under the Special Powers Act. In the past internment had been thought to be necessary by the government of the Irish Republic as well as by the Unionists in Northern Ireland. Its most recent use had been in 1956–62 when the two governments, North and South, had acted together and had been highly effective in bringing an IRA offensive to an end. The Republic was not, however, deterred by its own former actions from denouncing the new introduction of internment in the North. The Catholic hierarchy took a similar line. Joint action, North and South, of the kind used so successfully in the past, was not now obtainable and this was a great weakness. The efficiency of the operation was also greatly reduced by the fact that the intelligence records were out of date which was, in turn, partly the consequence of there being no-go areas which much hampered police intelligence.[10] Many of the wrong people were arrested while many of the real activists escaped except, surprisingly, in Derry where the local Provo leaders were picked up. There followed allegations about the brutal treatment said to be meted out to some of the internees. Moreover, Faulkner had disregarded the plea of the Home Secretary (then Reginald Maudling) by confining the arrests to Catholics. He was subsequently to explain that: 'The security forces were also adamant that there was no evidence of organized terrorism by 'Protestants' which would justify detention of persons other than IRA members.'[11] If so, it would have been prudent to have rejected the recourse to internment unless it could be used from the outset against both sides in a way that would have avoided the charge of sectarian bias. To quote a critical view: 'Internment was totally one-sided. No Protestants were arrested, and it was certainly not because every Protestant hand was clean from terrorism.'[12] At a later stage, Protestants were also to be interned but, by then, the harm had been done. There can be no doubt that this measure was badly mishandled and had the long-run effect of discrediting any form of internment.[13]

The introduction of internment was followed by intensified violence, made worse by a vicious Protestant backlash. The year 1972 was to be the worst of the whole tragic period, with 467 people killed as compared with an average for 1969–87 of 136, or about nine times the number killed in the relatively good year of 1985 before the Anglo-Irish Agreement had been announced.

LOYALIST PARAMILITARY FORCES

The situation facing the security forces in the early 1970s was particularly difficult with mob violence as well as paramilitary activity. The pressures making for civil war were not to be easily or quickly subdued. On the 'Loyalist' side there were soon a confusing number of organizations to cope with, and it seems appropriate at this stage to embark upon a digression about their formation and activities. Of these, the oldest was the Ulster Volunteer Force, founded in 1966 under the name of the Carsonite organization of 1913/14, although the new UVF was really an assassination gang. Two murders soon after its formation led to its being banned by the O'Neill Government, and one of its leaders was sentenced to life imprisonment. As an underground force it was active in the opening years of the 1970s, and continues to be so today, though now, apparently, on a reduced scale. In 1974, Merlyn Rees, the Secretary of State, removed the ban on the UVF in the hope that its members could be induced to abandon force for political activity, but the ban had to be reimposed in 1975 after the UVF had been responsible for fifteen deaths, including six of its own members killed by incompetence in the handling of explosives. Among the other victims were three members of the Miami Showband. With the UVF banned once more, the army directed a powerful operation against it.

The various other Loyalist paramilitary organizations have included the Red Hand Commandos, launched in 1972 and declared illegal the following year, and the Ulster Freedom Fighters, a splinter group from the Ulster Defence Association which was both founded and proscribed in 1974. The Tartan Gangs were formed in 1971 with a name designed to commemorate three young Scottish soldiers who had been treacherously murdered in cold blood by the IRA. The Tartan Gangs were said to be responsible for intimidation, especially during the Ulster Workers strike of 1974 which is described below, but they do not seem to have acquired the same reputation for assassination as the other organizations we mentioned.

The Ulster Defence Association, founded in 1971, requires separate treatment. Its declared objective initially was to coordinate the activities of the various Protestant groups but it professed to emphasize legal political activity rather than terrorism. Its membership has been assessed at as much as 40,000 in 1972.[14] Although this number was to drop to about 10,000 before the end of the decade, it was to remain a powerful organization. Like Sinn Fein, it is legal. Unlike Sinn Fein, it has not turned itself into a political party, but has been much concerned with political developments. The borderline between a hardline political organization and one concerned with violent activities has been thinly drawn which may be partly explained – though obviously not justified – by the fact that it seems to comprise people with somewhat different views, from the hard men to the larger number whose interest is mainly political. It is of particular importance to stress that the membership of the UDA has always been almost entirely working class – one of the many facts which has made nonsense of the claim by left-wing republicans that they were going to unite the Ulster proletariat against its Saxon capitalist oppressors.

A particularly tense situation arose in 1972 when the UDA organized a protest – by no means unjustified in principle – against the way in which the government was acquiescing in republican no-go areas. The protest took the form of threatening to erect barricades in Protestant areas, in particular one between the Protestant Shankill area and the Catholic Springfield area. A violent encounter with the army was only narrowly avoided at this point.

In the early 1970s the Loyalist paramilitary organizations were responsible for a large number of assassinations, some carried out with vicious cruelty. The ostensible objective was 'to take out' members of the IRA whom the security forces had failed to arrest or had chosen not to arrest from lack of sufficient evidence. An appalling succession of reprisals then followed with the Loyalists quite often killing the 'wrong' people. A particularly bad incident was the explosion in McGurk's bar in December 1971 when fifteen people were killed.

Although the vast majority of the murders took place in Ulster, the Republic did not escape unscathed. Two car bomb attacks in Dublin which claimed a large number of casualties have never been explained. One occurred in November 1971, with forty people injured. The second was in December when eighty-three people were injured, two of them fatally. The UDA denied any involvement. So did the IRA. The reason for suspecting all paramilitary organizations, including those that were republicans, was that the Dail was at that time debating an amendment to its Offences against the State Act which is directed against terrorism. As was, perhaps, to be expected some republicans placed the blame on the SAS. The matter has never been cleared up. In 1974 there were two more terrible car bomb outrages in the Republic, one in Dublin which killed twenty-two people, and one in Monaghan which killed five. In both cases, Protestant paramilitary forces must have been responsible.

THE END OF THE ULSTER PARLIAMENT

It is possible that the disappointing aftermath of the policy of internment to which Faulkner was so committed was one of the factors influencing Prime Minister Edward Heath when he decided, in 1972, to withdraw responsibility for security from Stormont. The more immediate factor was the political reaction at home and abroad to the shooting of thirteen young men in Derry on 30 January of that year. As 'Bloody Sunday' was to have such important consequences, it is appropriate to record the main course of events. The occasion was an illegal NICRA demonstration organized at a time at which the situation in Derry was particularly tense. Hume thought it 'a highly dangerous exercise' and refused to take part.[15] The local army commander decided to keep the demonstrators out of the city centre where young hooligans from the Bogside had recently done much damage and an army barricade was set up. The peaceful vanguard of the marchers turned aside at this point and had passed out of sight before trouble was started by the hooligan rearguard who at once attacked the soldiers. 'Not only stones, but objects such as fire grates and metal rods used as lances were thrown violently at the troops in a most dangerous way.'[16] This was not the peaceful crowd of some subsequent accounts, but it would also be absurd to claim that assaults of this kind could justify a volley of fire. As Harkness has observed: 'The truth of how 13 people came to be shot by paratroopers after an illegal march in Derry on 30 January 1972 will be disputed and perhaps never fully resolved.'[17] According to some of the soldiers and some of the witnesses, shots had first been fired at the troops. This charge was, however, hotly denied. The victims, for their part, were apparently unarmed and the forensic evidence failed to establish whether they had or had not discharged firearms. What seems beyond doubt is that some soldiers were under the impression that they had been fired upon, and they had reason to anticipate that this would happen for the IRA were adept at using a human screen in their attacks. In such circumstances, it would not have been surprising if one or two shots had been fired. A fusillade was a different matter. Lord Widgery, who conducted a subsequent official investigation, was satisfied that shots had been fired from the crowd, although he also concluded that the return fire had 'bordered on the reckless'[18] – surely an astonishing example of English understatement. No action was taken against the soldiers. The whole investigation was understandably denounced as whitewash by republicans, North and South.

Immediately after the tragedy took place, the British Embassy in Dublin was burned down, the Irish Ambassador was withdrawn from London, and the Irish Minister for Foreign Affairs (Hillery) was sent to the United Nations and Washington in order to discuss with friendly governments how 'to end the reign of terror which Britain is perpetrating against our people'. The Irish people, he said, 'are suddenly confronted with a brutal clarification of Britain's policies in our country.'[19] All this was nonsense, and presumably known to be so by all concerned.

The moral was rather that a sustained campaign of urban guerilla warfare may lead ultimately to a breakdown of discipline and to some over-reaction on the part of the security forces under attack. For long periods the troops had sustained a bombardment of stones and petrol bombs without using the weapons with which they could so easily have dispersed their tormentors. Moreover, in Derry itself, in the two weeks preceding Bloody Sunday, over 300 shots had been fired and almost 100 nail bombs had been thrown at the security forces.[20] With nerves kept on edge, there is always the danger of over-reaction, which will lead to more bitterness and more violence. It is also true that from the viewpoint of a hardline practitioner of urban guerilla warfare, such an outcome would appear satisfactory. From that point of view, Bloody Sunday could be cynically regarded as quite a success.

The responsibility for the behaviour of the security forces had rested on that occasion with the British army commanders, not with the Unionist government. Nor did it rest with the RUC. On the contrary, the Chief Superintendent in Derry had strongly advized against the tactics being followed by the paratroopers on the ground that these might lead to trouble, but his advice had not been accepted. Nevertheless the Heath Government decided that the time had come to remove the responsibility for security from Stormont to Westminster, and Faulkner was informed accordingly. When he and his colleagues resigned rather than accept, the parliament was prorogued and devolution after the 1920 model came to an end. It was scarcely surprising that this outcome provoked much indignation. Even if the case for suspending Stormont were to be accepted – and the Unionists of course did not do so – the suspension had been carried out at the wrong time for what appeared to be the wrong reason. The republicans, for their part, were correspondingly jubilant. Their revolt against Stormont had proved to be a resounding success. Moreover the 'Brits', who had shown no sign of wanting to remain in Ulster, might now be induced to leave altogether if the pressure were maintained.

In retrospect, it seems probable that, from their own point of view, the Unionists were wrong in not accepting the surrender of responsibility for law and order.[21] If the Westminster Government really wanted to hold that hot potato, they could have been allowed to do so. The Northern Ireland Parliament would then have remained in being and the Unionist position would have been a good deal stronger than it proved to be under Direct Rule.

NEGOTIATING WITH THE TERRORISTS

A further point of difficulty was the belief entertained by some British politicians that a settlement might be negotiated with the IRA. The pacesetter, initially, was the leader of the Opposition, Harold Wilson. In March 1972, he and Merlyn Rees met the Provo leaders in the course of a visit to Dublin – much to the dismay of the Irish Government.[22] The IRA demand for an almost immediate British withdrawal from the North was obviously unrealistic, but Wilson retained his illusions – or, as some might say, retained his desire to win the favour of the Irish vote in England. Of more immediate importance, the new Secretary of State, William Whitelaw, also decided to explore possibilities and contact was made in early 1972 through the SDLP and through the officials in his new secretariat, the Northern Ireland Office (NIO). As a gesture of goodwill, paramilitary prisoners were given military status, an act that was to be reversed much later but only at the cost of hunger strikes. When the IRA proclaimed a truce, Whitelaw announced that 'Her Majesty's forces will obviously reciprocate'[23] – a most illuminating remark which showed how the Government interpreted the duty of a state to maintain law and order. The Provo leaders were then flown to London for secret talks which proved futile, and the truce came to an end. Still in opposition, Wilson persisted, met the Provos once more and passed on a reassuring message to Heath on the very eve of one of the worst of the IRA outrages. This was the planting of some twenty bombs in Belfast, including one in a crowded bus station, on what became known as Bloody Friday. It is right to refer with some emphasis to the horror of that day, when the remains of innocent people had to be scraped off the pavements and put into plastic bags as a consequence of the action of republicans who claimed to be Irish patriots. The particular reason for doing so is that Bloody Friday is not remembered in the same way as Bloody Sunday – a contrast which is a tribute to the efficiency of nationalist propaganda.

With his illusions now apparently dispelled by this event, Whitelaw launched at last the much-needed operation against the no-go areas which was successful in partially restoring the authority of the security forces, although these areas were still not to be policed in anything like the normal way – and are not so even in the late 1980s.

The attempts to negotiate with the IRA betrayed a basic failure to understand that extreme republicans have no interest in compromise, only in domination. The harm done by entering into negotiations with them is threefold. First, the terrorists are encouraged to believe that the enemy is weakening, and they will therefore repeat and even intensify their pressure. Secondly, the terrorists are made to appear both more respectable and more powerful in the eyes of the Catholic population. Thirdly, Protestant opinion is outraged and may also become more favourable to the loyalist paramilitaries.

Unfortunately London ministers had not learned their lesson. In 1975, with Labour again in power and Merlyn Rees as Secretary of State, a new truce was negotiated after a meeting had been held in the Republic between a group of Protestant churchmen and the Provo leadership.[24] In this case, negotiations were carried so far that incident centres were established in a number of sensitive places in Belfast where civil servants could communicate at once with their superiors on the one hand and the IRA on the other in order, if possible, to prevent any escalation of violence. The corollary was a much reduced army presence and it was widely reported, perhaps with some exaggeration, that the IRA had taken over quite openly the task of policing the Catholic areas – even, in some reports, to the extent of acting as traffic policemen. Meanwhile talks between the Government and the IRA continued, though to little effect.[25]

The army believed that the truce gave the IRA a breathing space and allowed them to regroup. A different verdict on this period has, however, been given by Bishop and Maillie who point out that the IRA, no longer engaged in fighting the army, was locked in a bitter struggle with the Protestant paramilitaries and also with the Official IRA.[26] Once again some light is thrown on what might happen if the troops were to be withdrawn from Northern Ireland. For a time, the troops were, in effect, at least partially 'out', but the conflict between the different local factions then intensified. Thus, although the truce lasted for much of 1975, more people were killed (247) than in 1974 (216).[27]

The end of the so-called truce and of the futile negotiations was to be followed by a change within the IRA command which did not bode well for the future. For there was a shift of power from Dublin to the Northern Command under Adams and McGuinness with the result that the policy followed was to become, if anything, even more harsh than it had been before.

Let me conclude this chapter by observing that the terrorist campaign of recent years has differed substantially from those of earlier periods. Ireland, both North and South, is well enough accustomed to civil unrest and communal violence, but the disturbances that began in 1968 have persisted so long as to call for some special explanation. There is an obvious contrast between these events and those of 1956–62, when the IRA was launching an offensive. In that previous period the campaign was fought out between the security forces and the armed republicans without involving ordinary citizens to any significant extent. It was, so to speak, an old-fashioned campaign. The sequence of events from October 1968 onwards may be regarded as a textbook example of a well-planned exercise in modern guerilla warfare: begin by identifying some strongly felt grievances; exaggerate these grievances and give them intense publicity; ignore reforms or maintain that they are bogus; organize demonstrations and confrontations with the police; provoke police reaction and hope that it will be over-reaction; then do everything possible, with television assistance, to discredit the security forces, undermine confidence in them and weaken their own morale; try to create a situation where the police must either tolerate no-go areas or use force to end them on a scale that could be represented as grossly oppressive; establish the authority of the paramilitary force in the no-go areas by superseding the law courts as well as the police and by developing various forms of independent social policies; create bases in these areas from which guerillas can operate and seek to achieve the situation described by Chairman Mao where the guerilla can move around as easily and as unnoticed as a fish in the water; steadily raise the level of violence; rely upon new grievances being created as the police or the army persist with the increasingly difficult task of maintaining law and order; attempt, in all these ways, to wear down the government's resolve to maintain the struggle. The course of action so roughly sketched was, in effect, the course followed in Ulster.

We must assume that the IRA leadership is familiar with the techniques of urban guerilla warfare and has been ready to apply them when thought appropriate. It would be going much too far, however, to assert that the whole campaign has been master-minded from the outset by experts in the art. There does not appear to be positive evidence to support that view. But the whole campaign could scarcely have been more effective if it had, in fact, been planned in that way.

17

Power-sharing and the Council of Ireland – a Fatal Mixture?

The abolition of Stormont was to be followed by a long period of centralized government from Whitehall during which the electors of the Province and their parliamentary representatives could not exercise the normal rights of democratic government. There was some irony in this situation, as will be appreciated when it is recalled that inadequate minority representation in local government affairs had been one of the principal complaints of the civil rights movement. Under the new regime established in 1972, neither the majority nor the minority were to have any effective say over those matters that had previously been Stormont's responsibility, nor over the more important of the functions formerly exercised by local government. The only exception has been the brief period of devolution with power-sharing in 1973–4. It was a remarkable outcome to a campaign for better representation that representative government should be withdrawn almost completely. Some explanation is clearly required before we go on to look at the power-sharing experiment.

DIRECT RULE – AN OPPORTUNITY MISSED

When the Parliament of Northern Ireland was suspended, its former legislative functions were returned to Westminster. As it happened, the very last piece of provincial legislation had provided for the transfer to Stormont of much of the work formerly done by local government. This transfer had been carried out in accordance with the recommendation of the Macrory Report[1], for it was hoped in this way to reduce the risk of sectarian complaints about local boundaries and of sectarian complaints about the conduct of local business. Before the Ulster Parliament could assume these new responsibilities, it had ceased to exist, and both its old and its new responsibilities were transferred to Westminster. This transfer need not have implied the loss of responsible government for legislation relating to Northern Ireland could have been the subject of debate and vote at Westminster. As I have maintained in the previous chapter, the right course of action in 1969, after the troops had been deployed, would have been the suspension of regional representative government. That opportunity was missed but there was another chance to follow this course in 1972 after the Northern Ireland Parliament had, in effect, been abolished. Instead Westminster resorted to a form of Direct Rule which was clearly intended to be only a temporary expedient – but has lasted for sixteen years. Legislation relating specifically to Northern Ireland is passed by Orders in Council which can be debated, usually at night, but cannot be amended. Although some attempt may be made to sound opinion before an Order is drafted, this can be little substitute for the normal committee procedure and a second reading. Not only is the democratic process weakened, but such special treatment stigmatizes Northern Ireland as being, not a normal part of the United Kingdom, but a kind of colonial territory.

Constitutional stability was highly desirable and might have been achieved by adopting the Scottish model of administrative devolution, perhaps with some modifications appropriate to local conditions. Although Direct Rule in the form actually adopted has survived so long, it has failed to convey the assurance of stability that is so crucially important. For it has never been regarded as a permanent solution, and the succession of constitutional initiatives taken unsuccessfully over the years has perpetuated the feeling of uncertainty when stability was required. The harm done has been all the greater because Westminster has conveyed the implicit message that its desire to divest itself from direct responsibility for part of the public business conducted in the Province is a manifestation, not so much of any deep attachment to regional democracy, as of a desire to start the process of complete withdrawal.

DEVOLUTION WITH POWER-SHARING

The attempts to restore representative government within Northern Ireland have encountered the familiar obstacle that disagreement about the existence of the state itself could once more create a situation where the representatives of the Catholic minority would be excluded from government – or would exclude themselves. As we have seen, it was this basic disagreement that had ensured a Unionist majority at Stormont and could do so again even if members were elected by proportional representation. It should be noted that Faulkner had already put forward a proposal designed to ease this difficulty even before the old Parliament was prorogued. The arrangement he suggested, with the support of his party, was the establishment of three new functional committees, in addition to the existing Public Accounts Committee. The Opposition would always hold at least two of the salaried chairmanships. 'These committees', he explained, 'would be involved in policy-making at the formative stage, in reviewing and probing the performance of the Executive, and in giving expert consideration to legislation.'[2] It was an imaginative suggestion which, had it been made some years earlier, might have had an important effect on political events. Even in 1971 it was a constructive proposal. After some hesitation, the SDLP gave its qualified and – as it seemed – slightly reluctant approval. For the first time at Stormont, talks then began involving all the parties. It was a hopeful rapprochement but the SDLP brought it to an end in protest against the shooting of two unarmed Catholics by the army in the course of an encounter with the IRA in Londonderry. Hume's call for an inquiry was refused by Whitehall. The SDLP seized the opportunity and, with a certain want of logic, withdrew from talks with the Unionists at Stormont.

It was against this background that the new British administration in 1972 approached the task of devising an 'initiative', shortly after Direct Rule had begun. The Conservative Secretary of State (Whitelaw) was satisfied that some institutional arrangement for power-sharing was required and a committee system would not be adequate. The new proposals would provide, not just for proportional representation in elections for an Assembly, but also for something of the kind in the composition of the proposed Executive. Provision should also be made for the recognition of the 'Irish dimension' – a fatal addition, as we shall see. The Green Paper which set out these proposals was followed by discussions that led to the Northern Ireland Constitution Act of 1973 and thus, in June of that year, to the election by PR of a new Assembly.

The election revealed how deeply the Unionists were divided, and a faction opposed to the new departure allied itself to the parties led, respectively, by Paisley and Craig. Some of the protesters were noisy and even violent but this, as it turned out, did no good to their cause with the Protestant population. For it would be wrong to suppose that the Protestants were totally opposed from the outset to any form of power-sharing. There were some problems initially with the SDLP, the party that claimed to represent the Catholic minority, for this party was still supporting a rent and rates strike and was recommending its followers not to support the police. Moreover, there was the question of the oath of loyalty to the constitution which republicans might not wish to take. Sufficient progress was to be made, however, to allow the Faulkner Unionists, the SDLP, and the Alliance to set about the task of forming an executive. There was much haggling about which party should have which department but, by the beginning of 1974, the new executive was in being. Thus began an experiment in double-barrelled PR – that is to say, PR in both Assembly and Executive. It lasted until 29 May when it was brought to an end by the strike organized by the Ulster Workers Council.

Proportional representation in the Executive went much further than Faulkner's proposed committee system. Would it work? If the political future were still to be dominated by the basic constitutional issue, the Executive might be divided on traditional issues with the locus shifted to the Executive itself – issues on which agreement might still not be achieved, even if negotiations were helped in some measure by the personal relationships that had been established. If unresolved, how would such disagreements, or basic disagreements on any other issue, for that matter, be dealt with? Under the Faulkner committee proposal, the majority party would have the final say. Would this also be so under power-sharing with the final crunch coming at the Executive level? There would still be a Secretary of State and he would presumably have to cope with any such deadlock, so that the business of government would not be halted. Such intervention would, however, amount to failure. These were real difficulties but the experiment seemed to be well worth trying – given the assumption that representative government at the regional level was desirable. It was an almost unique experiment, somewhat remotely suggested by Swiss practice under very different conditions. In Ulster it was to be tried out in an area torn by civil strife. The basic disagreement about the existence of the state which created the situation in which power-sharing seemed appropriate, was also bound to make power-sharing hard to operate. Moreover, Westminster's insistence on PR in the Executive contrasted with the resolute rejection of PR for Westminster elections by both the Conservative and the Labour parties. Indeed, PR was even to be ruled out for election for the Assemblies proposed for Scotland and Wales in 1978. The fact that the Conservatives would have had little chance of ever forming an alternative government in those two countries did not seem to cause deep distress to the Labour Party. The Tories themselves were too frightened of establishing any precedent for PR to want to press the matter. Ulster people could therefore feel that they were being tested by a much more severe standard than that regarded as acceptable in Great Britain.[3]

The impression one gains is that the machinery of government worked well during this period in dealing with ordinary business, but this is no more than an impression from the sidelines. My own position on the sidelines was as a member of the Economic Council, an advisory body of ministers, trade unionists, civil servants and others which had been in operation since 1965. What was fascinating at these meetings was to see Faulkner and Hume sitting together at the head of the table and discussing the economic problems of Ulster in a cool, businesslike and friendly fashion. There can be no doubt that their experience in government was an instructive one for the SDLP. During the fifty years of the old Stormont regime, the Nationalists had been in opposition – when they were not simply boycotting the meetings of parliament. They had never had any responsibility for formulating or for executing policy. They could now, perhaps, begin to appreciate that official business at Stormont was not wholly dominated by sectarian affairs but was largely about matters of common concern to the Ulster people, whatever their respective religious or political allegiances. Faulkner was later to quote, as an example, the question directed at one of the Alliance ministers about their intention with regard to the physically handicapped. 'This, it seemed to me, was what the Executive and the Assembly were all about – getting down to the task of providing a better way of life for all our citizens and dealing with the bread and butter issues that mattered.'[4] I could not help reflecting that Hume, for his part, must have been forced to see that the lack of sufficient new industry in Derry was not simply the consequence of Unionist spite. The SDLP were also to learn that the civil servants were not the mere lackeys of the Orange Order. Faulkner recorded how John Hume and Paddy Devlin admitted that 'the Northern Ireland civil service had been much maligned.'[5] The Executive appears to have been able to deal smoothly enough with its devolved responsibilities, more smoothly than some cabinets in Britain based on majority rule have been able to do. What would have happened over a longer period is, of course, only a matter of speculation.

THE REASONS FOR FAILURE

The collapse of the Assembly is now often attributed to the bitter opposition of reactionary Orangemen, assumed to be led by Ian Paisley, who were prepared to stop at nothing rather than permit power to be shared with Roman Catholics. With varying degrees of elaboration this is the explanation that forms part of 'the conventional wisdom' outside Ulster. In media comments, a brief and categorical assertion to this effect is usually thought to be adequate: 'power-sharing with the Catholics was brought to an end by the Ulster Workers Council strike'. That strike was indeed the immediate cause of its collapse. To leave the matter there, however, would be quite wrong. It would be not only bad history but would endorse a deep misunderstanding of the Ulster situation from which new and possibly harmful errors of judgement could well arise.

The decisive issues can be divided into three groups:

1 Irish unity *versus* the unity of the United Kingdom, with Ulster included as part of it.
2 Security: both the IRA's response to the new situation and the attitude to security policy of the Irish Government and of the political parties in the South.
3 The sharing of power in the Executive between the political parties and the problems to which this might give rise.

There is good reason to suppose that, if the outcome had been more satisfactory under (1) and (2), then (3) would have survived for a much longer period, if not indefinitely.

THE 'IRISH DIMENSION'

The first point to stress is that the SDLP was, and is, deeply committed to the objective of a united Irish republic. Its leaders had reaffirmed this attitude in their statement of policy, 'Towards a New Ireland', published in 1972. Britain must declare its intention to withdraw and meanwhile there should be a London–Dublin condominium to supervise a coalition government in Ulster. This was scarcely a helpful prelude to the introduction of power-sharing. Hume, for his part, had adopted a narrow and unhelpful line when he declared that, of the three possibilities for discussion – integration with Britain, a restructured North and Irish unity – 'the only viable one is the last'.[6] But a 'restructured North' was the objective of power-sharing and bald assertions of the kind made by some of the SDLP leaders did nothing to help the Faulknerite Unionists in their attempt to persuade the large Northern majority that power-sharing deserved their support. Hume was to repeat statements of this kind on various subsequent occasions and advised the Irish Government not to yield 'to the false liberalism of placating the Unionists'.[7]

The SDLP made a serious mistake in deciding to boycott a poll held in March 1973 in order to establish what proportion of the population wished to remain within the United Kingdom. It was the belief of the British Government that by establishing clearly the attitude of the majority in the North by polls to be held every ten years, the unending dispute about the border could be set aside in order to allow business to proceed along more constructive lines. They were to find that they had seriously underestimated the intransigence of the SDLP. The boycott it recommended appears to have been fairly well observed by the Catholic minority – whose appearance at the polling booths could in any case have exposed them to punishment by the IRA – and reduced the participation of the population of voting age to 58 per cent. This SDLP boycott showed that, notwithstanding their own claims to fair representation, they did not wish any prominence to be given to a majority vote if it went against their nationalist objectives, and the boycott was helpful to them because it then allowed them to say that the test of opinion could not be taken seriously when two-fifths of the people had declined to record their views. The adoption of this attitude, however, was another discouraging prelude to power-sharing. Moreover, notwithstanding SDLP abstention, the poll conveyed a clear message. Of those who participated 98 per cent were in favour of remaining within the United Kingdom; only 1 per cent wanted to join the Republic. Even if the Protestant poll had been as high as 80 per cent of the Protestant population, it could be inferred that between a fifth and a quarter of the Catholic population had also voted in favour of preserving the union with Britain.[8] This need occasion no surprise except perhaps that the percentage was not even higher, as the opinion polls would lead one to expect (see chapter 21).

The Westminster Government had come to believe that the 'Irish dimension' should be recognized by reviving the idea of a Council of Ireland which had been contained in the Government of Ireland Act of 1920. Crucial questions had then to be answered. How should such a Council be organized? How would its members be selected? Should it be merely consultative or should it have executive powers? These were among the matters so hotly debated at the Sunningdale Conference (December 1973) between the heads of the Westminster and Dublin Governments and the leaders of all the Ulster parties apart from an important group of recalcitrant Unionists. It was finally resolved that there should be two tiers: (a) a Council of Ministers drawn from the Irish Government and the Northern Ireland Executive with executive powers which could, however, be used only with unanimous agreement; and (b) an advisory Consultative Assembly consisting of members of the Dail and of the Northern Ireland Assembly. There was to be a permanent secretariat. The illustrative list of topics with which it could deal was largely concerned with social and economic issues but also included the police. Would this be a decisive step towards Irish unity, especially if the second tier were to be established? Unity, after all, had been the explicit purpose of the Council of Ireland proposed in 1920. There was bound to be bitter hostility to any such Council in the North. Was it really worthwhile to incur this hostility? Faulkner maintained that the first tier of the Council would be innocuous because unanimity was required. But was it worth the risk its inclusion might entail for the acceptability of power-sharing in the North?

The constitutional guarantee

The UK Government hoped that the guarantee contained in Article 5 of the Sunningdale Agreement would dispel any anxiety on the part of the Unionists about the future constitutional position of Northern Ireland. For in this article the British Government affirmed its support for the wishes of the majority and went on to say: 'The present status of Northern Ireland is that it is part of the United Kingdom. If in the future the majority of the people of Northern Ireland should indicate a wish to become part of a united Ireland, the British Government would support that wish.' Unfortunately the Irish Government could not bring itself to admit that Northern Ireland was part of the United Kingdom, but agreed that 'there could be no change in the status of Northern Ireland until a majority of the people of

Northern Ireland desired a change in that status'. The fact that these two pledges were differently worded weakened their force, but the real trouble was to come. In Dublin, Kevin Boland, a hard-line republican imperialist, challenged the legality of Article 5 of the Agreement on the ground that it was in conflict with Article 2 of the Constitution of the Republic which already claimed the whole of the island. The Coalition Government responsible for the Agreement (Fine Gael and Labour) then protested that the guarantee did not really imply any abandonment of the view that Northern Ireland was properly part of the Republic. The Attorney General pleaded that: 'Any person living in this island and knowing our history could not possibly construe the declaration as meaning we did not lay claim over the Six Counties.'[9] The Prime Minister (Cosgrave) protested that the guarantee referred only to the *de facto* position. The Government's position was upheld by the Supreme Court.

What did this mean? De Valera had once explained to the more extreme republicans that the Twenty-Six Counties lacked the military power to take the Six. Was Cosgrave saying no more than this? That is to say, was he merely recognizing a fact he could not alter and representing this recognition as a concession? What was still implied was that Ulster had no *right* to remain outside the Republic. No official pronouncement has conceded any such right since the Boundary Agreement of 1925 was superseded by the Constitution of 1937. For to do so would involve a conflict with the 'right' to the whole of Ireland claimed for the Republic in Article 2. This was the clause that had caused much trouble already and was to do so again at the time of the Anglo-Irish Agreement. The pragmatic Lemass had made some attempt to have it revised in 1967 but had failed to do so. It was now reasserted with an over-riding force that at once depreciated the Sunningdale guarantee in Unionist eyes. The Unionists had already been suspicious. They were well aware that the SDLP was essentially an all-Ireland party and that the Council of Ireland was regarded by them as a first step.

At this point the British Government should have submitted a formal request for clarification. Faulkner, for his part, might also have been well advised to say that he would be obliged to resign unless the status of the constitutional guarantee contained in the Sunningdale Agreement was unequivocally restored, if necessary by a revision of the Republic's constitution. Bleakley, a Northern Ireland Labour Party member, did in fact recommend that that action should be taken, but was not heeded. When the British Labour Party came into power in 1974 the new ministerial team was not initially trusted by the Unionist population. Merlyn Rees, the Secretary of State, had been involved, together with Harold Wilson, in discussions with the IRA. Much worse, Stanley Orme, his second in command, was well known to be a supporter of Irish unity. Worst of all, from the Unionist viewpoint, was the fact that Wilson himself, the new Prime Minister, had expressed his support in the past for a united Irish republic.

THE ULSTER WORKERS' STRIKE

The second reason for growing hostility to the Sunningdale Agreement in Ulster was the continuing violence. Power-sharing did not bring peace. No one should ever have expected it to do so, for the IRA was, and is, no more interested in reforms than any other body of revolutionaries. During the period of power-sharing they actually increased their offensive. This intensification of terrorism would no doubt have been borne with patience if the Republic, for its part, had demonstrated that it was going to make a new effort to prevent its territory from being used as a comparatively safe haven by the IRA. It did not do so.

The Irish Government, for its part, was gravely at fault in continuing to withhold the long-demanded undertaking that suspected terrorists would be extradited for trial in Northern Ireland or in Great Britain, as might be appropriate. The case for extradition, which was so much in harmony with the general trend of security policy in Europe, was strongly urged at Sunningdale by Basil McIvor, a Unionist minister, though with inadequate support from the Westminster side. Dublin would not yield. It was agreed, however, that use should be made of an old legal power which would allow an offender to be tried for a crime in the area in which he was apprehended even if the crime had been committed outside the territorial jurisdiction of the court. This concession did little to impress the hard-line opposition back in Ulster. Nor did the proposal to establish a joint law commission. In both cases their scepticism proved in the event to be justified.

It is scarcely surprising that, in the circumstances, popular opposition to the Agreement should have become so strong and so general. The Protestant population – or, to put the point differently – the British population of Northern Ireland – felt that their position in the United Kingdom had been made less secure and, in return, they had gained nothing. The Republic had made no concessions, for the guarantee it offered amounted to nothing more than the recognition of a state of affairs it lacked the power to alter. It had refused extradition. The security position had not been improved. On the contrary, IRA attacks had increased. Power-sharing had not been rejected out of hand except by the more extreme Unionists whose bully-boy tactics in the opening sessions of the Assembly had lost them much Protestant support. But, as the months passed, attitudes had begun to change. It was one thing to share power with Catholics. Theological differences were not really the issue. It was a different matter to share power with committed nationalists who were using the Sunningdale Agreement as a step towards a united Irish republic. The strike in which this resentment culminated was directed primarily against this proposal to institutionalize the Irish dimension which, it was feared, would constitute that first step.

Although Paisley and Craig were on the strike committee, the strike was not led or organized by them. (Indeed some of its leaders were inclined to treat them with scant respect.) This really was a *workers'* strike. It amounted to an overwhelming vote of opposition to the Sunningdale proposals. This fact deserves considerable emphasis. For there has been a persistent failure on the part of nationalists in the South to appreciate that support for the preservation of the union with Britain has come from the great mass of the Protestant people. Naturally, this is a fact that the IRA, for its part, has preferred to ignore, but some leaders of the SDLP have also been guilty of self-deception. This appears to have been true even of John Hume himself, a Derry man who may not have had the same understanding of the industrial working class as Gerry Fitt or Paddy Devlin. Thus Bew and Patterson have remarked: 'From the constitutional nationalists of the SDLP to the Provisionals there was a consistent tendency to ignore the possibility of a substantial and relatively autonomous, Protestant mass response to anything construed as anti-partitionist.'[10] The lesson conveyed by the strike organized by the Ulster Workers' Council (UWC), should have been learned in Dublin and Londonderry, and, not least, in Westminster. The Anglo-Irish Agreement, and the procedures leading up to it, were to show only too clearly in 1985 that this had not been the case.

The strike might have been averted by the rejection of the Council of Ireland or even by toning down what was proposed. A toning-down was Faulkner's tactic and he and his supporters, backed by the Alliance, worked hard to persuade the SDLP to accept a modified version by dropping the proposed second tier, i.e. the advisory Consultative Assembly that was to consist of members of the Dail and of the Northern Ireland Assembly. They finally succeeded but it was too late. The SDLP had delayed too long and when it yielded – under pressure to do so from Dublin – the strike had already begun.

The Secretary of State, Merlyn Rees, was much criticized for alleged weakness in dealing with the strikers. Faulkner maintained that the army should have been told to remove the barricades. But there was little hope that any such action would have been effective against a mass opposition and, in any case, the crucial issue was the partial stoppage by the electricity workers. There proved to be no way of replacing them and keeping the supply going. The workers threatened to cut the supply down still more and it was feared that the social consequences would be horrendous – perhaps with the sewerage system disrupted and sewage appearing on the streets. Would they really have gone so far? Clearly there was a test of nerve. Apart from surrender, the only course for the Executive and, ultimately, the Secretary of State would have been to challenge them to do their worst – at the expense of their own people. In the event, the Faulkner Unionists resigned and the executive collapsed.

In the light of all the facts, it must be recognized that the action of the UWC was a good deal more understandable than is conceded in what has become the widely accepted account of events. But there is no escape from the conclusion that their action did far more harm than good to the unionist cause it was meant to defend.[11] A wiser course might have been to allow the Sunningdale proposals to be adopted, but with the intention of taking action later if it should appear that the Council of Ireland was really becoming a danger to the union with Britain. As Faulkner most sincerely believed, this danger was not inevitable. Indeed the proposed deliberations of the Council, while of some limited practical value, could also have shown very clearly that the scope for useful joint economic action was slight, that there were important differences in social legislation (e.g. on divorce and contraception) that could not be removed and that, on the crucially important issue of security, the Republic was not prepared to give the full cooperation its fellow member might reasonably expect. An example was the inherent contradiction between Dublin's demand for a Council of Ireland to promote goodwill and unity, and its refusal to extradite terrorists who were wanted for the most brutal atrocities committed on British soil. The Ulster members of the Council of Ireland could have turned a spotlight on this inconsistency.

All this, of course, is speculation. What is clear, however, is that by resorting to a preemptive strike, the Ulster-British exposed themselves to misrepresentation and denunciation as 'fascists'. Moreover, their attackers could assert that these

Protestants in Ulster were refusing to share power with Catholics, thus demonstrating the depth of their religious bigotry. Few people in Great Britain, or in America, would understand what was meant by 'power-sharing' in this particular context, or would appreciate that the point at issue was one of self-determination rather than theology. Unfortunately, neither the UWC nor the Unionist politicians succeeded in explaining to a wider audience that power-sharing would have met with far less disapproval without the proposed Council of Ireland.[12] By contrast the SDLP seemed moderate and statesmanlike, although in fact they might have saved the situation if they had not been so reluctant to accept even some reduction in the scope of this Council of Ireland. The Dublin politicians, for their part, had conceded nothing at Sunningdale but had managed, not for the first time, to conceal an intransigence that was even more firm and unyielding than that of many Unionists. Thus they appear to be reasonable persons confronting 'the thugs and bullies of the North', to use Harold Wilson's phrase. This Southern pose seems to have been widely accepted as genuine in Great Britain.

There was to be a re-run of much of this in 1985/6 after the Anglo-Irish Agreement had been introduced.

18

Constitutional Initiatives and Hunger Strikes

During the eleven years between the collapse of the Sunningdale Agreement and the announcement of the Anglo-Irish Agreement in November 1985, new attempts were made to establish devolved government in Ulster and, in the Republic, the New Ireland Forum was created in order to provide for inter-party discussion of the political future of the island. The initiatives taken in the North were to fail, but the deliberations of the Forum were to have an important influence on future policy, in particular on the shape of the Anglo-Irish Agreement.

Although it is scarcely necessary to describe in any detail the proposals put forward in the North, the main course of events must be briefly recorded, partly in order to show how the gap between the parties of the majority and those of the minority had widened even more since the early 1970s. It was not surprising that this widening should have occurred after the events leading to the collapse of the power-sharing Assembly. The Secretary of State (Merlyn Rees) proposed that a Constitutional Convention should be elected which would allow the various Ulster parties to express their own views about possible constitutional arrangements and find their own solution, instead of having one prepared for them by Britain. Elections were held in May 1975, but the convention was unproductive and was dissolved in March of the following year. The various Unionist groups had then shown themselves to be united in their opposition to any Irish dimension, but were divided about power-sharing.[1] The Ulster Workers' Council (UWC), for its part, had been hostile not so much to power-sharing as to an institutionalized expression of the 'Irish dimension' that could be regarded as a prelude to political unity, but this organization had existed for a specific purpose and soon disappeared. The SDLP, as might be expected, wanted power-sharing in the sense of PR in the Executive and so did the Alliance. The SDLP also continued to press for the Irish dimension. The gap between the parties was too large and no agreement was reached.

In 1976 the new Labour Party Secretary of State, Roy Mason, set his face against further constitutional 'initiatives' in such circumstances and concentrated his attention on improving security and strengthening the economy. He was also at pains to insist that Northern Ireland was part of the United Kingdom and would not be abandoned. It was a clear-headed policy based on experience.

When the Conservatives took office in 1979, it was reasonable to suppose that two changes would be made: (i) Northern Ireland business at Westminster would in future be handled in the same way as Scottish business, and (ii) an elected body of some sort would be made responsible for the more important local government functions taken away from the local authorities and transferred to the old Stormont Parliament on the very eve of its being prorogued in 1972. In the Convention discussions, James Molyneaux – who favoured full integration with Great Britain – had proposed that a top tier of local government be established for the Province as a whole, but had been turned down by Rees. The Conservative Shadow Secretary of State, Airey Neave, had also supported this course of action and it was included in the Conservatives' 1979 election manifesto. But Neave was murdered by the INLA, perhaps the most important assassination carried out by any republican group over the whole period of the disturbances. When the victorious Conservatives came into office they chose to ignore their election pledge. Nor did they retain Mason's policy. New initiatives were to follow.

Bew and Patterson may be right when they drily observe that: 'The desire of ordinary people for new local government is usually less burning than local politicians assume.'[2] Nevertheless, an outlet could have been provided for some expression of local views about local affairs and, more important, by reforming the conduct of Ulster business at Westminster, a greater element of stability would have been provided in an environment where stability was badly needed.

The new Secretary of State (Humphrey Atkins) did, however, put forward a proposal for devolved government with three possible ways of allowing the minority a measure of effective participation: some form of PR, which need not be arithmetical, for choosing the Executive; weighted voting; a bicameral arrangement providing checks and balances.[3] It was an ingenious scheme but was not acceptable to the SDLP because it made no provision for the 'Irish dimension'. The party split after this proposal was announced, and John Hume became leader in place of Gerry Fitt. With Fitt's departure which followed that of Paddy Devlin, the SDLP became even less 'Red' than it had been and more darkly 'Green', a change that did not bode well for subsequent agreement with the Protestant majority. It is important to appreciate that the SDLP feared the loss of votes to Sinn Fein, which was no longer proscribed – a change of dubious wisdom which had been made by Rees. This fear was and continues to be an important factor.

A further initiative was taken by the next Secretary of State, James Prior, who proposed an Assembly with powers yet to be determined and with the possibility that these powers could be extended with the passage of time – 'rolling devolution'.[4] The legislation that followed brought the proposed Assembly into being, but the SDLP, like Sinn Fein, refused to take the seats they had won. The Assembly had been expected to reach agreement on how devolved powers might be exercised with a 70 per cent majority required for this purpose, but in the absence of the SDLP, no devolution was permitted to take place. The Assembly was therefore restricted to the role of commenting, through its committees, on the work of the Northern Ireland departments, and this function was in fact well performed as can be seen by reading its reports. The Assembly was, however, abolished shortly after the conclusion of the Anglo-Irish Agreement, which its members had criticized – an ill-considered act on the part of Westminster for this was an occasion when it was particularly important to have an outlet for the expression of Unionist views, even if hostile.

Meanwhile there had been a new development in the relationship between Westminster and Dublin. At a summit meeting between the Prime Minister and the Taoiseach in 1980, recent progress in joint discussions at the official level, mainly concerned with economic issues, was noted, and it was decided to continue to cooperate by having a regular exchange of views about the totality of relationships. At a summit held in the following year, it was decided to set up an Anglo-Irish Intergovernmental Council which would meet at various levels. Further official meetings took place on economic issues, but the outcome has not been fully revealed – possibly because the scope for action between the two countries, both members of the EEC, was limited except with regard to matters of practical detail which, though useful, have little news value. Cooperation was not helped when a further change of government in Dublin brought Haughey back into power at the time of the war in the Falklands. After the sinking of the *Belgrano*, an Argentine warship, the Republic called for United Nations action *against* the British – a reversion to the traditional hostile posture of the republican movement. Subsequently, with the Falklands war over and Fitzgerald again in power in the Republic, the breach was healed. There was, however, a continuing difference of opinion about Northern Ireland. The British Government's 1982 proposals for devolution, described above, had been criticized on the ground that there was no provision for the Irish dimension. This problem, it was held, should be the concern of the Anglo-Irish Intergovernmental Council. Mrs Thatcher rejected any such suggestion and made her position clear in statements to the House. In view of what was to happen soon, it is appropriate to quote her remarks on two occasions:

no commitments exist on Her Majesty's Government to consult the Irish Government on matters affecting Northern Ireland.[5]

We try to work with the Republic of Ireland, because we believe that it is in the interests of the people of Northern Ireland to do so. The constitutional future of Northern Ireland is a matter for Northern Ireland and this Parliament, and for no one else.[6]

It is scarcely surprising in the light of such statements that the Ulster British should have felt themselves to be betrayed by the Anglo-Irish Agreement of 1985. The Prime Minister has, of course, rejected the notion that any betrayal had occurred and maintained that the consistency of her policy has been preserved.

The White Paper of 1982 that had preceded the establishment of the Assembly insisted (para. 21) that 'any new structures for the Government of Northern Ireland must be acceptable to both sides of the community.'[7] The same point was repeated in two other places (paras 39 and 42). The Assembly was not acceptable to the *minority* and, therefore, it remained a consultative body with no devolved authority. The application of the principle that acceptance must be forthcoming, at that stage deemed to be decisive, was to be neglected, as we shall see, when the Anglo-Irish Agreement – although not acceptable to the *majority* – was imposed on Northern Ireland in 1985.

HUNGER STRIKES

An important factor in Northern Ireland politics in the opening years of this decade was the decision by IRA prisoners to go on hunger strike in order to carry further their protest against the loss of 'special category status'. That status had been conferred upon internees when Whitelaw was Secretary of State and it allowed the prisoners, both republican and loyalist, to behave as though they were prisoners of war. The Government might indeed have asked the prisoners whether they were really serious in insisting that they were fighting a war and should be treated accordingly. For they had not been fighting in uniform and could be shot as *franctireurs*. As usual the terrorists liked to have it several ways at once.

The men in each 'cage' were under the command of their officers, drills took place and instruction classes were held. The prisoners were allowed to wear their own clothes. The Gardiner Committee held that the introduction of this special status had been a mistake and should be removed. When internment had been phased out by Merlyn Rees, all new prisoners were serving court sentences and the case for treating them like other prisoners seemed clear. After all no prisoner of war is tried in a court with defence counsel to support his case and with the chance of being declared 'innocent'. Prisoner-of-war status would also carry with it the prospect of release were peace declared – even if the peace did not last for long. The change to ordinary status, which involved the wearing of prison clothes was, however, bitterly resented by the republican prisoners and a substantial number 'went on the blanket' instead. They also behaved in a way which prevented routine sanitary procedures in their cells and the 'dirty strike' began. When negotiations with the authorities proved unsuccessful a hunger strike was started but was called off when it seemed that some agreement could be reached. The failure of this agreement led to a renewal of the hunger strike in March and the death, two months later, of Bobby Sands. Meanwhile he had been elected to the Westminster constituency of Fermanagh and South Tyrone in a by-election fought against a Unionist candidate in which the SDLP did not take part. That election presented Hume and his colleagues with an extreme instance of a problem that was to cause them so much trouble subsequently. To have put up a candidate would have had the effect of splitting the Catholic vote in a way that would probably have allowed the Unionist candidate to win. To refuse to do so laid the SDLP open to the charge of supporting an IRA terrorist.

The hunger strike went on and lasted until the autumn of 1981, by which time ten had died. The Government refused to yield to the pressure thus imposed upon them, in this respect following an example set by the Irish Government in 1946 when an IRA prisoner had been allowed to starve himself to death. The strikes were to demonstrate that by courage carried to the last extreme, determined prisoners could present the Government – any Government – with a grim dilemma. To yield would be to concede a defeat which would be followed, in all probability, by fresh demands. To resist would result in the deaths of prisoners and – even apart from any humane considerations – serious political harm could follow. The disapproval of the Catholic Church and the desperate pressure exerted by the families of prisoners have limited the use of this last-resort tactic, but there can be little doubt that the ten deaths won support for the republican cause, for a time at least, both in Ireland and abroad.

The next step by the republican leaders was the decision to take an active part in politics and, when elected, to abandon the old policy of abstention – with the exception, of course, of sitting in the 'foreign' House of Commons in London. From time to time, British politicians had expressed the hope that the republicans would turn to normal political activity but the response, when it came, was scarcely reassuring. 'Who here really believes that we can win the war through the ballot box?' demanded Danny Morrison at a republican gathering in 1981. 'But', he went on, 'will anyone here object if with a ballot paper in this hand and an Armalite in this hand we take power in Ireland?'[8]

The entry of Sinn Fein into local government politics has become a continuing problem for the SDLP which makes that party apprehensive of losing Catholic votes, and has put Unionist councillors in the unpleasant – and dangerous – position of having to serve with members of the propaganda wing of the IRA. It is scarcely surprising that some should ask why Sinn Fein, proscribed in Great Britain, is not proscribed in Northern Ireland as well.

THE NEW IRELAND FORUM

Let us now turn to developments in the Republic. In 1983 the New Ireland Forum began its deliberations on the political future of the island. It was an inter-party forum in which the SDLP was involved as well as the political parties of the Republic. Indeed Hume had been a principal initiator and played a leading role throughout.[9] The Unionist party of Northern Ireland were thus provided with a magnificent opportunity to state their case and, perhaps, to regain some of the sympathy lost in Great Britain by the UWC strike. They could have welcomed the establishment of the Forum and expressed their readiness to take part in an open exchange of views, and the organizers could not have repelled them without a disastrous loss of public esteem everywhere. The Unionist leaders could then have followed one of two courses. They could have attended sessions of the Forum and pressed, very properly, for reasoned answers to some basic questions. Thus the economic implications of unity could have been raised and the Republic's political leaders could have been asked to describe and elucidate the practical means by which they would hope to meet the undeniably serious difficulties that would then arise. They could also have raised the question of neutrality. As supporters of the Western Alliance, the Unionists could have explained that they would be deeply perturbed by any political change that would deprive it of the bases at its disposal in Northern Ireland. Would there be a consensus in the Republic in support of membership of the alliance? On both issues they could have counted on throwing the political leaders of the Republic – and of the SDLP – into some confusion. The other course of action would have been to say, at the very outset, that as they assumed the organizers wished the discussions to be conducted on a frank and open basis, with the merits of various measures fairly considered, they assumed that the Republic would clear the ground before discussions began by removing Articles 2 and 3 of the Constitution. That proposal would have led either to their removal or to the exposure of the Forum as something a good deal less fair than it claimed to be. But the Unionists missed their opportunities and remained at home, muttering angrily and achieving nothing.

The final report of the Forum which appeared in May 1984 rejected any solution imposed by force and said that: 'The validity of both the nationalist and unionist identities in Ireland and the democratic rights of every citizen on the island must be accepted; both of these identities must have equally satisfactory, secure and durable, political, administrative and symbolic expression and protection.'[10] In practical terms the following possible structures were considered: first, a unitary Irish state embodying the North; secondly, a federation or confederation; and, thirdly, a joint British-Irish authority for the government of Northern Ireland. There had been a disagreement between the leadership of Fianna Fail (Haughey) and of Fine Gael (Fitzgerald), and a real danger that two conflicting reports would appear. For Haughey was strongly in favour of a unitary Ireland and this line was also pressed by Hume's deputy, Seamus Mallon.[11] Fitzgerald pressed for consideration of the federal or confederal solutions, already foreshadowed in a Fine Gael policy document of 1979.[12] In the final report it was the unitary state that was described as: 'The particular structure of political unity which the Forum would have wished to see established.' The other suggestions left on the table would clearly present difficulties. The idea of a federation was really a revival of an old proposal which was discussed in the course of the Treaty debate in 1921 when Erskine Childers pointed to the difficulties (see pp. 53–4 above). De Valera had also suggested a federation[13] and so indeed had the IRA.[14] How would it be established on a secure basis? What constitutional arrangements would be adopted for dealing with the domestic responsibilities of the state governments? What foreign policy would the federation follow? Would the South support the Western Alliance, or would the North agree to withdraw? Would Westminster and Washington, for their part, feel more inclined, or less inclined, to welcome such an outcome when its implications had been properly understood? As for a confederation, this would not only imply the right of secession. It would do nothing in itself to solve the *internal* problems of the two constituent states, and Dublin would have no right whatsoever to express any views about domestic affairs in the North. The role of the confederacy would be in foreign policy – an area where serious difficulties would also arise.

The third possibility, a joint authority, would imply that Ulster would be governed by an outside body that was not responsible to the Ulster electorate. The Province would be treated like a backward area – indeed an area almost uniquely backward in the modern world – and administered by two countries who, to complicate the issue, might disagree between themselves. This was an unpromising suggestion but it was the one that, in a diluted form, got carried over, as we shall see, to the Anglo-Irish Agreement.

The economic difficulties posed by Irish unity had been clearly and forcefully presented in the evidence submitted to the Forum by Carter and Ryan,[15] but were dealt with by merely expressing the hope that outside assistance from some source, or sources, would be available. Haughey, for his part, sought to dispose of awkward economic facts, saying that 'if economics is the dismal science, politics must be the profession of hope.'

It should be observed that the proposals made by the Forum did not include any suggestion that the South should modify, still less abandon, its policy of strict republican detachment and neutrality. There was no question of returning to the Commonwealth, still less of exploring the possibility of a confederation of the British Isles. There was no hint of a willingness to join the Western Alliance.

The Irish unity desired by the Forum was to be 'achieved by agreement and consent, embracing the whole island of Ireland and providing irrevocable guarantees for the protection and preservation of both the unionist and nationalist identities' (p. 29).

This acceptance of the need for 'agreement and consent' as the basis for unity is immensely important if consistently adhered to. For it can only mean that unity must rest, not on a mere majority vote, but on a consensus. The Northern Protestants are not to be driven into the Republic by military force nor even by electoral strength which might perhaps follow from some future demographic change. They are expected to come only because they want to come. Passages such as this suggest a statesmanlike approach, and the qualities of fairness and sympathetic understanding were claimed for the Report, notably by Fitzgerald, when he said: 'The ideas we have put forward together show an openness to the other tradition in this island, and a sensitivity which, I believe, has no precedent in Irish history.'[16] Unfortunately this remark may be an adverse assessment of Irish history rather than a sustainable commendation of the Report. There was indeed some expression of moderate sentiments in the Report but a good deal of the space was devoted to an expression of traditional republican hostility towards both Great Britain and the British population in Northern Ireland. Thus the British Government was held to be responsible for the partition of the island in 1920/21 although the members of the Forum must have been quite well aware that this old accusation is contrary to the historical record. The Northerners who were to be won over and persuaded to come voluntarily into a United Ireland were subjected to sustained abuse. The faults of Unionist rule were indeed undeniable but the Forum showed itself to be deficient not only in charity but in fairness by the exaggerated and distorted account of the Northern faults which it chose to present.

To quote from a penetrating analysis of the work of the Forum: 'The key words "identity", "accommodate" and "structures", occur with almost hypnotic regularity throughout the document, giving it a deceptive solidity.'[17] For there is no question of recognizing that the Ulster majority has a different *nationalist* outlook. The new words are 'identity' and 'tradition' rather than sense of nationality. The author continues:

The new nationalist diagnosis was that culture, although not of course ethnicity, nor even, clearly, religion, lay at the root of the conflict . . . Thinly disguised by this tortuous prose was the demand for a united Ireland, founded on majority, that is, nationalist rule, which was deemed to be a part of the bedrock of the nationalist 'identity'. In order to fit in with this traditional demand, the characteristics of the unionist 'identity' were defined as strictly cultural in the narrowest sense, and excluded any right to choose to remain part of the United Kingdom.

Even this admission of legitimate cultural differences, inadequate though it is, can be regarded as a small step in the right direction. There is certainly a marked contrast between the imperialistic claim to the North as asserted by a de Valera or a Haughey and the more sympathetic approach of a Fitzgerald. There is, however, a certain play with words and perhaps a confusion of concepts that may prove to be harmful. In his book, *Towards a New Ireland*, Fitzgerald said that: 'History has created in the island of Ireland one nation with several different cultures and the concept of a mono-cultural nation-state simply does not fit the Irish case.'[18] But these cultural differences, the differences in religion, the differences in historical tradition, the differences in attitude to the neighbouring country across the Irish Sea – surely all these are the *components* of nationalism. Fitzgerald says that there is 'one Irish nation' but does not explain what he means by 'nation'. Of course the differences that separate different communities are a matter of degree, but there is a practical test that is surely appropriate in this case. Have these differences been sufficiently great to lead to the rejection of living together in the same nation state? The answer to that question is somewhat obvious. The South rejected membership of the British state of which the Ulster majority felt themselves to be a part, and that Ulster majority, in its turn, has rejected membership of the breakaway republic. It is hard to see how the concept of 'one nation' can be so stretched as to include these two communities.

Mrs Thatcher's reaction to the Forum Report was characteristically forthright. Her response to each of the proposals was 'Out', and it may have appeared at the time that that was the end of the matter as far as the British Government, under her leadership, was concerned. Events were soon to show, however, that this was by no means the case.

19

The Anglo-Irish Agreement and its Aftermath

The Anglo-Irish Agreement of November 1985 was to determine the framework of policy for an indefinite period ahead. Its centre-piece was an Intergovernmental Conference which would meet regularly in order to discuss a wide range of public business: political issues; security and related matters; legal matters, including the administration of justice; and the promotion of cross-border cooperation. The Conference would concern itself mainly with Northern Ireland, although some of its business might involve cooperative action in both parts of Ireland and in Great Britain. The Secretary of State for Northern Ireland and an Irish minister – in practice, the Foreign Minister – would take part and their governments would work together 'for the accommodation of the rights and identities of the two traditions which exist in Northern Ireland' (Article 4a). A dual role would thus be performed by the Irish minister: as advocate for the Catholic minority in the North, and as representative of the bond of national sentiment linking that minority to the Republic. The Irish Prime Minister, Garret Fitzgerald, explained the position as he saw it in the following way to the Dail. There would exist 'within the structures of the government of Northern Ireland a significant role for the Irish Government, towards which the Nationalist minority in Northern Ireland look – just as the Unionist majority look to the Government of the United Kingdom'.[1]

From this point of view, the Agreement could be regarded as an attempt to achieve a better compromise in a situation where different national loyalties were in conflict. The settlement of 1921 had gone a long way towards providing such a compromise, for the Irish nationalists had in effect achieved independence from Britain and the Ulster unionists had remained within the United Kingdom. But the preferences of other groups had not been accommodated – those of the Ulster Catholics and those of the Irish people in the South who wanted to retain close links with Britain. This last group was submerged and ceased to be important, but the former – that of the Ulster Catholics – has retained not only its identity but also – so it is often assumed – its sense of frustrated nationalism. Would an institutional link which stretched across the Border and allowed the Irish Government to concern itself with the affairs of these Ulster people not be a worthwhile way of improving upon the previous compromise? With the Republic accorded a role in this way, the Ulster minority should feel more secure and less alienated. Its members might therefore – so it was hoped – be less likely to vote for Sinn Fein rather than for the SDLP. In a less hostile atmosphere, the security forces should find their task was eased, especially if the SDLP and also the Catholic hierarchy were to respond to the Agreement by giving unequivocal support to a policy of restoring and maintaining law and order in the Province. Moreover the Republic itself would assist more fully in the campaign against terrorism both by consenting to extradition and by ensuring close cooperation between the police forces on both sides of the border. From the point of view of the British Government, the Agreement had the further merit of being a response to American pressure in the form of a new initiative taken in close and friendly cooperation with the Irish Republic.

This favourable assessment of the Agreement was reflected in a heavy vote in its support in both UK Houses of Parliament and by widespread approval abroad. It was widely believed that by these means the long crisis would be gradually brought to an end and violence stopped. A reading of the speeches made in Parliament confirms the view that the expected contribution to peace was the decisive consideration. That view was also expressed by foreign commentators. The general euphoria does not appear to have been seriously affected by the response of the IRA, which not only rejected the Agreement as quite inadequate but also claimed that, in so far as any ground had been yielded by the British, it was in response to its own military campaign. The Agreement was confirmation of the fact that the British were weakening and the pressure must therefore be maintained in order to get them out. It was not, however, on the IRA's response but on that of the Ulster Protestants that attention was concentrated. It was not favourable attention. On the contrary, it seemed that these people were behaving in a totally irresponsible way and demonstrating once more their inability to see any point of view other than their own. These were surely 'impossible people'.

THE GROUNDS FOR OPPOSITION

This Ulster opposition came from much the greater part of the Protestant population, not just from the leaders of the Official Unionist Party and the Democratic Unionist Party. The rejection of the Agreement was almost complete, with only about 8 per cent of the Protestants in support according to an opinion poll held at the time. As Harvey Cox has observed: 'What is so striking is not the expected hostility of the Protestant extremists, but the near unanimity of rejection by the Protestant community.'[2]

There were two reasons for their opposition: first, the way in which the Agreement had been imposed upon them without consultation, let alone consent, and secondly, the conviction that it was part of a plan to manoeuvre Northern Ireland into the Republic. Unfortunately the first of these reasons cannot now be set aside as nothing more than a regrettable incident in the past, for it undermined trust in Westminster to an extent that was bound to affect future relationships. During the eighteen months of negotiation, with two summits, that preceded the conclusion of the Agreement, no attempt was made to inform any of the Ulster leaders about the proposals under discussion or to seek their views. In all previous attempts to explore constitutional possibilities, successive British governments had been at pains to consult and to search for support all round if this could possibly be obtained, with much stress laid on the need for consensus. It may be assumed that it was partly because of these past failures that the British Government had decided to impose a settlement. In defence of this approach it could be said – realistically enough – that the Unionist leaders, if consulted, would have disagreed with what was being proposed, as would some of the Alliance leaders. There is, however, a vast difference between imposing a settlement after an unsuccessful discussion, and its imposition without any discussion at all. It is scarcely surprising that the procedure followed was bitterly resented as a massive snub – and resented by moderates who might otherwise have been more open-minded about what was proposed. On one point at least there could surely be no doubt: this was that all the Ulster parties should be treated alike. If the Unionist and Alliance leaders were being kept in the dark, so should the leaders of the SDLP. This did not happen. John Hume, the leader of the SDLP, was kept informed throughout by the Irish Government. Fitzgerald would appear to have shown a serious lack of judgement in doing so. Or, if Hume's advice was indeed indispensable, then the British Government should have abandoned the policy of completely excluding the other Ulster party leaders, leaving them to be informed by the press release after the Agreement had been signed. Nor did it help matters when it transpired that the Vatican had been consulted beforehand by the Irish Government and that some foreign embassies in Dublin and a number of politicians in the USA had been informed – all before the Ulstermen had been told anything at all. Westminster, formerly so much concerned about the alienation of the minority, had succeeded in deeply alienating the majority.

Apart from the opposition provoked in this way, there was much concern about the constitutional implications of the Conference at which important matters affecting the future of Northern Ireland would be dealt with in secret by a British and an Irish minister. The basis for this concern was expressed clearly by a former Secretary of State, Roy Mason, when he said: 'There is to be intrusion by a foreign state . . . in almost all Northern Ireland's affairs.'[3]

It was hardly surprising that the new arrangement should have been regarded as a means of gradually pushing Ulster out of the United Kingdom and into the Irish Republic. This fear had, of course, been anticipated and Article 1 of the Agreement was intended to provide the reassurance that was required. The signatories:

(a) affirm that any change in the status of Northern Ireland would only come about with the consent of a majority of the people of Northern Ireland;

(b) recognize that the present wish of a majority of the people of Northern Ireland is for no change in the status of Northern Ireland;

(c) declare that, if in the future a majority of the people of Northern Ireland clearly wish for and formally consent to the establishment of a united Ireland, they will introduce and support in the respective Parliaments legislation to give effect to that wish.[4]

The pledge under (a) and (b) was no more impressive than those that had preceded it. As we have seen, the Irish Free State had recognized the legitimacy of the partition of Ireland in 1925 after the deliberations of the Boundary Commission, and this recognition had been registered at the League of Nations – just as the Anglo-Irish Agreement was registered at the United Nations. But de

Valera had subsequently repudiated that recognition by inserting into the Constitution of 1937 the much debated Article 2 with its bold claim to *de iure* possession of Northern Ireland. At Sunningdale, the Coalition Government of the Republic had conceded that 'there could be no change in the status of Northern Ireland until a majority of the people of Northern Ireland desired a change of status' (chapter 15).

As Kenny has pointed out, the Anglo-Irish Agreement speaks of 'no change in the status of Northern Ireland; it does not determine that status.'[5] At Sunningdale, the British Government, for its part, had confirmed the status to be part of the United Kingdom, but it will be recalled that the Irish Government, in its parallel statement, had avoided doing so, and was thus able to defend itself against the charge of having infringed Article 2. The game then played out in the courts had confirmed the scepticism with which the Ulster majority regarded any Dublin pledge. That scepticism was to be vindicated and further strengthened when the 1985 pledge was denounced by the Fianna Fail Opposition in the Dail: 'We cannot [said Haughey] accept ... the abandonment of our claim to Irish unity or the recognition of British sovereignty over the North of Ireland which is involved in this agreement.'[6] The Foreign Minister felt able to assure him that the agreement is 'as it must be, of course, totally consistent with the Constitution' and therefore with Article 2. It was scarcely an impressive display of open and honest political dealing. As Kenny has observed, 'the very skill of the draftsmen had made the first article of the agreement so ambiguous that it was no surprise if it cast suspicions of doublespeak over the entire accord.'[7]

The unionists were convinced that their security depended, as it had always done, on their own determination. While that determination remained the Republic would be unable to absorb and govern the North against the will of the majority, and the guarantee was therefore regarded as merely a verbal embellishment. As the Leader of the Irish Labour Party had asked: 'Can anyone here imagine what it would be like to live in a united Ireland with one million people in rebellion?'[8] Biggs-Davison had good cause to say: 'I shall not cry hallelujah because once again the Irish Government have recognized, *de facto*, that Northern Ireland forms part of the United Kingdom.'[9]

If this *de facto* recognition had been accompanied by *de iure* recognition – that is to say, by the removal of Article 2 from the Irish Constitution – the situation in 1985 would have been transformed. The British Government might well have pressed for such a change during the negotiations. Even if, in the end, it had been thought right to accept an Irish refusal to change in order to save the Agreement, the British Government could have made it clear, in its public announcement, that it accepted this refusal only with reluctance. It is astonishing that any state could be so indifferent to the drawing of its own boundary as Britain appears to be. It seems profligate to make an implicit concession, without struggle or protest, instead of exacting some bargaining advantage. And it is surely somewhat naive to suppose that any gratitude or respect will be earned by doing so from intransigent Irish republicans.

For the Unionists in 1985 it was not just a matter of looking ahead apprehensively to some future time when the guarantee might be ignored. For it appeared that, in Article 2, the Anglo-Irish Agreement had *itself* changed, without consent, the constitutional status of Northern Ireland which was guaranteed in Article 1. This second article established the Intergovernmental Conference to which I have referred. The crucial point, then, was the status of that body. Was it to be merely a consultative body which, although it might exert its influence in important ways, could not take executive decisions? Or was it, in effect, the start of a condominium in which authority would be jointly exercised by the British and Irish Governments?

Article 2 of the Agreement contains sentences which must be quoted in full because their interpretation vitally affects the authority of the Conference and thus the significance of the Agreement itself:

In the interest of promoting peace and stability, determined efforts shall be made through the Conference to resolve any differences ... There is no derogation from the sovereignty of either the United Kingdom or the Irish Government, and each retains responsibility for the decisions and administration of government within its own jurisdiction.

Fitzgerald explained the role of the Conference as follows:

This provision – going beyond a consultative role but necessarily, because of the sovereignty issue, falling short of an executive role – provides in the Government's view, the most effective method by which to ensure the existence of the structures capable of eroding the alienation of the Nationalist minority.[10]

The Leader of the Irish Labour Party in the Coalition Government laid stress on the fact that: 'the two Governments for the first time commit themselves as a matter of obligation under an international agreement to the effect that "determined efforts shall be made to resolve any differences"'.[11]

The setting up of the Conference may have looked, at first glance, like a step towards the joint authority, or condominium, which was one of the options discussed by the Forum. On the British side, Mrs Thatcher had previously rejected all the Forum options, including this one, with an emphatic 'Out – Out – Out' She appeared, to apprehensive Unionists, to have changed her course in accepting the proposal for a Conference, but she insisted that it would have no executive authority either now or in the future. She went on to tell the House of Commons: 'We will listen to the views of the Irish Government. Yes, we will make determined efforts to resolve differences. But at the end of the day decisions north of the border will continue to be made by the United Kingdom Government.'[12]

Thus it became apparent in the course of the early parliamentary debates in London and Dublin that there was at least a difference in emphasis in the interpretation given to the status and authority of the Conference. Even when this fact was recognized, the Unionist opposition remained intense with strong resentment expressed against any kind of arrangement that allowed a foreign government to meddle in Ulster's affairs.

In reply it could be said that, to the Catholic minority in Ulster, the Republic is not a foreign state. This is a fair point, which the Unionists have preferred to ignore. To concede its validity is not to concede the further assumption that the majority of these Catholics would now wish to leave the United Kingdom for the Republic, for the evidence of the opinion polls has been strongly to the contrary over a long period of years. But the fact remains that there is far too much affinity with the Republic for it to be regarded by them as 'foreign'. It is a point that can scarcely be ignored, but even if it is accepted, the attempt to accommodate an irredentist viewpoint in the Agreement had some distinctly odd features. First it must be recalled that the minority already had the same political rights as the majority. They could put up candidates for the British Parliament and vote in elections, and the particular Government which emerged at Westminster would appoint the Secretary of State for Northern Ireland. It is true that for reasons we have considered elsewhere, these arrangements were, and are, seriously defective – with Northern Ireland legislation passed by Orders in Council, with the electorate denied even the possibility of belonging to the main British parties and with local government severely restricted. But this was so for the whole of the Ulster electorate, for the majority as much as the minority.

THE LACK OF SYMMETRY

The minority were, however, to be given additional representation of a kind peculiar to them. Their case would be presented and pressed at the new Conference by a minister from the Irish Republic, although the Northern Catholics did not take part in elections to the Dail and could not have voted for whatever government happened to be in power in Dublin. It had to be assumed, therefore, that the man from Dublin would interpret their views correctly and express them fairly. There also seemed to be an implication that no British Secretary of State could be trusted to provide equitable treatment for the Ulster Catholics. The Ulster majority, for its part, would have no such double representation. Yet it would be improper to accept any apparent implication that the Secretary of State was simply *their* advocate and defender against the minority's Dublin champion. His role was to hold the balance. But this left the majority's special interests unrepresented at the Conference, either directly by any elected politicians or indirectly – as are those of the minority. To quote from Carter:

The problem with the procedure envisaged by the Agreement is that it provides a means of pressure on the British Government by one side (using as its champion an independent state) without any provision for hearing the views of the other side. But the matters to be dealt with are complex, and open to reasonable differences of interpretation. No one in the majority community can be expected to believe that justice is done by institutionalising the pressures from one side and totally ignoring those from the other.[13]

The British Government for its part did not envisage a continuing role for the Conference on the scale of its initial deliberations. For that role would be curtailed to the extent that any of its responsibilities were transferred to a new assembly with devolved legislative authority in Northern Ireland. Indeed the British authors of the Agreement may have entertained the hope that a dislike of the Conference on the part of the Unionists would make the leaders more prepared than they had previously been to accept devolution with power-sharing. One can, again, detect a marked difference of emphasis between the British and Irish Governments, although both are committed to support devolution as well as to participate constructively in the Conference. To quote Fitzgerald: 'It is extremely important to understand that even in the event of devolution the Conference will still have a wide range of functions, concerning matters of particular interest to the Nationalist minority in Northern Ireland.'14 That was not the British emphasis.

Both countries agreed that devolution was desirable but it was also agreed that it could be achieved only 'with the co-operation of constitutional representatives within Northern Ireland of both traditions there'. Moreover the Irish Government would be able to put forward 'views and proposals on the modalities of bringing about devolution in Northern Ireland in so far as they relate to the interests of the minority community' (Article 4c). These are important passages, for they appear to mean that any proposal for devolution will be blocked unless it is thought satisfactory by the Irish Government and, in particular, by the SDLP. It is true that the British Government could override Irish views on 'modalities' if it saw fit because it retains sole executive power; but it would, in practice, be hard to do so on this issue. There is another difficulty. By withholding its cooperation the SDLP would be able to impose its veto on any scheme of which it disapproved. It would seem to be strongly in the interests of its leadership not to have any form of devolution at all. For it can express its views on any particular subject to the Irish Government and these views will then be transmitted to the Conference and will thus be dealt with at a higher level than would be the case under devolution. It is obvious that the leadership can exercise far more influence in this way than it could hope to do as leader of a minority party even in a 'power-sharing' executive. Although supported by only a fifth of the Northern Ireland voters, the SDLP has exerted greater influence for several years than any other Ulster party. It is ironic to reflect that the initial campaign was for 'one man, one vote'.

UNIONIST ERRORS

The Unionists, in their indignation, put themselves in a non-negotiating position by insisting that the Agreement must go.[15] They had good grounds for complaining about the invidious treatment they had received and the emotional reaction can be understood. It has, however, been hard to find a way out of the deadlock. It would have been possible to have taken a different line which placed more of the onus for change on the Republic. For it would have been possible to say that, notwithstanding the way in which the Agreement had been imposed, they would be prepared to accept its terms and work for its success provided the Irish Republic deleted from its constitution the clause which claims that Northern Ireland is by right part of its territory. They would, for their part, accept the possibility that an Irish minister should express what he believed to be the views of the Ulster minority, but they must then, in all fairness, be accorded formal recognition of the status of Northern Ireland. It can be assumed that this reasonable request would have been rejected by the Republic but it would then have been made quite clear that the intransigence was not just on one side. Alternatively acceptance of the Agreement could have been made conditional upon a further clarification, agreed and accepted by both Britain and the Irish Republic, of the status of the Conference as an advisory body with no executive role whatever. From every point of view that clarification would in any case have been beneficial and, in making it the central issue, the Unionists would have avoided the mistake, from which they were subsequently to suffer, of getting into a non-negotiating position. In the event, Mrs Thatcher's initial view is the one that has prevailed, as can be seen by the refusal to yield to Dublin pressure for changes in the Northern Ireland judiciary. The worst fears of the Unionists have not, therefore, been realized. With cooler heads they would not have prejudged the outcome by assuming – rather oddly – that the Dublin interpretation was the right one. Above all they should have acknowledged and emphasized the importance of the constitutional guarantee, even if not new and even if, in some respects, ambiguous. This is a point to which I shall return in the final chapter.

One effect of the Agreement was a worsening of relations between the British government and the Ulster majority. Confronted with a *fait accompli* and with other means of expression denied them, the Unionists took to the streets – both members of the Unionist parties and large numbers of others who were not. An immense demonstration of protest of about 200,000 people was held in Belfast and was conducted in a very orderly way. The message was ignored by Westminster, as was the request for a referendum, and it was hardly surprising that, on subsequent occasions, violence occurred in disregard of the appeals made by both Molyneaux and Paisley. The police then demonstrated to the Catholics that they would defend law and order against Protestants just as firmly as against Catholics, and thus helped to dispel – if only for a time – the lingering scepticism about their fairness which, according to the Scarman Tribunal, had already been demonstrated in 1969.[16] Some unfortunate police officers then had to endure attacks on themselves and on their homes. Several grim months were to elapse before the trouble subsided, and not before Ulster's reputation in Britain had been further damaged. Within Ulster, the feeling of betrayal weakened still further the old link with Britain but did not, of course, strengthen in any way the support for absorption into a united Irish Republic. The effect was rather to intensify the feeling of isolation and add further strength to the view that a future Ulster state might emerge which would be independent from both its neighbours.

PART IV
Central Issues

20

The Religious Divide

The historical importance of the religious factor requires no emphasis. What is much harder to understand and appraise is its effect on the current situation. The religious factor both in Ulster – and also, of course, in the rest of the island – is complex and difficult. To deal fully with it would not only require far more space than can be devoted to it in the present work but would also call for a scholarly knowledge of ecclesiastical matters to which I can lay no claim. Some attempt must be made however to cope with these issues if the closely related political and social consequences are to be understood.

The first part of this chapter will deal with religious attitudes in Northern Ireland and, to a lesser extent, in the Republic, including a reference to the attempts made to achieve closer relations and a better understanding between the Protestant Churches and the Catholic Church. The second will be concerned with the response of the Churches, acting singly or together, to violence in the community.

RELIGIOUS ATTITUDES

The most serious obstacle to an understanding of the situation in Ulster may be the fact that the two parties to the political conflict are normally identified as 'Protestants' and 'Catholics' respectively. The Unionist parties, with the exception of the Alliance Party, are supported exclusively by Protestants. The Catholics, for their part, give their support to the nationalist parties, splitting the vote between the SDLP and Sinn Fein in roughly the ratio of two to one. Thus the division between Protestants and Catholics seems to be sharp and clear – and anachronistic. For it appears to outside observers as though a seventeenth-century war of religion is being fought in the late twentieth century. It is hardly surprising that many people in Britain should then conclude that Northern Ireland's problems lie beyond rational analysis and sane solution. That must, indeed, appear to be so to many television viewers as they watch the incomprehensible behaviour of Orangemen on parade or listen to the thunderous oratory of the Reverend Ian Paisley. But this response, however natural, is unwise. It is one of the central themes of this book that any such attempt to ignore and forget will prove unsuccessful. The rational response is to try to understand, and in doing so full account must be taken of the emphasis given to the intensity of religious loyalties which may seem so strange to a secular eye.

If the support given to organized religion is a reliable guide, Ireland is one of the most 'Christian' areas in the world.[1] In Northern Ireland, church membership is believed to be something like 80 per cent as compared with a mere 13 per cent in England.[2] Admittedly these figures may exaggerate the contrast. Nominal declared membership is one thing, church attendance is another and degree of commitment yet another. Even the Catholic Church has complained about declining attendance at Mass and it has been suggested that Protestant working-class church attendance in the Shankill area had dropped to about 15 per cent in the early 1970s.[3] For many people in Northern Ireland, religious affiliation may have become little more than the scarification of tribal identity. The young yobbos who throw stones and petrol bombs are unlikely to do so from any intense conviction about the superiority of one theological doctrine over another – although they may hurl their missiles with a 'better conscience' because they believe themselves to be on 'the right side'. More generally those who prefer a newspaper to a church service on Sunday morning will continue to identify themselves as 'Protestants' or 'Catholics'. The old joke about 'Protestant agnostics' and 'Catholic agnostics' makes a real point, although the word 'agnostic' suggests a more carefully considered position than may be generally realistic. There can, indeed, be no doubt about the advance of secularism, but there is little sign of greater social harmony emerging as a consequence. When the cat has disappeared, the smile – or rather the snarl – may still remain behind.

As well as the differences in degree of commitment, there are also differences in doctrine not only between, but also within, the larger Protestant denominations. In the nature of the case such differences are not easily assessed, but it has been suggested that one Anglican in four may adhere to evangelical beliefs, and one out of two may hold such views in both the Methodist and Presbyterian Churches.[4] Some of the smaller sects, such as Dr Paisley's Free Presbyterian Church and the Church of God, are strongly evangelical. There are also a large number of evangelical mission halls.

By contrast the Roman Catholic Church is a unified disciplined organization. It was brought firmly under papal discipline by Cardinal Cullen in the last century and retains this ultramontanist relationship with the Vatican. The scope for diversity of belief is correspondingly restricted, although the Church may be less monolithic than is often assumed to be the case.

For our purposes it seems best to begin with the more conservative doctrines, both Catholic and Protestant, for the social implications may be more easily perceived when religious beliefs are sharply defined. The implications may be far reaching in any society where there is substantial acceptance of the ancient doctrine, as expressed by Augustine, that: 'There is no salvation outside the Church'. Nothing can then matter so much as membership of that Church and access to its sacraments, for on this eternal salvation depends. Heresy is the worst of all evils and must be unrelentingly opposed. That was the old doctrine, but it may be objected that there is no longer any point in dwelling on any such exclusive claims on behalf of the Catholic Church, for these have been abandoned. A real, if gradual, change has taken place which was acknowledged and endorsed at Vatican II (1962–5). This is so, although the older view has had its adherents even in modern times. A remarkable instance was Cardinal MacRory's assertion, recorded by Lyons,[5] that the Protestant Churches did not form part of the true Church of Christ. Lyons goes on to observe that it would be easy but pointless to give further examples of opinions of this kind.

Important implications for social policies followed from acceptance of the belief that the Catholic Church alone could open the door to salvation. Whatever other purposes these social policies could be shown to serve, the basic objective must be the protection of the faith against any harmful influences that might emanate from heretical Protestantism or from agnostic secularism. It will suffice to mention two examples from modern times. The first was the insistence that Catholic children should attend Catholic schools that were effectively under clerical control. Schooling thus segregated would divide the community with consequences that might be deeply harmful, but even this price would simply have to be paid. Another example was the *Ne Temere* decree of 1564, subsequently relaxed but reinstated in full rigour in Ireland in 1908, by which the non-Catholic partner in a mixed marriage was required to give consent to any children being brought up as Catholics. It was a ruling that, naturally, caused much Protestant resentment.

The claim that the Catholic Church alone could open the way to salvation was formally abandoned at Vatican II. Although the Council still held to the view that 'This is the sole Church of Christ which in the Creed we profess to be one, holy, Catholic and apostolic', it went on to say:

The Church knows that she is joined in many ways to the baptised who are honoured by the name of Christian, but who do not profess the Catholic faith in its entirety or have not preserved unity or communion under the successor of Peter. [It is also held that] Catholics must gladly acknowledge and esteem the truly Christian endowments from our common heritage which are to be found among our separated brethren.[6]

Thus the ecumenical path was opened.

I cannot presume to assess the doctrinal significance of these pronouncements but it is apparent, even to the lay observer, that the Protestant Churches are no longer regarded as heretical in the ancient – and damning – sense of the term. Vatican II had thus led to discussions with these Churches and, even in Ireland, relations are much closer than has ever formerly been the case, with regular meetings held to discuss theological matters and matters of social concern. There are also a number of interdenominational associations of a kind that would have been unusual in the past.[7] Indeed it has been suggested that the long period of violence has had the effect of drawing the Church leaders closer together instead of forcing them apart. There have been regular discussions between the Cardinal, the Church of Ireland Primate, the Presbyterian Moderator and the Methodist President. There have also been discussions between Catholics and members of all the denominations belonging to the Irish Council of Churches. The main Protestant Churches have been represented at these discussions – Presbyterian, Church of Ireland, Methodist, Lutheran, Moravian, Unitarian, the Society of Friends and the Salvation Army. This much has been recorded. What is naturally much harder to assess is the extent to which ecumenical tendencies have reached the ordinary congregations on both sides. On the Protestant side, Dr Paisley's Free Presbyterian Church has held indignantly aloof, and his political party has derived some of its strength from the disapproval with which these ecumenical gatherings have been watched by evangelicals in other Protestant denominations. To this extent the effect has been to raise, rather than lower, sectarian tension in the Province.

It was to be expected that the more tolerant attitude adopted at Vatican II would have implications for Catholic views on social policies. The two examples taken above can now serve as test cases and it then appears that there has been one partial concession to record and one disappointment. The concession has been the replacement of the *Ne Temere* decree by a new ruling. Since the publication of *Matrimonia Mixta* in 1970, 'the Catholic partner promises to do all he or she can do to have the children of the marriage baptised and raised as Catholics'.[8] The former obligation is no longer imposed on the other partner. The obligation placed on the Catholic partner may, however, be interpreted in different ways and can be supported by varying degrees of social pressure. As the Catholic Directory fully recognizes, a mixed marriage can still encounter very serious problems. Some relaxation has, however, been permitted.

The second example is segregated education. In this case, Vatican II has not been followed by any relaxation of the policy of preserving Catholic schools with only Catholic teachers and a strong clerical presence. This may seem strange. An Irish Episcopal conference declared that: 'The Catholic Church does not claim that its members are necessarily more faithful to these truths of Christ or more earnest in availing themselves of the means of grace than other Christians.'[9]

The 'spiritual dangers' in integrated education would seem, therefore, to be less serious than was previously anticipated, and it is genuinely puzzling to find that even such a limited experiment as Lagan College (see p. 143 above) has met with so much disapproval that no Catholic chaplain has been appointed, and priests have been forbidden to work there – although a Catholic sister works in the school with the knowledge of the bishop. Sometimes the emphasis has been shifted to ethical considerations. For example, Bishop Francis Brooks has said that the Catholic school should 'always encourage pupils to co-operate with people of other faiths' but has also defended segregated schooling. In doing so he has held that 'a fully Catholic school will ensure a way of life utterly opposed to all hate and divisions.'[10] This is a bold claim which might carry more conviction if the members of the IRA were not former pupils of these schools. It is only fair to add that the Protestant Churches have displayed only restrained enthusiasm for the principle of integrated education. As might be expected the Democratic Unionist Party has opposed it – but Paisley's Church has not yet had its Vatican II and there is no reason to suppose it to be imminent.

The non-Catholic community constitutes just over three-fifths of the Ulster population. Its distribution over the various Protestant denominations is shown in table 20.1. It is commonly assumed outside Northern Ireland that this Protestant population is almost entirely Presbyterian. In fact Presbyterians, though the largest group, are less than half. Over one-third belong to the episcopal Church of Ireland which is a member of the Anglican Communion.

It will also be observed that Dr Paisley's Free Presbyterian Church is quite small, although its size is no indication of the political support accorded to its founder. In order to prevent any misunderstanding, it is in place to add that his Church is quite

TABLE 20.1   Distribution of the non-Catholic community
among Protestant denominations (per cent)

Church of Ireland	35.6
Presbyterian Church in Ireland	46.5
Free Presbyterian Church	1.6
Methodist Church	8.0
Baptist Church	1.8
Others	6.4
	100.0

Source: Northern Ireland Attitude Survey (BIAS) as
reported by Moxon-Browne (1983, p. 89)

unconnected with the Presbyterian Church in Ireland. Moreover it would appear
that the Church is not Calvinistic and is not, therefore, even formally in the
Presbyterian tradition.[11]

Although there is a wide diversity of opinion within the non-Catholic population,
an overwhelming majority are opposed to membership of the Irish Republic. On
this issue, at least, there is almost complete agreement. Is this opposition really
based on religious considerations? Or does it largely reflect other issues that lie
behind misleading sectarian labels? The diversity of beliefs would seem to support
the second interpretation, but a closer look is clearly required. It seems best to begin
with the evangelical wing of the Protestant Churches because their opposition to
Catholicism has been such a powerful factor in the past and, even in modern times,
a substantal proportion of evangelical Protestants – though not all – have opposed
ecumenical discussions. There is therefore some irony in the fact that both
evangelical fundamentalists and Irish Catholics have a number of basic beliefs in
common, with both opposed to liberal modernist theology and to secular humanism.
The crucial difference of view relates, of course, to 'the means of grace', and on this
issue the conservative evangelical can accept no compromise. Ecumenical
approaches will therefore be either futile or dangerous and should be avoided. So
much seems to follow clearly enough from the premises. There might, perhaps, be
a considerable evangelical measure of agreement with the interpretation of the
Catholic attitude put forward by O'Malley: 'Ecumenism is simply a way of bringing
erring Christian brethren back into the True Fold. Catholics see it as requiring no
compromises on their part, no theological concessions, no substantial doctrinal
changes. In short ecumenism is palatable to Northern Catholics because they do not
take Protestantism seriously.'[12]

Church unity is rejected, but it is not apparent that the rejection of Irish political
unity must therefore follow. The Irish Republic tolerates other religions. Indeed
toleration is required by its constitution. What, then, have the evangelicals to fear
from incorporation? There is a puzzle here which must seem strange and baffling to
moderate and reasonable Catholic proponents of Irish unity. The more extreme
evangelicals do, however, have an answer, of which Paisley has been the most
vehement exponent. The answer is to present an elaborate apocalyptic scenario in

which the Church of Rome plays the central Mephistophelian role, and does so with skill and duplicity behind a deceptive screen that suggests toleration and compromise. It follows that Irish unity must be resisted because it would bring the Ulster Protestants under a power which is adept at controlling events and effectively stifling opposition to its views and its objectives. It is a gripping plot, full of melodrama, and narrated with a generous use of metaphor. 'There is no doubt about it, the Jesuits in England are flying a kite testing the temperature of the water.' The plot is not – one would suppose – something that is regarded as fully credible by the evangelical movement as a whole. Even, however, from a more sober view-point, non-Catholics would view with apprehension their absorption in a state that is so much under Catholic influence. That influence is, of course, revealed by the way in which the Catholic ethical position has been supported by legislation with regard to divorce, abortion, contraception and pornography; but here we encounter another paradox. For the ethical position of the evangelicals happens to coincide with the Catholic position on a number of these issues, though not on all. Those who would be most affected by this legislation would be the liberal-minded Christians, the agnostic humanists and those who belong to other religions. What can also be said, however, is that all non-Catholic groups including the evangelicals, would resent the fact that these legal restraints have been imposed and retained in order to give expression to the ethical views of the Catholic Church.

It is important to understand the basis of this opposition to Irish unity. Attention should not be confined to the traditional picture of Catholics and Protestants glaring at each other in mutual atavistic hostility. For there are many non-Catholics who have no sympathy for the views of the Protestant ultras but are nevertheless strongly opposed to becoming members of a state where clerical influence is as strong and pervasive as it continues to be in the Irish Republic. The point has been taken by some of the politicians in that country – notably by Dr Garret Fitzgerald and by Senator Mary Robinson – and attempts have been made to have the restrictions on divorce and contraception removed. So far these efforts have failed. Moreover no serious attempt has been made to challenge the tight hold of the Church on the educational system, and none would be likely to succeed. It is not only, or even mainly, the Protestant minority in the Republic that is affected for they have their own schools, at least in areas where their numbers make this possible. In this modern age there are Catholic parents and Catholic teachers who would prefer an educational system less under the domination of an ecclesiastical institution. They would also presumably resent the recent renewal of pressure to ensure that all teachers in Catholic schools – that is to say, nearly all schools – are not only Catholics but practising Catholics. It is hardly surprising if many liberal-minded people in Ulster are opposed to Irish unity. Their attitude should be intelligible enough in Western Europe, especially in France, Italy and Spain.

Non-Catholics – whether in Ulster or England or anywhere else – could also be expected to have reservations about becoming citizens of a country whose government felt impelled to consult the Papacy before any important political decision was taken. To non-Catholics the sense of simply not belonging to such a state would clearly be a deterrent. Religious differences are then to be regarded as one of the several factors that have contributed historically to the emergence of two different senses of nationality. This seems to be the right way of explaining the situation for there is no point in becoming embroiled in the old debate about the relative importance of religion and nationalism as though these were alternative explanations.

When some of the other ingredients of nationalism begin to lose their power, it may be natural that more attention should be devoted to religion. This is the theme that has been developed by some sociologists in Northern Ireland.[13] The Protestant people are described as bemused and insecure. They can no longer rely with the same confidence on support from Britain and have, moreover, come to realise somewhat belatedly that they are not accepted as fully 'British'. They are not, however, prepared to accept incorporation into the Irish Republic. Ulster nationalism is a third possibility but in the opinion of these sociologists it fails to carry full conviction. With the future so uncertain Protestants may at least be able to sustain their ethnic identity in Ireland by an intense commitment to evangelical fundamentalism. The support given to Dr Paisley is, they suggest, to be explained in this way. No one can, indeed, deny that, in times of stress and uncertainty in Ulster or anywhere else, a firm belief of some kind can provide assurance and support. If the sense of identity is to be strengthened by an intensified religious commitment, the doctrinal variant chosen had better be one with clear lines and sharp edges. For this purpose, fundamentalism is to be preferred to liberal Christianity with its emphasis on the humane virtues and social reform and its readiness to seek some form of accommodation with other beliefs. The contrast of views may be illustrated by an incident described by Callaghan in his memoirs when he appealed to Paisley on the basis of Christian humanism by saying that we are all 'children of God'. But Paisley would have none of it: 'No we are not Mr. Callaghan, we are children of wrath'. Callaghan admits that he could think of nothing more to say.[14] This incident is also worth recalling for another reason. It illustrates how Paisley's way of expressing his views makes them seem not only intolerant but strangely parochial and unintelligible. Yet Paisley would seem to have been enunciating the ancient doctrine of Original Sin which occupied so central a place in traditional Christian belief and presumably continues to do so in the teaching of the Roman Catholic Church.

By contrast with both evangelicals and Catholics, liberal Christians may appear to be 'light half-believers [in their] casual creeds'. That assessment may be totally misleading, but our concern is not with its fairness or unfairness, any more than it is with the creeds themselves. What is relevant is that by combining a strong personality with strong opinions Paisley has won support at a time of crisis. Unfortunately the strength of his opinions has been carried, in the opinion of many people, to the point of extravagance which has prevented him from becoming the shrewd and able leader of the whole community which he might otherwise have been. The extent of the support he has actually received must not be exaggerated. Although presented on British television in such a way that he has appeared to be the leader of the Ulster Protestants, Paisley's leadership has not been overwhelmingly endorsed at the polls. Even in the years of his prime, the DUP did not win half of the Protestant vote and, by 1987, it received less than one-third of the votes cast for the Official Unionist Party and not much more than Sinn Fein or the Alliance, although the low figure in the last year was to be partly explained by the fact that some potential DUP supporters, as a consequence of a political disagreement, were sulking in their tents.[15]

THE CHURCHES AND VIOLENCE

If attention is now directed to the Churches' attitude to violence, a number of questions suggest themselves. Have the Churches, by their disagreements among themselves and by their dogmatic exclusiveness, encouraged or even inspired some of the violence that has occurred over the past twenty years? Even if they have not done so in any direct and overt way, have they done so indirectly by helping to create a moral atmosphere in which violence against 'the other side' is a minor offence, or no offence at all? Or, if they have not actually encouraged violence, have they nevertheless failed to resist it, and to make the sustained and unequivocal protest that the situation would seem to require? It would be no extravagant use of language to say that we Irish – we assertively religious people – are a scandal of Christendom. The leaders of the Churches can scarcely have failed to see that this is so. What has been the response on their part?

In attempting to answer questions such as these a distinction must be drawn between, on the one hand, the appeals and pronouncements of church leaders and, on the other, the views expressed by parish clergy and ministers. It is possible to ascertain fairly easily from the press and from pamphlet literature what has been said at the former level but it would obviously be a much harder task to obtain information about what has been said at the parish level. At that level, there may, perhaps, be a wider dispersion of views – but this is no more than speculation.

As was only to be expected, there has been very little overt support for terrorist activities from churchmen. Much more importance must be attached to the possible influence of any Church or religious organization that inflames denominational antagonism to the point where it may erupt in violence. To the outside observer there are two bodies that appear likely to behave in this way: the Orange Order and Paisley's Free Presbyterian Church. Indeed there may be an inclination to identify the two which would, of course, be inaccurate. The Orange Order is not only much the older but also much the larger organization with membership drawn from all the main Protestant denominations – though without complete support from any of them. The Order has performed the function of holding together a substantial proportion of the Protestant population in a defensive alliance within an island that has a Catholic majority. It has also served to unite Protestants of different classes.[16] Its members are pledged to display toleration in personal relations, but opposition to Catholicism and to Irish nationalism is a central objective. It must be said at once that the Order does not in any way organize or advocate terrorist activities and has incurred the contempt of some Loyalist paramilitary spokesmen as a consequence. In so far as the Order has contributed to violence over the past twenty years, it appears to have done so indirectly by insisting on traditional parades along traditional lines of march. In times of relaxed tension, these parades had become sectarian pageants which, though noisy and assertive, may not have seriously troubled many Catholics. It has been a different matter at a time of heightened tension when parades have become a provocation. Hence the apprehension with which the 'marching season' has been awaited each year by the authorities responsible for law and order. Even so, the Order has sought to impose discipline on its members, and it is quite conceivable that, without these organized traditional marches, there would be other demonstrations organized by more extreme groups with greater violence as a consequence.

There seems an obvious overlap between the Orange movement and the Paisleyite movement although Paisley belongs, not to the main Order, but to an old breakaway group, the Independent Orange Order. His real channels of communication, however, have been his Church and his political party. The Paisleyite world is infested with traitors – or 'Lundies'[17] – who are dedicated to the betrayal of Ulster and the Protestant tradition. Mrs Thatcher has been included in their number – which at times also included a Grand Master of the Loyal Orange Order. In this atmosphere of heightened anxiety and distrust, violence is all the more likely to occur. Paisley has *not* advocated terrorism, but he has raised sectarian hostility to the boiling point, especially in the early years of the distubances, and cannot be allowed to escape responsibility when it has boiled over. Apart from the harm thus done to social relations in the Province, this harsh sectarianism has greatly damaged its image in Britain and abroad. Ulster Protestants may feel that they have not received as much sympathy and understanding as they were entitled, on the merits of the case, to receive, but they need not, perhaps, be altogether surprised when the hard-liners are assumed to be Ulster's chosen spokesmen. Of course this is unfair. A large proportion of Ulster Protestants do not share these extreme religious views. It is also unfair that Ulster Protestants are supposed to have a monopoly of intolerance because some are so direct and forthright in expressing their views. When Catholics are bigoted, they usually manage to be so in a better tone of voice.

What has been particularly damaging has been the association of Protestant religious bigotry with loyalty to Britain. Indeed it would be hard to find anything less 'British' in modern times than the way in which loyalty to Britain has been proclaimed by ultra-Protestant spokesmen. However unwittingly, they have done great harm to the Union. Sinn Fein should be grateful.

Violence has been repeatedly condemned over the years by the Church leadership, both Catholic and Protestant. It might seem unnecessary to add that these leaders include those of the Presbyterian Church in Ireland but it does in fact seem appropriate to do so explicitly in order to meet some of the misrepresentation that has taken place. For it has become something of a habit for media commentators to describe Presbyterians as unrelenting Calvinists, obsessively committed to an early tradition of militant Protestantism and harshly indifferent to the rights of their Catholic fellow citizens. A denunciation along these lines can even be encountered in so surprising a place as the *Oxford Children's History*, where children, at an early age, will learn to accept the following view of Ulster Protestants: 'As for the Protestants, they aren't like our Church of England people. They are the descendants of Scottish settlers, so they are strong Presbyterians and have extreme views. They just hate Catholics in a way that we find difficult to understand.'[18]

Although it is undeniable that, like all other Churches, the Presbyterian Church has a substantial quota of bigots, the remark above is quite indefensible. It seems in place, at this point, to record that, as early as 1965, the General Assembly of this Church resolved 'to urge upon our own people humbly and frankly to acknowledge and to ask forgiveness for any attitudes and actions towards our Roman Catholic countrymen which have been unworthy of our calling as followers of Christ'. Of the various other appeals made along similar lines it may suffice to refer to one expressed – in unmistakably Presbyterian language – in the grim conditions of 1970, when it was declared that 'the awful wrath of the living God must fall upon all who intimidate or help to drive from their houses or work Roman Catholics or Protestants who have lived and worked together in peace'.[19]

Similar quotations could be given from statements made by the leaders of other Churches, both Protestant and Catholic, and by various interdenominational bodies, and no doubt from many others who are not in top positions. As well as these appeals for peace and mutual understanding, both Church leaders and local clergy of all denominations have tried to cool the situation on the streets and to provide shelter and other forms of assistance for the victims of communal rioting of the kind that occurred especially in the early years of the disturbances. For example, to quote from a Presbyterian report about the early 1970s:

'Many church halls became centres for peace-keeping patrols of clergy and citizens. Up to one hundred of our own ministers in Belfast and neighbouring Presbyteries, not to mention hundreds of others, were involved in Belfast both by day and at all hours throughout the night, especially at weekends and for weeks on end, patrolling streets, reasoning with individuals and groups, facing crowds and interposing themselves as a last line between them and the soldiers or police, looking after refugees or comforting the frightened and the sorrowful. While in these efforts, ministers, elders and Church members were often met with scorn, anger, accusations, obscenities and rejection, there were also signs of increasing respect . . .

The authors go on to observe that the news media paid little attention to these efforts 'by our own and sister churches' and refer, by contrast, to the attention given to 'more bellicose or flamboyant spokesmen.'[20]

Why, one may ask, should the media be so selective? After all, efforts such as these could scarcely be said to be lacking in interest, or even in sensationalism. Was it no more than the usual bias in favour of bad news? Was it also because such behaviour by church members, Protestant and Catholic, in pursuit of peace did not correspond at all to the stereotype picture of Northern Ireland? A cynic might suggest that a stereotype that is so old and carefully cherished must never be exposed to any danger of damage from the facts.

The various churchmen have tried to combat violence but have clearly achieved no more than limited success. The explanation lies partly in the fact that they cannot speak for all their members – not even in the disciplined Catholic Church. So much is obvious. But there may be other explanations of which one may sometimes have been a failure to say what has to be said unambiguously and with clarity and consistency. The need for definition becomes apparent when one considers what is meant by the denunciation of 'violence'. In what sense is the term 'violence' being used when some distinguished cleric condemns violence in forthright terms, whether used by terrorists or by the security forces themselves? Presumably this is not to be taken as a plea for pacifism carried to the point of anarchy where force would not be used even to maintain law and order. In 1976/7, an interdenominational committee produced a report – *Violence in Ireland* – which offered the following clarification:

There is a place in human affairs for the use of 'force'; we should like to keep the word 'violence' for a use of force that is not justifiable . . . In this report 'violence' always has a pejorative sense and the word is not employed as synonymous with 'force'. The pejorative sense derives partly from the idea of 'illegitimacy' and partly from the idea of 'destructiveness'. We believe that the state must avoid, to the utmost possible extent, any element of unnecessary destructiveness when it uses force to restrain the violent. We believe that the use of force by those who oppose the State is more difficult to justify and therefore more easily constitutes 'violence' on grounds of illegitimacy.'[21]

The distinction between 'force' and 'violence' is crucial and should invariably be made clear. For a Catholic bishop who denounces 'violence' on television, 'whether used by the police or the terrorists', may well be taken to mean that both are equally guilty in resorting to 'force'. If both are equally to blame, the police are no more entitled than the IRA to support from the general public. Unfortunately the clarification needed to prevent this mistaken inference has often been omitted – perhaps more often than not.

An example of the clerical treatment of these issues is to be found in the address delivered by Cardinal Tomas O'Fiaich at the funeral in February 1988 of a young Catholic tragically killed in passing a guard post by the discharge of a sentry's gun. For the Cardinal thought it proper to describe this shooting as 'murder'. He explained that he had previously condemned all killings by paramilitary groups as murder, even if accidental, and asked how he could avoid using 'the same term of murder towards the killing in broad daylight of one of the best liked young men of the parish'.[22]

According to an inquiry that was subsequently held in the Republic itself, the death had been caused by a ricochet bullet which clearly conveys the presumption of an accidental discharge. By way of comparison, we may take the IRA 'accident' at the La Mon Hotel in February 1977 where members of a cycle club and a dog club were having dinner. The bomb, which was of a particularly powerful kind, created a fireball and twelve people were incinerated. The IRA explained that this was an 'accident'[23]. They had intended to phone a warning but the callbox was out of order. On many other occasions, the murderers have accidentally murdered the 'wrong people'. Apart from the falsity of the comparison between 'accidents', the Cardinal's choice of words was liable to convey the impression that the paramilitary organizations are as fully entitled to use force as are the security forces, with the implication that when an accident occurs both can be judged in the same light.

It has seemed appropriate to direct attention in this way to the Cardinal's statement on that occasion because an unqualified pronouncement of that kind from a person in so senior a position can undo the many appeals for the cessation of violence put forward by the leaders of all the Churches, including the Cardinal himself. It is necessary to add at once that, on other occasions, the Cardinal has spoken very differently. For example, in an address given in Germany in 1987[24] he said that:

While the victims [of terrorism] were more evenly balanced in the 1970s, most of the killings in the past few years have been carried out by the IRA and most of the victims were Ulster Protestants. These are the crimes for which we Catholics, as the community from which they sprang, must ask forgiveness from our Protestant brothers and sisters.

The violence of the IRA has been strongly condemned on many occasions by members of the Roman Catholic episcopate. Observers of the Ulster scene may therefore feel some surprise that masked terrorists should be able to come forward and fire salutes at burial services. As a press correspondent has observed: 'Ulster is replete with macabre incongruity, but little can compare with the sensation of sitting in a packed cathedral taking part in a Requiem Mass for convicted terrorists who are known to have committed unspeakable acts against their fellow men.'[25] Dr Edward Daly, Bishop of Derry, explained that the funeral liturgy is in·no sense a commendation of the acts of the dead persons, but he felt impelled to bar the practice of carrying the bodies of dead IRA men into churches in his own diocese. No such ban has been generally applied. Moreover it is clear that some members of the priesthood are strongly sympathetic towards the IRA. When the three terrorists shot in Gibraltar were buried in Ulster they were accorded the respect due to martyrs. The officiating priest at the funeral of Mairead Farrell said that she had been 'done to death in a barbarous assassination by a gunman as she walked on a Sunday afternoon'. According to the *Guardian* correspondent, he likened her death to that of Christ. At none of these funerals was any reference made to the fact that these were experienced terrorists who had been about to explode a bomb in the middle of Gibraltar which would have killed anything from 100 to 200 innocent people.[26] By contrast, Bishop Cahal Daly delivered a very strong condemnation of the IRA and its activities. Clearly there are divided counsels. These would appear – superficially at least – to be more divided about violence than about the evils that might follow from integrated education. To the outside observer who is trying to understand the different attitudes adopted by the leaders of the community, such contrasts are puzzling.

To denounce the terrorists does not mean that the security forces must be uncritically supported. That is obvious enough and the need for a clear statement on these different issues was recognized some years ago by the group of leading churchmen, Protestant and Catholic, who were responsible for producing the report *Violence in Ireland*. Its authors say:

While we recognize that the authorities can make mistakes or be guilty of abuses, we recommend that the Churches jointly remind their members that they have a *prima facie* moral obligation to support the currently constituted authorities in Ireland against all paramilitary powers and that to do so is not in any way to prejudge longer-term political and constitutional developments. In particular, where an individual has information about violent activities of paramilitary organizations he or she may be assuming a personal moral responsibility if, after taking account of all the personal, family and other dangers involved, he does not put such information before the authorities.[27]

If that advice – which Bishop Cahal Daly had helped to draft – had been consistently repeated over the years by all Church leaders, including the leaders of the Catholic church, the level of violence might have been substantially reduced. There have been occasions when such advice has indeed been given. After the IRA bomb explosion in November 1987 at the Cenotaph in Enniskillen which killed eleven people, the Catholic bishops, in a joint statement, expressed their sympathy with the police forces, North and South, who were trying to uphold the law in most difficult and dangerous circumstances. They went on to say that: 'We call on all our people to co-operate with the police in bringing the guilty to justice.'[28] It was a firm statement but, to be effective, this attitude would have to be consistently maintained. That condition has not been satisfied.

For example, Cardinal O'Fiaich himself had said in December 1986 that the Stalker case – when, in three incidents, members of the police force had been accused of shooting to kill (see pp. 243–4) – had created difficulties about pursuing a policy of urging Catholics to join the RUC. He did not believe they had reached that point yet until the issues arising from the Stalker investigation had been cleared up.[29] But the hierarchy had been holding back from supporting the security forces long before the Stalker affair, and to continue to do so until it had been settled was unreasonable. *Were the terrorists to have a free hand meanwhile?* Indeed even when the Attorney General made his controversial decision in February 1988 not to authorize prosecutions, it could not be reasonably maintained that a *boycott* of the police was therefore justified. Nor is it convincing to advocate the establishment of a number of different police forces, as the Cardinal had done.[30] Not only would this add to the problem of coordination, but the new area police forces might, in some cases, be under the control of the IRA! Bishop Cahal Daly, for his part, has referred with sympathy to the difficult conditions under which the RUC has to work,[31] but has also said that, as Catholic policemen are prime targets for the IRA, it was not for him to tell people to put their lives at risk. His critics could then say that Protestants were being left to bear the risks for the whole community. Only about 10 per cent of the RUC is Catholic – some in senior positions. (Sir Jamie Flanagan, Chief Constable between 1973 and 1976, was a Catholic.) The force has tried hard to recruit more Catholics. Support from the hierarchy would clearly be a help.

It should be hardly necessary to add that the use of force by opponents of a particular regime may sometimes be fully justified. The Catholic Church, for its part, concedes that there may be a 'just rebellion'. In 1917, the need for definition was felt to be acute, and a Catholic episcopal report was prepared in which the theory of the 'just war' was applied. It was concluded that rebellion would be justified only when '(i) the government was widely held to be tyrannical, (ii) there was no constitutional means of redress, and (iii) rebellion had a good chance of success'.[32]

The violence now taking place in Northern Ireland cannot possibly be defended by these standards – as the authors of *Violence in Ireland* made clear. This is not a 'just rebellion' and the violence of the IRA is therefore morally indefensible, if this standard of judgement is applied. This verdict has been clearly given on many occasions, in one form of words or another, by the leading clerics of all denominations, including Cardinal O'Fiaich and the Catholic bishops. Bishop Cahal Daly has been very firm and clear: 'I pronounce this campaign to be morally wrong and unjustifiable . . . I am proclaiming teaching that is binding on Catholics . . . Judged by every single criterion of the traditional "just war" theology, the present physical force campaign is morally wrong and the operations to which it obliges its members are morally wrong.'[33]

The Catholic hierarchy has not, however, resorted to the policy adopted in 1923 when the republicans who were in arms against the Government of the Irish Free State were excommunicated. No doubt, in this more secular age, some of the terrorists would be indifferent, but there are others of whom this would not be true. Indeed some members of the IRA, even some of its leaders, are said to be devout Catholics. Moreover their families and those who shelter them might well be seriously perturbed. There might, however, be enough sympathetic priests to reduce the effectiveness of a hierarchical pronouncement. At all events excommunication does not appear to have been seriously considered.

Without going nearly so far as the excommunication of the IRA terrorists, the Church could at least give positive support to the authorities responsible for restoring and maintaining law and order. Of course these authorities should be criticized if they appear to be behaving wrongly, and the latter, in turn, are under an obligation to pay regard to responsible criticism and try to respond as fully as possible. Unfortunately, disagreements are likely to persist if only because it is often so hard to establish the true facts of the case when some complaint is laid against the security forces. Much bitterness has also been caused by an incident of a different kind – the release from prison of a soldier convicted of murder who had served only a short part of his sentence. Situations of this kind are liable to recur, often with valid points on both sides, and this is one reason why a short period of stronger action against terrorism might be better than milder measures extended over a period of indefinite length – a point taken up in chapter 22. The crucially important fact is that, in the opinion of the Catholic hierarchy, the IRA is not fighting a 'just war'. It cannot then be right to boycott the judiciary and the security forces – a point very clearly made in the interdenominational report, *Violence in Ireland*, to which I have referred above (p. 214). To say, in this context, that 'it cannot be right' to do so is not to express a political opinion. All that is being said is that the verdict on terrorist activities, given by the Catholic leaders themselves, must as a matter of logical inference lead inescapably to the conclusion that the authorities responsible for law and order are entitled to support. It is only fair to recognize that, for a variety of historical reasons, the Catholic leaders may find it more difficult to give that support than do the leaders of the Protestant Churches. But the difficulty cannot remove the obligation.

21
The Republic and its Three Minorities

According to the Constitution of the Republic of Ireland, the national territory extends to the whole of the island. On this assumption, the Republic has three minority groups within its *de iure* frontiers: the Protestant minority in the North, the Catholic minority in the North and the Protestant minority within the Twenty-Six Counties. The first two of these groups are still outside the area under the effective authority of the present Republic but are within what is claimed, as of right, to be part of the national territory. The abolition of the border which excludes them is therefore regarded by politically active Irish nationalists as a primary objective of policy.

ULSTER MAJORITY, IRISH MINORITY

The Ulster Protestant population would, of course, reject with some firmness the suggestion that they could be regarded as a minority within the legitimate boundaries of the Republic. Nor is it my purpose in this chapter to endorse so contentious a claim. My purpose is quite simply to consider how those who do advance such a claim could be expected to behave towards these separated minorities. One might suppose that both minorities – the Protestants as well as the Catholics – would be treated with the affection and understanding due to fellow citizens. That would be only a natural approach. But is it really the approach that is adopted by Irish nationalists towards the Ulster Protestants? Or is it rather the case that these Northerners are treated as foreign aliens – and rather disagreeable aliens at that?

In view of their unrelenting determination to absorb the Northern counties, it would seem reasonable to suppose that nationalists in the South would have made themselves very familiar with those counties, with their characteristics and with the people who live there. This has not happened. *Irish irredentism is based on abstract aspiration rather than on love of a well-known country or affection and respect for its people.* Even as tourists, comparatively few Southerners have ever come to Ulster. It is an old saying, and a fair commentary on attitudes, that it is 'one hundred miles from Belfast to Dublin but one thousand miles from Dublin to Belfast'.

Certainly it was much more customary in the past for Northerners to visit the South than for southerners to visit the North. It is true that in quite recent years, a substantial number of Southerners have come to the towns on the British side of the border in search of cheaper shopping, but rather more than that would be required in order to obtain a reasonable understanding of the views of the Ulster people, whether Protestant or Catholic. As a recent investigator has shown, the opinions held over the years about the Ulster Protestants have largely consisted of a number of dubious stereotypes.[1]

The attitudes adopted towards the Northern Protestants have been puzzling and contradictory. Protestant opposition to a united Ireland has been bitterly resented but constitutional nationalists have held that this opposition should not, or could not, be crushed by force. It is not altogether clear whether force has been rejected as improper or as ineffecual. When the IRA had tried to make Ulster ungovernable in 1921–2 both the signatories and the opponents of the Treaty had supported the assault. De Valera, for his part, made many statements on the subject. In 1918, Ulster's opposition was 'a rock in the road' and 'They must if necessary blast it out of their path'. In 1927, he held that the Unionists who 'have wilfully assisted in mutilating their motherland can justly be made to suffer for their crime'. When pressed to explain what was meant by the slogan, 'We must punish Ulster', he admitted that 'They were not in a position to declare war on the six counties with England behind them'. As Bowman has shown,[2] de Valera was less extreme than many other republicans but, even so, there were occasions when the reason he gave for not attacking Ulster was simply lack of sufficient military force, rather than respect for self-determination.

Let us now, however, assume that any possibility of using force has been rejected in favour of constitutional nationalism. The objective is a united Ireland, but it is to be obtained only by peaceful means. What form should these means take? The Ulster Protestants are to be persuaded to come willingly into the Republic because they have been brought to regard themselves as members of the Irish nation. That would require a very great change in outlook on their part and also – as a prior condition – it would require a very great change of attitude on the part of the Irish nationalists who are trying to win them over. It would mean abandoning the notion, suggested by the map image, that, as an island, Ireland can contain only one nation. It would mean sacrificing the much cherished myth of a historic Irish nation. It would call for sufficient honesty to admit that there never was such a nation in the past and also to concede that there is not yet any sense of common nationality today capable of drawing together all the people of the island. As I said in concluding the opening chapter, the first step must be the abandonment of false ideas that are only an impediment in seeking to achieve the objective of unity. A united Irish nation is not something that has to be restored; it is something that has yet to be created. If that fact were recognized – and it is scarcely an obscure fact – a large step forward would have been taken.

If even the genuinely constitutional nationalists cannot quite bring themselves to kill the old myths that have been so dearly cherished, they might perhaps go so far as to concede that the Ulster Protestants, although truly 'members of the Irish nation' – in some sense that can be left undefined – have yet to realize that this is so. How, then, can a 'true consciousness' be fostered? A positive answer would be difficult, but it should at least be possible to see what ought *not* to be done. Not only is it foolish to try to take the border by force, as the IRA are trying to do, but it is also foolish to suppose that it can be taken by direct political assault. This would be the case even if Britain were not involved or even if Britain were fully prepared to collaborate. For the partition with which we are concerned is in the hearts and minds of the island's inhabitants and cannot be removed by merely altering the map. The harm done by Article 2 of the Republic's constitution illustrates the folly of asserting an imperialistic claim. In so far as that article has had an effect on political attitudes, the effect has been to sharpen the conflict. The sensible approach is then to accept the fact that partition will remain for an indefinite period. The more partition is execrated and the more its supporters are vilified, the longer the true division – that division in the hearts and minds – will persist. It is long since time for Irish nationalists to realize that their traditional policies are self-contradictory and tend to defeat the very objective they are meant to serve.

Although the fact of the border must be accepted, every effort can be made to ensure that its effect on the lives of ordinary people is as slight as possible. To this end, complete freedom of trade has always been desirable and so, from this point of view, has been monetary union. The Anglo-Irish trade agreement of 1965 was therefore a hopeful sign, and there was another and somewhat stronger glimmer of hope when both Britain and the Republic became members of the European Economic Community. For the two parts of Ireland were thereafter part of a larger unity which would reduce the practical importance of the border and might even encourage the people of Ireland to adopt a less narrowly parochial outlook. A greater measure of harmony might then be achieved without any abandonment of national sentiment on either side. But it was also clear that any advance along these lines would be halted and even reversed if the Republic were to yield to the old temptation of trying to take a short cut.

It may seem unrealistic to suggest that Irish nationalists should adopt a pragmatic rather than a doctrinaire approach, but it is worth recalling that, after the Boundary Commission had completed its work in 1925, the Free State Government did, for a time, pursue the kind of policy that commonsense suggests. The outcome of that inquiry had been bitterly disappointing to the Irish Free State, but Cosgrave and the other leaders of the Cumann na nGaedheal party, then in power, resigned themselves to accepting what they could not alter. The boundary corresponding to a six-county Northern Ireland was officially endorsed in a treaty registered with the League of Nations – just as the Anglo-Irish Agreement was registered with the United Nations many years later. It was a courageous step for the Irish Government to take, for the deep divisions that had led to the civil war within the Free State were by no means closed. The opponents of the Treaty of 1921 were still boycotting the Dail and the gunmen were still sporadically active.[3] The Irish Government was also accused of deserting the Catholic minority in the North but, on this issue, its leaders again took a bold and constructive line by advising the Nationalists in Ulster to take their seats in the Belfast parliament. This was a very marked change of attitude from that adopted four years before when non-cooperation had been the policy recommended to Ulster Catholics by both the moderates and the more hard-line republicans in the South. In response to the new and more helpful approach adopted by the Dublin government in 1925, the Unionists, for their part, should have been at pains to respond. When the Nationalists finally took their seats in Parliament, an effort should have been made to draw them as fully as possible into the process of policy-making, and this could have been done without an elaborate arrangement for power-sharing of the kind ultimately tried in 1973/4. There would then have been at least some chance of breaking the vicious circle of resentment, suspicion and discrimination, with cooperation now withheld and now rejected, that was to be the sad characteristic of the years ahead. What concerns us, in the immediate context, however, is that, for a few years, an Irish Government was adopting a constructive approach which was described at the time as follows: 'Our policy should in its broad general sense aim rather at attracting towards [us] these Northern Irishmen rather than alienating them still further from us with a view to shortening the period to the ultimate and inevitable union.'[4] That union would at best lie far ahead, but it was better to move slowly in the right direction than to rush away in the wrong direction.

The Fianna Fail Government did in fact choose to rush away in the wrong direction when it came into power in 1932. Or rather it chose as the basic objective, the further separation of the Free State from England with no regard to the fact that, in moving away from Britain, they were moving away from Ulster. The traditional republican policy of economic nationalism was adopted which was scarcely the way to attract Ulster's support. Worse was to come in the form of the Irish Constitution of 1937, which has been one of the factors consolidating and perpetuating the partition of Ireland. 'Eire' – the new name that replaced Irish Free State – became, in effect, a republic whose establishment apparently vindicated the Unionists who had always prophesied that a limited measure of autonomy granted to Ireland would be only the first step towards independence. Moreover the notorious Article 2 – to which we have had much cause to refer – laid imperialistic claim to the possession of the whole island. It may be held that this was merely empty rhetoric of no practical importance, but that was not so. It amounted to the repudiation of the 1925 agreement which was not in the least protected by having been registered with the League of Nations. It was a lesson for Ulstermen to remember. Subsequently this Article has proved to be 'a rock in the path' towards a better understanding between the two parts of Ireland and, by formally enshrining a misleading myth, has encouraged nationalists to evade the uncomfortable fact that an Irish nation is something that has yet to be created.

Another Unionist warning – that Home Rule would mean Rome Rule – seemed to be vindicated by Article 44 of the 1937 Constitution, which recognized 'the special position of the Holy Catholic Apostolic and Roman Church as the guardian of the Faith professed by the great majority of the citizens'. In the past, membership of that Church had been most unfairly punished and, although that past was by then rather distant, one can understand the desire to make an assertion of this kind. Moreover it is only fair to add that the main Protestant denominations and the Jewish faith were also recognized, and religious discrimination was forbidden. Nevertheless, Article 44 was damaging to Irish unity – as was in effect conceded when it was removed in 1972. Another Article declared that divorce would not be allowed. Another proclaimed that Irish was the first language with English – the real language of the country – accorded second place. The next constitutional step was to be taken in 1948 when a republic was formally declared and Ireland withdrew from the Commonwealth. As we have seen in tracing the history of the nineteenth and early twentieth centuries, Irish nationalists had pursued their objectives with a total disregard for the views of the majority in Ulster. That unfortunate practice was to be maintained in modern times. The conflict of opinions and the division of territory to which such behaviour so generously contributed, was then greeted repeatedly with expressions of surprise and outrage and followed by attempts to attribute to others – usually the British – the full blame for developments that were so much the consequence of their own actions. If commonsense had not been extinguished by nationalistic fervour it would have been recognized that every new move that further weakened the link betwen the South and Britain also weakened the link between the South and the North.

The Second World War provided a magnificent opportunity to take a long step forward towards a closer unity of sentiment in the island. By this I do not mean that Britain should have been offered full support in return for removing partition. The Ulster people would have resented being used as a pawn in that way, and even if Britain could have implemented a constitutional transfer, the disunity of sentiment would have remained. Unconditional support against the Nazis was what was required but was, of course, withheld. Even at the most desperate stage in the Battle of the Atlantic, Britain was denied the use of the ports so unwisely surrendered on the eve of the war. There is no need to elaborate on further incidents such as the protest when the US forces landed in Ulster on their way to participate in the liberation of Europe, the rejection of the US request for bases and the stiff-necked regard for protocol that led de Valera to send Germany a message of sympathy when Hitler's death was announced. There can be no doubt that de Valera favoured the Allied side but he was determined to demonstrate that Eire, as an independent nation, could choose to be neutral if she wished.[5] It was not, then, altogether surprising that the Soviet Union should have vetoed the Republic's entry to the United Nations for many years after the war. Nor was it surprising that after the newly proclaimed Republic had left the Commonwealth in 1948, Britain's Labour Government should have guaranteed Ulster's constitutional position for as long as it was supported by a majority in the Northern Ireland Parliament. Yet this guarantee came as a shock to the politicians in the Republic. The Taoiseach (Costello) moved a resolution which referred to the 'indefeasible right of the Irish nation to the unity and integrity of the national territory' – a resolution which rested on the empirically false assumption that there really was an Irish nation of this kind. The words 'indefeasible right', though empty of meaning, were to be constantly reiterated over the years – notably, in modern times, by Charles Haughey. When Costello moved a resolution of protest in the Dail, De Valera supported it and declared:

Every time this question of the partition of our country loomed up as a question to be considered between the Irish and British governments you had immediately an election call to pretend that the people in the Six Counties were democratically supported in their attitude. They told us that it is only by the will of this Northern Ireland Parliament that we can ever hope to get our unity – through the will of a Parliament that is specially designed to deny it. We are told that no part of that territory can be taken from them except by the will of that Parliament – a Parliament that is empowered to gerrymander, as they have done in many cases, to any extent they wish.[6]

These remarks, which would have had widespread support in the Dail, encapsulate in a few sentences the errors of fact and inference so characteristic of the republican attitude to partition. Although the Unionists laid themselves open to attack by gerrymandering in local government in a way that was both improper and stupid, the *parliamentary* strength of the opposition to a united Ireland did not depend upon electoral malpractices but upon the near-unanimous attitude of the Protestant majority. It required no great research to establish that this was the case. The refusal to accept so unpleasant a fact has, however, persisted down the years and is still a barrier to political progress in the island.

It may seem strange that the British guarantee should have provoked so much indignation in the Republic with the Minister for External Affairs, Sean MacBride, playing the leading role. An attempt was even made to persuade the US administration to intervene. The State Department reported that there was a distinct possibility of violence involving MacBride's Clann na Poblachta and the IRA, but it was also reported that: 'Until recently the agitation on this issue has been largely the concern of Irish politicians. Our Legation in Dublin has reported general apathy towards both the question of partition and the entering into force last month of the Republic of Ireland Act.'[7] Not for the first time and not for the last, the politicians were determined to keep the pot boiling.

In the same year, the Republic was invited to join NATO but declined with the problem of partition given as the reason. Support for the Western alliance could of course be provided without formal membership of NATO but, by adhering strictly to its policy of neutrality, the Republic has put itself in a somewhat delicate position as a member of the European Community. Some concern has been expressed in Britain about the 'undefended frontier',[8] and this, together with economic considerations, may have been a reason, on the British side, for establishing the Anglo-Irish Intergovernmental Council in 1980. Clearly it had been hoped that some fuller recognition of the common interests of the two islands would begin to supersede the disputed question about political unity in the island of Ireland, but the Anglo-Irish Agreement appears in turn to have restored the traditional emphasis.

There has also, in recent years, been a growing, if still rather slight, willingness even on the part of politicians to admit that nationality in Ireland is not so simply and clearly defined as used to be implied. There has been no question of conceding that there is more than one nation, but it has been recognized that, within this nation – with its supposedly 'indefeasible rights' – there are different 'traditions'. This admission is at least a first step towards reality, and that is progress. But it is far from clear how a 'tradition', in this particular context, differs from a 'nation'. Boulding was endorsing a point that has long been widely accepted when he said: 'In the formation of the national image the consciousness of great *shared* events and experiences is of the utmost importance. A nation is a body of people who are conscious of having 'gone through something' together.'[9] 'Tradition', in this sense, is what makes a nation. What is of some interest is that the participants in the Forum made so little attempt to show that the 'two traditions' in Ireland have anything in common. For example, the specific reference to the battle of the Somme as part of the Northern Protestant tradition is not followed by any reference to the fact that volunteers from both parts of the island fought on the same side in both of the great wars. For these wars are still regarded as Britain's wars and of no concern to Ireland. Even those citizens of the Republic who played a distinguished part in defeating Hitler's Nazi tyranny are not officially remembered in this inward looking Republic where the preserved tradition is that of the old struggle against the British. A somewhat divisive approach, one might suppose.

As was recorded in chapter 18, none of the constitutional suggestions put forward by the Forum envisaged an arrangement by which Northern Ireland would remain part of the United Kingdom, as does the Anglo-Irish Agreement. The Forum's largest concession – for which Garret Fitzgerald was presumably responsible – was contained in the option by which Northern Ireland would become a condominium under the joint authority of the United Kingdom and the Republic. But the preferred option was a unitary Irish republic for the whole of the island. This was the only option to which Haughey was prepared to give full support. For there has been only a little political progress in the Republic, and its leaders are still a long way from accepting the wisdom in a remark made long ago by Kevin O'Higgins: 'It is useless to seek to abolish the Boundary in law until we have abolished it in our hearts.'

There is an immediate problem of much more pressing importance than any future constitutional arrangement. This is the problem of ending terrorist attacks in the North when the terrorists can escape across a frontier that the security forces are not allowed to pass. Here is a basic test of the *moral foundation* on which the Republic must base its claim to the whole of Ireland. If Ireland is indeed a single nation, then the Protestant minority in Northern Ireland have an 'indefeasible right' to protection to be accorded to them by the Government of the Republic of Ireland. That Government must not expect to have it both ways. In asserting the 'indefeasible claim to unity', with which we are so familiar, it is also accepting the obligation to protect its citizens. To do so is not to make a concession which may be more generous or less generous, perhaps as a part of some political bargain, such as the Anglo-Irish Agreement. It is to recognize a basic duty of any government in any country. It is true that partition makes it impossible for the Republic to carry out this function inside the Six Counties, but it falls within its present jurisdiction to ensure that the Twenty-Six Counties do not provide a haven for those guilty of acts of terrorism in the North. It is scarcely necessary to add that, in fact, action of this needed kind has been taken but it can also be held that the action was taken too slowly and is still on too limited a scale. It was a different matter in 1956–62 when the Irish Government collaborated with the Ulster Government – although at that time it was a Unionist Government of the days before reform. The present terrorist phase began, as we have seen, in a different way and did not elicit cooperation of an equally effective kind. So much was conceded in the Anglo-Irish Agreement itself which was to be followed by closer cooperation between the police, North and South. In Westminster this prospect of improved security was much emphasized when the Agreement was debated and was clearly regarded as one of its principal merits. For any such improvement the Ulster people, for their part, could be deeply thankful; but they were also entitled to ask why full-scale cooperation had been withheld for so many years. They could also be forgiven for expressing some hesitation before taking it for granted that the new undertaking would be fully and ungrudgingly honoured. To quote from a speech made by Ian Gow at that time: 'Is it really suggested that without the agreement such cooperation would have been less effective? All civilized Governments, with or without a formal agreement, should commit themselves unreservedly to the elimination of terrorism.'[10] Security matters are discussed in chapter 22, but there is a point of some importance that can properly be made at this stage. The IRA has provided successive governments in the Republic with an opportunity to demonstrate to Northern Protestants what is meant by belonging to an 'Irish nation' that encompasses all the people living on the island. By accepting fully and without evasion or hesitation their obligation to protect all Irish citizens from terrorist violence, these Governments might have made substantial progress towards winning the support and sympathy they claim to deserve in *Hibernia Irredenta*.

THE ULSTER CATHOLICS

The second of the minorities, the Catholic minority in Ulster, is, of course, regarded in a quite different light. To both the more moderate Irish nationalists in the South and to the more extreme republicans, this minority is without question part of the Irish nation although condemned to artificial separation by a Border that the English – allegedly – imposed. It is of some real interest to observe that this recognition of the Ulster Catholics as 'our people' accords a different meaning to the concept of nationality from that implied in the familiar assertion that the nation embraces the whole of the island and all its people. As we have seen, the latter interpretation is derived from the myth of an ancient Irish nation and supported by the psychological impact of the map-image. In the treatment of the Ulster Catholics, however, the decisive importance of national sentiment is implicitly conceded.

The Southerners had, therefore, two reasons for deploring the plight of the Northern Catholics: first, they were treated unfairly by the Unionist Government and, secondly, they were denied self-determination which in itself was a wrong that ought to be righted. We have devoted a good deal of attention in previous chapters to the first of these points. The Unionists did not establish a police state and discrimination was not practised on anything like the scale that has been so often alleged. The Catholic minority was not 'deprived of the means of social and economic development' as the Forum, with a flourish of untruthful rhetoric, proclaimed. The fact remains that there was some discrimination and the Forum was also justified in referring to the denial 'of the right of nationalists . . . to effective participation in the institutions of Government.' As I have already observed, with some emphasis, the Unionists should have tried to draw the nationalist politicians into the business of policy-making. Admittedly there is little reason to suppose that Catholics would have been encouraged by the hierarchy to respond and cooperate, but the attempt should have been made, even in face of repeated rebuffs. There should also have been an attempt by Protestants at all levels of society to break down the 'social apartheid' which resulted in Catholics being regarded as, in some sense, inferior. Again there might have been no response and might even have been resistance. For, from a Catholic viewpoint, social apartheid had the important incidental merit of being a shield against dangerous thoughts and bad example.

Stormont has gone. For almost twenty years the Province has been governed directly from Westminster with no local parliament or assembly to complicate the situation – apart from a brief spell in 1973–4 – and with even the role of local government severely curtailed. In circumstances such as these, political responsibility has rested squarely with successive British Governments which can surely not have wished to oppress the Catholic minority. It may be objected that these governments failed, for many years, to exert as much effort as they should have done in coping with discrimination in employment – that still sore topic discussed in chapter 12. Suppose, however, that the further measures adopted in 1988 prove in the event to be effective. Suppose that, in this and in all other respects, the minority is to be treated with scrupulous fairness, or even to be given the benefit of positive discrimination on its behalf. Could we then assume that the political parties and their leaders in the Republic would be satisfied? The answer is that they would not, for the irredentist complaint would remain. The island would still be partitioned and the Ulster Catholics would still be denied self-determination, or would *appear* to be so. The other grievances of this minority – in, say, housing or employment – have served the useful purpose of bolstering the case for political change and their removal may have been viewed with mixed feelings in Dublin. The Southern nationalists have, in fact, been engaged for many years in an unacknowledged trade-off. That is to say they have constantly emphasized and greatly exaggerated the unfair treatment of the Northern Catholics in order to discredit partition, but any gain thus achieved has been bought only at the cost of a further alienation of the Northern Protestants.

What opinions do the Ulster Catholics themselves really hold? 'Opinions' – for one can expect some variation in outlook and certainly some difference in the degree of emphasis attached to different issues. The main parties in the Republic claim to know the answer for, under the Anglo-Irish Agreement, they claim to represent the minority. It is an interesting claim that calls for attention. At the Conferences held under this Agreement, the Foreign Minister of the Republic will be able to regard himself as the spokesman for the Catholics although they will have taken no part in the election that brought his party into power. He will know what they want – or what they *ought* to want if faithful supporters of Fine Gael or Fianna Fail as the case may be. The Secretary of State cannot, it is implied, be expected to act as the spokesman of the Catholics but he will be left to perform that function for the Protestants and must, by implication, have a *dual role* both as 'president of the court' and as counsel for one of the parties. In practice, of course, the Secretary of State is likely to be as close to the leadership of the SDLP as to that of the Official Unionists and a great deal closer than he will be to the leadership of Paisley's Democratic Unionist Party. The same SDLP leadership also maintains close contact with Dublin and, in these ways, has in effect two voices – one in the Westminster Parliament and one in the Dail through Fianna Fail, and even Fine Gael. The SDLP has become increasingly concerned with Irish unity, to be prefaced by various other links between Northern Ireland and the Republic.

The views of the ordinary Catholic people are more difficult to ascertain than are the views of the ordinary Protestants. There can be no doubt that the vast majority of the Protestants are firmly opposed to being absorbed into the Irish Republic; but we cannot take it for granted, as used to be done, that the Catholics are as unanimous in their desire to be so. One of the most commonly made assumptions used to be that almost two-thirds of the Ulster people were against unity and slightly over one-third in favour, but there have been many changes in Northern Ireland over the past twenty years which may have evoked some response on the part of the minority. Even in the heyday of Unionist rule, Catholics voted with their feet in favour of Northern Ireland and rarely, in this way, in favour of the Republic. When opinion polls came to be held, the answers given showed that the Catholic minority was divided in its sympathies. Even in 1968 only 76 per cent of these Ulster Catholics felt that the term 'Irish' best described the way they felt about themselves. Only 56 per cent of these Catholic respondents were in favour of a united Ireland.[11]

It is hardly necessary to stress that polls of this kind, however well designed, must be interpreted with caution. A number of questions have to be asked for attitudes to Irish unity will obviously be affected by the nature of the alternatives. A united Ireland as against a Northern Ireland with power-sharing? Or one without power-sharing? And so on. The possibilities presented over the years by different pollsters have naturally varied which makes it all the harder to identify and summarize any changes in opinion that have taken place. And there are always the 'don't knows'. Notwithstanding these and other difficulties, it is clear that a substantial proportion of the Catholics in Northern Ireland has not expressed itself to be in favour of unity with the Republic. A poll held in May 1973 recorded that, of the various possibilities put before them, only 48 per cent accorded first preference to unity. In 1974, the figure was only 23 per cent. In 1976, although power-sharing had been swept away and there had then been a further period of murder and disruption, the figure was still 23 per cent. Almost half the Catholics stated that 'they would regard a policy of encouraging a united Ireland as unacceptable'. In 1978 only 69 per cent of Catholic respondents described themselves as 'Irish' while 15 per cent said 'British' and 6 per cent 'Ulster'. In 1980, however, 69 per cent had fallen to 38 per cent but by 1984 it had risen again to 50 per cent. Later polls suggested that 47 per cent favoured unity in 1985 but only 22 per cent in 1987 and 1988. Thus, over 90 per cent of Ulster's total population seemingly want to remain in the United Kingdom.

The reason for quoting so many results is to show that, although the proportion of the Catholic population in favour of a united Ireland has varied from poll to poll, there has been sufficient consistency to discredit the commonly made assertion that all the Northern Catholics – now nearly two fifths of the total population of Northern Ireland – want the Six Counties to be absorbed into the Republic. This is clearly not the case, and was not the case even before the Unionist regime came to an end.

The inference is important. It means that we are not faced with quite such a hopeless conflict of national loyalties as the more strident republican claims would imply. It means that the Unionists, when still in power, might have built up a more stable political system if they had been at pains to avoid both the fact and the appearance of discrimination, and had accorded the minority a larger measure of tolerance and respect. For the future it means that it is not necessary to despair of reaching some tolerable solution. Our immediate concern, however, is with the lesson for the political leaders in the Republic. They are not justified in taking it for granted that the Ulster Catholics are 'our people'. They are so in religious beliefs but not in political outlook. On the contrary, there is a marked division of opinion about the desirability of leaving the United Kingdom in order to join the Republic. These political leaders can scarcely be unaware that this is so but have preferred to ignore such troublesome facts and to remain content with the old rhetoric about the 'indefeasible right' to unity.

What have also been ignored have been the opinions expressed in polls by members of the Republic's own electorate. The answers neglected include those given by Dubliners and reported by Father Michael MacGriel in a book published in 1972.[12] One of the questions related to this very issue of the unity of the nation and 43 per cent supported the view that there are, in fact, two Irish nations. About 58 per cent regarded unity as an essential condition for a just solution of the Northern Ireland problem, but 36 per cent disagreed. One of the questions asked whether Catholics in Northern Ireland have more in common with Northern Protestants than they have with Catholics in the Republic, and to this the answer from 60 per cent supported the first alternative – surely an interesting assessment on the part of the respondents. In 1980 a poll carried out by RTE – the Irish radio and television authority – came up with the result that only 56 per cent favoured Irish unity and, a further interesting point, that 13 per cent supported the idea of an independent Northern Ireland. The respondents also expressed, by a substantial majority, their willingness to share oil and gas finds with the North but only 29 per cent were prepared to pay higher taxes as part of the cost of unity. The number broadly in favour of unity appeared to have risen to 76 per cent in 1983 but to have declined to 67 per cent in 1987. Even the 67 per cent dropped sharply to 39 per cent when it was suggested that unity might mean higher taxes. What attracted most attention in the 1987 poll results was the fact that almost a half of the respondents expressed the view that Ireland would never be united.

When all the qualifications appropriate to any poll results have been made, it is clear that the ordinary citizens of the Republic who gave these answers are well in advance of most of their political leaders in political perception and in a readiness to accept the truth of the situation.

THE SOUTHERN PROTESTANTS

The third of the Republic's minorities – the only one that is normally so described – consists of the Protestants living in the Twenty-Six Counties. Their fate has had some influence on attitudes in the North, although it would be rash to suppose that the treatment accorded to a small minority can be taken as a reliable guide to the treatment that could be anticipated by a very much larger minority. When the Irish Free State was formed, about a tenth of the population was Protestant, but their numbers have declined over the years and they now constitute roughly 4 per cent. This decline, closely observed in Ulster, contrasts sharply with the growth of the Catholic minority in the latter area. Why has it occurred?

During the war of independence and the period of turmoil that followed, the Protestants were harassed and threatened in some parts of what is now the Republic but, when stability had been achieved, this minority was well treated in a number of respects. The Protestant Churches were recognized, and Protestant schools were given some financial support. A few Protestants with the right personal or family backgrounds achieved high positions in the state. 'Home Rule' was not harsh rule. That much must be said at once. The fact remains that the Protestants were living in an assertively Catholic country and – to use the modern jargon – were bound to feel 'alienated'. It would therefore seem natural to infer that the Protestant emigration rate would be high. The inference may be valid for some periods but in that studied by Professor Brendan Walsh – 1946–61 – the evidence showed a substantially higher rate of Catholic emigration.[13] There were other reasons for the fall in the Protestant population, in particular an older age structure which meant a higher mortality rate and a lower birth rate. Another explanation of the Protestant decline was the effect of the *Ne Temere* ruling on mixed marriages (see chapter 20). This ruling was not, of course, peculiar to the Irish Republic but was liable to be particularly severe in its effect in such a society where the non-Catholics were in a small minority. First, there was a greater likelihood that Protestant young people would marry Catholics simply because there were fewer Protestant young people around. Secondly, in a local society that was overwhelmingly Catholic, intense social pressures could be brought to bear on any family with one Catholic parent that tried to defy the Catholic church by bringing its children up as Protestants, humanists or whatever. Walsh's investigation suggested that about 25 per cent of each generation of Protestants was lost to the Protestant faith in this way. As we have seen, *Ne Temere* has now been superseded, but it remains to be seen whether the new ruling will bear much less heavily on non-Catholic families (see chapter 20).

In their report of 1982, the parties comprizing the Forum expressed satisfaction at the way in which the non-Catholic minority had been treated, and claimed that 'constitutional, electoral and parliamentary arrangements in the South specifically sought to cater for the minority status of Southern unionists and did so with considerable, if not total, success.'[14] It is puzzling that the explicit reference is to 'unionists', not Protestants or non-Catholics, for it is hard to see how the 'constitutional, electoral and parliamentary arrangements' have catered in any way for those persons – Catholic as well as non-Catholic – who wished to preserve the Union with Britain in one form or another. On the contrary, the unionist case was simply ignored and even the more moderate form of Irish nationalism was a lost cause after Fianna Fail came into power in 1932.

The minority problem in the Republic has been a good deal easier than in Ulster for two related reasons. The first has been the small size of the minority group, which has prevented it from being a serious challenge in any part of the country. Members of the minority have therefore accepted their position – or have left the country. In Ulster the minority has, of course, been very much larger and – the second factor – it declined to cooperate with the Unionist governments, and was not much pressed to do so. In more recent years, the possibility of cooperation within some form of government in Ulster appears to have increased but, with everything overshadowed by violence, it is not easy to discern what can be achieved. The immediate point to observe is that generosity towards a small and harmless minority should be cheap and easy. That generosity has been curtailed, however, for three reasons. First, there has been the resolve to assert complete independence from Britain in all possible respects, from cultural heritage to the conduct of practical political affairs – a resolve which ought to have weakened with the achievement of maturity but has shown slight sign of doing so. Secondly, the attempt to revive the Irish language and to concentrate attention on Gaelic culture has been a tiresome exercise. Thirdly, the special role accorded to the Catholic Church has made it clear that a non-Catholic is 'not really one of us'; and the embodiment of Catholic moral values in legislation has entailed a restriction of personal freedom.

There is no need to add to what has been said already about the first of the points above, but the second point – the consequence of the Gaelic revival – requires further attention. The Gaelic revival was a natural accompaniment of burgeoning nationalism but it developed in unfortunate ways. The crusade for the revival of the Irish language derived some of its force and fervour from the belief that its decay was simply attributable to the deliberate efforts of the English oppressors. In fact we are now informed that the Catholic school teachers, even at the time of the hedge-schools, perceived that English was a more useful language and set out to teach it.[15] To attempt to revive Gaelic when it had become only the language of a remote minority may appear to have been a somewhat quixotic effort and one that, in so far as it could be achieved, would be at the expense of teaching in other subjects. Such a policy was also bound to strengthen the division between the Catholic and Protestant communities. A revival of interest in early Irish culture was a different matter which could have been imparted to school children without their being required to learn the language – perhaps better imparted with less time devoted to the linguistic side which could have been left to specialists. (After all elementary courses on the civilizations of Greece and Rome are now given, even in universities, without the non-specialists being required to show proficiency in the languages.) But the enthusiasts – of whom initially some of the leading figures were untypical Southern Protestants – were determined that the language, notwithstanding its limited usefulness, must be revived as must everything else that could be associated with that ancient Gaelic ascendancy – even Gaelic sports. There seems to have been no awareness – or no willingness to concede – that the movement would have further divisive consequences in an already too divided country. So much was implicit in Pearse's famous plea for 'Ireland . . . not free merely, but Gaelic as well; not Gaelic, merely, but free as well.'[16] A somewhat unpleasant racist theory came to be emphasized, as is clearly shown in the following assertion by Corcoran:

The Irish nation is the Gaelic nation; its language and literature is the Gaelic language; its history is the history of the Gael. All other elements have no place in Irish national life, literature and tradition, save as far as they are assimilated into the very substance of Gaelic speech, life and thought. The Irish nation is not a racial synthesis at all . . .[17]

Admittedly Corcoran was an extremist, but he was giving sharp and clear expression to a view that was also expressed, sometimes more moderately, sometimes with equal force, by many others, including such practical politicians as de Valera himself. This racist doctrine was not only as bogus as racism elsewhere (see chapter 1) but it was also politically harmful for it was scarcely likely to evoke a sympathetic response from British/Irish people whether in the Six Counties or in the Twenty-Six Counties. In practical terms, it meant compulsory Irish for school teachers, compulsory Irish in schools, compulsory Irish for civil service entrants – in its way, a disguised form of discrimination. It was not until 1974 that the requirement for the civil service and for school certificate was removed, but by then much harm had been done. The richer members of the minority could, of course, view this Gaelic enthusiasm with a measure of indulgence and detachment because their children would be sent to English schools and would not have to find careers in the Republic unless they chose to do so. It was a different matter for the less affluent.

The dominant position of the Catholic Church – the third of the points mentioned above – meant that Catholic morality was imposed with regard to divorce, contraception and abortion and continues to be so today, with only a slight relaxation which allows doctors to prescribe contraceptives in appropriate cases. The authority of the Catholic Church was also asserted in such a way as to affect the development of the welfare state in the Republic. In 1950 the famous Mother and Child case demonstrated to non-Catholics on both sides of the border that this Church could exert decisive authority when it decided to do so. In that year the young Minister of Health, Dr Noel Browne, proposed to provide free medical care for mothers and expectant mothers and for children under the age of sixteen. It was scarcely a revolutionary proposal as compared with developments in Great Britain and Northern Ireland. It was, however, strongly condemned, not only by the Irish Medical Association, but by the Catholic hierarchy for a number of reasons which may be summarized as follows:[18]

1 'The right to provide for the health of children belongs to parents, not to the state. The State has the right to intervene only in a subsidiary capacity, to supplement, not to surplant. It may help indigent or neglectful parents; it may not deprive 90% of parents of their rights because of 10% necessitous or negligent parents.' (The inference was that any assistance provided must be subject to a very severe means-test.)
2 'Education in regard to motherhood includes instruction in regard to sex relations, chastity and marriage. The State has no competence to give instruction in such matters. We regard with the greatest apprehension the proposal to give to local medical officers the right to tell Catholic girls and women how they should behave in regard to this sphere of conduct at once so delicate and so sacred.'

The bishops' insistence upon confining assistance to low income families committed them strongly to one side in the general debate about the welfare state which, of course, still continues in a number of countries.[19] In the Republic itself, even today, comprehensive free health care continues to be provided only for people with incomes below certain limits, the poorest quarter of the population, although the state heavily subsidizes the voluntary contributory health insurance system which covers the rest of the population. (It would of course be unwarranted to assume that this continues to be so solely because of any views expressed by the Catholic hierarchy.) Our concern is not, however, with the intricacies of the debate about 'selectivity' but rather with the way in which the power of the Catholic Church was demonstrated by the famous Browne case. The message to non-Catholics on both sides of the border seemed to be clear. In the words of the supposedly radical Sean MacBride: 'You cannot afford to fight the Church.'

As is well known, the Catholic Church also asserted its views on morality by imposing a tight censorship of publications. For many years the works not only of 'foreigners' but of some of the greatest Irish authors were officially banned – though no doubt often smuggled in from England or from more liberal Ulster. It would, however, be a serious misrepresentation to imply that such rulings were passively accepted or that nothing has changed over the years. A hard-fought campaign against censorship led to some relaxation in 1967 when books that had been published *twelve years before* were removed from the banned list, which in itself meant the release of 5000 titles.[20] But the censors are still at work. For example, in May 1987 it was reported that a book called *The Joy of Sex* and another book about erotic Hindu sculptures had been banned.[21] There have also been strong campaigns against the law prohibiting the sale of contraceptives. John Hume put the matter very clearly as follows: 'The real issue is whether the law should impose the religious viewpoint of one section of the community on another.'[22]

There are, of course, many people in Britain who believe that society has become too 'permissive' and would like to see rather more control. For example, it is held that television should be more restrained in its treatment of sex and violence. Again it must be emphasized that we are not directly concerned with these controversies but only with the social and political repercussions in Ireland. It is, however, in place to comment when inconsistent attitudes have been adopted, and this has long been true of the attitudes adopted towards Northern Ireland by the Liberal/Left in Britain. The traditional attitude to the non-Catholic majority has been one of moral disapproval. The Protestants are regarded as stiff-necked bigots who ought to be pushed into the Irish Republic by every means except, possibly, force. For a united Ireland is seen as the right objective – even if it means that the non-Catholics will then find themselves in a state whose laws have been shaped by the Catholic ethic and a state where that most venerated institution of the Left is missing – a free universal health service. It is puzzling to understand why English socialists should wish to see the Ulster workers living under a regime which they would regard as unacceptable for English workers – and from which, if threatened with it, they themselves would recoil in dismay.

As we have noted, conditions have begun to change in the Republic. The British television programmes which can be watched there, with the secular and permissive approach to life which they so strongly reflect, may have gradually fostered the adoption of more liberal views. The Catholic attitude to Trinity College, Dublin, may serve as an example. Catholics had long been discouraged from going to that college; they were forbidden to do so in 1944 by the Archbishop of Dublin – J. C. McQuaid who was every bit as rigid in his views as is Ian Paisley. That ban was removed in 1970 and 'integrated education' has been accepted, at least for this particular institution. More generally there appears to have been some weakening of the Church's hold, especially over the younger generation. The Republic, moreover, is no longer the same inward-looking stagnant society of the 1950s. The opening of the economy to foreign trade was followed by further measures to open up the society to outside influences and by some crumbling away of the old parochial walls. The decision to join the European Community was clearly important in these wider respects as well as in its effect on trade. More generally, it is clearly impossible in the television age to insulate Ireland from the powerful secular influences of the outside world. In short the Republic has changed and is changing, and it is desirable that people in Ulster should be aware of these facts, although the process is likely to be slow.

22
Security – Maintaining the Law
and Respecting the Law

The defeat of terrorism is the most urgent of the tasks to be performed in dealing with the complex of issues that constitute the 'Ulster problem'. Over the years 1969 to 1987, 2618 people have been killed and about 20,000 injured. When it is recalled that the population is only 1.5 million, the scale of the suffering can be better appreciated. Moreover, after almost twenty years, the end is not yet in sight and it is this discouraging fact, more than any other, that makes the Ulster problem seem insoluble. The gloom is relieved, though not dispelled, when account is taken of the improvement that has been achieved. As figure 22.1 records, the number of casualties rose sharply in 1971 and reached a peak in 1972 with 467 people killed in that year. The fact that this increase occurred *after* a large number of social reforms had been carried out should serve as a warning against any assumption that violence can be readily and quickly stopped by measures for the betterment of social conditions. By 1985, the best year, the number killed had fallen to about one-eighth the number of victims in 1972. It will also be observed that the curve, after dropping in the mid-1970s, remained fairly flat but with a sharp percentage rise since 1985, the year when the Anglo-Irish Agreement was announced. A further upsurge occurred in 1987/8 as the new supplies of arms and explosives from Libya were brought into use. This was a bad setback, although the number of casualties remained far below those for the early 1970s. In these circumstances, it is hard to convey an accurate impression of conditions in Belfast which would show how normal life goes on cheerfully enough but would, at the same time, convey the sense of suffering and strain.

In dealing with terrorism, the security forces have been obliged to operate under three constraints:

1 The Border which they cannot cross has provided a base and a refuge for republican terrorists.
2 There are urban areas within Northern Ireland where law and order have never been fully restored since those disastrous early days in the 1970s to which I have referred in chapter 16.
3 Although emergency powers are in force, the normal rights of the citizen must be infringed as little as possible.

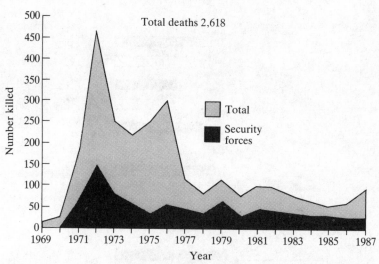

FigURE 22.1 The security situation: deaths arising 1969–87 (source: RUC, Chief Constable's Annual Report)

The continuing failure of the security forces to put an end to terrorist activities is scarcely surprising when proper account is taken of these three constraints within which they are required to operate.

The Border

The importance of the Republic as a base for the IRA in the 1970s when violence was at its height, has been described as follows by former Secretary of State Merlyn Rees: 'As I, and presumably also the Irish government, already knew, its leaders – the Army Council [of the IRA] – met in Dublin on Thursdays, and it was from the South that the violence in the North was orchestrated.'[1] After various charges in the IRA command, it was from a Dublin headquarters that the campaign was again being directed in the 1980s. Moreover, during the whole period of close to twenty years, the IRA has also been able to use suitable training areas within the inadequately policed Republic. When operations have been carried out, they have been able to find a refuge across the Border which the security forces in Ulster are not allowed to cross. The importance of the Border is illustrated by the statistics for incidents in South Tyrone and Fermanagh, where a systematic campaign, sometimes described as being close to genocide, has been directed against Protestant farmers and their sons. It is strongly suspected that the objective has been to drive the families off the land which can then be acquired by Catholics in these sensitive areas. Most of the victims have also served at one time or another – sometimes many years ago – in the police or its reserve, or in the British army, and that is a crime which, in republican eyes, can never be expunged. The convenience of the escape route provided by the Border is shown by the fact that 158 murders

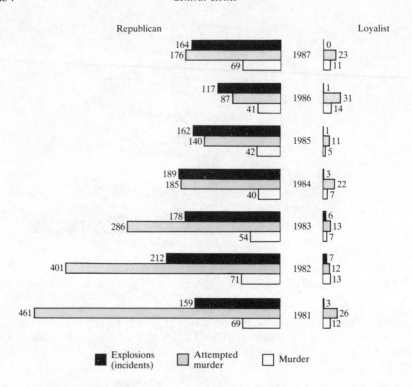

FIGURE 22.2　Known terrorist activity 1981–7 (source: RUC, Chief Constable's Annual Report)

were committed by republicans in these areas from the beginning of 1971 until September 1987, but only fourteen republicans were convicted. Over the same period twenty-two people were murdered by Loyalists in these areas but convictions were obtained in half of these cases.[2]

It would be unfair to imply that the terrorists were completely safe in the Republic, even in the earlier period of the disturbances, for many were arrested and imprisoned. But they were then in no danger of being tried for crimes committed in Ulster and might get away with a light sentence for membership of a proscribed organization. This, of course, was the reason why an extradition arrangement was sought, but without success, over a long period of years.[3] As we have seen (chapter 17), a compromise emerged from the Sunningdale conference in 1973, after the request for extradition, strongly pressed by Unionist representatives, had again been rejected. The compromise was that arrangements should be made for extra-territorial trials at which a person could be tried where he had been apprehended for an offence committed on the other side of the Border. In practice, however, this arrangement proved so difficult to organize as to be largely ineffective. Subsequently a few extraditions from the Republic to Northern Ireland were carried out, but in some other cases the warrants were said to be technically faulty and the suspects held in the Republic were then released. A proper international

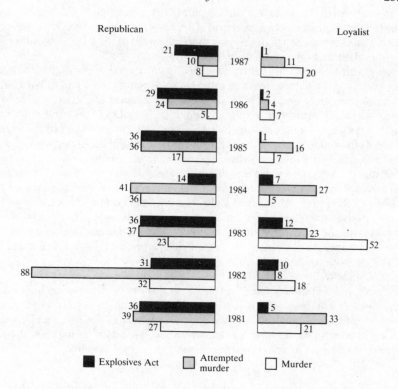

Republican   Loyalist

FIGURE 22.3   Persons charged with terrorist offences 1981–7 (source: RUC, Chief Constable's Annual Report)

understanding was required and appeared to have been achieved by the Anglo-Irish Agreement of 1985 under which the Irish Government undertook to adhere to the European Convention on the Suppression of Terrorism. But two further years were to elapse before extradition was sanctioned by the Dail and this undertaking was qualified by a ruling that each case would have to be examined and approved by the Irish Attorney General in a way that implied less favoured treatment than that accorded to other European countries. It was therefore necessary to resume negotiations in order to obtain a rather less invidious approach. Even then obstacles were encountered – or raised. For there can be no doubt about the strength of nationalist opposition to extradition. Although the brutality of the IRA may be sincerely condemned, the 'boys' are often seen to be fighting in the wrong way for the right cause and it goes against the grain to surrender them for trial to the traditional enemy.

What may sometimes be crucial is the extent to which the party in power in Ireland depends directly upon hardline republican support or is threatened by another party to which such support will gravitate. Other considerations may then be over-shadowed and perhaps completely neglected. Unfortunately the customary attacks – even by constitutional nationalists – on Britain's administration of the law can scarcely fail to convey to members of the IRA, and to those who aid and shelter them, that they really have a great deal of justice on their side. As a consequence the Ulster majority is bound to be still more alienated from Irish nationalism with further damage to the cause of Irish unity.

In practice, cooperation between the security forces on both sides of the Border is an even more important factor than extradition, and there is said to have been a large improvement over the years with a further advance as a consequence of the Anglo-Irish Agreement. The coordination of the activities of the security forces on both sides of the Border appears to have benefited from the small establishment of officials from the Republic in an office on the shore of Belfast Lough. As well as the need to coordinate police activities, there is a further complication created by the fact that the Republic will have no direct dealings with one part of the security forces in Ulster – that is the British army which is regarded as a 'foreign' force on Irish soil. The RUC, for all its alleged faults, is at least deemed to be 'native'. If an Irish unit observes some suspicious movement in a Border area, it will send a radio message to the gardai in Dundalk who will pass on the message to the RUC in Newry who will, in turn, pass it on to the British army unit. For Article 2 of the Irish Constitution must be respected.

The effectiveness of joint action in security matters must also depend upon the strength, training and equipment of the forces that can be deployed on both sides of the Border. The Irish army is one of the largest in Europe, relative to population, but training and equipment are apparently inadequate. Security has imposed a heavy burden on the Republic's economy and, with the fiscal savings now imposed, it may not be easy to achieve the improvements that are required.

SAFE AREAS

The second obstacle to the preservation of security has been the continued existence of comparatively safe areas within Northern Ireland itself, notably in the Bogside–Creggan districts of Londonderry and in West Belfast for the republicans and, to a much lesser extent, in East Belfast for the Loyalists. For the terrorists these areas serve two purposes: they are bases from which to operate and also bases for the various rackets from which they obtain part of their funds. The ordinary people of these areas have been urged from time to time to repudiate the terrorists – but without their being given any clear instructions about how they should set about doing so. They live under harsh regimes. Offences against the 'godfathers' are severely punished with offenders shot or beaten or tarred-and-feathered. Knee-capping is a penalty much favoured by the IRA. Since 1973, over 1200 people – nearly all Catholics – have had their knees shattered by IRA revolver bullets which has left them lame for life.

Increasing attention has been directed in recent years to the fact that terrorism has become an industry, and one that the godfathers will do their utmost to protect. Naturally there is no precise information about IRA finances. One guess is that total expenditure comes to about £5 million a year of which about £1.5 million may be obtained from rackets. The RUC reports that the money involved in forty large operations conducted by all the main paramilitary operations came to about £2 million in 1987. These figures may be too low especially when account is taken of money made by smuggling across the Border. There has even been a very high estimate of £20 million for the total annual income of the IRA. Where the truth lies can only be a guess.[4]

It was particulrly desirable for the IRA to extend its various rackets after the murder of Lord Mountbatten in 1979 had caused the US authorities to take more effective action in exposing the true nature of an ostensibly charitable organization, Noraid, which had in fact been a fund-raiser for the IRA. With the sharp decline in American financial support that followed, indigenous Irish sources of funds had to be more fully exploited. Various ways of raising money have been developed in both the republican and Loyalist areas: fruit machines and drinking clubs that earn substantial profits – to the disgust of many an honest inn keeper – protection money, extracted from numerous sources, including 'loans' that need not be repaid from certain finance companies, and a fleet of IRA-controlled taxis. Such practices, as well as financing terrorism, have had damaging social consequences in the areas concerned, as Bishop Cahal Daly has stressed:

When policing breaks down it is the weakest and the innocent who suffer, the aged, the housebound, the children and the young people. In many areas, particularly in what we used to call working class areas, ordinary policing has broken down to a disturbing extent. The result is that the quality of life has been seriously damaged through the almost uncontrolled social epidemic of car-stealing, mugging, robbery and burglary, vandalism and general misbehaviour on the part of a lawless minority. These communities have a right in justice to normal policing.[5]

It is not unfair to interpolate at this point that the police, for their part, may feel that they have a right to less equivocal support from the leaders of the Catholic community.

In October 1987, a strong public protest against racketeering was made by a group of Catholic and Protestant clergy with parishes in West Belfast from which the following extracts are taken:

In our part of Belfast, and indeed in much of Northern Ireland, the rule of law has broken down. The paramilitaries and their acolytes dominate our communities. This is nowhere more obvious than in the 'Protection Rackets', in which building contractors and other businesses are forced to pay 'Protection Money', often in the region of several hundred pounds a week, in order to be allowed to continue trading. Sometimes this money is demanded with overt threats; more often the threat is implied. The various paramilitaries, even those supposedly 'at war' with each other, are known to collude with each other in the organization of these rackets.[6]

They called on the Churches to be more forthright in condemnation and on the business community to explore possible strategies. And also

We call on the government, statutory bodies and police, who so often appear to acquiesce in these practices, to tackle them impartially by tightening up the tax laws still further and by effective accounting-rules and policing.

Father Denis Faul of Dungannon added his denunciation of 'the so-called republican movement which is now a big gangster racket' and proposed that the clergy should compile lists of cases and then expose the facts in their pulpits, but not the identities of those concerned because 'the Provisional IRA would, in Mafia style, murder anyone who complained publicly. The proposed action by the clergy is called "consciousness raising" and it worked in the Phillipines. It is working throughout Latin America.'[7]

Action along these lines by the various Churches might help, and should, of course, be directed against Loyalist as well as republican racketeers. The case for more vigorous action by government, often stressed in the past, was again officially recognized in April 1988 when it was announced that a new task force composed of representatives of the relevant government departments would collaborate with the police in investigating and assessing the scope for action. The Home Secretary also announced that action would be taken to freeze terrorists' funds and possibly confiscate them along lines similar to the action already directed against drug traffickers.[8] A full-scale campaign of this kind is surely overdue.

A return to normal policing and the effective restoration of law and order in these areas would be no easy task. As the police sought to assert their authority more thoroughly they could expect to be attacked by terrorist-organized mobs and by the terrorists themselves. Incidents might then take place which would provide grounds for new complaints about 'police brutality' – complaints which would be accepted with little regard to the context by vocal and credulous commentators in Britain and the USA. Yet strong action for a short period might be preferable to a festering sore. To this point we shall return.

RESPECTING THE LAW

The third of the constraints imposed on the judiciary and the security forces is the requirement to respect, as far as possible, the normal rights of the ordinary citizen under the law. To do so fully in such difficult circumstances is impossible. Let us begin with the judiciary.

Trial by jury with witnesses appearing in open court becomes impracticable when the lives of both the jury and the witnesses are at risk. The South has found this to be so. In 1927 it was thought necessary to introduce special legislation after the assassination of the Minister of Justice by IRA gunmen. Ten years later the Irish Constitution provided, in Article 38(3), for the establishment by law of a Special Court 'for the trial of offences where it may be determined in accordance with such law that ordinary courts are inadequate to secure the effective administration of justice and the preservation of public peace and order'. Senator Mary Robinson has pointed out that special measures of temporary duration could have been introduced whenever it seemed necessary, but the Offences against the State Act of 1939 introduced a permanent arrangement which allowed action to be taken at any time by Government Proclamation.[9] It is interesting to note that the same option had already been chosen in Northern Ireland by the Unionist Government when it decided to keep the Special Powers Act in being although particular orders issued under that Act had been withdrawn (chapter 8). In the Republic, the Special Criminal Court was composed initially of three army officers but, from its reinstitution in 1972, it has consisted of three judges. Since that year trial by jury has been suspended for subversives. The gardai have been given the right to arrest and search without warrants and those arrested could be held on suspicion for periods that have varied from forty-eight hours to ten days.

As in the Republic, trial by jury with witnesses in open court has been suspended in Northern Ireland for 'scheduled offences', though retained for other cases which are much more numerous. A committee under the chairmanship of Lord Diplock held in 1972 that 'Unless the state can ensure [witnesses'] safety, then it would be unreasonable to expect them to testify voluntarily, and morally wrong to compel them to do so.'[10] This committee recommended the establishment of what came to be known as the 'Diplock Courts', brought into being by the Emergency Provisions Act of 1973. In these juryless courts a Court judge, sitting alone, has to determine the guilt or innocence of the accused. (It is always a High Court judge in murder cases.) With detention or internment phased out, these courts have therefore the responsibility of dealing with terrorists.

The central problem of law enforcement is still that of obtaining evidence that will stand up in court – whether or not it is a Diplock court. The methods of interrogation used to obtain both confessions and general information about terrorist activities had already been the subject of two committees of inquiry before these courts were established. The Compton Committee had reported in 1971[11] that the methods of interrogation included hooding, deprivation of food and sleep and standing for long periods against a wall, but regarded this as 'ill-treatment', not 'brutality'. A similar conclusion was reached in 1972 by two of the three members of the Parker Committee but the third – Lord Gardiner – recommended that such practices must stop. It was this minority recommendation that was then accepted by the Prime Minister (Heath). In 1978 a third investigation was carried out under the chairmanship of Judge Bennett after an Amnesty Report had alleged the ill-treatment of prisoners.[12] The committee accepted the fact that some of the injuries to prisoners had been self-inflicted – for self-inflicted cigarette burns and bruises can be used both to discredit the police and to provide the prisoner with a defence when subsequently cross-questioned by other prisoners about what he has said in an interrogation. But there were other cases where the hurts did not appear to be self-inflicted. Elaborate arrangements for supervising interrogations by means of closed-circuit television were then adopted.[13] One cannot help wondering whether the care taken to protect prisoners is any greater in, say, the USA or France. In the Republic itself, two reports appeared which were critical of strong-arm methods used there – one report by Amnesty (1977) and one by Judge O'Briain (1978).

As might be expected, the Diplock Courts have been seriously handicapped by the difficulty of obtaining evidence from witnesses. This has been a problem when the defendants have been Loyalists but has been particularly troublesome in the case of IRA defendants because – even apart from intimidation – there is a long tradition of Catholic hostility to 'informers'. Witnesses could be regarded in that light in cases of this kind. There was, however, another possibility: information might be obtained from persons who were themselves prisoners. That is to say, a prisoner could 'turn Queen's evidence' and, for a time, the RUC came to rely heavily on this traditional method of obtaining evidence. What was not traditional was the scale on which this method came to be used, with large numbers of prisoners convicted on the evidence of 'super-grasses' who were offered concealment and financial assistance to induce them to cooperate. It has not, apparently, been so unusual for a large number of prisoners to appear in the dock at the same time in Italy, but it was a strange procedure by British standards. The judiciary did not approve. Some of these witnesses were corrupt and quite dishonest. In 1986 the Lord Chief Justice ordered the release of the prisoners who had been convicted in this way, notwithstanding the fact that most of them, if not all, were members of paramilitary organizations. The police had unwisely overplayed their hand.

With super-grass evidence ruled out and ordinary witnesses in fear for their lives, the problem of obtaining evidence that would stand up in court has become acute. To add to the difficulty, the accused have the right to say nothing when questioned. As was only to be expected the IRA has exploited this right to the utmost, and all their operatives are advised to maintain complete silence. The question then is whether such silence should be taken to imply an attempt to thwart the course of justice and should therefore incur a penalty? It should be observed that, whereas in the Republic the Special Court was empowered to accept the statement of a senior police officer that he believed the accused to be guilty, such evidence has not itself been regarded as sufficient in the Diplock Courts. The former practice has now been modified in the Republic to the extent that some additional corroborative evidence is required – but only when a prisoner *himself* controverts the charge – *thus recognizing the court by breaking silence.*

The experience of these years appears to show that both the government and the judiciary have sought to ensure that those arrested and accused of terrorist offences are tried in ways that depart as little as may be from normal legal procedures. It is true that trial by jury has not been restored but it does not follow that, in a community so deeply divided, jury trial would provide any better assurance of fair treatment than trial by a judge. On the contrary, concern about possible bias on the part of jury members has been one of the arguments for juryless courts, even if some effective way of protecting juries could be devised. So much appears to have been implicitly conceded by both Fine Gael and Fianna Fail governments in Dublin. Their criticism has been directed at a different feature of the judicial system in the North – the fact that only one judge sits in the Diplock Courts. In order to ensure a fair trial, there should, it is held, be three judges as in the Special Court in the Republic.

We are now on highly controversial ground, but it is surely relevant to observe that a judge in a Diplock Court is required to explain in writing the reasons for his verdict whereas a jury's verdict is uninformative about reasons. Moreover, in the difficult circumstances of Northern Ireland, all convicted persons have an unrestricted right to have their cases brought before the Appeal Court with its three judges, so that the demand for 'reform' is in effect a demand for trial by six judges rather than four. The practical difficulty of appointing the additional judges for the Diplock Courts without depleting the senior criminal bar was stressed both by Lord Diplock himself and by Lord Gardiner and was fully recognized by Sir George Baker who agreed with the Lord Chief Justice of Northern Ireland that 'even allowing for the appointment of some new QCs the Bar's ability to provide counsel for the defence of persons charged with scheduled offences could not be guaranteed.'[14] The accused themselves could therefore lose from the depletion of the criminal bar as the price of having three judges – from which they might gain nothing at all. It cannot, in any case, be taken for granted that enough senior counsel would be willing to exchange their far more lucrative practices for the Bench. In the case of Catholic counsel, the certain loss of income would be accompanied by the serious risk of loss of life. All members of the judiciary are targets for the IRA – several have been shot since the troubles began – but Catholic judges are viewed with particular hatred as 'traitors' who have gone across to the other side. They have immediately become priority targets for the gunmen who have killed three and severely wounded a fourth.

Admittedly the Republic can find three judges for its Special Court but it sits only on a very few occasions during the legal term whereas the Diplock Courts are at work more or less continuously. The comparison, therefore, does not hold, as Lord Baker made clear.

There is one possibility of easing the pressure on the Diplock Courts. This would be to transfer from them all those cases in which, even if there has been violence, it has not been terrorist violence. For it is the nature of the alleged offence (e.g. murder) and not the motive that determines whether a case will be set to a Diplock Court. I have seen no estimates of the quantitative importance of such 'descheduling', as it is called.

Apart from the practical difficulties of instituting three-judge courts in Northern Ireland, there is understandable resentment on the part of the Northern judiciary at the implied slur on the fairness and competence of its members. In this as in other respects the somewhat contemptuous attitude adopted in the Republic towards law enforcement in Ulster is hard to reconcile with the procedures that have been followed in the Republic itself. Michael Farrell has made this general comment:

Indeed there is more than a touch of irony about the Dublin government complaining, through the Anglo-Irish Agreement, about Diplock courts, the conduct of the security forces and restrictions on political expression by the nationalist minority in the North, when its own record on such issues does not bear too close an examination.[15]

It is interesting to observe that the two cases where the justice of previous verdicts was subjected to severe Irish criticism in 1987–8 were English cases where those accused of terrorism had been tried in the normal way by a jury court. One acquittal in particular may be recalled – that of Dominic McGlinchey, a particularly notorious and self-declared terrorist, who was acquitted on appeal in 1984 because the evidence was thought to be insufficient. After reviewing the operation of the Emergency Provisions Act, Baker concluded by saying: 'So I have heard of no instances of a person wrongly convicted nor has the LCJ [Lord Chief Justice].'[16]

Another interesting illustration of the attitude of the Northern Ireland judiciary has been afforded by the upholding of the rights of individual members of Sinn Fein to participate in local government. Their presence has been both resented and feared by Protestant councillors. It has been resented because these councillors do not want to have, as their colleagues, persons who are no better than publicity agents for the IRA – some of them formerly active terrorists themselves, many of them liable to become so if this was required of them. It has been feared because the IRA is thus kept fully informed about what is happening in local government and about the personal movements of councillors who may be targets for assassination.

(At the time of writing, in 1988, one had already been murdered.) In these circumstances attempts were made by the Unionists on one local council to quarantine the Sinn Fein members by excluding them from a special committee appointed to handle the real business of the council in place of the council itself. When this case was taken to court in 1985, the Unionists lost. A second attempt was then made by requiring all sitting members to sign a declaration repudiating violence but, once again, the court upheld the legal right of individual members of Sinn Fein to serve as councillors. To quote from the statement made by the Lord Chief Justice (Lord Lowry) in the Court of Appeal:

I do not subscribe to the view that Sinn Fein can be regarded as a lawful organization (or by necessary implication as a 'legitimate political party') just because it has been allowed since 1975 to operate as a political party without being proscribed. That is a different thing from saying, in the present state of the law, that individual members of Sinn Fein, if not otherwise disqualified, cannot legally stand for election and take their seats as councillors if elected; but they are entitled to do so despite their membership of Sinn Fein and not because of it.[16]

Notwithstanding rulings of this kind, some leading politicians in the Republic have committed themselves to a sustained campaign against the Northern Ireland judiciary on the ground that its members deny fair treatment to the republican movement. It must, of course, be assumed that some of the critics of single-judge Diplock Courts have been sincere in believing that three-judge courts would be both desirable and feasible. But it is rarely made clear that their own Special Court consists of one High Court judge sitting with a circuit court judge and a district justice, i.e. a stipendiary magistrate or RM. The alleged deficiency in Ulster can be urged as a reason for impeding extradition. Another possible reason for pressing for three-judge courts is that success in achieving their adoption might then make it possible to ask for two further measures. One of these would be the re-trial of all those previously convicted in single-judge courts which would, of course, impose a crushing burden on the judiciary. A further demand might be for a ruling to the effect that there should be at least one Catholic in every three-judge team. Any such proposal would be strongly resisted for what would be entailed would be the abandonment of the belief that the judiciary is capable of enforcing the law with fairness and impartiality. It would then be implied that judges were so biased that nothing better could be expected than a compromise verdict from three unfair judges biased in different directions. Before long there would be a campaign in favour of acting on the precedent thus set by the appointment in Great Britain as well of panels of judges, perhaps with lay assessors, in such a way as to ensure that different ethnic groups were represented.

LAW ENFORCEMENT AS A GRIEVANCE

Obviously security policy cannot be taken out of its political and social context and, depending upon circumstances, there may be various forms of complementary action that will reinforce the effect of security policy in undermining the terrorist organizations. Official policy in Northern Ireland has, after all, been based on this premise for many years. It would appear to be the case, however, that the grievances now most bitterly felt – if bitterness of expression is a guide – relate to the behaviour of the security forces themselves. As we have observed, the original demands for social reform put forward by the Northern Ireland Civil Rights Association have long since been met and further reforms, far beyond anything then envisaged, have been carried out. The qualification is that some of the security measures resented in the past are still in force, though under different legislation. But it is hard to see how the use of such measures could possibly be avoided so long as terrorist activity continues. For example, the right to stop and question would appear to be indispensable but is also the cause of new grievances. In the vast majority of cases, those who are obliged to submit to this treatment will be innocent – innocent and sometimes outraged. This action is then denounced as harassment. And, of course, matters are made worse if discipline is not strictly observed, and those stopped are dealt with far more roughly than could possibly be justified. Some officers may behave badly. All of them are acting under stress with the knowledge that they are liable to be shot in the back by IRA gunmen at any time and in any place.

The RUC has been accused of a shoot-to-kill policy and it has been further maintained that, in doing so, they have been implementing a decision adopted by government at a high level. The accusations relate to three incidents that occurred in the Lurgan/Armagh area in November/December 1982. In two of these cases, the police opened fire on cars containing IRA terrorists, according to intelligence reports based on close surveillance on both sides of the Border. The men were killed but were, surprisingly, found to be unarmed. The third incident was the shooting of two young men in a hay shed which, it was known, had been a store for explosives used recently in the murder of three policemen. The shed had been bugged by MI5 and a trap thus carefully set for larger fish than those that were eventually caught. The files on all three cases were sent by the RUC to the Northern Ireland Director of Public Prosecutions, Sir Barry Shaw, and some police officers were tried for murder in the cases of the two car deaths. They were acquitted, but it also transpired that faulty evidence had been given and certain distortions introduced.

The Director of Public Prosecutions (DPP) then formally requested the Chief Constable, Sir John Hermon, to organize a new investigation into all three cases and Deputy Chief Constable John Stalker of the Greater Manchester Police was appointed, in 1984, to be in charge of the inquiry. In his own account of the inquiries carried out by him and his team,[17] Stalker reports that the high command of the RUC obstructed their work and did not provide them with all the information they required. In May 1986 he was suspended from his duties pending a high-level investigation by English police relating to alleged disciplinary offences in an earlier period in the Manchester area. The investigation in Northern Ireland was then taken over by Colin Sampson, Chief Constable for West Yorkshire. In January 1988 the Attorney General, Sir Patrick Mayhew, informed the House of Commons that no further prosecutions would follow. The DPP, for his part, had reached the conclusion that, although there was insufficient evidence to warrant new prosecutions with regard to the shootings, there was evidence of offences in perverting or attempting to pervert the course of justice. The Attorney General had decided, however, that it would be against the public interest to proceed, and the DPP, when given all the facts, had concurred.

The Stalker inquiry had already attracted much interest and aroused much indignation. It had been held, for example, by Cardinal O'Fiaich to afford sufficient reason for declining to support the RUC.[18] It was only to be expected, therefore, that the Attorney General's decision would be met with a fresh storm of protest.

Inexpert comment on the details of this immensely involved affair must clearly be avoided – although even expert comment would have to be inconclusive when the facts have not been fully revealed. What must be obvious to anyone is that, for some reason, things went badly wrong at an early stage and continued to do so. The harm done to the RUC, even on a cold basis of calculation, and more generally to the fight against terrorism, must have far outweighed whatever was gained by eliminating those IRA activists in 1982. We can accept the fact that, by 1988, the Attorney General had to make a hard choice between a further cover-up, on the one hand, which was bound to cause deep suspicion and resentment, and on the other hand, the revelation of secret activities that would, apparently, have led to the destruction of an intelligence network, with a loss of life not only within that network, but also among ordinary people as the consequence of a weakening of the entire security service. Whether he made the right choice is a matter that will be long debated but can scarcely be resolved until more of the facts have been revealed. It is also undeniable that the shooting of the three IRA terrorists in Gibraltar on 6 March 1988 – whatever the reason – diverted much public attention from the massacre they were planning to carry out.

There are, however, some more general questions that can be raised and some general points that can then be made. First, the arguments against shoot-to-kill are both familiar and powerful. If generally adopted, quite innocent people might be killed in error. Moreover, even if those killed were always terrorists, they too were entitled to a fair trial and, should they be found guilty, the sentence is imprisonment, not execution. There are basic principles which must not be set aside. Unfortunately difficult issues can arise. If, in a particular case, it is known that those concerned are terrorists, is it better to shoot than to allow them to escape? Should they escape, even if one of them is believed to be a particularly notorious terrorist, as was the case in 1982? It is not unlawful for a policeman to open fire if he can be reasonably thought to be in danger. The question then turns upon what is 'reasonable'. As Conor Cruise O'Brien has observed, those who have to make the arrests may view things differently from those not in danger.[20] The point was made rather neatly in a cartoon by 'Mac' published some years ago[21] in which Gerry Fitt admonishes a group of soldiers: 'In future don't shoot till you FEEL the thump of their bullets.' O'Brien informs us that in the shoot-out on 27 November 1987 between the Irish army and a notorious terrorist – O'Hare, the Border Fox – and a companion, it may have been the army that fired first. He adds that if it had been established that this had been so, 'most Irish people at the time would have favoured giving the soldier a medal'.

This is not, of course, to say that the highly dangerous policy of shoot-to-kill should be adopted. But it is unfair, and a little hypocritical, to imply that this kind of thing can never happen except in Ulster. It would, in fact, be rather interesting to see the results of a comparative study of the regulations and the practice with regard to the use of firearms by the police in, say, various cities in the USA, in Northern Ireland, Great Britain, the Irish Republic and France.

In this difficult and confusing area it is at least quite clear that 'shoot to kill' has not been the usual and accepted policy followed by the security forces in Northern Ireland. Apart from official denials, the evidence is overwhelmingly against drawing any such inference from the Stalker affair. If that were official policy, leading members of the IRA would not still go openly around in Belfast, confident in the knowledge that, as there is too little evidence for their conviction in court, they have nothing to fear from the authorities. With such a policy, they would have been 'taken out' long ago – and the question of detention would not even arise. With such a policy in force, the RUC and the army would not have been required to hold their fire, even when under heavy attack, as has so often been the case over a period of many years. Two illustrations may suffice. The first is the death of a young soldier in Londonderry in 1973 who was surrounded by a group of angry women. Presumably he could have freed himself at once by using his firearm – and what an outcry that would have caused. He did not do so and his captors held him until an IRA assassin could be fetched who shot him dead. Another incident is the account given by a senior army commander of a young officer dying in the street with people spitting down on him. But the dying officer's men held back and maintained their self-control.[22]

Whatever view is taken about such immensely complicated questions as those posed by the Stalker enquiry, there is a more general conclusion which can be firmly maintained. Although the campaign may be conducted with skill, care and moderation, from time to time things will go wrong. Mistakes will be made. Faulty intelligence will be received. One or two police officers or soldiers will over-react – as happened with such appalling consequences on Bloody Sunday. New grievances will be created and the terrorists will gain fresh support. Thus a society may be caught, year after year, in an evil spiral of violence. An intensified campaign of law enforcement may then be a better option than one that is more restrained but also indefinitely prolonged.

DETENTION

The problem is to determine what form that campaign should take – and that is a matter for expert judgement. It is, however, of particular interest to note that Patrick Cooney, a former Fine Gael Minister of Justice, has presented a strong case for detention, thus endorsing a proposal that has been put forward by various people on different occasions. He conceded that detention in the 1970s in Northern Ireland was not an encouraging precedent partly because intelligence had then been faulty, but went on to say: 'I would be satisfied that the security forces would be very accurate at this stage in pinpointing the persons who should be interned.'[23] To quote from the Annual Report for 1987 of the Chief Constable of the RUC: 'It cannot be right that known murderers can walk the streets with apparent immunity and that the community can be intimidated and coerced.'[24] In Belfast, it has long been understood that leading members of the paramilitary organisations could move around freely because there was insufficient evidence to convict them.

It is of particular interest to recall the events of 1955–62, when an IRA offensive was broken by similar official action on both sides of the border. The two governments then resorted to detention and the terrorists were removed for a time from the scene. It is true that the IRA campaign had not, at that time, evolved from a civil rights movement along what we now regard as the orthodox course for urban guerilla warfare, for those were early days. The paramilitaries had not then established bases, as they were allowed to do in the early 1970s with such unfortunate consequences.

Two questions were raised by the proposal to resort once more to detention in 1988. The first was whether, in the circumstances of the time, imprisonment without trial along normal lines could be morally justified. The second was whether detention would be likely to prove effective.

Detention must always be viewed with repugnance. It is something to be used only as a last resort, when there are grounds for believing that it would be a lesser evil than the indefinite prolongation of a terrorist campaign. It should always be remembered that the terrorists continue to claim their victims in the community at large and that, inside the areas they dominate, they impose a brutal tyranny where people are tried by kangaroo courts and cruelly punished. It may seem, therefore, to many people that the paramilitaries are not in a strong moral position to claim for themselves the traditional right to a fair trial under the law! But the law must, of course, be respected, and respect may be gradually undermined if normal procedures are set aside. It is a danger, however long-term, that should never be incurred unless the case for doing so is very strong. So much may be agreed.

The infringement of civil rights implied by 'detention without trial' will vary according to the methods used. The words 'without trial' are in themselves misleading, for it has not been implied that those detained would be held in custody without any serious attempt being made to assess their guilt or innocence. 'Without trial' really means without trial in a court where the normal rules of evidence apply. It does not, or should not, mean that the cases of the detained will not be individually considered. At this point a distinction must be made, as Diplock insisted, between arbitrary imprisonment which he called 'internment' and 'detention' after an extrajudicial process carried out according to special rules. [25] In the event this use of terms has not been adopted in ordinary usage, which may be a pity, but I shall attempt to do so.

There is also a further distinction that might be drawn between 'executive detention' and what may be termed a form of 'quasi-judicial detention'. The former was the method adopted in Northern Ireland in 1971 and would be the method followed if there were to be detention under the Emergency Powers Act. In the earlier period, the Prime Minister was responsible for considering every case and that duty, under Direct Rule, would fall upon the Secretary of State. Within 14 days of arrest on suspicion, a person's case would have to be referred to an Adviser who would determine (1) whether that person had been involved in terrorist activity and (2) whether detention was necessary in the public interest. After considering the Adviser's report, the Secretary of State would decide whether to make a detention order or sign a release. The case of each person detained would then be reviewed at regular intervals. The term 'quasi-judicial detention' can be applied to those cases where the imprisonment of the suspect has been ordered by a court of law to which abnormal powers have been granted. Such powers can be exercised by the Special Court in the Republic of Ireland which can order detention under the

Safeguarding of the State Act. There may, perhaps, be an inclination to suppose that the danger of detaining the wrong people will be less when the decision to detain is reached in each case, not by a minister acting on advice from an adviser, but by three judges as in Ireland's Special Court. The contrast should not, however, be drawn too sharply for, in Northern Ireland, the detainees could be given (as in 1973) a right of appeal to a tribunal composed of three senior lawyers. In both Ulster and the Republic, there would be two departures from the usual legal procedures: (1) the normal rules of evidence would not be fully applied and (2) detention would be for a period of unspecified length.

The second much-debated question has been the effectiveness of detention as a means of reducing the level of terrorist activity. Special knowledge and experience would obviously be required in attempting to answer that question but it may be possible for even a non-expert observer to perceive the errors in the over-confident assertion that detention must fail because it failed in 1971. To begin with, the final verdict on that earlier experiment is not altogether clear, for a number of different factors have to be disentangled and a distinction drawn between its initial and its longer-term effects. Moreover, as Cooney stressed, police intelligence was far better in the late 1980s than in the early 1970s, and there was much less danger that the wrong persons would be arrested. There should also be no question of confining the action to the IRA, as was done initially in 1971. All paramilitaries should be liable to detention. There is a further reason for resisting the over-facile dismissal of the case for detention and it is one of crucial importance. This is the fact that the Border provided an easy escape route in 1971 but that route would be blocked if, as Cooney proposes, detention were to be introduced simultaneously in Northern Ireland and in the Republic. The relevant model should not have been the action taken in 1971 in Northern Ireland alone but the highly successful action taken on both sides of the border in 1956–62. Such joint action, if taken once more, would not only close the escape route but would have other far-reaching consequences. In such circumstances, Sinn Fein would find it difficult to mount a propagands campaign against 'oppressive British policy' in order to sway ill-informed 'liberal' opinion in Britain and the USA. Nor would the IRA/Sinn Fein leadership be able to solicit so much sympathy in the North or organize protesting mobs. Detention in Northern Ireland alone could be regarded as a course of dubious wisdom but, on the most sober basis of calculation, it seems highly likely that joint action in both parts of the island would succeed in severely weakening, and perhaps, in ending, the terrorist campaign.

In the course of the debate in the late 1980s, there was surprisingly little attempt to distinguish between a situation where detention would be introduced in both parts of the island at the same time and one where it would be attempted in Ulster alone. There has, of course, been little reason to suppose that the Republic would be prepared to take that step, but its curt refusal in September 1988 to do so need not have been accepted without question or without protest. If joint action along these lines would curb the violence and permit the restoration of law and order in the areas under terrorist domination, why should the Republic be opposed to such action? Why should the SDLP also be opposed, as has clearly been the case? These were questions that might have been strongly pressed both in public and at meetings of the Anglo-Irish Conference which was specifically designed for such a purpose.

Ultimately the persons detained would be released. Meanwhile others might take their place until they too were arrested. One of the difficulties is the decentralized command structure of the IRA. The crucial question is whether the authority of the paramilitaries could nevertheless be sufficiently weakened in this way to permit the restoration of the rule of law in the difficult areas and a gradual return to normal policing and law enforcement. There can be no doubt that many people would welcome that restoration with the ending of the rackets and the ending of the brutally enforced rule of the paramilitaries. More generally there is said to be great weariness after so many years of violence and a longing for peace which cannot, however, find expression until the power of the terrorist organisations has somehow been greatly reduced. Detention may be needed in order to achieve that end.

There are, of course, other possible courses of action. One of them – apparently at the opposite end of the spectrum – would be the early release of those who are already prisoners. The case for doing so has been repeatedly urged by Father Denis Faul who maintains that family pressure against the subsequent resumption of terrorist activity would be decisive.[26] In some instances this might well be so, especially in the case of young prisoners under the age of 18 at the time of the offence who are held 'at the Secretary of State's pleasure' – the SOSPs. But it would surely be a highly risky operation unless accompanied, or preceded, by firm new action to break the power of the godfathers. As an accompaniment rather than as an alternative to detention, some early releases might deserve consideration but, even then, the risk would be considerable for some of the most fanatical offenders may also be young. Unfortunately, official estimates of recidivism were not available until November 1988, when it was announced that a fifth of those released were convicted again within two years.[27] As the conviction rate is low in the case of republican terrorists, the proportion who return to violence must be substantially higher than a fifth. There is the further point that a number of early releases might foster the belief that a general amnesty could be extracted, and this would weaken the force of imprisonment as a deterrent.

In considering Father Faul's suggestion, it must also be recognized that the sentences served in Northern Ireland are already very short by normal British standards. For the judicial system – though habitually described by even constitutional nationalists as intolerably severe – has permitted a one half remission of sentences as compared with the normal British one third. It was also announced in November 1988 that, for terrorists serving fixed sentences of five years or more, the remission time in Northern Ireland would be reduced to the proportion customary elsewhere in the UK. Moreover, anyone serving a year or more who committed a new offence during the unexpired period of the original offence would then have to serve that unexpired period as well as the new sentence.[28]

The case for tougher sentencing and less remission has, therefore, been widely discussed. Paul Wilkinson has strongly supported such changes and can see further advantages. For he has gone on to say: 'If sentences were really severe, if life meant life, the Government could introduce a system such as the Repentant Law which helped the Italian Government to defeat the Red Brigade terrorists in the early 1960s. We could offer real inducements of remission to terrorists prepared to give concrete information.'[29]

What I have said about some of these possibilities has of necessity been exploratory. There is nothing speculative or tentative about the proposition that further action of *some* sort has appeared to be required in order to break the grip of the paramilitary forces. Apart from the human suffering for which they are responsible, the social consequences in the areas they control are deeply harmful, as we have recorded. At a less melodramatic, but immensely important level, the prospects for economic expansion, discouraging in the best of circumstances, are bound to be bleak in a country where terrorist activities continue indefinitely with no end in sight. Thus unemployment will remain high, and the unemployed will provide more recruits for the terrorist organizations with the two evils reinforcing and perpetuating each other. For Sinn Fein is deliberately exploiting the grievances caused by hardships which the IRA has helped to create and seeks to prolong.

23
Prospects

It is hardly surprising that many people have come to regard the Northern Ireland problem as insoluble. Over a long period of twenty years, various proposals have been put forward and various efforts made, but the hopes that inspired them have been followed by disillusionment and continuing violence. Moreover the present unrest is no isolated affair but only the most recent incident in a long history of political disagreement. Richard Rose has expressed this widely held pessimism in a somewhat cryptic way by saying that: 'The problem is that there is no solution'.[1] It may be a grim verdict but it has the appearance of resting on a firm foundation of prolonged experience. There is nothing to be gained by pretending that the facts are other than they are – provided, of course, that what are assumed to be the facts have been correctly observed and their message rightly interpreted. That rather obvious qualification is needed because, on a closer view, one may feel inclined to doubt whether these conditions have been adequately satisfied. Let us, however, set aside any such reservations and simply assume for the moment that, on a cool and balanced assessment, 'no solution' appears to be available. What would follow from such a conclusion? What inferences for public policy could then be drawn? In what respects, if any, would certain changes then seem to be required? Should some measures be dropped and some new ones, perhaps, introduced in their stead?

These are necessary questions to ask, and when proper consideration has been given to them, this deeply pessimistic conclusion may not have such important practical implications as might initially be supposed. After all government action is taken, in this as in other contexts, in the belief that things will be made better by doing so. If, in the event, a particular difficulty can be truly and finally disposed of that will be splendid; but even if so satisfactory an outcome is too much to expect, the measures adopted will still be justified if their net effect is to ameliorate what would otherwise have been a much worse situation. The point is scarcely an obscure one, but it has to be made because some of those who maintain that the Ulster problem is 'insoluble' then go on to argue that a complete British withdrawal from Northern Ireland would therefore be the logical response – a *non sequitur* that the IRA will most assiduously wish to foster. The case for such a withdrawal seems to rest on two underlying assumptions. The first is that, if a complete solution cannot be found, Britain might just as well rid herself of this encumbrance, and can do so with no loss in other respects. The second is the notion that, if left to themselves, the 'Irish' would reach agreement and thus demonstrate, in some miraculous way, that the allegedly insoluble problem had become soluble after all. Such reasoning – if it can be so described – is very confused. A clear warning about the dangerous consequences of a British departure has come from many sources, including John Hume, the leader of the SDLP:

The most likely, immediate response would be that the vacuum left by the British army would be filled by people with arms. Seizing territory as a bargaining counter is par for this course. If you need examples, just look at Cyprus and the Lebanon . . . I am not interested in getting the British army out of Ireland if it leaves behind an even more divided society.[2]

Thus the apparent realism of those who advocate withdrawal may turn out to be, not realism, but self-deception after all. For Britain could not stand aside, indifferent and detached, if civil war were to break out in Northern Ireland – as it was starting to do in 1969. Apart from any humane concern about the fate of British subjects, Catholic and Protestant, who had been brusquely expelled from the United Kingdom, there would be good ground for concern if trouble-makers like Libya then began to exploit, for their own ends, a position so close to Britain's western coastline. On a lower, but still troublesome, plane of inconvenience, Britain would have to cope with a flood of immigrants who would come from both sides of the Ulster community.[3]

So far we have been clearing the ground. If the discussion is to be carried further, we shall need to consider again the current meaning of that omnibus term, the 'Ulster problem'. We shall also have to determine what state of affairs – this side of Utopia – might be deemed to constitute an adequate 'solution'. As previous chapters have shown, the problem consists of several components which, though connected, have their own different aspects and special features. For example heavy unemployment is one of the difficulties of the region but it is a difficulty shared with many other places in Europe and, however hard to cure, is not what people have in mind when they say that 'the Ulster problem is insoluble'. What has obviously given so much apparent support to the conclusion that there is 'no solution' is the persistence of violence. As we have seen, however, in the previous chapter, the measures adopted to deal with violence have been by no means unsuccessful and its level, as measured by the number of deaths, had been greatly reduced by 1985 and, even after a subsequent increase, was still in 1988 well below the level reached in the early 1970s. Many more were killed in road accidents. Moreover we should be applying a standard that would, unfortunately, be inappropriate in the modern world if we were to decree that a solution to this aspect of the Ulster problem would require nothing less than the complete cessation of violence. A more suitable standard by which to judge success may be the level of violence in mainland Britain – a standard that has itself been lowered since the early days of the disturbances in Northern Ireland. For those initial encounters between the police and the Ulster mobs would have seemed less shocking – though still certainly deplorable – if they had been preceded by the miners' strike or the demonstrations at Wapping. In those early days we had not yet had experience of the organized thuggery which has subsequently been displayed at football matches – with the disastrous events at the Heysel Stadium a particularly tragic example. Moreover it has transpired that even in England juries may sometimes be at risk of reprisals. The fact remains that even by this sadly subsiding British standard, the level of violence in Northern Ireland remains high, with the 'Ulster problem' in that sense still very inadequately resolved.

It may be asked whether it is appropriate to refer to violence as a *component* of the Ulster problem rather than as a *symptom* of that problem. In fact, of course, it is both. As I have said in the previous chapter, the vicious circle of violence is not to be regarded as simply a response to other grievances, for violence feeds on itself and becomes an independent cause of bitterness and hate – now a more important cause, I suspect, than anything else. Moreover the scale on which violence occurs is not at all closely correlated with the hardship caused by other grievances. Thus violence may intensify even at a time when some apparently basic causes of discontent are being removed or greatly ameliorated – as happened in Ulster in the late 1960s and early 1970s when the implementation of social reform was accompanied by an upsurge of violence. Or, in different circumstances, violence may be reduced or even eliminated altogether for long periods, although some important political issues remain unresolved. There were very few deaths from violence – roughly 30–35 – during the whole period of Unionist rule between 1923 and 1969.[4]

The assertion that the Ulster problem is insoluble is usually made without any attempt to define either problem or solution. Richard Rose has not, of course, left the matter there but has sought to explain his own pessimistic pronouncement by saying: 'In this strife-torn land where the United Kingdom meets the Republic of Ireland there is no solution, if a solution is defined as a form of government that is consensual, legitimate and stable.'[5] 'Consensual' government can be taken to mean a regime that is universally supported, or nearly so. People will naturally differ about the particular parties they favour and the particular policies they prefer, but not about membership of the particular country. The absence of a consensus in this sense has, of course, been a longstanding feature of political life not just in Ulster but in the island as a whole. It is widely believed to be so still. But it is not enough to identify the problem. It is also necessary to decide how much significance should be attached to this lack of consensus at any particular time and place. Clearly it cannot be taken for granted that when some conflict of national sentiment occurs, it must always do so with such disruptive force that no tolerable state of affairs can then be hoped for. A lack of consensus may lead to instability and revolt, but the outcome must naturally depend upon the importance attached to a particular political allegiance and thus upon the intensity of feeling should this allegiance be frustrated for those on the wrong side of a political frontier. Moreover, this outcome will obviously be much affected by other social conditions and by the constitutional framework within which political affairs are conducted.

Devolution may be helpful in a situation where the devolved authority can be conferred on a disaffected minority within a nation, but for it to work really well there should be a geographical concentration of those affected. In Northern Ireland, however, devolution has meant autonomous government for the whole region *within* which the conflict of loyalties occurs, and a false comparison must not therefore be drawn with devolution in, say, Brittany, or the Basque country, or the Tyrol. In Northern Ireland, devolution may well have aggravated the situation by isolating the two protagonists in hostile confrontation. It might, therefore, have been better if the Government of Ireland Act of 1920 had been withdrawn from the North when it proved unacceptable to the South. For, as we have seen, both the Nationalist leaders and the leaders of the Catholic church were inclined to withhold cooperation, and the Unionists, content with their own supremacy, showed too little inclination to seek it. It was scarcely an ideal arrangement for coping with an absence of consensus, and the best we can say is that, to the credit of both sides, the outcome was less unsatisfactory than might have been expected in such unpromising circumstances.

The next chapter will be concerned with certain strategies that might be adopted for the future. Before turning to that discussion, however, there are three important matters to which we must address attention if the Ulster problem in its present form is to be viewed in proper context.

First, there is the possibility of reducing the area within which the alleged conflict of national identities takes place by a redrawing of the frontier. Fewer Catholics would then have their nationalist inclinations frustrated, and the smaller 'Ulster' – if that name may still be permitted – would be more stable.

Secondly, it is widely believed that demographic change will steadily alter the religious composition of the population and bring about a Catholic majority in the not far distant future. Although this prediction may not be fulfilled and is certainly not immediately imminent, the anticipation of a future change of that kind would be bound to cast long shadows before it with effects for current political attitudes that could well be important.

Thirdly, the strategy chosen must be based on a realistic assessment of economic prospects. Let us consider these points in turn.

CHANGING THE BORDER

If the Protestant and Catholic populations were neatly distributed with the latter concentrated in areas contiguous to the Republic, a change in the frontier would be an obvious solution. No doubt some republican zealots, their minds now distorted beyond remedy by romantic nationalism and that insidious map-image, would even then complain, and some might still resort to gun and bomb in a futile attempt to enforce their claims. But the violence would presumably be on a much smaller scale and could be more easily contained with the area of the North so reduced and with a border re-drawn with more regard – one hopes – to ease of defence.

A glance at the map in Appendix 3 (page 300) will serve as a reminder that the Ulster population is not so obligingly distributed. Even in the predominantly Protestant Belfast urban area with a total population in 1981 of about 640,000, there were about 160,000 Catholics – or five times as many as in the Border district of Fermanagh. With so complex a distribution, it is essential to avoid the old mistake made during the Home Rule debate in the early years of the century, of confining attention to such large areas as counties. The finer analysis in terms of local authority wards – on which the map is based – is clearly more appropriate. When the implications of an exercise of this kind are pursued, a number of options can be presented which would reduce the Catholic population in Northern Ireland by varying amounts.[6] Some of the possible changes, if determined solely with regard to the distribution of the population, would be quite unrealistic from the point of view of public administration, but there are other more feasible changes which could have important political consequences, notwithstanding the fact that a substantial proportion of the present Catholic population would still be left in Northern Ireland. For example, by transferring the area west of the river Foyle together with Fermanagh, West Tyrone and Newry, the proportion of Catholics in Northern Ireland could be reduced from the current figure of about two-fifths to about one-fifth. The change in the sectarian composition would be still greater if, as would seem likely, movements of population in both directions were to take place in response to the change in the frontier.

Those left on the 'wrong side' of the new border would complain bitterly of betrayal, and some assistance with resettlement might be required. More generally, there would be protests about 'surrender' from the whole Protestant community – but protests that would be less strong nowadays than would at one time have been the case. For it would presumably be appreciated that, thereafter, they would be 'safe' from the demographic pressure which, with the existing border, may ultimately bring about a Catholic majority – or so it is feared. For precisely the opposite reason, the resistance from the Republic to a redrawn frontier might well be intense. Although, in principle, the nationalists should be glad to gain these fragments of 'Hibernia Irredenta', they would not be easily reconciled to losing the chance of having the whole of Northern Ireland voted into the South by a Catholic majority. For the nationalist movement – even the constitutional nationalist movement – does not seem to have appreciated the full implications of their own professed objective of *a united Ireland based on consensus* but have their eyes fixed on a mere majority vote. This confused approach has been discussed in chapter 21 and we shall return to it again below in order to consider its implications.

We can reasonably assume that any change of the border would have to be carried out by Britain in face of protests from Dublin. When it came to the crunch the Republic could hardly refuse to accept these areas which are already held to be – as of right – part of the national territory. The famous Article 2 of the Republic's Constitution would then become a boomerang. The fact remains that the operation would be hard to carry out and probably costly. Furthermore it might also be unnecessary. Not only may there be other ways of dealing with a lack of consensus, but the division of opinion about continuing membership of the United Kingdom may not really be as deep and bitter in Northern Ireland as is often supposed. For, as was shown in chapter 21, caution is necessary in generalizing about Catholic preferences. Nevertheless there is a strong case, in my view, for giving serious consideration to what would be implied in practical terms by a redrawing of the border and even for having certain contingency plans prepared which could be brought forward if a deteriorating situation should, at some stage, make this appear the best of the bad options. One of the factors that might bring about just such a deterioration would be an approach towards equality in the Protestant and Catholic populations. For, as we shall see, such an approach could have explosive consequences. Another possible reason would be a refusal by the Irish Republic to take the joint action required in order to cope much more effectively with the terrorist campaign of the IRA. These contingency plans for the border should be kept ready as a shot in the locker which could be used if required.

Demographic change

The belief that partition cannot continue indefinitely has derived support from certain demographic prophecies which have brought consolation to committed Irish republicans but deep concern to Ulster Protestants. For many years, the number of Catholics has been increasing more rapidly than the number of Protestants, and the simple extrapolation of this trend would lead ultimately to a Catholic majority in the voting population. If it proved to be the case that virtually all of Ulster's Catholics were in favour of Irish unity, the British and Irish Governments would then be obliged to take 'appropriate action' under the Anglo-Irish Agreement, although the precise nature of this action has not been defined. In article 1(c), the two governments have declared that: 'if in the future a majority of the people of Northern Ireland clearly wish for and formally consent to the establishment of a united Ireland, they will introduce and support in their respective Parliaments legislation to give effect to that wish.'

Much of what has been said about the political consequences of demographic change rests on the assumption that the Protestant population would accept without protest a vote of something over 50 per cent in favour of joining the Republic. But this can by no means be taken for granted. Admittedly the Unionists have talked themselves into a position where resigned acceptance would appear to be required of them, for they have conferred upon the area of Northern Ireland a sanctity scarcely warranted by its pragmatic origin and have claimed that a majority vote in favour of union with Britain must be respected as the clear expression of democratic choice. Consistency should then require that a majority vote in favour of unity with the Republic should be treated with the same respect. But it cannot be assumed that, in practice, this conclusion would be universally accepted.

When James Molyneaux, the leader of the Official Unionist Party, was questioned on this point by Padraig O'Malley, he did in fact maintain a consistently democratic attitude by replying that:

> If 51 per cent of the people of Northern Ireland in a free and open election voted in favour of some form of unification, my party would accept it democratically. When you say 'accept', presumably you are asking whether we would take up arms to resist it. I don't think we would. But then you'd be leaving out of account the people who wouldn't be under the influence of any politicians – and there would be a growing number of them in those circumstances who would, if they felt they were being pushed into a united Ireland against their will, without adequate safeguards and all the rest of it; then I think you'd find the strength of the paramilitaries vastly increased. You'd have a terrorist situation, the reverse of what it is now. It would be a question for the South of Ireland to decide, if it would be either prudent or desirable to go for unification if they were going to have that kind of problem on their hands.[7]

This was both a fair response on Molyneaux's own part and also a necessary warning that a change in the demographic balance might bring, not social harmony, but a new period of difficulty. Another Unionist, Robert McCartney, reacted still more strongly against possible unity, even in those circumstances. O'Malley, for his part, found 'something profoundly disturbing in these remarks by moderate Unionists'. He went on to complain: 'For what they are saying is that as a group of people, Unionists, who presumably consider themselves part of the civilised world, are opposed to the point of physical revulsion to the thought of any association, under all sets of circumstances, with the rest of Ireland.'

Even if this were a fully accurate comment on what they are reported to have said, it would be unclear whether O'Malley's remark was an empirical proposition or an expression of moral disapproval. If it is an empirical proposition, then it amounts to the implicit dismissal of any claim that there already exists, or is likely to exist in the foreseeable future, anything that could be remotely described as an Ireland united by national sentiment. If, however, his comment is to be taken as an expression of moral disapproval, that disapproval should then be extended to the political leaders in the Republic, both Fine Gael and Fianna Fail, who would also 'presumably consider themselves as a part of the civilised world' but have always reacted with just as much dismay and distaste against the thought of any association, even in so loose an organization as the Commonwealth.

Here we are touching once more on the issue discussed in chapter 21 that is of such basic importance. This issue is the way in which the Irish leaders expect to achieve unity in the island, and the conditions which would, in their view, have to be satisfied. According to their often stated opinion, unity must be by *consent*, not by compulsion. The North must be won over and helped to acquire a 'true consciousness' of its position as part of the Irish nation. Let us do these leaders the courtesy of assuming that they are sincere and mean what they say when they refer to the need for consent. There can then be no question of dragging the non-Catholic population of the North unwillingly into the Republic. That is to say, there can be no question of merely transferring the problem of government-without-consensus from Northern Ireland to Ireland as a whole. *Neither* the ballot *nor* the Armalite will serve for this purpose. For a mere ballot-box majority would be inadequate if unity has really to be based on consensus, which implies far more than that. If consensus were indeed the objective, then the constitutional nationalists would have to be prepared to wait, and to acquiesce in a separate existence for Northern Ireland – perhaps a Northern Ireland reduced in size by a frontier change – until that consensus had finally been won. To try to enforce the verdict of a simple majority vote would be to invite a sharp clash of opinion which could again erupt into violence.

If a delicate situation of this kind were to be reached, it would be helpful, as I have suggested, to have some contingency plans prepared for a redrawing of the border and for a transfer of population, rather than to have to resort to improvised measures hurriedly devised at a time of crisis.

Of course this situation may never arise, for there may never be a Catholic majority in Northern Ireland. Moreover, even if such a majority were to emerge, we need not take it for granted that all Catholics would vote for membership of the Republic. What we can predict with certainty is that the situation would be highly dangerous if, at a time when parity in the voting population had been reached, there was still as much hatred and distrust as there appears to be in the late 1980s. It is really rather fortunate that no such pressure from demographic change is at all imminent. Time is available, and time would certainly be required, in order to bring about the change of 'heart and mind' on which the achievement of *genuine* Irish unity would depend. It would, therefore, be a great mistake for Irish nationalists to suppose that they had only to wait until, with a shift in population, the North was quietly dropped by majority vote into their lap. *Whether or not a Catholic majority ever emerges in Northern Ireland – and that, as we shall see, is far from certain – the task of achieving their objective of Irish unity by willing consent remains basically unaltered.* It is a task that will not be easily or quickly accomplished and therefore – from the point of view of those who are committed to this particular objective – there should be no delay in making a more substantial beginning.

Demographic forecasting is always a hazardous business, and in Northern Ireland is made more difficult by uncertainty about the religious composition of the population even in the two *previous* census years, 1971 and 1981. In 1971, 9.4 per cent refused to state their religious denomination partly because there was some Catholic political resistance and also because some non-Catholics were reluctant to do so in conditions of political uncertainty. Paul Compton has attempted to apportion the refusals with the aid of information from other sources, and has estimated that the Catholic population was 36.8 per cent of the total in 1971, as compared with the officially enumerated 31.4 per cent.[8] This revised calculation indicated a substantial relative increase since 1961 when the proportion was 34.9 per cent, and still more since 1937 when it was 33.5 per cent. The rise in the Catholic proportion would, of course, have been greater still if a higher rate of natural increase had not been partly offset by a higher rate of emigration. In the next census year, 1981, political resistance to the census was much stronger and even led to violence in some Catholic areas. (One unfortunate enumerator was killed in Derry.) There were also heavy abstentions on the part of non-Catholics. After making three different assessments, Compton has come to the conclusion that the Catholic population accounted for 37.6–38.6 per cent of the total in that year.

If, then, the denominational birth and death rates were to be maintained, with no offset from relatively greater Catholic emigration, a simple majority would be reached by 2026, but another fifteen years or so would have to elapse before there was a majority of voting age – a point that is sometimes overlooked. Naturally a simple projection of this kind is unlikely to give the right answer. Thus it is apparent that there has already been a decline in the fertility rate of Catholic females, which is estimated to have fallen from 3.64 to 3.24 – i.e. by 11 per cent – between 1971 and 1983 for the Province as a whole. In the city of Belfast, however, a much larger fall occurred, from 3.47 to 2.81 – i.e., 19 per cent – and something similar may be taking place with a time-lag in the smaller towns and country districts. It is true that the corresponding rates for non-Catholics were only 2.29 for the Province in 1983 and 2.14 in Belfast, but the gap between the Catholic and Protestant rates has clearly been narrowing. A similar decline in the Catholic birth rate has been observed in the Republic, and may continue in both parts of the island, notwithstanding the opposition of the Roman Catholic Church. A wide variety of assumptions can be made about the speed with which Catholic and non-Catholic fertility rates will converge, but it is quite possible, as Compton shows, that the denominational ratio will be stabilized with the non-Catholics *still* the larger group. 'In other words, the likelihood of an eventual Roman Catholic majority, despite superficial appearance to the contrary, is now receding and is more remote than seemed possible a decade or so ago.'[9] The outcome may, of course, be affected by the respective rates of emigration and it cannot be taken for granted that the

Catholic rate will continue to exceed the Protestant rate to the same extent as in the past.

Two conclusions emerge quite clearly from this analysis: first, a Catholic majority is by no means to be taken as inevitable; secondly, on any reasonable assumption, many years are likely to elapse before Catholics of voting age outnumber non-Catholics.

The conclusion thus derived from demographic forecasts is endorsed and fortified by economic considerations. For it must be assumed that, for an indefinite period ahead, political unity will also be precluded by economic difficulties which are already acute enough in both areas and would only be further intensified by their political union.

THE ECONOMIC CONSTRAINT

The economic factor has long been an obstacle to the political unity of the island, but its nature has changed. In the past the dispute centred around free trade or protection. The Irish nationalist leaders were usually protectionists who, in their more romantic moments, dreamed of a self-contained Ireland whose many farmers and whose few industries would provide all that was required for the simple traditional life with which Irish people ought to be content. But the industrial North, dependent upon British and indeed world markets, was not prepared to adopt so introverted an attitude and had therefore a strong economic reason for resisting any Home Rule proposals that might finally allow a Dublin government to adopt an independent tariff policy. This Ulster attitude was, of course, vindicated when de Valera embarked upon a highly protectionist policy; but a critically important change occurred in the 1950s when Lemass and Whitaker began to lead the Republic towards a more open and more progressive economy. With both parts of the island now members of the EEC and with the Single European Act about to come into operation in 1992, the emphasis has now shifted away from trade barriers to fiscal and financial policies.

During the 1960s and part of the 1970s economic progress proceeded at a satisfactory pace in the Republic, with industrial development fostered by a lively promotional agency and assisted by generous subsidies and tax concessions. Membership of the EEC brought further assistance to the farmers and the combined effect of all these changes was a rise in prosperity to a level never before experienced. But Irish prosperity depended substantially upon world prosperity and the difficulties that followed the oil crises required appropriate adjustments on the part of the Republic, as elsewhere. It was, however, at the time of the second oil crisis (1979) that the Fianna Fail Government under Haughey chose to embark upon an ambitious expansion of the welfare state. Social benefits in cash were then raised to levels close to those thought appropriate for Britain where output per head was about one-third higher. The penalty of this overambitious expansion was heavy indebtedness at home and abroad. By 1982, the exchequer borrowing requirement was 15.7 per cent of GNP. The Fine Gael/ Labour coalition which had taken over was insufficiently strong to cope with the situation and a state of crisis had been reached when Fianna Fail, again under Haughey, came into power in 1986. The exchequer borrowing requirement was then 14.4 per cent of GNP and the accumulated national debt was equivalent to eighteen months' gross national product. That debt had been doubled in four years and interest alone absorbed a third of tax revenue. Two-fifths of the debt – equivalent to more than seven months' national output – was owed abroad and a foreign surplus was therefore necessary for many years to come. Public expenditure was 60 per cent of GNP.

The new Fianna Fail Government, with a fine disregard for electoral pledges, then embarked upon an austerity programme, and financial control is now being gradually restored. According to one team of forecasters, the growth rate of GNP may have recovered to about 3.5 per cent a year by the early 1990s.[10] The exchequer borrowing requirement may be stabilized at about 5.5 per cent of GNP by 1992 with some decline in the debt/output ratio perhaps in 1990. But taxation is extremely high – for those who pay it. The Irish Republic has the highest starting rate for income tax in Western Europe, as is illustrated by a tax rate of 35 per cent for a single person with an annual income corresponding to a mere £1800 a year and for a married couple with £3,600.[11] In Britain no income tax at all would be paid at these levels. A single person on average wages has a marginal tax rate of 58 per cent. Apart from the tax burden, there is no prospect that unemployment will fall much below 20 per cent, without more emigration.

The moral is clear. The Republic is starting to extricate itself slowly from a disastrous situation but will be in no position to take over responsibility for Northern Ireland for an indefinitely long period ahead.

It has been pointed out often enough that the standard of living would be reduced if Northern Ireland were to leave the United Kingdom in order to join the Republic. Like the other, less prosperous areas of Britain, Ulster receives a subvention which is ultimately derived from the more prosperous areas – as described in chapter 9. Local expenditure reflects local needs, and locally collected revenue reflects local taxable capacity. Net transfers between different areas thus take place which can be regarded as the implicit consequence of progressive taxation on the one hand and the welfare state on the other. These transfers are not even estimated for the various regions of Great Britain but, as a consequence of the 1920 Government of Ireland Act, are still presented for Northern Ireland with the result that that area is represented in a particularly unfavourable light.

The large increase in the subvention in recent years helps to account for the emphasis it has received. After a long period in which Ulster was treated less well than the other poor areas of Britain, the scale of assistance was greatly increased, and much more generous provision was made for dealing with the accumulated deficiencies of social capital. These adjustments, together with the impact of the recession, have raised the subvention to about a third of public expenditure or about a fifth of personal income per head.[12]

It is merely realistic to accept that the Ulster electorate cannot be expected to abandon willingly its position in the United Kingdom for membership of the Irish Republic. The loss that such a change would entail has been substantially increased as a consequence of the financial deterioration in the Republic in recent years. Not only would the ordinary Ulster people, both Protestant and Catholic, lose the assistance they receive from Westminster but they would have to accept responsibility for a share of the Republic's massive debt of about £25,000 per household.

There is no reason to suppose that Britain, for her part, would continue to pay a subvention on anything like the current scale if Ulster had joined the Republic. Perhaps some transitional assistance might be provided for a short period on a reduced scale, but that would be all that could realistically be expected. After all, one of the main attractions of a united Ireland, from the British point of view, would be the possibility of ending the subvention to Ulster.

It may be objected that no account has been taken so far of the economic benefits that would follow from Irish unity. With the border removed, would the two parts of the island not be able to trade together to their mutual benefit and to achieve the advantages of larger economies of scale? We need not repeat what has been said in previous chapters about the limited scope for mutual trading and the far greater importance to both areas of British and world-wide markets. But there is another answer which, though rather obvious, tends to be strangely neglected by proponents of a united Irish economy. This is the fact that the border, as an obstacle to trade, has already largely disappeared and should do so completely when the Single European Act comes into full operation after 1992. Nor is there anything, even now, to prevent joint ventures in industrial promotion or public investment of the kind much discussed in recent years, with particular reference to the Derry/Donegal and Newry/Dundalk areas. Such possibilities should, of course, be sympathetically explored and, where appropriate, implemented, but without extravagant antici- pations about the gain to general prosperity that might be achieved thereby. As Charles Carter remarked to the Forum, 'their effects on unemployment would be equivalent to the products of nine bean rows on the Isle of Innisfree, when set against a requirement of new jobs in the North in the coming two decades which is of the order of 200,000'.[13] Neither he nor Louden Ryan, Governor of the Bank of Ireland, could offer the Forum much prospect of economic advantage from unity.

Nevertheless there still appears to be a lingering misunderstanding about the supposedly neglected scope for cooperation which calls for further comment. For example, Neil Kinnock has complained that it is an absurdity 'that Britain can exchange electricity supplies with continental Europe but that Northern Ireland and the Republic cannot'.[14] There are indeed economies of scale in this particular industry but it is also the case that no political or constitutional obstacle prevents their exploitation. Even under the old Unionist regime at Stormont, there was cooperation with the Republic in this field. But the possibility of continuing cooperation was removed by the enthusiastic efficiency with which the IRA destroyed the power lines – a point apparently overlooked by the author of Mr Kinnock's brief. More generally, there is a tendency to exaggerate the importance of the border as an obstacle and to assume a political reluctance to cooperate on a scale that was not present even when the Unionists were in power when there was cooperation in transport and fisheries policy as well as in electricity supply. Banking was another example. In our study of banking in 1966, which was commissioned by the Unionist government, we naturally spent some time in Dublin as well as in Belfast.[15] Everyone recognized that it would have been impossible otherwise to do the job, but political unity was not required.

A different line of speculation concerns the possible effect of taking Northern Ireland out of the sterling currency area and into the area of the punt. It might be urged that the currency depreciation thus implied would surely make Ulster industry more competitive and thus foster expansion. There is indeed no reason to assume that the national exchange rate of the United Kingdom is the most appropriate one for all its constituent regions, and given relative wage levels and levels of productivity, the pound may be at too high a level to suit Ulster's needs.[16]

What would then be implied would be a currency depreciation for the North of about a tenth, if the punt held its present value. In fact the punt may still be overvalued and may have to fall further with the implication that Ulster could expect a larger depreciation, apart from any further repercussions from the act of unification itself. Unfortunately it does not follow that the lower currency would have more than a short-term beneficial effect on competitiveness. For dearer import prices would lead to higher production costs, both directly through higher prices for energy and other inputs and indirecty through higher wage demands in order to offset the rise in the consumer price level. Prices to the consumer would be further raised by the high rates of value added tax. Income tax in the Republic would also cut severely into the size of take-home earnings in the North and lead to fierce demands for higher pay. Roughly four-fifths of the unionized Ulster labour force belong to British trade unions, but the difficulty of wage inflation would not be removed even if their members could be persuaded to move into the far from quiescent unions of the Irish Republic. In short, depreciation, to be effective, must not be offset by rising domestic costs. The twenty-six-county Republic has yet to demonstrate that it can maintain the *effective* depreciation needed in order to achieve the balance of payments surplus required by its weak debtor position; for its own domestic costs, especially labour costs, will not be easily controlled. Or, if the foreign surplus can be achieved, it is most unlikely that this will be accomplished at a tolerably high level of employment and low level of emigration. The advent of the Ulster workers caused by a removal of the Border would give a further and immensely strong impetus to cost inflation and thus to further currency depreciation, with the danger that the newly unified Ireland would be in still greater danger of being sucked into a downward spiral.

Nor is this all. For, if there were sufficient control of the Ulster labour market to permit an effective devaluation of the currency, the exercise of that same control could be used to make Ulster industry more competitive *without* currency devaluation. This could be achieved by simply ensuring that wages and salaries in Ulster did not rise as much relatively to rising productivity as in Britain as a whole. Even in Thatcher Britain, there is scope for relative progress in any region that can show itself to be capable of a little more discipline in its own particular labour market.

In discussing these possibilities, as in the previous discussion of the welfare state, we have been touching on large and controversial issues, hedged with technical complexities which cannot, of course, be pursued further in the present volume. But these issues, though obviously in need of further development, could not be neglected even in our present review of the situation.

The conclusion of this section is clear enough. With both parts of the island faced with serious economic problems, political unification is not now a relevant option and, for this reason alone, apart from any other reasons that may be adduced, will not become an option for an indefinite period ahead. In this chapter we have established three firm conclusions which should constitute part of the basis for future policy:

1 Although demographic change will gradually strengthen the voting power of the Catholic population in Northern Ireland, there is no prospect of a Catholic

majority of voting age for an indefinite period ahead and only a doubtful possibility that such a majority will ever be reached. It follows that the likelihood of Ulster being voted out of the United Kingdom and into the Republic is remote and uncertain.

2   A mere majority in Northern Ireland in favour of Irish unity would in any case fall far short of the professed objective of constitutional nationalists, which is the achievement of a consensus of opinion in its support. Unity is to come by general agreement, not just by majority vote. Such agreement is not yet even remotely in sight.

3   For many years ahead, the Republic will have to contend with serious economic difficulties and, with its own battered economy, will be in no position to attract the North into a political union. Both areas will have plenty to occupy them in coping with unemployment and other ills.

24
Strategies

I ended the previous chapter with the quite firmly established conclusion that a united Ireland will not come about for an indefinitely long period. If it is to be achieved at all, it is much more likely to be achieved by some later generation. If, however, it is agreed that this conclusion is inescapable, does it follow that political life in Northern Ireland must continue to be blighted by an enduring conflict between different national aspirations, with a large Catholic minority compelled, against their will, to live in the United Kingdom? Must it be anticipated that the resentment thus provoked will be sufficiently intense to sustain a guerilla campaign of indefinite duration – a campaign which would be all the more tragic because its barbarity would be futile? When the more pessimistic forecasters claim that the Ulster problem is insoluble, is this the prospect they have in mind?

If such a conclusion were indeed inescapable, there would appear to be an overwhelming case for changing one of the present parameters. That is to say, there would be sufficient ground for regarding a change in the Border as a lesser evil. As we have observed, a change of this kind would allow more Catholics to live in the Republic, though at the cost of taking many unwilling Protestants with them; it would remove for good the prospect of a Catholic majority in Northern Ireland, and the new Border could be so drawn as greatly to ease the problems of the security forces. But we have also observed that this change would be difficult and costly to effect. It is not therefore to be regarded as a preferred solution if others are available, but it is one that should be held in reserve, not prematurely discarded.

There would be a positive advantage in including a pronouncement about the Border in a comprehensive official presentation of the options available. It might be clearly stated that, although other options were to be preferred, a situation could arise where the government would feel compelled to resort to an alteration of the Border preferably with, but if necessary without, the agreement of the Republic.

A more hopeful approach can be adopted when it is recognized that Ulster Catholics have no unanimous and strongly felt desire to leave the United Kingdom and become citizens of the Republic of Ireland. No doubt Irish unity is widely cherished as a long-term ideal but, for the more relevant future, Northern Catholics seem inclined to be pragmatic. They are well aware of the grass-roots resistance to unity from the majority in the North and also of the practical disadvantages that they themselves would have to accept, with the British subvention replaced by a share in responsibility for the very large national debt of the Irish Republic. It is true that they would not nowadays have to face a big loss in cash social benefits provided some arrangement could be made for dealing with the claims of new entrants to the Republic's benefit system.[1] But the penalty would be a very high rate of VAT which would reduce the real value of all incomes, whether derived from work or benefits, and they would not appreciate a penal income tax levied at the rates illustrated in the previous chapter. Nor would there, one supposes, be any great enthusiasm for a health service with a means test or for an educational system where the state no longer met 100 per cent of the costs.

As we have seen in chapter 21, the opinion polls have never recorded any large majority of Ulster Catholics in favour of unity. Recent polls, on the contrary, record only a minority of between 20 and 25 per cent. Let us also recall that, in the Republic, only two-thirds of those responding to a large poll in the summer of 1987 declared themselves to be in favour of a united Ireland. Even when this number – two-thirds of 3.5 million – is added to that of the Northerners who favour unity now – about a tenth of 1.5 million – the majority in its favour, in the island as a whole, is slightly less than a half. It is also very important, in speculating about future trends, to recall that support for a united Ireland comes predominantly from the older generation and from the rural population. As the *Irish Times* put it: 'There is above average support for the idea of a 26-county nation (that is to say, a partitioned island) in all age groups up to 50, below average support for a 32-county nation (a united Ireland) in the same age groups.'[2] The contrast of views between the older and the younger generations affords some grounds for hope that, as the former are removed by the passage of time, a cooler and more rational approach may become more general – which would benefit relations with the North and improve the longer-term likelihood of finding an agreed and harmonious solution.

We must always distinguish between aspirations and anticipations. Let us again recall the figures. Although two-thirds of all those questioned in the Republic would favour a united Ireland, only a half expected that unity would ever be achieved, only two-fifths anticipated unity in the next 100 years and only 29 per cent in the next 50 years. Almost a fifth did not want a united Ireland and a seventh were undecided. It would seem that these respondents had a firmer grip on reality than some of their political leaders. Admittedly poll results must always be treated with caution, as I have stressed in chapter 21, but the results of a succession of polls both North and South have been too consistent to be ignored. If their results do not mislead, then neither the partition of the island nor the conflict of nationalist aspirations would seem to be the cause of as much bitterness and frustration as some rhetorical politicians would have us believe. As Padraig O'Malley has put it:

If a majority of Northern Ireland's Catholics are not actively seeking a united Ireland, and if a large number will settle for an outcome that does not necessarily involve a link with the South, and if there is no real depth of commitment to unification in the South herself, then the question must be raised: who does want a united Ireland?[3]

SECURITY POLICY

The traditional way of viewing the Ulster problem as a hopeless conflict between divergent national aspirations now begins to seem less appropriate. Yet the killing goes on. The initial social grievances of the minority could not possibly justify twenty years of terrorist activity, and most of those original grievances have long since been removed. What, then, is the point of this violence? What purpose is it designed to serve?

Part of the explanation lies obviously in the fact that the leaders of the IRA and Sinn Fein are fired by a specially intense fanaticism and are quite prepared to act 'on behalf of the nation' with no mandate for doing so, on the strength of their own vision of its rights and its future. For the members of these paramilitary forces, especially for the leaders, terrorism has also become a way of life. It gives them occupation, authority and power. It allows them to dominate their respective areas. Moreover, whatever its origin in ancient grievances, violence takes on the character of an independent evil, itself the cause of new grievances, fresh bitterness and a further widening of the sectarian divide. Thus terrorism and the means used to control it acquire a continuing momentum of their own. The most vehemently expressed grievances of the Catholic minority now appear to be those attributed to the behaviour of the security forces. These complaints, when not simply unfounded, may often be greatly exaggerated, but the fact remains that, in so tense a situation, some mistakes are bound to be made, and some of the actions taken will go wrong. A policy of simply trying to contain the activities of the terrorists must therefore be attended by great dangers. Their force needs to be broken – but that is not easy when the Republic provides at least a partial refuge and when, within Northern Ireland, strict limits are placed on any infringement of the rights normally enjoyed by the citizens of a free society. Yet some further action has clearly been required.

The various possibilities may now be summarized. The first is an intensified attack on the rackets run by the paramilitary forces in order to obtain finance. As was observed in chapter 22, a new interdepartmental operation was launched in 1988 with the net extended to deal with abuses in the letting of government contracts and to catch finance companies that might be involved in handling terrorist cash or in paying protection money themselve. In these ways the paramilitaries may be seriously hampered – although, in the case of the IRA, the loss of funds could, perhaps, be made good from Libya and even from the USA. The real domestic obstacle to enforcing the policy is bound to be that of finding victims or witnesses who will be prepared to risk the terrorists' wrath by testifying. Although this operation is so obviously desirable and may well bring valuable results, success on the scale that is really needed may be elusive until normal policing can be restored. In short, the attack on paramilitary sources of finance should be regarded as complimentary to other measures directed against the power of the godfathers, not as a substitute for them.

The second proposal has been longer terms in jail for convicted terrorists in order both to increase the deterrent and to extend the period before they are again free to commit new atrocities. Although the Northern Ireland judiciary is usually described by nationalists as a worthy successor to Genghis Khan, the sentences served are, in fact, substantially shorter than elsewhere in the United Kingdom. A reduction of the remission period from 50 per cent to the usual one-third was announced in November 1988. For the worst offenders, some believe that the life sentence might really be for life.

A third possibility, actually adopted in 1988, has been the removal of the *right to silence* exploited to the full by the IRA. That is to say, a refusal to answer questions would become an offence. It is relevant to recall that, in the Republic, silence could entail the presumption of belonging to an illegal organization. Section 3, subsection 2, of the Offences Against the State Act provides that: 'Where an officer of the Gardai Siochana, not below the rank of Chief Superintendent, in giving evidence in proceedings relating to an offence under the said Section 21, states that he believes that the Accused was at a material time a member of an unlawful organization, the statement shall be evidence that he was such a member.'

The power thus accorded to the court was, I believe, greater than any power accorded to a Diplock Court, and was much criticized. In the event, it was allowed that such evidence could be controverted by the accused and fresh evidence would then be required for a conviction. *But it has been necessary for the accused to put his case even at the cost of recognizing the court.* Senator Robinson records that 'The newspaper reports of cases show that the belief of the Chief Superintendent would be sufficient to convict unless it was controverted either under oath or even by unsworn statements made by the accused.'[4] Silence would then be punished.

The fourth possibility has been the introduction of internment or detention by which is meant imprisonment for an unspecified period, not without trial but after a trial of a special kind at which the normal rules of evidence would be relaxed. This course of action has been regarded as one to be avoided except in a situation of extreme gravity, but it could be argued that such a situation has existed for many years in Ulster. Would it not, therefore, be better to resort to detention than to permit an indefinite continuation of terrorist activity and an indefinite prolongation of the brutal rule of the paramilitaries in the areas largely under their control? The answer was bound to depend largely upon the anticipated effectiveness of detention. That effectiveness would obviously be much less if introduced in Northern Ireland alone than it would be if adopted at the same time on both sides of the Border. Action of this kind, taken jointly as in 1956–62, would be a very different matter and might well break the power of the terrorists and bring their campaign to an end. The crucial question has therefore been the willingness of the Republic to take such action. Given the assumptions, the refusal curtly given in September 1988 can only mean that a substantial part of the responsibility for allowing terrorist activity to continue must rest with the Government of the Irish Republic.

SOCIAL REFORM AND POLITICAL STABILITY

Oracular commentators on the situation in Ulster are wont to asseverate that the IRA cannot be defeated by military measures alone. Notwithstanding the suggestion of original insight with which this proposition is sometimes enunciated, it is one that has long been accepted. The action required may then be considered under two headings.

First, measures to improve social conditions and meet reasonable complaints about discrimination; second, constitutional reforms. We will leave this second point to the next section.

With regard to the first, many changes have long since been made and bulwarks against discrimination erected. The outstanding problem is the very much heavier rate of unemployment among Catholics. Although this differential has a number of explanations of which deliberate discrimination is no longer regarded as the most important, the fact remains that the gap is there and the grievance is strongly felt. The new measures introduced by the Government in 1988 have been described in chapter 12, and some emphasis was placed on the difficulty of coping satisfactorily with the problem in Ulster where only a small rise in employment has occurred during the current cyclical expansion in the world economy. For any substantial improvement to be achieved, a strong and well-sustained rise in the rate of growth of output would be required, and one of the several obstacles is, of course, the continuing activity of the terrorists themselves. It is a point that should be driven home. It should also be recognized that the paramilitary organizations have nothing that could be even remotely described as a coherent economic policy. If the Brits were in fact to leave, what would Sinn Fein then do about the houses and jobs and social benefits they now claim as of right for their supporters? There is no answer.

What is true for the economy generally can be illustrated with particular sharpness by referring to the situation at the shipbuilders Harland and Wolff, and the aircraft component manufacturers Short and Harland. Both firms have belonged to highly subsidised sectors of British industry and special efforts have been made to prevent their collapse, especially in the case of the shipyard. In both firms, however, the workforces have been predominantly Protestant, and Ulster Catholics have felt, quite understandably, that they have had a grievance. In 1988 it was announced that the two firms were to be privatized and would then have to fight even harder for survival in a competitive world. In such circumstances it will be exceedingly difficult to change substantially the sectarian composition of their respective labour forces, in particular at the skilled level. Nor is it obviously in the interest of young Catholics to seek to acquire such skills, especially in the shipyard where their future careers would be linked to an industry with such dubious prospects. More hopeful may be the attempts to foster new industrial development along new lines in the Catholic areas and it would, therefore, be a serious error to test the effectiveness of the Government's policy by directing attention too narrowly to the changes in individual firms.

The Government may attempt in this way to persuade the ordinary working-class people that the terrorists are holding back the rise in prosperity from which all would gain, but the chance of achieving success is greatly reduced by the attitude of the constitutional nationalists. When a new wave of violence occurs, as in the summer of 1988, the response of the constitutional nationalist party – including the SDLP – is to assert that the fundamental solution must be political. In this way attention is diverted from the need for tighter security. Indeed it should be more widely recognized in Britain that when the leadership of the SDLP was expressing regret at the IRA atrocities of that year and was pleading for 'reconciliation', they themselves were still withholding support from the security forces. Their demand for reform also conveys, by implication rather than demonstration, the conclusion that reform is still desperately needed and, furthermore, that the onus rests with the British, not with themselves. When the British yield to such demands, the IRA for its part can then claim – as it did with regard to the Anglo-Irish Agreement – that the constitutional nationalists are ready enough to accept the prizes won by terrorism, however much its brutality may shock their sensibilities. Nationalists may seem to have behaved cleverly but their approach may be rather short-sighted and dangerous. First, the IRA is at war with the Republic as well as Britain, and its aim – now to be won with the support of its Libyan allies – is to overthrow the 'bourgeois state' and replace it with an Irish Socialist Republic. (It is surely time that US sympathizers understood this fact.) Secondly, in so far as the constitutional nationalists gain ground in this indirect way they do so only at the cost of widening still more the gap that separates them from the Ulster majority. Thus the basic questions are raised once more. Are they aiming at conquest? Or do they want an island that is truly united by the agreement of its people?

It may not be fully appreciated in Britain that concessions designed to deprive the IRA of sympathy can have the opposite effect. If the terrorists have forced the government to concede this and grant that, perhaps they deserve continuing sympathy! A vote for Sinn Fein is not unequivocal evidence of an immediate desire to leave the United Kingdom with all the disadvantages that would entail. Still less is it clear support for an outright IRA victory and a new 'Socialist' Republic under Gerry Adams! A vote for Sinn Fein may indeed be an expression of traditional hostility for Brits and Prods, but it may also be an electoral method of extorting further benefits. Of course it is true that certain reforms had to be made, and have in fact been made. But the prospect of yet more benefits should not be allowed to constitute a continuing incentive to support Sinn Fein. The government might well consider the case for adopting a different stance by making it absolutely plain that there would be no more concessions and no more 'initiatives' until there had been a substantial decline in terrorist activity.

CONSTITUTIONAL REFORM

The second line of action – constitutional reform – can be followed at both the provincial and the national level. The main emphasis has been on the former with attention concentrated on the possible restoration of some form of representative devolved government. It is undeniable that naive expectations have sometimes been entertained about the benefit that might follow from an 'initiative' along such lines. It was certainly naive to suppose that the IRA, for its part, would respond by calling off its offensive. It cannot be too often emphasized – because it is so frequently forgotten – that the IRA is not in the least attracted by any mere reform of the present system. This is a revolutionary body which will be content with nothing less than the overthrow of the system, both North and South of the border. Reforms will be welcomed only in so far as they may open up new paths to revolution, but are to be opposed if there should be any danger of their leading to a stable and contented society. So much has been made clear in their own pronouncements, and so much was demonstrated by their contemptuous rejection of power-sharing in 1973/74 and of the Anglo-Irish Agreement in 1985. This crucially important lesson may have been learned at last, but the hope is often expressed that further reforms might lead ordinary people to repudiate the paramilitaries. As I have stressed, however, that act of repudiation is both difficult and dangerous. For the proposed reforms to have their desired effect, it would be essential that they should be accompanied by an intensified effort to break the grip of the terrorist organizations, in particular the stranglehold of the IRA.

The problem of *devolved government* in Northern Ireland in the past has been discussed at some length in other chapters, and I shall not attempt any comprehensive summary. There are, however, some central points that must be singled out for comment. If the local political scene were still to be dominated by the debate about a united Ireland, the outcome would be Protestant domination of the regional Assembly, unless special provision had been made for power-sharing in some sense of that term.[5] The polls suggest that there would be quite a lot of support, Protestant as well as Catholic, for another experiment but, in practice, the difficulties would be even greater than in 1973/4. Sinn Fein's entry into representative politics has clearly created new and very serious difficulties for local government. Some of its members might be elected to a new Assembly – and might choose to take their seats. Any action to exclude them would then be represented as an attempt to disenfranchise part of the electorate. It is hard to envisage a regional Assembly with Sinn Fein representatives, and an Executive containing Sinn Fein members would be impossible, even if security policy were not to be devolved. It is useless to suppose that Sinn Fein members could be excluded by simply requiring them to sign some declaration condemning the use of violence. That proposal, when made with regard to local government, was treated with derision by Sinn Fein. Its members will cheerfully sign anything without any feeling that an undertaking given to an enemy government with which they are at war need be taken at all seriously. Some means of enforcement would have to be devised.

The total rejection of the Anglo-Irish Agreement by the Unionist leaders has been an obstacle to negotiation which produced stalemate. By the early months of 1988, however, the role of the Conference had been sufficiently clarified to have warranted a more relaxed approach. For it had then been established beyond all doubt that this body was a consultative, not an executive, organization. Mrs Thatcher had meant what she had said. So had the Secretary of State, Tom King. Even the undertaking accepted by both Britain and Ireland to seek to achieve agreement had not conferred on the Conference the *de facto* executive authority the Unionists had feared. So much had been demonstrated by the rejection of the demand for three-judge Diplock Courts and by the dispute about an alleged shoot-to-kill policy. It was unfortunate that the limitation of the role of the Conference had to be demonstrated in these particular ways, which aroused so much bitter controversy, but the demonstration had been clear enough. The Unionists who had put themselves out on a limb had an honourable means of withdrawing now that this clarification had been made – withdrawing not to the point of acceptance of the Agreement as it stood, but to the point of negotiation.

The arrangements that operated over the first three years of that Agreement perpetuated the exclusion of the Ulster majority. The meetings of the Conference were held in private with no representatives of the Ulster electorate present – just as none were allowed to take part in the discussions that led up to the 1985

Anglo-Irish Agreement. But the leadership of the SDLP was able to express its views and exert its influence through its association with the Irish Government. Thus the one-sided arrangement which was a feature of the period when the Agreement was being negotiated, has been allowed to continue. The Unionist parties and the Alliance had therefore an incentive to negotiate because any business that was devolved would be taken away from the secret meetings of the Conference – an inducement which, as noted in chapter 19, may have been introduced deliberately by the British Government with precisely this objective in mind. But, as we also noted, the Agreement provided both the Irish Government and the SDLP with an incentive to *resist* devolution because their influence over business so devolved would then be diluted. This resistance could be exerted effectively by the terms they demanded for any new assembly. Whether such opposition will be exerted and sustained on the nationalist side is not clear. For there has clearly been some nationalist disillusionment with the Conference which may conceivably revive their support for devolution. The SDLP might well press for the responsibility for law and order to be among the services to be devolved,[6] in order to take it away from the 'oppressive' British. The Unionists, for their part, would also have their price. They might reasonably maintain that they would consent to take part in a new devolved and power-sharing administration only if the Republic's bureaucratic outpost at Maryfield on Belfast Lough were to be closed down – or were to be restricted to the work of a security-liaison office, for which, indeed, a case can be made. But the gain they would achieve by getting rid of Maryfield would be mainly symbolic. Much more important would be a new arrangement for consultation between the Secretary of State and the Northern Ireland parties before meetings of the Conference, in the same way as the Irish Government consults the SDLP. A further step would be to invite members of those parties to attend the meetings of the Conference itself, or some part of those meetings.

In the continuing debate about representative devolution, attention has been concentrated in recent years on the constitutional arrangements, in particular on the possibility of power-sharing, and on the functions a new assembly might be expected to perform. Not much attempt has been made to assess the differences that devolution might bring in practice.

It would presumably be accepted without question that the powers to be devolved should include those normally exercised by the top layer of local government which had been transferred to the old Stormont parliament on the recommendation of the Macrory Report (p. 175 above). If to these there were to be added responsibility for the health service and for educational policy, the extent of devolution would be roughly that contemplated for a Scottish assembly in 1979. Its scope could, in fact, be further increased to cover all the services for which the old Stormont parliament was responsible, including industry, but with the exception of law and order and security. For it would obviously be absurd to consider devolving responsibility for law and order if there were Sinn Fein members in any new Executive, or even in a new Assembly. With Sinn Fein somehow excluded from both, there would still be great difficulties. The SDLP would presumably be highly suspicious of a Unionist Minister for Home Affairs, and the Unionists, for their part, could scarcely be expected to forget that the SDLP had withheld its full support from the police even after the Anglo-Irish Agreement had come into force. Moreover, the old questions about the role of the army under devolution would have to be faced once more.

What advantages would follow? On the positive side, the government of the Province might be more representative of public opinion with a new Assembly and Executive better informed about local needs and ways of meeting them – though also less objective about them. (Whether with devolution or without, the Northern Ireland civil service would be the principal source of expert information and guidance.) The politicians, for their part, would have their attention substantially diverted from the old sectarian issues to such common problems as unemployment and economic development. The experience of working together should be helpful, as I believe it was in 1973/4, and as it is said to be in the European Parliament. The fact that there is now a block grant permits more freedom of manoeuvre than was possible in the old Stormont days when fiscal transfers were determined by parity of service on a more or less item by item basis. Unfortunately, it would always be easier to think of services that might be expanded than of those where contractions could be made, and the exercise of autonomy, when it came to the point, might be limited. A similar consideration would arise if some taxing power were to be devolved. Although there could be support for the view that public expenditure, at 70 per cent of GDP, is far too high, and could be reduced with a corresponding reduction in locally raised revenue, it is far from easy to envisage a situation where that option would be exercised. More generally, there is a real danger that too much might be anticipated from devolution and disenchantment would follow.

A case can be made for devolution on the doubtful assumption that the various parties can work together harmoniously. There have been some hopeful signs. For example, as long ago as 1984, the Official Unionist Party published its proposals for the future in a pamphlet which recognized that: 'it is the responsibility of the majority to persuade the minority that the Province is also theirs'.[7] It may be more difficult, however, to achieve the necessary degree of harmony now than in 1973/4. That earlier period also had its tensions, largely because some members of the SDLP were so obviously looking impatiently beyond power-sharing to a united Ireland. Nevertheless there was sufficient goodwill on the part of all to allow the system to work surprisingly well during its short life-time. Subsequently personalities have changed. The SDLP has become even more 'green'. Nor does it help when John Hume talks about the need 'to lance the boil of unionism'. The Democratic Unionist Party would now have to be fitted into the team with Paisley and, presumably, Robinson playing leading roles. Overshadowing even these difficulties is the one already mentioned – the election of members of Sinn Fein, an organization that is not even legal in Great Britain.

It is doubtful whether, in these circumstances, devolution is really a practical possibility. If it were to be attempted, it would surely be prudent to restrict the scope of devolved business, initially at least, to those matters that are the normal concern of the upper level of local government, with a further extension left for the time being as a possibility to be decided in the light of experience.

Removing constitutional uncertainty

Violence thrives in an atmosphere of uncertainty, but it is not uncertainty about devolution that is the most important question. What is of central importance is the widespread feeling of doubt about Northern Ireland's future position as part of the

United Kingdom. Unfortunately the British political parties, both in office and in opposition, have somehow succeeded in conveying a false impression of impending departure. This is so although there is no question of a united Ireland in the foreseeable future. Government policies must not only be based on that fact but should be clearly *seen* to be so.

The IRA has repeatedly asked for an undertaking that Britain will withdraw at some specified date in the immediate future. Mercifully its request has been ignored. In 1971 a similar request was put forward in a more moderate but still unrealistic form by Harold Wilson, then Leader of the Opposition, who proposed that Britain undertake to leave within 15 years, provided political violence had ceased. Even if his recommendation had been accepted in principle, it is unlikely that the proviso would have been satisfied. For it would be very hard for any government to maintain its authority during an interregnum when every paramilitary force would have a flood of recruits and all would seek to strengthen and extend their positions in preparation for an impending conflict.

Nevertheless the British political parties have somehow managed to suggest that they are responding to the earnest plea of Irish nationalists which Conor Cruise O'Brien has paraphrased: 'Please say you're going but for God's sake stay.'[8] Thus a hazy impression of impending withdrawal has somehow been created which has provided the IRA with an obvious incentive to keep up its pressure and speed the parting guest. The apparent insecurity of the future has also impressed upon the Protestant paramilitary organizations the need to maintain their strength in case there should soon be a struggle for power. The consequence is that the government of the Province has been made more difficult than it need have been. For it is hard to retain authority when looking backwards from what seems to be the threshold of a half-opened door.

This uncertainty is not only harmful; it is entirely unwarranted.[9] The Anglo-Irish Agreement makes that quite clear. In Article 1 of that Agreement, the two Governments 'affirm that any change in the status of Northern Ireland would only come about with the consent of the majority of the people of Northern Ireland'. The Agreement received overwhelming support from all parties in both of Britain's Houses of Parliament. In so far as there was opposition, it was not opposition to this clause with its constituional guarantee. Moreover, the Agreement was formally registered as a treaty with the United Nations. There can, then, be no question of any British Government yielding to IRA pressure by deciding to expel Northern Ireland from the United Kingdom. Even if, in the absence of such a binding obligation, a majority of UK voters might prefer such a course, that course is effectively blocked. The Sinn Fein inspired agitation for 'troops out' is, therefore, a futile waste of time. Ulster will remain British until a majority of its voters think otherwise and, so long as it is a part of the United Kingdom, it must be defended like any other area. Britain is firmly bound by an international treaty that must be respected by her political parties – unless, indeed, they are prepared to commit an act that would flagrantly dishonourable. Indeed there can have been only a few cases in British history when Parliament has been quite so firmly bound by its almost unanimous acceptance of an international undertaking.

Oddly enough, the significance of that undertaking has been concealed by the reaction of the unionists themselves. For the various reasons given in chapter 19, they have been so outraged by other aspects of the Agreement and by the way in which it was negotiated and concluded, that they have failed to appreciate and bring out the importance of this first clause of Article 1. It is true that there have been earlier constitutional guarantees given in the past, notably at Sunningdale in 1973, but it is hard to see why that fact should make the new pledge any the less significant. There is also a certain irony in the fact that the IRA, for its part, claimed that the Agreement which established the Anglo-Irish Conference would never have been accepted by Britain if British politicians had not been convinced by the terrorist campaign that a 'political solution' involving the Republic was required. To this extent the Conference was the achievement of the IRA! But the same Agreement destroyed, as firmly as any such document could possibly do, their own hope that Britain would be bombed into abandoning Ulster. Not for the first time, the leaders of the IRA demonstrated that they were clever at tactics but hopeless at strategy.

It is therefore important that both the Prime Minister and the Secretary of State should persist in their attempt to impress upon the British electorate the meaning of the commitment given to Northern Ireland in 1985. They could do more than that for they could go on to demonstrate the fact that current expressions of preference and demographic forecasts afford no reason to anticipate a change of attitude. British policy must of necessity be founded on the assumption that Northern Ireland will remain part of the United Kingdom for a future period of indefinite length. That is the crucial point. It needs to be firmly made with no scope for any further ambiguity.

The situation would be further improved if the Labour Party, for its part, would abandon the position described by Mr Kinnock: 'As a matter of policy and commitment, the Labour Party wants to see Ireland united by consent.'[10] It is hard to see why the party should feel impelled to commit itself on this issue – apart from a desire, which cynics will stress, to win Irish votes in British constituencies. For, if Northern Ireland were to leave the United Kingdom, or be expelled from it, a regard for consistency should oblige the Labour Party to concede that the future of that area would be no more its concern than would be that of the rest of the island. Any such intrusion would now be resented by the South and would then be equally resented by the North. Of more immediate concern is the harmful effect of Labour's attitude in encouraging republicans to hope, and unionists to fear, that a Labour victory at the polls in Britain would put Irish unity on the immediate agenda. It is highly unlikely that anything of the kind would happen – for Labour has always been more realistic about Irish affairs when in office than out of it and would moreover be bound by the Anglo-Irish Agreement. But meanwhile the Labour party, out of office, is contributing to the general feeling of instability and insecurity.

Reforming the legislative procedure

It is highly desirable that the practice of passing nearly all legislation relating to Northern Ireland by Orders in Council should be abandoned and the Province treated, in this respect, in the same way as Scotland. If the responsibility for some services were later to be devolved to a representative assembly, then the scope of

Westminster's direct responsibility would be correspondingly reduced, but not eliminated, because responsibility for some services would be retained at the centre. Northern Ireland has already been governed for 16 years under these emergency arrangements while the possibility of restoring some form of devolution has been explored in vain. The uncertainty thus perpetuated has been interpreted to mean uncertainty about the Province's position as a member of the United Kingdom, and this could have been prevented if a Scottish form of devolution had been introduced in 1969 or 1972. Such a step would have dispelled the illusion, fostered initially by the success of the civil rights movement, that with the Unionists discredited and the British uninterested, it would be possible in the near future to edge Northern Ireland into the Republic.

On both of these occasions, Westminster followed a different course and continued to do so in 1979 after the Conservatives returned to power. The impression thus given was that Ulster was not really part of Britain and could therefore have its legislation treated differently. It would be a helpful contribution to stability if the emergency procedure by Order in Council were now to be brought to an end.

Unfortunately Westminster would have to cope with a domestic difficulty, which would be quite simply the unwanted addition to the volume of public business carried by a parliament that is already obliged to sit for a larger part of the year than similar bodies in other countries. The opposition to treating Ulster legislation in the same way as Scottish legislation is partly explained by this practical consideration and is not simply to be taken as evidence of a desire to treat the Province as less than fully British.[11] Nevertheless it is unfair that, because the House of Commons is overburdened, Northern Ireland should be treated worse than other areas, and it is also most unwise to do so because, in the case of Ulster, the political ramifications are so harmful. Moreover, this unfair treatment of a single region can achieve no more than a slight marginal easement of pressure on the parliamentary time-table. That problem needs to be tackled in some different way on a much wider front.

To say this is not to exclude the possibility of reducing any additional burden caused by treating Ulster business in the same way as Scottish. First, advantage could be taken of the fact that a very large part of that business follows precisely the same lines as business for England and Wales – possibly rather more than in the Scottish case. To this extent, separate legislation is not required. Secondly, there would be a further easement if some kind of assembly could be established in order to deal at least with those matters that were handled at the higher level of local government before 1972. It is, however, a very different matter to regard devolution as an alternative arrangement which would make it possible to avoid recognition of Ulster's right to fair treatment at Westminster, like other parts of the United Kingdom. With devolution, Ulster could be thrust to the shadowy edge of national affairs with its constitutional status left vague and undefined – in a way, let it be said, that was never contemplated for Scotland and Wales when devolution for those countries was proposed in 1978. It is this second approach, however, that seems to attract a good deal of quiet, but strong, support in Britain, and it is most unfortunate that this should be so. For there can be no case for attempting in this way to obscure the fact that Northern Ireland is part of the United Kingdom. The consequence will only be continuing political instability and continuing political unrest – and part of the cost will continue to fall inevitably on the rest of the United Kingdom. Evasion of the central constitutional issue will not pay.

Another possible reform that has received some attention in recent years has been the removal of the ban on membership imposed by the main British parties on people in Northern Ireland (see chapter 8 above). In recent years, the agitation for 'equal citizenship' has been successful at least to the extent of informing more people in Great Britain that such a ban exists. For it has not been generally known that people resident in Ulster cannot join the Conservative Party or the Labour Party. If the ban were to be lifted, it is unlikely that there would be far-reaching political consequences at Westminster – not, at least, in the short run. But the removal of this improper form of political discrimination would help in dispelling the constitutional uncertainty which is the cause of so much damage.

THE MOMENT OF TRUTH FOR CONSTITUTIONAL NATIONALISM

The situation in Northern Ireland would be greatly eased if the leaders of the main political parties in the Republic, in particular Fianna Fail, were to admit that Irish unity lies far in the future. I am very well aware that any such suggestion is likely to be dismissed out of hand as absurdly unrealistic. Perhaps it is. But what then is to be made of the statement that the constitutional nationalists seek only a unity that will be based on agreement and consent, not on coercion? As in previous chapters, I am continuing to do these political leaders the courtesy of assuming that they really mean what they say. If so, they must concede that unity will be indefinitely postponed. For the basic condition of agreement and consent has clearly not been satisfied, and there is no prospect, on the most optimistic assumptions, that it will be satisfied for many years to come. They must not be permitted to evade the issue by simply repeating the old and empty claim that the Irish constitute 'a single nation'. Clearly we do not. If we did, there would be no call for any qualification about the need for agreement and consent, because that condition would already be satisfied. Manifestly it has not been satisfied. Nor is this all. For the party leaders in the Republic, and also the party leaders of the SDLP, must be well aware that there is only limited support for unity in the Republic and still more limited and qualified support among the Catholic population in Ulster. The practical economic difficulties are also apparent to all.

It is therefore hard to understand why even those politicians who claim to be pragmatists should feel they are helping towards a solution by simply reiterating that Ireland has 'an indefeasible right to unity'. If they then went on to maintain that they would, therefore, be justified in using force to subdue the recalcitrant Protestants – almost a million of them – their position could at least be credited with a certain logic, sour and disagreeable though that logic might be. But *consent* is a different matter. It implies that the nationalist aim is to win over the Protestants – not just to score over them. The nationalists should, therefore, be earnestly considering how that winning over might be accomplished and, if they are prepared to accept the rather obvious facts of the situation, they must acknowledge that it will take, not only a lot of effort, but also a lot of time. By admitting that Irish unity – true unity – will be unattainable for many years to come, these leaders of constitutional nationalism would do much to undermine support for the imperialistic nationalism of the IRA which seeks a quick and brutal solution. The IRA will not, in fact, achieve that solution, but much blood will be needlessly shed so long as they persist. The possibility of preventing such bloodshed would be all the stronger if the Roman Catholic hierarchy, for its part, were also to make the same explicit admission that the attainment of consent and reconciliation, as the necessary basis for Irish unity, will require many years of patient constructive effort. So long as moderates imply that their aim can be attained in the near future, they are laying themselves open to the charge of being eager to grasp a prize which they can only expect will be won, not by their own efforts, but those of the terrorists. In short, it is not only the terrorists' methods that need to be condemned but also their time scale.

There would be no betrayal of the aspiration of Irish unity in admitting that it will not come about for many years ahead. On the contrary, by lifting the seige-like pressure to which the Ulster Protestants have so long been subjected, a more relaxed situation would be created and better relations could then be developed with those Northern people whose young children may one day become fellow-citizens, within some new political structure, of those who are now young children in the Republic.

> We had fed the heart too much on fantasies,
> The heart's grown brutal from the fare

These lines by Yeats written at a time of the Civil War in the Twenty-Six Counties retain their relevance in all thirty-two counties more than half a century later. It is time for a change of fare.

National unity is not a question of 'right'. It is a question of tradition, sentiment and common purpose. Will national unity in this true sense ever be achieved in Ireland? Even with a constructive and humane approach of this kind, could it really be assumed that a united Ireland would ultimately emerge? Obviously that question cannot be answered, but the whole matter has to be viewed in a different light as soon as we accept the fact that we are looking ahead to an outcome that will be resolved by the views and sentiments of another generation. So much will have changed by then that even the hard old contours of the Irish question may have altered. There may then be less resistance in Ulster to some form of close association with the Republic, and less resistance in the Republic to a closer unity of the British Isles – a vital component in any final settlement. Both islands will by then have had long experience of membership of the European Community and both will also have had extended practical experience as members of other international organizations whose policies cross national frontiers. The old nationalism, the old emphasis on exclusive sovereign rights and the old devotion to self-determination may by then have been complemented, and perhaps diluted, by other objectives and obligations. Although predictions of this kind are only guesswork, they have the merit of bringing out the fact that Irish unity, if it is ever achieved, will be achieved in a world environment vastly different from our own. There is an important moral that is immediately relevant. As soon as it is recognized that unity is not a matter for the present generation, the Ulster problem, as it confronts us today, can be approached with a greater sense of realism and with a stronger belief in success.

Notes

CHAPTER 1   ISLAND, STATE AND NATION

1 *Handbook of the Ulster Question*, 1923, p. 91.
2 Sinn Fein Election Manifesto, 1918, reproduced by A. C. Hepburn in *The Conflict of Nationality in Modern Ireland*, 1980, p. 111.
3 John Bowman, *De Valera and the Ulster Question, 1917–1973*, 1982, p. 38.
4 Sean Lemass, *One Nation*, 1959, pp. 4–14. Emphasis added.
5 Dail Debates, 19 November 1985, cols 2580–600.
6 New Ireland Forum, *Report*, 1984, para. 4.1.
7 K. E. Boulding, 'National images and national self-determination', in *International Politics and Foreign Policy*, ed. J. N. Rosenau, 1969, pp. 422–3.
8 M. W. Heslinga, *The Irish Border as a Cultural Divide*, 1962, p. 41.
9 Bowman, *De Valera*, p. 13.
10 Ronald H. Buchanan: 'The Planter and the Gael: cultural dimensions of the Northern Ireland problem', in *Integration and Division*, eds Frederick W. Boal and J. Neville Douglas, 1982, p. 60.
11 Thomas F. O'Rahilly, *Early Irish History and Mythology*. Dublin Institute for Advanced Studies, 1946, pp. 15–17; 193–207; 417–29.
12 Bowman, *De Valera*, p. 34
13 Estyn Evans, 1967 Conference paper, 'The Irishness of the Irish', pp. 2–3.
14 Peter Levi, *The Flutes of Autumn*, 1983, p. 132.
15 Francis J. Byrne: 'Early Irish society', in *The Course of Irish History* eds T. W. Moody and F. X. Martin, 1967, p. 59. In the same volume Kathleen Hughes, in writing about the seventh and eighth centuries, gives the following translation of an Ulster hero's boast: 'I swear by that by which my people swear, since I took spear in my hand, I have never been without slaying a Connachtman every day and plundering by fire every night, and I have never slept without a Connachtman's head beneath my knee' (p. 79).
16 J. C. Beckett, *The Making of Modern Ireland*, 1966, p. 13.

CHAPTER 2   THE EMERGENCE OF A UNIFIED STATE WITHOUT CONSENSUS

1 New Ireland Forum, *Report*, 1984, para. 3.1.
2 M. W. Heslinga, *The Irish Border as a Cultural Divide*, 1962, p. 118.
3 Ronald H. Buchanan, 'The Planter and the Gael: cultural dimensions of the Northern Ireland problem', in *Integration and Division*, eds Frederick W. Boal and J. Neville

Douglas, 1982; J. C. Beckett, *The Making of Modern Ireland, 1603–1923*, 1966; Patrick Macrory, *The Seige of Derry*, 1980; A. T. Q. Stewart, *The Narrow Ground*, 1966; Margaret MacCurtain, *Tudor and Stuart Ireland*, 1972.

4 Urban planning received remarkably close attention at that time as was shown by G. Gamblin in *The Town in Ulster*, 1951.

5 Stewart, *The Narrow Ground*, p. 49.

6 Beckett, *The Making of Modern Ireland*, p. 118.

7 This is the Talbot whose name occurs in the song 'Lillibulero'. It was the tune of this song that was broadcast to the resistance movement by the BBC during World War II.

8 Beckett, *The Making of Modern Ireland*, pp. 151 and 157.

9 J. L. McCracken, 'The social structure and social life, 1714–60', in *A New History of Ireland*, eds T. W. Moody and W. E. Vaughan, 1986, p. 34. The estimate of 5 per cent relates to 1776 but there can have been little change by the end of the century. The 95 per cent was owned by 5,000 Protestant landowners.

10 Patrick J. Corish, *The Catholic Community*, 1981.

11 Beckett, *The Making of Modern Ireland*, p. 144.

12 The landlord system was less oppressive in the North because the 'Ulster Custom' gave the tenant security of tenure and the right to sell his tenancy.

13 The first of these restrictions, Poyning's Law, was imposed in 1494 during Henry VII's reign by Governor Poyning after an unsuccessful Yorkist revolt. All bills had to be approved by the Privy Council before being presented to the Irish parliament where they could not be amended. An ingenious way round this prohibition, followed for many years, was to introduce 'Heads of Bills'. The superiority of the British parliament was formally asserted in 1720: 'Sixth of George I'.

14 Beckett, *The Making of Modern Ireland*, p. 244.

15 L. M. Cullen, 'Economic development, 1750–1800', in *A New History of Ireland*, eds T. W. Moody and W. E. Vaughan, 1986, vol. iv, p. 186.

16 Edith Mary Johnston, *Ireland in the Eighteenth Century*, 1974, p. 170.

17 Beckett, *The Making of Modern Ireland*, pp. 259–60; Thomas Pakenham, *The Year of Liberty*; R. B. McDowell, 'The age of the United Irishmen: reform and reaction, 1789–94', in *A New History of Ireland*, eds T. .W. Moody and W. E. Vaughan, 1986, vol. iv.

18 Adam Smith, *The Wealth of Nations*, Glasgow edn of the Works of Adam Smith, 1976, vol. 2, p. 944.

CHAPTER 3   IRISH UNITY WITHIN THE UNION

1 Patrick J. Corish, *The Catholic Community*, 1981, p. 136.

2 J. C. Beckett, *The Making of Modern Ireland*, 1966, p. 285.

3 Gearoid O'Tuathaigh, *Ireland before the Famine 1798–1848*, 1972, p. 74.

4 Ibid., p. 315ff; R. B. McDowell, *Public Opinion and Government Policy in Ireland*, 1952, chs 3 and 7.

5 R. J. Lawrence, *The Government of Northern Ireland*, 1965, pp. 105–9.

6 Beckett, *The Making of Modern Ireland*, p. 322.

7 The blight which devastated the 1845–6 crop was much less serious in the following year, but a dispirited peasantry had not planted on an adequate scale. In 1847–8 the blight returned and persisted for two years.

8 Kenneth H. Connell, *The Population of Ireland, 1750–1845*, 1950.

9 Cormac O' Grada, 'Malthus and the pre-famine economy', in *Economists and the Irish Economy*, ed. Antoin E. Murphy, 1984, pp. 85–92.

10 Beckett, *The Making of Modern Ireland*, p. 350. A famine did indeed occur in mainland Britain at the same time. This was the famine in the Western Highlands of Scotland. It was, however, on a smaller scale. See *The Great Highland Famine* by T. M. Devine (1988) – a book which only appeared as this book went to press.

11 O'Tuathaigh, *Ireland before the Famine 1798–1848*, 1972, p. 220; Liam Kennedy, 'The rural economy, 1820–1914', in *An Economic History of Ulster, 1820–1939*, eds Liam Kennedy and Philip Ollerenshaw, 1985, p. 29.

12 O'Tuathaigh, *Ireland before the Famine*, p. 215.

13 L. A. Clarkson, 'Population change and urbanisation', in Kennedy and Ollerenshaw, *An Economic History of Ulster*, pp. 138–9.

CHAPTER 4   INDEPENDENCE OR UNITY – THE HOME RULE PHASE

1 Liam Kennedy, 'The rural economy, 1820–1914', in *An Economic History of Ulster, 1820–1939*, eds Liam Kennedy and Philip Ollerenshaw, 1985, p. 41. R. W. Kirkpatrick, 'Origins and development of the land war in mid-Ulster, 1879–85', in *Ireland under the Union*, ed. F. S. L. Lyons and R. A. J. Hawkins, 1980.

2 Joseph Lee, *The Modernisation of Irish Society 1848–1918*, 1973, sections 2 and 3.

3 Kennedy, 'The rural economy', pp. 38–9. (Hence the old complaint from the landlord side: 'Tenant right, landlord wrong.')

4 Kirkpatrick, 'Origins and development of the land war'.

5 One of Butt's reasons for commending Home Rule was as a defence against the importation of socialism (J. C. Beckett, *The Making of Modern Ireland*, 1966, p. 377).

6 The reference here is to the accusation in *The Times* in March 1887 that Parnell sympathized with the terrorists, including the murderers of Lord Cavendish and T. H. Burke in 1882. The basis of the accusation was in a famous forged letter prepared by Richard Pigott.

7 For a modern discussion of Gladstone's change of opinion and its consequences, see John Vincent, *Gladstone and Ireland*, British Academy (Raleigh Lecture) 1977; James Loughlin, *Gladstone, Home Rule and the Ulster Question*, 1986.

8 Cf. Joseph Lee's observation: 'It is a travesty of the dedication of grassroots unionists to imply, as nationalist propagandists were prone to do, that they were prodded into activity against the Home Rule Bill only when Lord Randolph Churchill played the Orange card in February 1886 by bequeathing to Belfast the slogan "Ulster will fight and Ulster will be right".' (*The Modernisation of Irish Society*, p. 132).

9 Cf., e.g., Loughlin, *Gladstone, Home Rule and the Ulster Question*, pp. 69–80.

10 'Home Rule All Round' was recommended by a minority in the *Report of the Royal Commission on the Constitution 1969–73* (Crowther/Kilbrandon), vol.II, 1973. The members who dissented were Lord Crowther-Hunt and Sir Alan Peacock. See also Vernon Bogdanor, *Devolution*, 1979, ch. 2, and Thomas Wilson, 'Matters of public policy', in *Fiscal Decentralisation*, ed. Thomas Wilson, 1984; John Kendle, 'The Round Table Movement and 'Home Rule All Round'', *Historical Journal*, 1968.

11 L. M. Cullen 'Economic development 1750–80', in *A New History of Ireland*, eds T. W. Moody and W. E. Vaughan, 1986, vol. iv, pp. 186–7.

12 Tom Garvin, *Nationalist Revolutionaries in Ireland, 1858–1928*, 1986, p. 14.

13 F. S. L. Lyons, *Ireland since the Famine*, 1973, p. 306.

14 Roy Jenkins, *Asquith*, 1964, p. 280.

15 Quoted by H. Montgomery Hyde, *Carson*, 1953, p. 342.

16 F. S. L. Lyons, *Ireland since the Famine*, 1973, p. 307. For a documentary history of Unionism, see Patrick Buckland, *Irish Unionism 1885–1923*, 1973.

17 This Unionist belief about the Government's intentions is said to have been based on a confidential document which fell into their hands. Hyde, *Carson*, p. 358.
18 For a vivid account of the gun-running, see A. T. Q. Stewart, *The Ulster Crisis*, 1967.
19 The respective roles of Bonar-Law and Walter Long are described by Richard Murphy, 'Faction in the Conservative Party and the Home Rule crisis, 1912–14', *History*, 71, no. 232.
20 Lyons, *Ireland since the Famine*, p. 302. An interesting comment by Bogdanor on the 1886 proposals also applies to those that followed: 'The idea of a devolution of power to satisfy the principle of nationality was, as we have seen, based upon the model of colonial self-government, and especially upon the granting of responsible government to Canada. The particular division of powers governing devolution was based on the federal-type division of powers between the Canadian province and the Dominion Parliament', *Devolution*, p. 17.
21 The inherited notion of the 'contract' and the role of the 'loyal band' are described by David W. Miller in *Queen's Rebels*, 1978.
22 Loughlin, *Gladstone, Home Rule and the Ulster Question*.
23 Hyde, *Carson*, p. 344.
24 Quoted by Conor O'Clery in *Phrases Make History Here*, 1987, p. 46. Unfortunately Dillon's phrase did not make history in Ireland.
25 Jenkins, *Asquith*, pp. 279 and 294.
26 Quoted by O'Clery in *Phrases Make History Here*, p. 44.

CHAPTER 5   INDEPENDENCE OR UNITY – TOWARDS A REPUBLIC

1 J. C. Beckett, *The Making of Modern Ireland*, 1966, p. 436.
2 F. S. L. Lyons, *Ireland since the Famine*, 1971, p. 364.
3 Conor O'Clery, *Phrases make History Here*, 1987, p. 74.
4 Conor Cruise O'Brien, *Neighbours*. The Ewart-Biggs Memorial Lectures, 1980, p. 64.
5 John J. Horgan, *Parnell to Pearse*, 1948, p. 289.
6 Lyons, *Ireland since the Famine*, p. 370.
7 David W. Miller, *Church, State and Nation in Ireland 1898–1921*, 1973, pp. 329–58.
8 Quoted in R. Kee, *Ireland: a History*, 1980, p. 172.
9 Padraic Pearse, *Political Writings and Speeches*, 1952, p. 217.
10 Lyons, *Ireland since the Famine*, p. 337.
11 Garret Fitzgerald, *Towards a New Ireland*, 1972, pp. 10–11.
12 HC Debates, 25 May 1916, col. 2309.
13 A detailed account of the proceedings of the Convention is given by Horgan, *Parnell to Pearse*. See also Sir John Biggs-Davison and George Chowdharry-Best, *The Cross of St. Patrick*, 1984. The authors include an account of the role of Catholic Unionists, often overlooked.
14 Miller, *Church, State and Nation*, p. 405.
15 Patrick Shea, *Voices and the Sound of Drums*, 1981, pp. 28–9.
16 Charles Townshend, *The British Campaign in Ireland 1919–1921*, 1975, p. 204.

CHAPTER 6   THE RESPONSIBILITY FOR PARTITION

1 D. G. Boyce, *Englishmen and the Irish Troubles*, 1972, p. 113.
2 HC Debates, 29 March 1920, cols 948 and 957; 30 March, col. 1110.
3 Tom Garvin, *Nationalist Revolutionaries in Ireland, 1858–1928*, 1987, p. 150.
4 Boyce, *Englishmen and the Irish Troubles*, p. 102.

5   HC Debates, 18 May 1920, col. 1289.
6   HC Debates, 29 March 1920, col. 989.
7   Richard Murphy, 'Walter Long and the making of the Government of Ireland Act 1919–20', 1986, p. 86.
8   The offer was qualified in some important respects with regard to defence, the sharing of the national debt and protective duties. Correspondence relating to the Proposals of His Majesty's Government for an Irish Settlement, Cmd 1502, 1921.
9   Ibid., p. 4. For a discussion of De Valera's attitude as expressed in Document 2 prepared for the Dail, see the Earl of Longford, and Thomas P. O'Neill, *Eamon de Valera*, 1970, ch. 14; John Bowman, *De Valera and the Ulster Question, 1917–1973*, 1982, ch. 2.
10 Bowman, ibid., p. 85.
11 Ibid., pp. 51.
12 Ibid., pp. 58–60.
13 K. C. Wheare, *Federal Government*, 1964.
14 Bowman, *De Valera*, ch. 8.
15 Ibid., pp. 34–35.
16 Dorothy McCardle, *The Irish Republic*, 1968, p. 455.

CHAPTER 7   HOME RULE IN THE NORTH – A HARD BEGINNING

1   F.S.L. Lyons, *Ireland since the Famine*, 1973, p. 397.
2   Sir Arthur Hezlet, *The B-Specials*, 1972.
3   Michael Farrell, *Northern Ireland: The Orange State*, 1976, ch. 2.
4   Patrick Buckland, *A History of Northern Ireland*, 1981, p. 36.
5   Patrick Buckland, *James Craig*, 1980, p. 76.
6   J. C. Beckett, *The Making of Modern Ireland*, 1966, p. 459. See also Younger, *Ireland's Civil War*, 1970.
7   Eoin Neeson, *The Civil War in Ireland, 1922–23*, 1969, p. 291n.; Lyons, *Ireland since the Famine*, p. 468n.
8   Tim Pat Coogan, *The IRA*, 1980, p. 58.
9   John A. Murphy, *Ireland in the Twentieth Century*, 1975, p. 58.

CHAPTER 8   DEVOLUTION IN NORTHERN IRELAND: AN OVERVIEW, 1920–1972

1   Nicholas Mansergh, *The Government of Northern Ireland*, 1936, p. 323.
2   *Report of the Royal Commission on the Constitution, 1969–73*, HMSO, 1973, vol. 1, ch. 6.
3   John Mackintosh, *The Devolution of Power*, 1968, pp. 181–2.
4   Mansergh, *The Government of Northern Ireland*; A. S. Quekett, *The Constitution of Northern Ireland*, 3 vols, 1928, 1933, 1946; F. H. Newark, 'The Law and the Constitution', in *Ulster under Home Rule*, ed. Thomas Wilson, 1955.
5   This point has been made by a former Northern Ireland civil servant John A. Oliver in 'The evolution of constitutional policy', in *Political Co-operation in Divided Societies*, ed. Desmond Rea, 1982, p. 74.
6   10 and 11 Geo. V, ch. 67, 3, 2(1), 1920.
7   K. C. Wheare, *Federal Government*, 1964.
8   Vernon Bogdanor, *Devolution*, 1979, pp. 206–10.
9   H. C. Debates, 7 March 1922, col. 1085.
10 T. Wilson, 'Regional government', in *Royal Commission on the Constitution, Written Evidence. 6: Northern Ireland*, 1972.

11 R. J. Lawrence, *The Government of Northern Ireland*, 1965, pp. 34–5.

12 Newark, 'The Law and the Constitution', in *Ulster under Home Rule*, ed. Wilson, p. 35; Patrick Buckland, *A History of Northern Ireland*, 1981, pp. 52–4.

13 Christopher Hewitt, 'Catholic grievances, Catholic nationalism and violence during the civil rights period: a reconsideration', *British Journal of Sociology*, 1981, pp. 362–80.

14 John Whyte, 'How much discrimination was there under the Unionist regime', in *Contemporary Irish Studies*, eds Tom Gallagher and James O'Connell, 1983, p. 4.

15 Denis P. Barritt and Charles F. Carter, *The Northern Ireland Problem*, 1962, pp. 41–3.

16 Hewitt, 'Catholic grievances'.

17 Barritt and Carter, *The Northern Ireland Problem*, p. 43.

18 James Madison in Alexander Hamilton, James Madison and John Kay, *The Federalist*, ed. Max Beloff, 1948, pp. 46–7.

19 John E. Sayers, 'The political parties and the social background', in *Ulster under Home Rule*, ed. Wilson.

20 Tim Pat Coogan, *Disillusioned Decades. Ireland 1966–87*, 1987, p. 18.

21 H. C. Debates (NI), 21 April 1934, col. 1095. Emphasis added.

22 Eric Gallagher and Stanley Worrall eds, *Christians in Ulster 1968–80*, 1982, p. 13.

23 On Craigavon's final phase in office see Patrick Buckland, *James Craig*, 1980.

24 Conor O'Clery, *Phrases Make History Here*, 1987, p. 93.

CHAPTER 9 FISCAL CONSTRAINTS AND THE SUBVENTION

1 *Fiscal Federalism* by Wallace E. Oates, 1972. 'Approaches to a fiscal theory of political federalism' by Richard Musgrave, in *Public Finances, Needs, Sources and Utilisation*, 1961; reprinted in *The Economics of Federalism*, eds G. Grewal, T. Brennan and R. Mathews, 1980, a volume which also contains some other important contributions to the subject, including papers by the editors. 'Federalism and fiscal equity' by James Buchanan, *American Economic Review*, September 1950. *Mechanisms for Fiscal Equalisation in an Integrating European Community*, EEC, 1977. 'Matters of public policy' by Thomas Wilson, in *Fiscal Decentralisation*, ed. Wilson, 1984.

2 *Devolution: Financing the Devolved Services*. Cmnd 6890, HMSO, London, July 1977.

3 K. S. Isles and Norman Cuthbert, *An Economic Survey of Northern Ireland*, 1957; R. J. Lawrence, *The Government of Northern Ireland*, 1965; F. H. Newark, 'The law and the constitution' and Thomas Wilson, 'Devolution and public finance', both in *Ulster under Home Rule*, ed. Thomas Wilson, 1955; A. J. Green, *Devolution and Public Finance: Stormont from 1921 to 1972*, Studies in Public Finance, 1979; John V. Simpson, 'The finances of the public sector in Northern Ireland', 1980–81, and 'Northern Ireland: the Financing of Devolution' in *Fiscal Decentralisation*, ed. Thomas Wilson, 1984; Patrick Buckland, *A History of Northern Ireland*, 1981.

4 Lawrence, *The Government of Northern Ireland*, p. 37.

5 Ibid., p. 45.

6 Isles and Cuthbert, *An Economic Survey of Northern Ireland*, p. 457.

7 Buckland, *A History of Northern Ireland*, pp. 75–6.

8 *Ulster Year Book*, 1950, p. 11.

9 Lawrence, *The Government of Northern Ireland*, p. 62.

10 J. P. Mackintosh, *The Devolution of Power*, 1968, p. 174.

11 HC Debates, 1936, cols 1708–9.

12 Isles and Cuthbert, *An Economic Survey of Northern Ireland*, p. 405.

13 Lawrence, *The Government of Northern Ireland*, pp. 68–73. Lawrence observes that: 'To gain Britain's recognition of that claim was Mr. Andrews' crowning achievement.' Andrews was then Prime Minister of Northern Ireland.

14 *Report of the Royal Commission on the Constitution 1969–73*, 1973, vol. 1, p. 180. Also T. Wilson, 'Devolution and public finance', *Three Banks Review*, December 1976.
15 Northern Ireland Economic Council, *Public Expenditure Comparisons between Northern Ireland and Great Britain*, 1981, updated in mimeograph for 1985–6.
16 The recent increase in subsidies provided for public housing has raised the demand for means-tested assistance. In Scotland and Wales the burden has to this extent been shifted to the DHSS and buried there in the national GB accounts. In Northern Ireland, however, responsibility for cash benefits as well as for housing assistance cannot be shifted in this way because both services have been devolved.
17 For example, in 1938 de Valera told the US Minister at Dublin, John Cudahy, that Northern Ireland could not exist without British subsidies and explained that Craigavon would be persuaded to adopt a more reasonable attitude if they were withdrawn (Sean Cronin, *Washington's Irish Policy 1916–86*, 1987, p. 56).

CHAPTER 10   ECONOMIC PROGRESS AND STRATEGIES FOR DEVELOPMENT

1 Kieran A. Kennedy, Thomas Giblin and Deirdre Waugh, eds, *The Economic Development of Ireland in the Twentieth Century*, 1988.
2 K. S. Isles and Norman Cuthbert, *An Economic Survey of Northern Ireland*, 1957.
3 *Report of the Joint Working Party on the Economy of Northern Ireland*, 1962.
4 *Belfast Regional Survey and Plan*, 1963.
5 *Economic Development in Northern Ireland*, 1964, p. 3.
6 *Development Programme 1970–5*, 1970.
7 *Review of Economic and Social Development in Northern Ireland*, 1971.
8 *Economic and Industrial Strategy for Northern Ireland: Report by Review Team 1976*, 1976.
9 In the course of preparing a report on the Scottish economy, the committee of which I was vice-chairman had visited France in 1963 and had discussed regional policy with members of the Commisariat au Plan and of other public departments (*Report on the Scottish Economy*, Scottish Council for Development and Industry, 1963). I had published a critique of indicative planning in *Planning and Growth*, 1964.
10 When the National Plan appeared in 1965 I was a member of the Board of Trade Committee on the shipbuilding industry. Although we were all supplied with copies of the plan, I do not recollect that it was sufficiently detailed to be of much assistance and was soon forgotten.
11 Leo Pliatzky, *Getting and Spending*, 1982.
12 S. J. Prais, *National Institute Economic Review*, November 1981 and February 1988; *Oxford Review of Economic Policy*, vol. 4, no. 3, 1988.
13 It was not represented on the committee that used to be responsible for industrial development certificates over the period when this form of control was used in order to divert industrial expansion, where possible, to the development areas. The inadequate reason for Ulster's exclusion was the fact that the region had its own devolved government. The committee did, however, inform the Ministry of Commerce of its decisions and of any firm that was dissatisfied, and the Ministry could then act swiftly in order to try to persuade the firm to consider what Ulster had to offer.
14 *Report of the Committee of Inquiry into Bank Interest Rates*, 1966. In the report of this committee, of which I was chairman, as in the Wilson Plan itself, rather too much stress was laid on what might be achieved by inducing the Industrial and Commercial Finance Corporation to extend its activities to Northern Ireland. The reason was our feeling of pessimism about the likelihood of an indigenous organization being established. Happily we were to be proved wrong when the government finally decided to establish the Local Enterprise Development Unit (LEDU).

CHAPTER 11 INDUSTRIAL LOCATION AND DISCRIMINATION

1 The borderline between 'East' and 'West' is bound to be somewhat arbitrary. I have followed the division by ESO areas made by James F. Bradley, Victor N. Hewitt and Clifford W. Jefferson in *Industrial Location Policy and Equality of Opportunity in Assisted Employment in Northern Ireland 1949–1981*, 1986, p. 48. The ESOs deemed to be in the 'East' are Ballymoney/Ballymena, Antrim/Carrickfergus/Larne, Belfast, Lisburn, Portadown/Lurgan, Banbridge, Newry/Kilkeel, Ballynahinch/Downpatrick, Newcastle, Bangor/Newtownards. Those in the 'West' are Londonderry (an area somewhat larger than the city), Enniskillen, Armagh, Dungannon, Omagh, Coleraine, Magherafelt, Limavady, Strabane, Cookstown.
2 Ibid., p. 87.
3 New Ireland Forum, *Report*, 1984, p. 11.
4 Peter Neary, 'The failure of economic nationalism', in *Ireland: Dependence and Independence*, 1984, p. 71.
5 *Economic Development in Northern Ireland* (the Wilson Plan), 1965, p. 39.
6 *The Belfast Regional Survey and Plan*, 1963.
7 New Ireland Forum: *The Economic Consequences of the Division of Ireland since 1920*, Dublin, 1983, pp. 29–30.
8 *Regional Physical Development Strategy, 1975–79*, 1975. Also *Economic and Industrial Strategy for Northern Ireland: Report by Review Team*, 1976. The new approach amounted to adding a few towns to the old list of growth and key centres. As it had never been suggested that any town should be denied an improved infrastructure, the change of emphasis can easily be exaggerated.
9 Just before I undertook the work of consultant in Northern Ireland, I had been consultant in Canada and had seen the consequences there of confining attention to areas of need without regard to potentiality. For industrial assistance at that time was confined to places where unemployment had been high and output stagnant for at least ten years. For example, St John's, Newfoundland, was excluded because it had made some progress. As we bounced along dirt roads to visit small factories in remote outposts, I felt that even the formidable premier, the Hon. Joe Smallwood, would find it hard to achieve the development he desired while the federal straitjacket remained.
10 Bradley et al., *Industrial Location Policy*, p. 94.
11 Ibid., p. 78.
12 *Development Programme, 1970–75*, 1970, p. 21.
13 Bradley et al., *Industrial Location Policy*, p. 79.
14 Ibid., p. 98.
15 I am deeply indebted to Dr Clifford W. Jefferson of the Queen's University, Belfast, for providing me with the data on which the observations in the text and table 11.2 are based. Dr Jefferson must not, however, be held responsible for any errors of interpretation that may have been committed.

CHAPTER 12 DISCRIMINATION, SOCIAL STRUCTURE AND UNEMPLOYMENT

1 The Continuous Household Survey is a sample inquiry comparable to the Family Expenditure Survey in Great Britain. The figures for unemployment are based on statements by those interviewed that they are unemployed and seeking employment. The estimates thus obtained exceed those for persons claiming benefit.
2 E. A. Aunger, 'Religion and class: an analysis of the 1971 census data' in *Religion, Education and Employment*, eds R. J. Cormack and R. D. Osborne, 1983.

3 The Forum consisted of the leaders of the main parties in the Republic and of the Social Democratic Labour Party. The words quoted come from p. 11 of their *Report*. This was ostensibly a conciliatory document.

4 Richard Rose, *Governing without Consensus: an Irish Perspective*, 1971, p. 289.

5 R. C. Murray and R. D. Osborne, 'Educational qualifications and religious affiliation', in *Religion, Education and Employment*, eds Cormack and Osborne.

6 Paul A. Compton, John Coward and Keith Wilson-Davis, 'Family size and religious denomination in Northern Ireland', *Journal of Biosocial Science*, 17 (1985), 137–45.

7 Paul A. Compton, 'Demographic dimension of integration and division', in *Integration and Division*, eds Frederick W. Boal and J. N. H. Douglas, 1982.

8 Paul Doherty, 'The unemployed population of Belfast', in *The Contemporary Population of Northern Ireland and Population-related Issues*, ed. Paul A. Compton, 1981.

9 Paul A. Compton, 'Demographic and geographical aspects of the unemployment differential between Protestants and Roman Catholics in Northern Ireland', in *The Contemporary Population of Northern Ireland*, ed. Compton.

10 Denis P. Barritt and Charles F. Carter, *The Northern Ireland Problem*, 1962, pp. 95–7.

11 R. D. Osborne and R. J. Cormack, eds *Religion, Education and Employment*. This volume contains updated FEA reports on a number of these investigations. See also *Integration and Division*, eds Boal and Douglas.

12 Osborne and Cormack, 'Conclusions' in *Religion, Education and Employment*, eds Osborne and Cormack, p. 228.

13 David J. Smith, *Equality and Inequality in Northern Ireland. Part 1: Employment and Unemployment*, 1987.

14 David J. Smith and Gerry Chambers, 'Positions, perceptions and practice', *Fortnight*, December 1987; Paul Compton, Bob Cormack and Bob Osborne, 'Discrimination research "flawed"', *Fortnight*, January 1988. Although the authors explain that they 'do not share a common perspective on policy matters', they are united in the criticism of the report by Smith. The same issue contains a reply by him and the February issue a rejoinder by Compton.

15 Smith, *Equality and Inequality*, p. 38.

16 Ibid., p. 39. Emphasis added.

17 Smith and Chambers, 'Positions, perceptions and practices'.

18 Stephen Smith, *Britain's Hidden Economy*, 1986.

19 Sir Charles Carter in a letter to the author, quoted with permission.

20 John Whyte, 'How much discrimination was there under the unionist regime 1921–68?', in *Contemporary Irish Studies* eds Tom Gallagher and James O'Connell, 1983, p. 8.

21 Barritt and Carter. *The Northern Ireland Problem*, pp. 95–7.

22 *Northern Ireland Civil Service Equal Opportunities Unit*, 1987, table 12(b).

23 Patrick Shea, *Voices and the Sound of Drums*, 1981, pp. 112–13. Shea, who was not a graduate, was recruited into the clerical grade. He was, I believe, the first person to be promoted to the assistant principal grade from that position.

24 *Northern Ireland Civil Service Equal Opportunities Unit*, paras 3.30–3.46.

25 *Report of an Investigation by the Fair Employment Agency for Northern Ireland into the Non-industrial Northern Ireland Civil Service*, 1983, p. 41.

26 Whyte, 'How much discrimination . . .?', p. 10.

27 *Disturbances in Northern Ireland* (Cameron Report), 1969, para. 138.

28 Barritt and Carter, *The Northern Ireland Problem*, p. 97.

29 *Report into the Non-Industrial Northern Ireland Civil Service*. There are some revealing sentences in the Fair Employment Agency Report on the civil service: 'It is important that effort is not expended in justifying past practice or the results of past practice.' Then, a few lines later: 'Generally, however, the Civil Service in the past has paid insufficient attention to the pattern of recruitment and insufficient attention has been

taken to ensure that the departmental distribution of staff has not had a discriminatory effect on promotion opportunities.' One must not *justify* the past record but need feel no inhibition about *blackening* it.

30 Smith, *Equality and Inequality*, p. 39.
31 Barritt and Carter, *The Northern Ireland Problem*, ch. 6.
32 Gerald Chambers, *Equality and Inequality in Northern Ireland*. Part 2: *The Workplace*, 1987.
33 Ibid., p. 26.
34 *Religious Equality of Opportunity in Employment*, Department of Economic Development, 1988.
35 Chambers, *Equality and Inequality*, p. 199.
36 This point is emphasized by C. McCrudden, 'The experience of the legal enforcement of the Fair Employment (Northern Ireland) Act 1976', in *Religion, Education and Employment*, eds Cormack and Osborne, pp. 201–21.

CHAPTER 13   THE HOUSING SHORTAGE AND DISCRIMINATION

1 *Royal Commission on the Housing of the Working Class*. C.1402, HMSO London, 1885.
2 J. G. Calvert in 'Housing policy in Northern Ireland', eds Derek Birrell and Alan Murie, 1972.
3 The Mortgage and Rent Restrictions Act of 1915 applied to the whole of the United Kingdom.
4 Liam Kennedy and Philip Ollerenshaw, *An Economic History of Ulster, 1820–1939*, 1985, pp. 208–9.
5 *Economic Development Plan, 1965–70* (Wilson Plan), 1964.
6 *Development Programme 1970–75*, 1970; Derek Birrell and Alan Murie, 'Facts and findings', in 'Housing policy in Northern Ireland', 1972.
7 *Review of Recent Developments in Housing Policy*, 1985.
8 *Disturbances in Northern Ireland*, 1969, para. 128.
9 H. C. Debates (NI), 1 January 1968, vol. 68, cols. 288–335.
10 Quoted by Dale Singleton in 'Housing allocation policy in Northern Ireland', *Housing Review*, 1985.
11 John Whyte, 'How much discrimination was there under the unionist regime, 1921–68?', in *Contemporary Irish Studies*, ed. Tom Gallagher and James O'Connell, 1983. Whyte is now professor of politics at University College, Dublin.
12 C. E. B. Brett, *Housing in a Divided Community*, 1986.
13 Richard Rose, *Governing without Consensus*, 1971, pp. 292–6.
14 *Fourth Report of the Northern Ireland Commissioner for Complaints*, Annual Report for 1971, HC 2181, 1971.
15 *Development Programme 1970–75*, 1970, paras 38–39.
16 I recall being chided for advocating such a centralized body by my old friend and former colleague the late Sir Norman Chester, Warden of Nuffield College, Oxford, whose views had also been sought by the Government of Northern Ireland.
17 Dale Singleton, 'Housing in a divided community', *Housing Review*, May–June 1982.
18 *HM Treasury: Needs Assessment Survey*, 1979.
19 Northern Ireland Economic Development Office, *A Review of Recent Developments in Housing Policy*, 1985.
20 Northern Ireland Housing Executive: *Housing Strategy Review 1988/89–90/91*; and *The Belfast Experience* (1984).
21 It will be recalled that Sir Robert Matthew's 'stopline' was designed to check the growth of Belfast. In the event, a number of factors – in particular sectarian violence – led to a

move of population away from the city. Thus the modern problem became, in Belfast as elsewhere, one of inner city rehabilitation after a drastic fall in population to about 300,000.

22 The grouping of houses in this way follows the Essex design guide adopted in dealing with overspill from inner London. High density without loss of privacy is thus possible.

23 Frederick W. Boal, 'Segregation and mixing: space and residence in Belfast', in *Integration and Division*, eds Frederick Boal and J. N. H. Douglas, 1982.

CHAPTER 14   EDUCATION – DEVELOPMENT WITHIN A SEGREGATED SYSTEM

1 Monsignor Arthur H. Ryan, *Mirroring Christ's Splendour*, 1986, p. 185.

2 Quoted by Gemma Loughran in her essay, 'The rationale of Catholic education', in *Education Policy in Northern Ireland*, eds R. D. Osborne, R. J. Cormack and R. L. Miller, 1987, p. 116. The author also quotes other passages from this pronouncement and from a statement by Cardinal MacRory.

3 It has been suggested by John Darby and Seumas Dunn that the teaching of Irish history may now be rather less partisan. See 'Segregated schools: the research evidence' in *Education Policy in Northern Ireland*, eds Osborne, Cormack and Miller, p. 88.

4 R. J. Lawrence, *The Government of Northern Ireland*, 1965, pp. 107–8.

5 HC Debates (NI), 17 April 1923, col. 351.

6 Prior to the Government of Ireland Act of 1920, denominational schools received 60 per cent of their capital costs: Patrick Buckland, A History of Northern Ireland, 1981, p. 56.

7 Government of Ireland Act, 1920, 10 & 11 Geo. v, ch. 67, 5(1).

8 Donald Harman Akenson, *Education and Enmity*, 1973, p. 6.

9 Lawrence, *The Government of Northern Ireland*, p. 112.

10 Patrick Buckland, *A History of Northern Ireland*, 1981, p. 78.

11 Education Act (Northern Ireland) 1947, 22(1).

12 *Local Education Authorities and Voluntary Schools* 1967, para. 4. See also *Public Education Northern Ireland*, 1970.

13 Lawrence, *The Government of Northern Ireland*, p. 125.

14 Eric Gallagher and Stanley Worrall, *Christians in Ulster, 1968–80*, 1982, p. 153.

15 Ibid., p. 161.

16 Ibid., p. 167.

17 Ibid., p. 164.

18 Ibid., p. 159; Darby and Dunn, 'Segregated schools: the research evidence', pp. 91–2.

19 J. Harbison and J. Harbison, *A Society under Stress*, 1980; J. Harbison, 'The children of Northern Ireland', *New Society*, 17 April 1980.

20 *The Future Structure of Teacher Education in Northern Ireland* (Chilver Report), 1980.

21 *Higher Education in Northern Ireland* (Lockwood Report), 1965.

22 Frank Curran, *Derry – Countdown to Disaster*, 1986.

CHAPTER 15   FROM CIVIL RIGHTS TO CIVIL STRIFE

1 De Tocqueville, *L'Ancien Regime*, 1966, p. 195.

2 In collaboration with D. J. Wilson, the author has discussed these issues in *The Political Economy of the Welfare State*, 1982.

3 NICRA had been preceded by the Campaign for Social Justice in Northern Ireland, founded in 1964. At no time did either of these organizations submit evidence to the economic consultants or attempt to meet them.

4　Patrick Bishop and Eamonn Mallie, *The Provisional IRA*, 1987, pp. 50–1.
5　Ibid., p. 55.
6　*Disturbances in Northern Ireland* (Cameron Report), 1969, para. 46. The other two members of the Commission were Professor Sir John Biggart of the medical faculty at Queen's University, and James Joseph Campbell, a nationalist academic. Nothing could be further from the truth than the suggestion sometimes made that this was a white-washing committee.
7　Terence O'Neill, *The Autobiography of Terence O'Neill*, 1972, chs XI and XII.
8　The full statement was reproduced later in para. 13 of *Development Programme, 1970–75*, 1970.
9　The importance of this point was recognized by the Tribunal of Inquiry under the chairmanship of the Hon. Mr Justice (now Lord) Scarman. *Violence and Civil Disturbances in Northern Ireland in 1969* (Scarman Report), para. 1.4.
10　*Disturbances in Northern Ireland*, paras 72–88.
11　O'Neill, *Autobiography*, p. 121.
12　Paul Arthur, *The People's Democracy*, 1974; Michael Farrell, *Northern Ireland: the Orange State*, 1976, ch. 11.
13　Scarman Report, para. 10.4.
14　Brian Faulkner, *Memoirs of a Statesman*, 1978, p. 60.
15　Scarman Report, para. 20.5.
16　Desmond Hamill, *Pig in the Middle*, 1985.
17　Cameron Report, para. 177.
18　Scarman Report, p. 17.

CHAPTER 16　WESTMINSTER AND THE SECURITY PROBLEM

1　James Callaghan, *A House Divided*, 1973, p. 97.
2　The need for stability in constitutional arrangements has been strongly urged by Professor A. E. Alcock. See *Minutes of Evidence to the Committee on the Government of the Northern Ireland Assembly*, 1986, vol. III, pp. 161–64.
3　Richard Rose, *Is the United Kingdom a State?*, Centre for the Study of Public Policy, University of Strathclyde, 1983.
4　Callaghan, *A House Divided*, p. 907 records an interview with Wolseley, the Commissioner of Police for Belfast, who 'confirmed to me that the RUC had been unaccepted in parts of Belfast and Londonderry for the previous two years'. He therefore rejects the view that it was the disarming of the RUC on the recommendations of the Hunt Report that led to there being no-go areas.
5　Michael Dewar, *The British Army in Northern Ireland*, 1985, p. 64.
6　Desmond Hamill, *Pig in the Middle*, 1985, p. 53.
7　James Callaghan, HC Debates, 7 April 1970, col. 318.
8　*Report of the Advisory Committee on Police in Northern Ireland* (Hunt Report), October 1969, para. 27, p. 12.
9　A Record of Constructive Change, 1971. See also David Harkness, *Northern Ireland since 1980*, 1983, p. 170.
10　Brian Faulkner, *Memoirs of a Statesman*, 1978, p. 112.
11　Ibid., p. 119.
12　Hamill, *Pig in the Middle*, p. 62.
13　Martin Dillon and Denis Lehane, *Political Murder in Northern Ireland*, 1973.
14　W. D. Flackes, *Northern Ireland: a Political Directory 1968–79*, 1980, p. 138.
15　Barry White, *John Hume*, 1984, p. 120.

16 Report of the Tribunal appointed to enquire into the events on Sunday 30th January 1972 which led to the loss of life in connection with the procession in Londonderry on that day (Widgery Report), 1972, p. 9.
17 David Harkness, *Northern Ireland since 1980*, p. 171.
18 Widgery Report, p. 38.
19 Sean Cronin, *Washington's Irish Policy 1916–1986*, 1987, p. 304.
20 Hamill, *Pig in the Middle*, p. 88.
21 This verdict has also been given by a former senior civil servant at Stormont, John A. Oliver, 'The evolution of constitutional policy' in *Political Co-operation in Divided Societies*, ed. Desmond Rea, 1982.
22 Merlyn Rees, *Northern Ireland: a Personal Perspective*, 1985, p. 15.
23 Patrick Bishop and Eamonn Mallie, *The Provisional IRA*, 1987, p. 176.
24 For an account of the meeting at Feakle between some leading Protestant churchmen and the IRA, see *Christians in Ulster 1968–1980* by Eric Gallagher and Stanley Worrall, two of the participants.
25 Paul Bew and Henry Patterson, *The British State and the Ulster Crisis*, 1985, p. 84.
26 Bishop and Mallie, *The Provisional IRA*, pp. 220–1. See also Rees, *Northern Ireland*, ch. 7.
27 Hamill, *Pig in the Middle*, pp. 89–92.

CHAPTER 17 POWER-SHARING AND THE COUNCIL OF IRELAND – A FATAL MIXTURE?

1 Report of the Review Body on Local Government in Northern Ireland (Macrory Report), 1970.
2 Brian Faulkner, *Memoirs of a Statesman*, 1978, pp. 103–4.
3 An interesting suggestion has been made by John A. Oliver: 'When urging power-sharing or coalition on politicians in the extremely difficult circumstances in Ulster . . . it would surely be becoming to display something of the same attitude in the immeasurably easier circumstances of Westminster. In other words, what better example of power-sharing than for H.M. Government of the day to have appointed (in consultation with the Leader of H.M. Opposition) someone from the opposing party to be one of the Junior Ministers under direct rule?': 'The evolution of constitutional policy', in *Political Co-operation in Divided Societies*, ed. Desmond Rea, 1982, p. 85.
4 Brian Faulkner, *Memoirs of a Statesman*, p. 248.
5 Ibid., p. 240.
6 Barry White, *John Hume*, 1984, p. 127.
7 Ibid., p. 157.
8 *Irish Times*, 22 February 1974.
9 John Bowman, *De Valera and the Ulster Question, 1917–1973*, 1982, p. 101.
10 Paul Bew and Henry Patterson, *The British State and the Ulster Crisis*, 1985, p. 56.
11 R. Fisk, *The Point of No Return: the Strike which Broke the British in Ulster*, 1975.
12 Gerry Fitt himself was later to concede as much (White, *John Hume*, p. 210).

CHAPTER 18 CONSTITUTIONAL INITIATIVES AND HUNGER STRIKES

1 Paul Bew and Henry Patterson, *The British State and the Ulster Crisis*, 1985, p. 100. The authors quote from the *Ulster Loyalist* of 14 March 1974 where it was explained that power-sharing, in the opinion of the UDA, should not be ruled out.

2 Bew and Patterson, *The British State and the Ulster Crisis*, p. 112.
3 *The Government of Northern Ireland, A Working Paper for a Conference*, November 1979, followed by *The Government of Northern Ireland, Proposals for Further Discussion*, 1980.
4 *Northern Ireland, A Framework for Devolution*, 1982.
5 *HC Debates* 29 July 1982, vol. 28, col. 1226.
6 *HC Debates* 17 May 1984, vol. 60, col. 503.
7 *Northern Ireland, A Framework for Devolution*. 1982.
8 Patrick Bishop and Eamonn Mallie, *The Provisional IRA*, 1987, p. 301.
9 Barry White, *John Hume*, 1984, pp. 243–5.
10 New Ireland Forum, *Report*, 1984, p. 27, para. 5.2(4).
11 When Seamas Mallon was elected to Westminster in 1986, thus defeating an abstentionist Sinn Fein candidate, this was greeted in London as evidence of the fact that the Anglo-Irish Agreement has secured a triumph for moderation. The fact that Mallon was a totally uncompromising Irish nationalist was overlooked.
12 Fine Gael, *Ireland – Our Future Together*, 1979.
13 John Bowman, *De Valera and the Ulster Question, 1917–1973*, 1982, pp. 186–7.
14 Bishop and Mallie, *The Provisional IRA*, pp. 164–5. This was the Eire Nua proposal adopted by the IRA in 1972 but dropped in 1981 in favour of a unitary republic with 'no sops to Loyalists'. See Coogan, *Disillusioned Decades*, 1987, pp. 233–4.
15 *New Ireland Forum: Presentations by Sir Charles Carter and Professor Louden Ryan*, 21 September 1983.
16 Quoted by Clare O'Halloran, *Partition and the Limits of Irish Nationalism*, 1987, p. 195.
17 Ibid., pp. 194–210.
18 Garret Fitzgerald, *Towards a New Ireland*, 1972, p. 175.

CHAPTER 19   THE ANGLO-IRISH AGREEMENT AND ITS AFTERMATH

1 The Taoiseach (Dr Garret Fitzgerald), Dail Debates, 19 November 1985, col. 2562.
2 W. Harvey Cox, 'Public opinion and the Anglo-Irish Agreement', *Government and Opposition*, Summer 1987, pp. 336–51.
3 Roy Mason, HC Debates, 26 November 1985, col. 788.
4 *Agreement between the Government of the United Kingdom of Great Britain and Northern Ireland and the Government of the Republic of Ireland*, 15 February 1985.
5 Anthony Kenny, *The Road to Hillsborough*, 1986, p. 96.
6 Charles Haughey, Dail Debates, 19 November 1985, col. 2581.
7 Kenny, *The Road to Hillsborough*, p. 101.
8 The Tanaiste (the Leader of the Irish Labour Party in the Coalition Government), Dail Debates, 20 November 1985, col. 2717.
9 Sir John Biggs-Davison, HC Debates, 26 November 1985, col. 798.
10 The Taoiseach, Dail Debates, 19 November 1985, cols.2564.
11 The Tanaiste, Dail Debates, 20 November 1985, col. 2721.
12 The Prime Minister, HC Debates, 26 November 1985, cols 750 and 752.
13 Sir Charles Carter, *Two Years of Peace, Stability and Reconciliation?*, 1987, p. 21.
14 The Taoiseach, Dail Debates, 20 November 1985, col. 2563.
15 The views of the Official Unionist Party (Molyneaux) were already expressed in a pamphlet, *Ulster Must Say No* published in 1986.
16 'The Shankill riots of the 2/4 August establish beyond doubt the readiness of the police to do their duty against Protestant mobs, when they were disturbers of the peace': *Violence and Civil Disturbances in Northern Ireland in 1969* (Scarman Report), p. 15.

CHAPTER 20   THE RELIGIOUS DIVIDE

1   Edward Moxon-Browne, *Nation Class and Creed in Northern Ireland*, 1983.
2   Steve Bruce, *God Save Ulster*, 1986, p. 237.
3   Frank Wright, 'Protestant ideology and politics in Ulster', *European Journal of Sociology*, 1973, p. 236.
4   Fred Boal and David Livingstone, 'Protestants in Belfast', *Contemporary Review*, April 1986, p. 170.
5   F. S. L. Lyons, *Ireland since the Famine*, 1971, p. 726.
6   Irish Episcopal Conference, *Directory on Mixed Marriages*, 1983, pp. 14–16.
7   An account of these developments is given by Eric Gallagher and Stanley Worrall in *Christians in Ulster 1968–1980*, 1982. This book has the great merit of setting the ecclesiastical developments in the wider context of political events over these years. A number of statements have also appeared by groups of Catholic and Protestant clergy and laity working together. For example *Choose Life* (1986) and *Towards an Island that Works* (1987), both by an Interchurch Group on Faith and Politics.
8   *Directory on Mixed Marriages*, p. 18; Austin Plannery, *Vatican Council II*, 1981.
9   Ibid., p. 15.
10   Reported in *Irish News*, 3 December 1985.
11   Peter Brooke, *Ulster Presbyterianism*, 1984, pp. 211–14. Clifford Smyth, *Ian Paisley*, 1987, pp. 123–4.
12   Padraic O'Malley, *The Uncivil Wars: Ireland Today*, 1983, p. 175.
13   Bruce, *God Save Ulster*; Roy Wallis, Steve Bruce and David Taylor, *'No Surrender'*, 1986.
14   James Callaghan, A House Divided, 1973. p. 82.
15   See appendix 2 on election results p. xxx.
16   Wright, 'Protestant ideology and politics'.
17   'Lundies' – local name for traitors. Colonel Lundy was Governor of Londonderry when the city was invested by James II's forces. Although a supporter of William III, Lundy proposed to surrender the city but was foiled by the apprentices who closed the gates. Hence the annual 'Apprentice Boys Parade'.
18   Peter and Mary Speed, *Oxford Childrens' History*, Oxford, Oxford University Press, 1983, p. 219.
19   *The Northern Ireland Situation*, Church Statements 1968–85, pp. 20 and 25.
20   Ibid., pp. 23–4.
21   *Violence in Ireland*, 1977, pp. 9–10. This report was prepared by a committee under the joint chairmanship of Bishop Cahal Daly and Rev. R. D. Eric Gallagher.
22   *Irish News*, 24 February 1988.
23   Patrick Bishop and Eamonn Maillie, *The Provisional IRA*, 1987, pp. 267–8.
24   Catholic Press and Information Office, Dublin: press release of 14 September 1987, p. 4.
25   *Daily Telegraph*, 17 April 1987.
26   Alan Rusbridger, 'Pulpits of faith and fury', *Guardian*, 26 March 1988.
27   *Violence in Ireland*, pp. 90–1.
28   *Irish Times*, 10 November 1987.
29   *Belfast Telegraph*, 22 December 1986.
30   Ibid.
31   *Belfast Telegraph*, 6 January 1986.
32   David W. Miller, *Church State and Nation in Ireland 1898–1921*, 1973, pp. 397–8.
33   Quoted by Eric Gallagher in 'The faith and its forms in times of strife', in *Northern Ireland: Living with the Crisis*, ed. Alan J. Ward, 1987, p. 115

CHAPTER 21   THE REPUBLIC AND ITS THREE MINORITIES

1   Clare O'Halloran, *Partition and the Limits of Irish Nationalism*, 1987.
2   John Bowman, *De Valera and the Ulster Question, 1917–1973*, 1982.
3   Kevin O'Higgins, one of the ministers who lent strong support to this constructive approach in 1925, was assassinated two years later.
4   The quotation is from a memorandum by Kevin O'Shiel, quoted by O'Halloran, *Partition and the Limits of Irish Nationalism*, p. 105.
5   For an account of the negotiations that did in fact take place during the War, see Robert Fisk, *In Time of War*, 1983; Sean Cronin, *Washington's Irish Policy*, 1987.
6   The Earl of Longford and Thomas P. O'Neill, *Eamon de Valera*, 1970, p. 434. An account of American reactions is given by Sean Cronin in *Washington's Irish Policy 1916–1986*, 1987, pp. 258–65.
7   Sean Cronin, ibid., p. 262.
8   John Biggs-Davison and Patrick Macrory, *Britain's Undefended Frontier: a Policy for Ulster*, European Security Studies, no. 2, 1984.
9   K. E. Boulding, 'National images and national self-determination', in *International Politics and Foreign Policy*, ed. J. N. Rosenau, 1969, p. 424.
10   HC Debates, 26 November 1985, col. 763
11   Sources of poll results used in this discussion are as follows: The 1968 poll was organized by Professor Richard Rose and his research team and the results are given in his book: *Governing without Consensus: an Irish Perspective*, 1971, p. 213. The 1973 poll was carried out by Carrick James Market Research for *Fortnight* and *The Sunday Times*. In this case respondents were asked to accord preferences to various possibilities. For more detail see the review of poll results by Richard Rose, Ian McAlister and Peter Mair, *Is There a Concurring Majority about Northern Ireland?*, 1978, p. 18. This monograph also includes summaries of the NOP polls held in 1974 and 1976. The quotation in the text is from *Fortnight*, 2 April 1976. The figure quoted for national identity in 1978 is derived from an investigation described by Edward Moxon-Browne in *Nation, Class and Creed in Northern Ireland*, 1983, p. 6. The 1981 and 1984 figures are from MORI polls organized for London Weekend Television, the second in connection with Mary Holland's programme, 'From the Shadow of a Gun'. The 1985 survey was by BBC 'Spotlight'. The last two reported were the polls carried out by Coopers & Lybrand in 1987. The results for the Republic are taken from Father Michael MacGriel's *Prejudice and Tolerance in Ireland*, 1972. The results for 1980 are from the *Irish Independent*, 29 November 1980 and for 1987 from the *Irish Times*, 1 September 1987.
12   Father Michael MacGriel, *Prejudice and Tolerance*, 1972.
13   His evidence is summarized by Garret Fitzgerald in *Towards a New Ireland*, 1972, pp. 34–6.
14   New Ireland Forum, *Report*, 1984, para. 3.2.
15   Joseph Lee, *The Modernisation of Irish Society 1848–1918*, 1973, p. 28.
16   F. S. L. Lyons, *Ireland since the Famine*, 1973, p. 635.
17   Terence Brown, *Ireland: a Social and Cultural History 1922–79*, 1981, p. 62.
18   Noel Browne, *Against the Tide*, 1986, pp. 158–9. Browne records how he was told by Sean MacBride that: 'You cannot afford to fight the church.' MacBride, a former IRA veteran and a future Nobel Prize winner, was then the leader of Browne's minority party, Clann na Poblachta, in a coalition with Fine Gael. See also John Whyte, 'Church, state and society, 1950–70', in *Ireland 1945–70*, J. J. Lee ed. 1979, pp. 73–82.
19   For a commentary, see Thomas Wilson and Dorothy J. Wilson *The Political Economy of the Welfare State*, 1982.

20 Brown, *Ireland: 1922–79*, p. 297. Brown has also recorded how the importance attached to the control of reading matter could be expressed not only in censorship but, right down the line, in the appointment of a county librarian. In 1930 the Mayo Library Committee rejected a Protestant woman librarian as a candidate and were defended in the Dail by de Valera who insisted that, if a librarian has any interest in and control over what books are available, then in a Catholic country the people were 'justified in insisting on a Catholic librarian.' (p. 150). In Ulster such an incident would have been quoted as an example of discrimination.

21 Nuala O'Faolain, *Irish Times*, 18 May 1987.

22 *Irish Independent*, 17 May 1971.

CHAPTER 22   SECURITY: MAINTAINING THE LAW AND RESPECTING THE LAW

1 Merlyn Rees, *Northern Ireland: A Personal Perspective*, 1985, p. 48.

2 I am indebted to Mr Ken Maginess MP for these statistics.

3 Edgar Graham, *The Case for Extradition*, published by the Human Rights Unit with editorial assistance from the Publicity and Research Department of the Ulster Unionist Party, 1982.

4 Articles on the financing of terrorism appeared in *The Sunday Times* and the *Belfast Telegraph* respectively on 10 and 11 April. For the RUC estimate, see 1988 Annual Report of the Chief Constable for 1987, p. 10.

5 *Irish News*, 18 March 1988.

6 Mimeographed handout. The statement was summarized in the Irish newspapers for 16 October 1987.

7 *Belfast Telegraph*, 23 October 1987.

8 *The Times*, 23 April 1988.

9 Mary T. W. Robinson, *The Special Criminal Court*, 1974, and the 'Special Criminal Court almost Eight Years On', mimeo, 1982.

10 *Report of the Commission to consider legal procedures to deal with terrorist activities in Northern Ireland* (Diplock Report), December 1972, p. 9. For a discussion of this and other issues, see D. S. Greer, 'The impact of the Troubles on the law and legal system of Northern Ireland', in *Northern Ireland: Living with the Crisis*, ed. Alan J. Ward, 1987.

11 *Report of the enquiry into allegations against the security forces of physical brutality in Northern Ireland arising out of events on 9th August 1971* (Compton Report), November 1971.

12 *Report of the Committee of Inquiry into Police Interrogation Procedures in Northern Ireland* (Bennett Report), March 1979.

13 HC Debates, 24 October 1983, cols 3–5.

14 Gardiner Report, Cmnd 5847, 1975; Baker Report, Cmnd 9222, 1984.

15 Michael Farrell, *The Apparatus of Repression, a Field Day Pamphlet*, 1986, p. 26.

16 Baker Report, para. 125.

17 Rt Hon. Justice Lowry, *Civil Proceedings in a Beleaguered Society*, The Child & Co. Lecture, 1987.

18 John Stalker, *Stalker*, 1988.

19 *Belfast Telegraph*, 22 December 1988.

20 *The Times*, 16 March 1988.

21 Reproduced in Desmond Hamill, *Pig in the Middle*, 1985, p. 67.

22 Ibid., pp. 137–8.

23 *Belfast Telegraph*, 15 January 1988. See also John Cole, 'Security Constraints' in *The Constitution of Northern Ireland*, ed. David Watts, 1981, p. 138.

24 *Annual Report for 1987*, p. xiv.

25 Diplock Report, para. 28. See also Baker Report, ch. 6. Baker recommended that the section of the Prevention of Terrorism Act which permits detention should be repealed. This recommendation, made in 1984 when the situation was relatively good as compared with the early 1970s or the late 1980s, was qualified by the remark that 'If "doomsday" arrives in whatever form it will be the duty of the then Government to bring any necessary legislation before Parliament immediately' (para. 236).

26 See his letter to *The Times*, 19 June 1987. Fr Faul has expressed the same view in discussion with the author. It is relevant to add that Northern Ireland has already been operating what has been described as 'a release policy strikingly more lenient than that operating in Britain' (David McKettrick, *The Times*, 19 June 1987).

27 *The Times*, 23 November 1988.

28 Ibid.

29 Paul Wilkinson 'Taking the war to the terrorists', *The Times*, 2 September 1988.

CHAPTER 23   PROSPECTS

1 Richard Rose, *Northern Ireland: Time of Choice*, 1976, p. 139. See also his 'Northern Ireland: the irreducible conflict', in *Conflict and Peace-making in Multi-ethnic Societies*, eds J. H. Montville and H. Binnedijk, 1988.

2 *Belfast Telegraph*, 28 December 1985.

3 This prospect of a flow of refugees has been discussed by Frank Wright, *Northern Ireland Comparative Analysis*, 1987.

4 Patrick Buckland, *A History of Northern Ireland*, 1981, pp. 76 and 105.

5 Rose, 'Northern Ireland: the irreducible conflict', p. 1.

6 Liam Kennedy, *Two Ulsters: a Case for Repartition*, 1986.

7 Padraig O'Malley, *The Uncivil Wars: Ireland Today*, 1983, pp. 140–1.

8 Paul A. Compton, 'An evaluation of the changing religious composition of the population of Northern Ireland', *The Economic and Social Review*, April 1985. See also his paper, 'The Demographic Background', in *The Constitution of Northern Ireland*, ed. David Watt, 1981.

9 Compton, 'An evaluation . . .', p. 222. See also Paul A. Compton, John Coward and Keith Wilson-Davis, 'Family size and religious denomination in Northern Ireland', *Journal of Biosocial Science*, 1985.

10 J. Bradley, J. Fitzgerald and R. A. Storey, *Medium Term Review 1987–1992*, December 1987, p. 1.

11 Frances Cairncross, 'Republic of Ireland', *Economist Survey*, 16 January 1988; Robert Hutchinson and John Sheehan, 'Ireland: economic problems and policy issues', *Economic Review*, March 1985.

12 See chapter 9 for details where, it will be noted, an Economic Council calculation would warrant a much larger reduction in the estimate of the subvention.

13 Charles Carter, New Ireland Forum, *Report*, Proceedings of 21 September 1984, p. 5. Louden Ryan's evidence is contained in the same volume. See also Charles McCarthy and William J. Blease, 'Cross-border industrial co-operation: limits and possibilities', *Administration*, 1978.

14 HC Debates, 26 November 1985, col. 759.

15 *Report of the Committee of Inquiry into Bank Interest Rates*, 1966.

16 Norman Gibson, in a short but stimulating paper on these issues, has raised the possibility that 'economic integration has in a sense distorted the Northern Ireland economy and contributed to a weakening of the private sector'. 'Integration and devolution', in *Political Co-operation in Divided Societies*, ed. Desmond Rea, 1982, ch. 2.

CHAPTER 24 STRATEGIES

1 In technical jargon, a pay-as-you-go social security system allows new entrants to be given a full entitlement to rights without delay. An historical example is the introduction of complementary pensions in France. It is probable, of course, that the burden on the Republic would be eased by a payment from Britain related to the national insurance contributions previously made by pensioners or their employers.

2 *Irish Times*, 1 September 1987.

3 Padraig O'Malley, *The Uncivil Wars: Ireland Today*, 1983, p. 84.

4 Mary T. W. Robinson, *The Special Criminal Court*, 1974, p. 32.

5 Power-sharing may imply an approximation to PR in an Executive as well as PR in elections to the Assembly. This was the 1973/4 model. Or a minimum number of votes above 50 per cent may be required for the approval of proposals, with the minimum variable according to the gravity of the subjects. Or there may be a committee system broadly based on the local government model. A convenient and well-documented review of possibilities is to be found in the *First Report of the Committee on the Government of Northern Ireland of the Northern Ireland Assembly*, Jan. 1986. A reference is included to proposals prepared for the assembly by Sir Charles Catherwood. The respective proposals of the Official Unionist Party and the Democratic Unionist Party are to be found in *Unionism: A Policy for all the People*, 1987. The proposals of the Ulster Defence Association were presented in *Common Sense* by John McMichael, 1987.

6 A demand for the inclusion of security powers in any future scheme for devolution has been made by Austin Currie, one of the SDLP leaders, *Irish News*, 12 June 1987.

7 *The Way Forward*, Ulster Unionist Council, 1984.

8 Conor Cruise O'Brien, *Neighbours*, 1980, p. 45.

9 The importance of achieving constitutional stability has been stressed by Professor A. E. Alcock in a submission to the Northern Ireland Assembly. See *Minutes of Evidence*, vol. III, 1986.

10 HC Debates, 26 November 1985, col. 760.

11 The importance of this point has been stressed in an interview with former Secretary of State, Merlyn Rees.

Appendix 1   Political Parties and other Organizations

DUP	Democratic Unionist Party
INLA	Irish National Liberation Army. Breakaway group from Official IRA
IRA	Irish Republican Army. Provisional branch (Provos) the more important, sometimes indicated by PIRA, but normally by IRA: Officials by OIRA
NICRA	Northern Ireland Civil Rights Association
NILP	Northern Ireland Labour Party
SDLP	Social and Democratic Labour Party
UDA	Ulster Defence Association
UDR	Ulster Defence Regiment
UUP or OUP	Ulster Unionist Party or Official Unionists
UPNI	Unionist Party of Northern Ireland; formed by Faulkner after UUP majority rejected Sunningdale. Faded gradually away
UUAC	United Unionist Action Council – for 1977 strike
UUUC	United Ulster Unionist Council: UUP together with DUP and Craig's Vanguard Party after Sunningdale. Collapsed after disagreement about strike of 1977. After Hillsborough, OUP and DUP formed coalition
UWC	Ulster Workers Council
VUPP	Vanguard Unionist Progressive Party, founded by William Craig

Note

'Unionist' with an initial capital refers to one or other of the Unionist Parties. Without a capital, the term 'unionist' referst to persons who support the union with Britain. Many unionists belong to no party, and some belong to the Alliance Party which is 'unionist' in this sense.

The term 'nationalist' is used to refer to supporters of a united Ireland to be achieved by constitutional means. With a capital, the historical reference is to the Nationalist (or Irish Parliamentary) party which had been superseded by Sinn Fein by 1919. In more modern times, it refers to the Northern Ireland party which was superseded by the SDLP in 1970. 'Republican' refers to strong-arm supporters of a united Ireland although this customary use is somewhat arbitrary in view of the fact that 'nationalists' also support the Irish Republic and seek to extend its boundaries.

'Loyalist' – always with a capital – is a collective term for the various groups of Protestant militants.

Londonderry is the official name of the city, but it is usual, in ordinary speech, to revert to the still older and shorter 'Derry'. The abbreviation is sometimes used to convey a nationalist protest at the link with London. I have used both names indifferently without political intent.

Appendix 2 Party Percentage of the Vote, 1979 to 1987

Party	Election								
	UKGen. 1979	Euro. 1979	NICo. 1981	NIAss. 1982	UKGen. 1983	Euro. 1984	NICo. 1985	UKBy-E. 1986	UKGen. 1987
Official Unionist	36.6	21.9	26.5	29.7	34.0	21.5	29.5	51.7	37.9
Democratic Unionist	10.2	29.8	26.6	23.0	20.0	33.6	24.3	14.6	11.7
Other Unionist	12.2	7.3	5.2	5.8	3.1	2.9	3.1	5.2	5.2
Alliance	11.9	6.8	8.9	9.3	8.0	5.0	7.1	5.5	10.0
SDLP	18.2	24.6	17.5	18.8	17.9	22.1	17.8	12.1	21.1
Sinn Fein	nc	nc	nc	10.1	13.4	13.3	11.8	6.6	11.4
Other nationalist	8.1	5.9	5.3	0.3	nc	nc	2.4	nc	nc
Workers party	1.7	0.8	1.8	2.7	1.9	1.3	1.6	3.1	2.6
Others	1.1	2.9	8.2	0.3	1.7	0.3	2.4	1.2	0.0

Notes:
1   UKGen., UK General; Euro., European; NICo., Northern Ireland Council; NIAss., Northern Ireland Assembly; UKBy-E., UK By-election.
2   nc, not contested.
3   European, Northern Ireland Assembly and Northern Ireland Council elections are held under the Proportional Representation system and these figures refer to the percentage of first preference votes won by each group. United Kingdom elections use a plurality system.
4   After 1983 Northern Ireland had 17 seats instead of its previous 12 at Westminster.
5   In 1986 by-elections were held for 15 of the 17 NI seats at Westminster. Foyle and West Belfast were the two exceptions.
6   Others includes a range of candidates of which the most prominent are various Labour candidates. It also includes Independent, Liberal, Communist and Ecology Party Candidates.

Sources: D. Butler and D. Kavanagh, *The British General Election of 1979* and *The British General Election of 1983*; S. Elliot and F. J. Smith, *Northern Ireland: The District Council Elections of 1981* and *1985*; S. Elliot, *Northern Ireland: the First Election to the European Parliament* and *the Second Election to the European Parliament*; S. Elliot and R. A. Wilford, *The 1982 Northern Ireland Assembly Election*.

Appendix 3 Roman Catholics as a Percentage of Total Persons in Northern Ireland

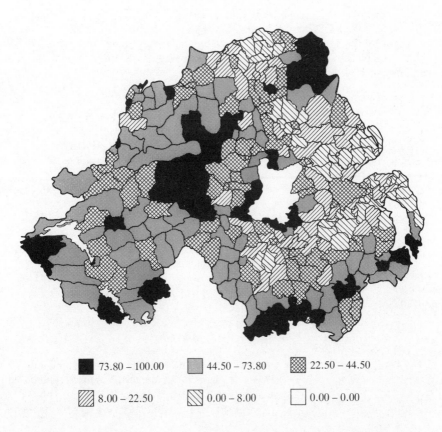

73.80 – 100.00　　44.50 – 73.80　　22.50 – 44.50

8.00 – 22.50　　0.00 – 8.00　　0.00 – 0.00

The figures are estimated and are based on the 1971 Census of Northern Ireland.

Chronology

The record of events for the years 1968 to 1979 has been prepared with the aid of the three volumes *Northern Ireland Chronology of Events*, prepared by Richard Deutsch and Vivien McGowan and of *Northern Ireland: a Political Directory 1968–79* by W. D. Flackes. Mr Gordon Gillespie has prepared the record from 1980 to 1988 and has advised throughout.

1968: Killed 0; injured n.a.

5 October	Banned civil rights march in Londonderry attacked by police. Followed by demonstrations and riots there and in Belfast in subsequent weeks.
22 November	Government announces five-point reform programme.
30 November	Civil rights march in Armagh blocked by Paisley and supporters.
9 December	O'Neill stresses reform and appeals for peace. Civil rights moderates respond: extremists do not.
11 December	O'Neill dismisses Wiliam Craig, Minister of Home Affairs.

1969: Killed 13; injured n.a.

3–4 January	Catholic mob attacks Guildhall in Londonderry. Marxist People's Democracy (PD) march ambushed and attacked at Burntollet by Protestant mob.
10–11 January	Banned PD demonstration in Newry with attacks on police.
15 January	Cameron Commission appointed. Split in Unionist Party.
24 February	Election with disappointing result for O'Neill.

11 March	Ombudsman takes office.
19 April	Serious rioting in Londonderry followed by violent action by some policemen in Bogside.
20 April	Water installations bombed by Loyalists to discredit O'Neill.
28 April	O'Neill resigns, succeeded by Chichester-Clark.
May–August	Several riots and communal confrontations.
12 August	Apprentice Boys Parade in Londonderry followed by prolonged conflict between police and Bogsiders. Sympathetic Catholic rioting in Belfast with strong Protestant response.
14 August	Army called in.
19 August	Downing Street Declaration.
10 September	Peace line separating warring factions completed in Belfast. No-go areas for security forces allowed, especially in Londonderry and West Belfast.
12 September to October	Sporadic rioting.
9 October	'One man, one vote' in local government granted.
10 Coctober	Hunt Report accepted: disbanding of Specials and disarming of police. Protest riot.
27 November	Commissioner for Complaints assumes office.
18 December	Police authority established.

1970: Killed 25; injured n.a.

January	IRA splits into Officials (OIRA) and Provisionals (PIRA).
29 March – 2 April	Commemoration of Easter rising in 1916 leads to riots.
21 April	Alliance Party (unionist and interdenominational) formed.
19 June	Conservatives win election. Maudling becomes Home Secretary.
23 June	Second Economic Development Programme published.
25 June	Catholic hierarchy allows Catholics to attend Trinity College, Dublin.
27–28 June	Further communal conflicts.
3–5 July	Troops raid Lower Falls in arms search.
21 August	Social Democratic Labour Party (SDLP) formed with Fitt as leader and united Ireland as primary goal.
14 September	Reconstituted Economic Council holds first meeting.
22 September	Charles Haughey and others charged with conspiracy to import arms illegally (for IRA).
12 November	Northern Ireland Housing Executive formed.

1971: Killed 174; injured 2592

3–5 February	Search for arms by troops in Catholic districts of Belfast resisted by rioters and by machine-gun fire.
6 February	First soldier killed.
10 March	3 young off-duty soldiers murdered.
23 March	Faulkner succeeds Chichester-Clark as Prime Minister.
22 June	Faulkner proposes committee system to provide role in government for opposition parties.
7 July	Bill to legalize contraceptives in the Republic defeated.
5–9 July	Rioting in Londonderry with shots fired at troops. Two Catholics shot by troops. Army refuses inquiry.
16 July	SDLP withdraws from Stormont in protest, and also rejects Faulkner's initiative.
9 August	Internment introduced. SDLP calls for rent and rates strike. Heavy rioting.
September	Ulster Defence Association (UDA) formed.
12 September	Cardinal Conway and bishops denounce IRA for trying to 'bomb a million Protestants into a United Ireland'.
30 September	Paisley founds Democratic Unionist Party (DUP).
24 October	O'Brady, IRA, says North must be made ungovernable.
25 November	Harold Wilson proposes that Britain should promise to withdraw in 15 years with Republic as member of Commonwealth.
4 December	McGurk's bar bombed by Loyalists with 15 killed.

1972: Killed 467; injured 4866

January	Succession of incidents with exchange of fire between troops and IRA.
30 January	'Bloody Sunday': 13 members of illegal demonstration killed.
1 February	Heath appoints committee of inquiry under Lord Chief Justice Widgery. Harold Wilson says that a united Ireland is the only solution. William Craig suggests ceding Bogside and Creggan to Republic.
2 February	OIRA bomb at Aldershot barracks; British Embassy in Dublin burned down.
4 March	Government of Northern Ireland refuses to surrender responsibility for law and order. Parliament

	prorogued and Direct Rule follows with Whitelaw as Secretary of State.
26 May	Special Criminal Court reinstituted in Republic of Ireland with trial by jury suspended for subversives.
26 June	IRA (Provo) truce.
7 July	Whitelaw meets IRA leaders secretly in London.
21 July	'Bloody Friday': 26 bombs exploded by IRA (Provos) in Belfast killing 11 people.
31 July	Army enters 'no-go areas': Operation Motorman. Three IRA bombs explode in Claudy killing 6 people.
18 September	Darlington Conference on devolution with power-sharing. Boycotted by SDLP and more hard-line Unionists.
20 September	SDLP proposes joint British and Irish sovereignty ('Towards a New Ireland').
16–17 November	Heath warns against UDI.
1 December	2 killed by bomb in Dublin.

1973: Killed 250; injured 2651

1 January	Britain joins EEC.
8 March	Border poll confirms strength of opposition to a united Ireland. Bombs in Belfast and Londonderry. Bomb in central London with one death.
20 March	White Paper proposes devolution with power-sharing and Council of Ireland. Rejected by more hardline Unionists (UUUC) and by IRA.
14–15 May	Martin McGuiness, former Chief of Staff of IRA in Londonderry, released in Republic after 6 months' imprisonment.
30 May	Election with PR for new Assembly.
12 November	Composition of power-sharing Executive announced.
3 December	Pym succeeds Whitelaw as Secretary of State.
6 December	Sunningdale Conference between British and Irish Ministers and NI Executive. Agreement on Council of Ireland. Weak compromise on extradition.

1974: Killed 216; injured 2398

11 January	Executive takes office. Loyalist oppposition mounts.
28 February	British general election won by Labour.
5 March	Merlyn Rees becomes Secretary of State.

4 April	Proscription of UVF, imposed by O'Neill in 1966, lifted by Merlyn Rees. Proscription of Sinn Fein also lifted with SDLP approval.
15–28 May	UWC strike leading to collapse of Executive. Direct Rule resumed.
17 May	Car bombs kill 22 in Dublin and 5 in Monaghan.
8 May	Emergency Provisions Act dispenses with juries.
10 October	Westminster elections strengthen position of anti-Faulkner Unionists.
6 November	Mass escape of IRA prisoners.
21 November	Bombs in Birmingham pubs kill 19.
10 December	Group of Protestant churchmen meet IRA at Feakle in Republic.

1975: Killed 247; injured 2474

12 February	Ceasefire with incident centres manned by IRA and government officials.
1 May	Polling day for new Constitutional Convention.
31 July	Miami Showband assassinations by UVF.
3 October	UVF proscribed once more.
5 December	The last of the detainees released.
22 December	Gang of IRA gun-runners broken up in USA.

1976: Killed 297; injured 2729

4 January	5 Catholics killed.
5 January	10 Protestants killed.
1 March	Special category status abolished for new prisoners.
3 March	Constitutional Convention ends in failure.
30 March	NICRA calls off rent and rates strike started in August 1971.
21 July	British Ambassador to Republic murdered.
18 August	SAS deployed in South Armagh.
1 September	State of Emergency in Republic.
10 September	Roy Mason becomes Secretary of State.
4 November	Plan for UDI put forward by hard-line Unionists.
1 December	Fair Employment Act.

1977: Killed 112; injured 1383

1–13 May	UUAC strike, supported by Paisley, fails.
16 June	Fianna Fail regains power under Lynch.
27 July	Feud between Official and Provisional IRA.

| 12 September | Mason says that 'myth of British withdrawal from NI' is now dead forever. |
| 14 October | Dr Tomas O'Fiaich becomes Cardinal. |

1978: Killed 81; injured 985

18 January	European Court holds that interrogation of internees in 1971 did not involve torture but had been 'inhuman and degrading'.
17 February	IRA fire bomb in La Mon restaurant kills 12.
6 March	Official Unionists reject talks with Paisley.
7 April	Neave, Conservative Shadow Secretary of State, says that power-sharing is no longer practical politics.
1 August	De Lorean car project for West Belfast announced.
22 September	Mason and Neave simultaneously make statements denouncing idea of British withdrawal.
October – November	Heavy rioting and IRA bomb attacks.

1979: Killed 13; injured 875

30 March	Airey Neave murdered by Irish National Liberation Army, offshoot from Official IRA.
3 May	Conservatives win General Election. Atkins becomes Secretary of State.
18 July	Paisley, Hume and Taylor become NI European MPs.
31 July	US State Department bans private arms shipments to NI including sales to RUC.
27 August	Lord Mountbatten murdered by IRA. 18 soldiers killed at Warrenpoint by bombs exploded by radio from Republic.
29 September	Pope in Ireland: pleads for peace.
30 October	Plea rejected by IRA.
25 October	Atkins proposes conference for political settlement. OUP insists on top-tier local government. DUP reserves position. SDLP and Alliance accept.
3 November	SDLP proposes joint British and Irish approach to NI problem.

1980: Killed 76; injured 801

| 24 March | The 'Atkins Talks' end without agreement. |
| 1 April | Special category status for terrorist prisoners ended. |

2 July	Government document (Cmnd 7950) proposing further discussions makes no impact.
27 October	7 H-Block prisoners begin hunger strike.
8 December	First Anglo-Irish summit held in Dublin.
18 December	Hunger strike called off.

1981: Killed 101; injured 1350

1 March	Bobby Sands starts new hunger strike.
9 April	Sands elected to Westminster in Fermanagh–South Tyrone by-election.
5 May	Bobby Sands dies.
11 June	Fine Gael/Labour minority government elected in Eire. Two H-Block prisoners elected to the Dail.
20 August	Owen Carron wins Fermanagh–South Tyrone by-election for Sinn Fein.
13 September	James Prior becomes Secretary of State.
29 September	British Labour Conference votes to 'campaign actively' for a united Ireland by consent.
3 October	Hunger strike ends after 10 have died.
14 November	MP for South Belfast, Rev. Robert Bradford, murdered.

1982: Killed 97; injured 525

18 February	Fianna Fail minority government elected in Eire.
2 April	Argentinian invasion of Falkland Islands.
21 April	White Paper proposing 'rolling devolution'.
20 July	8 soldiers killed by two IRA bombs in London: 3 other people die later.
20 October	NI Assembly election. SDLP and SF refuse to take their seats.
25 November	Fine Gael/Labour government formed in Eire.
6 December	17 people, including 11 soldiers, killed in INLA bombing of 'Droppin Well', Ballykelly.

1983: Killed 77; injured 510

16 January	County Court judge William Doyle (Catholic) shot dead by IRA.
11 April	14 UVF men jailed on evidence of 'supergrass' Joe Bennett. First of many 'supergrass' trials continuing throughout 1984 and into 1985.
9 June	UK General Election returns Conservatives. Unionists win 15 of the 17 NI seats.

7 September	Abortion rejected in referendum in the Republic.
25 September	Maze prison break.
20 November	Darkley massacre by INLA who fire into church congregation. OUP withdraw from Assembly in protest at security policy.
7 December	OUP Assembly member and law lecturer, Edgar Graham, murdered by IRA.

1984: Killed 64; injured 866

2 May	New Ireland Forum Report released.
23 May	OUP announce ending of Assembly boycott.
14 June	European Parliament elections.
11 September	Douglas Hurd becomes Secretary of State.
12 October	Brighton bomb kills 5 people at Conservative conference.
19 November	Thatcher rules out three main proposals of the Forum Report.

1985: Killed 54; injured 916

28 February	9 RUC officers killed in IRA mortar attack on Newry police station.
15 May	NI Council elections.
3 September	Tom King becomes Secretary of State.
15 November	Anglo-Irish Agreement signed at Hillsborough Castle.
23 November	200,000 unionists attend demonstration against Anglo-Irish Agreement at Belfast City Hall.
5 December	Unionists set up 'Grand Committee' in Assembly to examine the effects of the Anglo-Irish Agreement on NI Government departments.
11 December	First session of Anglo-Irish Conference at Stormont marked by protests and clashes between police and loyalists.

1986: Killed 61; injured 1450

24 January	By-elections in 15 NI Westminster seats. 420,000 unionists vote against the Anglo-Irish Agreement but OUP lose Newry and Armagh seat to SDLP.
3 March	Loyalist day of protest shuts down much of NI commerce and industry. Snipers later fire on the RUC during rioting in Protestant areas.

20 May	Nicholas Scott, Minister of State, tells the House of Commons there have been 368 cases of intimidation against the RUC during recent loyalist violence against the Anglo-Irish Agreement.
5 June	Stalker suspended from duties in Manchester police. In Ulster replaced by Sampson.
23 June	NI Assembly dissolved by Secretary of State.
26 June	Divorce rejected in referendum held in the Republic.
7 August	DUP Deputy Leader Peter Robinson arrested in Clontibret, Co. Monaghan, when loyalists temporarily take over the village.
2 November	Sinn Fein conference votes to end abstention from Dail.
15 November	200,000 unionists protest against Anglo-Irish Agreement at Belfast rally.

1987: Killed 93; injured 1129

19 February	General Election leads to Fianna Fail minority government.
25 April	Lord Justice Gibson and his wife killed by IRA bomb.
8 May	8 IRA men shot dead during attack on Loughgall RUC station.
11 June	Conservatives win UK General Election. Enoch Powell, OUP, loses South Down to SDLP.
2 July	Unionist Task Force report calls for opening of discussions with government.
1 November	150 tonnes of arms and ammunition seized on the *Eksund* at Brest.
8 November	11 killed, 63 injured by IRA bomb at Remembrance Day ceremony in Enniskillen.
22 December	UDA Deputy Leader John McMichael killed by IRA bomb.

1988: Killed 59; injured 581 (to end August)

25 January	Attorney General Sir Patrick Mayhew announces there will be no prosecutions arising from the Stalker/Sampson inquiry.
6 March	3 IRA members on 'active service' shot dead in Gibraltar.
16 March	3 mourners killed during attack on funerals of 'Gibraltar bombers'.

19 March	2 soldiers beaten by a mob and killed by IRA during the funeral procession of one of those killed earlier in the week.
15 May	3 Catholics killed in a UVF machine-gun attack on the Avenue Bar in central Belfast.
15 June	6 off-duty soldiers killed in Lisburn by IRA bomb after charity fun-run.
28 June	IRA bomb causes injuries in school bus carrying Catholic and Protestant children.
23 July	IRA bomb kills three people by mistake when attempting to murder a judge.
5 August	Archbishop Robin Eames criticizes Lambeth Conference motion in favour of 'armed struggle'. New motion on Ulster carried. (Eames also rumoured to be negotiator between constitutional parties.)
20 August	8 off-duty soldiers killed and 28 injured when their bus is blown up by IRA bomb.
30 August	IRA 'active service unit' of 3 killed by army. IRA booby trap kills two Catholics in Londonderry, raising number of 'mistaken killings' by IRA to 20 since Eniskillen bombing of 8 November 1987.
4 September	At Anglo-Irish Conference, the Republic's government asks for *less* emphasis on security and more on political change.
5 September	End of talks between SDLP and Sinn Fein.
21 September	GB Labour Party urges All-Ireland economic institutions and harmonized social security as prelude to unity.
19–20 October	Home Secretary announces ban on direct broadcasts by terrorist spokesmen, and curtailment of right to silence in court. (Similar measures already in force in Republic.)

Bibliography

Adamson, Ian, *Cruthin: the Ancient Kindred*. Donard Publishing Co., Bangor, 1974.
Akenson, Donald Harman, *Education and Enmity*. David and Charles, Newton Abbot, 1973.
Alcock, A. E., *Minutes of Evidence to the Committee on the Government of the Northern Ireland Assembly*, vol. III, pp. 161–4, 1986.
Arthur, Paul, *The People's Democracy*. Blackstaff Press, Belfast, 1974.
Arthur, Paul, *Government and Politics of Northern Ireland*. Longman, London, 1980.
Arthur, Paul, 'Independence', in *Political Co-operation in Divided Societies*, ed. Desmond Rea, Gill and Macmillan, Dublin, 1982.
Arthur, Paul and Jeffery, Keith, *Northern Ireland since 1968*. Basil Blackwell, Oxford, 1988.
Barritt, Denis P. and Carter, Charles F., *The Northern Ireland Problem*. Oxford University Press, Oxford, 1962.
Beckett, J. C., *The Making of Modern Ireland, 1603–1923*. Faber and Faber, London, 1966.
Beckett, J. C., *The Anglo-Irish Tradition*. Blackstaff Press, Belfast, 1983.
Bew, Paul, *C. S. Parnell*. Gill and Macmillan, Dublin, 1980.
Bew, Paul and Patterson, Henry, *The British State and the Ulster Crisis*. Verso, London, 1985.
Biggs-Davison, John and Chowdharry-Best, George, *The Cross of St. Patrick*. The Kensal Press, Bucks, 1984.
Biggs-Davison, John and Macrory, Patrick, *Britain's Undefended Frontier: A Policy for Ulster*, European Security Studies, no. 2, 1984.
Birrell, W.D. 'The Stormont relationship', *Parliamentary Affairs*, XXVI (1972–73), 471–91.
Birrell, Derek and Murie, Alan (eds), 'Housing policy in Northern Ireland', *Community Forum*, no. 2, 1972.
Bishop, Patrick and Mallie, Eamonn, *The Provisional IRA*. Heinemann, London, 1987.
Black, R. D. C., *Economic Thought and the Irish Question*, Cambridge University Press, Cambridge, 1960.
Boal, Fred and Livingstone, David, 'Protestants in Belfast: a view from the outside', *Contemporary Review*, 248, no. 1443 (April 1986), 169–75.
Boal, Frederick W., and Douglas, J. N. H. (eds), *Integration and Division*. Academic Press, London, 1982.
Bogdanor, Vernon, *Devolution*. Oxford University Press, Oxford, 1979.
Boulding, K. E., 'National images and national self-determination', in *International Politics and Foreign Policy*, ed. J.N. Rosenau. The Free Press, New York, 1969, pp. 422–3.
Bowman, John, *De Valera and the Ulster Question, 1917–1973*, Oxford University Press, Oxford, 1982.
Boyce, D. G., *Englishmen and the Irish Troubles*. Jonathan Cape, London, 1972.
Boyce, D. G., *Nationalism in Northern Ireland*. Croom Helm, London, 1982.
Boyce, D. G. (ed.), *The Revolution in Ireland, 1879–1923*. Macmillan, London, 1988.

Boyle, Kevin and Hadden, Tom, *Ireland: a Positive Proposal*. Penguin, London, 1985.

Bradley, J., Fitzgerald, J. and Storey, R.A., *Medium Term Review 1987–1992*. The Economic and Social Research Institute, no. 2, Dublin, 1987.

Bradley, J. F., Hewitt, V.N. and Jefferson, C.W., *Industrial Location Policy and Equality of Opportunity in Assisted Employment in Northern Ireland 1949–81*. Research Paper 10, Fair Employment Agency, Belfast, 1986.

Brett, C. E. B., *Housing in a Divided Community*. Institute of Public Administration, Dublin, 1986.

Brinton, Crane, *The Anatomy of Revolution*. Vintage Books, New York, 1965.

Bristow, John, 'All-Ireland Perspectives', in *Political Co-operation in Divided Societies*, ed Desmond Rea, Gill and Macmillan, Dublin, 1982.

Brooke, Peter, *Ulster Presbyterianism*. Gill and Macmillan, Dublin, 1987.

Brown, Terence, *Ireland: a Social and Cultural History 1922–79*. Fontana, London, 1981.

Browne, Noel, *Against the Tide*. Gill and Macmillan, Dublin, 1986.

Bruce, S., *God Save Ulster*. Oxford University Press, Oxford, 1986.

Buchanan, J., 'Federalism and fiscal equity', *American Economic Review*, vol. xl, no. 4 (September 1950), pp. 582–99.

Buchanan, Ronald H., 'The Planter and the Gael: cultural dimensions of the Northern Ireland problem', in *Integration and Division*, eds Frederick W. Boal and J. Neville Douglas. Academic Press, London, 1982.

Buckland, Patrick, *Irish Unionism 1885–1923*. HMSO Belfast, 1973.

Buckland, Patrick, *The Factory of Grievances, Devolved Government in Northern Ireland, 1921–1939*. Gill and Macmillan, Dublin, 1979.

Buckland, Patrick, *James Craig*. Gill and Macmillan, Dublin, 1980.

Buckland, Patrick, A History of Northern Ireland. Gill and Macmillan, Dublin, 1981.

Butler, D. and Kavanagh, D., *The British General Election of 1979*. Macmillan, London, 1979.

Butler, D. and Kavanagh, D., *The British General Election of 1983*. Macmillan, London, 1984.

Byrne, Francis J. 'Early Irish society', in *The Course of Irish History*, ed. T. W. Moody and F. X. Martin. Mercier, Cork, 1967.

Cairncross, Frances, 'Republic of Ireland', *Economist*, Survey 16, January 1988.

Callaghan, James, *A House Divided*. Collins, London, 1973.

Carter, Charles, *Two Years of Peace, Stability and Reconciliation?* Policy Studies Institute, London, 1987.

Chambers, Gerald, *Equality and Inequality in Northern Ireland*. Part 2: The Workplace. Policy Studies Institute, London, 1987.

Clarkson, L.A. 'Population change and urbanisation', in *An Economic History of Ulster, 1820–1914*, ed. Liam Kennedy and Philip Ollerenshaw. Manchester University Press, Manchester, 1985.

Clifford, Brendan, *Parliamentary Sovereignty and Northern Ireland*. Athol Books, Belfast, 1985.

Clifford, Brendan, *Government without Opposition*. Athol Books, Belfast, 1986.

Cole, John, 'Security Constraints', in *The Constitution of Northern Ireland*, ed. David Watts. Heinemann, London, 1981.

Compton, Paul A., *Northern Ireland: a Census Atlas*. Gill and Macmillan, Dublin, 1978.

Compton, Paul, 'The demographic background', in *The Constitution of Northern Ireland*, ed. D. Watt. Heinemann, London, 1981.

Compton, Paul A. (ed.), *The Contemporary Population of Northern Ireland and Population-related Issues*. Institute of Irish Studies, The Queen's University, Belfast, 1981.

Compton, Paul A., 'An evaluation of the changing religious composition of the population of Northern Ireland', in *The Economic and Social Review*, 16, no. 3 (April 1985), 201–21.

Compton, Paul, Cormack, Bob and Osborne, Bob, 'Discrimination Research "flawed"', *Fortnight*, January 1988.

Compton, Paul A., Coward, John and Wilson-Davis, Keith, 'Family size and religious denomination in Northern Ireland', *Journal of Biosocial Science*, 17 (1985), pp. 137–45.

312   *Bibliography*

Connell, Kenneth H., *The Population of Ireland, 1750–1845*. Oxford University Press, Oxford, 1950.

Coogan, Tim Pat, *The IRA*. Fontana, London, 1980 (sixth expanded impression).

Coogan, Tim Pat, *Disillusioned Decades, Ireland 1966–87*. Gill and Macmillan, Dublin, 1987.

Corish, Patrick J. *The Catholic Community*. Helicon, Dublin, 1981.

Cormack, R.J. and Osborne, R.D. (eds), *Religion, Education and Employment*. Appletree Press, Belfast, 1983.

Cox, W. Harvey, 'Public opinion and the Anglo-Irish Agreement', *Government and Opposition*, Summer 1987.

Cronin, Sean, *Washington's Irish Policy 1916–86*. Anvil, Dublin, 1987.

Cullen, L. M., *The Emergence of Modern Ireland 1600–1900*. Gill and Macmillan, Dublin, 1981.

Cullen, L. M., 'Economic development 1750–1800', in *A New History of Ireland*, vol. iv, ed T. W. Moody and W. E. Vaughan. Oxford, 1986.

Curran, Frank, *Derry – Countdown to Disaster*. Gill and Macmillan, Dublin, 1986.

Curtis, Edmund, *A History of Ireland*. Methuen, London, 1961.

Darby, John (ed.), *Northern Ireland: the Background to the Conflict*. Appletree Press, Belfast, 1983.

Deutsch, Richard and Magowan, Vivien, *Northern Ireland 1968–73: A Chronology of Events*, 3 vols. Blackstaff Press, Belfast, 1973, 1974, 1975.

Devine, T. M. *The Great Highland Famine*. John Donald, Edinburgh, 1988.

Devlin, Bernadette, *The Price of My Soul*. Pan, London, 1969.

Dewar, Michael, *The British Army in Northern Ireland*. Arms and Armour Press, London, 1985.

Dillon, Martin and Lehane, Denis, *Political Murder in Northern Ireland*. Penguin, London, 1973.

Edwards, Owen Dudley, *The Sins of Our Fathers*, Gill and Macmillan, Dublin, 1970.

EEC, *Mechanisms for Fiscal Equalisation in an Integrating European Community*. Brussels, EEC, 1977.

Elliott, S., *Northern Ireland: the First Election to the European Parliament*. The Queen's University, Belfast, 1980.

Elliott, S., *Northern Ireland: the Second Election to the European Parliament*. The Queen's University, Belfast, 1985.

Elliott, S. and Smith, F. J., *Northern Ireland: the District Council Elections of 1981*. The Queen's University, Belfast, 1982.

Elliott, S. and Smith, F. J., *Northern Ireland: the District Council Elections of 1985*. The Queen's University, Belfast, 1987.

Elliott, S. and Wilford, R., *The 1982 Northern Ireland Assembly Election*. Centre for the Study of Public Policy, University of Strathclyde, 1983.

Evans, Estyn E., *The Irishness of the Irish*. Irish Association for Cultural, Economic and Social Relations, Belfast, 1967.

Farrell, Michael, *Northern Ireland: the Orange State*. Pluto Press, London, 1976.

Farrell, Michael, *The Apparatus of Repression*. Field Day Pamphlet no. 11, Derry, 1986.

Faulkner, Brian, *Memoirs of a Statesman*. Weidenfeld and Nicolson, London, 1978.

Fine Gael, *Ireland – Our Future Together*. Fine Gael, Dublin, 1979.

Fisk, R., *The Point of No Return: the Strike which Broke the British in Ulster*. Deutsch, London, 1975.

Fisk, Robert, *In Time of War*. Deutsch, London, 1983.

Fitzgerald, Garret, *Towards a New Ireland*. Gill and Macmillan, Dublin, 1972.

Fitzgerald, John D., *The National Debt and Economic Policy in the Medium Term*. The Economic and Social Research Institute, Dublin, 1986.

Flackes, W. D., *Northern Ireland: a Political Directory, 1968–79*. Gill and Macmillan, Dublin, 1980.

Flannery, Austin, U. P., *Vatican Council II*, Dominican Publications, Dublin, 1981.
Gallagher, Eric, 'The faith and its forms in times of strife', in *Northern Ireland: Living with the Crisis*, ed. Alan J. Ward. Aldwych Press, London, 1982.
Gallagher, Eric and Worrall, Stanley, *Christians in Ulster 1968–80*. Oxford University Press, Oxford, 1982.
Gallagher, Michael, *Political Parties in the Republic of Ireland*. Gill and Macmillan, Dublin, 1985.
Gamblin, G., *The Town in Ulster*. Mullan, Belfast, 1951.
Garvin, Tom, *Nationalist Revolutionaries in Ireland, 1858–1928*. Oxford University Press, Oxford, 1986.
Gibson, Norman J. (ed.), *Economic and Social Implications of the Political Alternatives that may be open to Northern Ireland*. New University of Ulster, Coleraine, 1974.
Gibson, Norman, 'Political and economic integration', in *Political Co-operation in Divided Societies*, ed Desmond Rea, Gill and Macmillan, Dublin, 1982.
Gibson, N. J. 'The impact of the Northern Ireland crisis on the economy', in *Northern Ireland: Living with the Crisis*, ed. Alan J. Ward. Aldwych Press, London, 1982.
Graham, Edgar, *Ireland and Extradition*. European Human Rights Unit. Belfast, 1982.
Gray, John, *City in Revolt*. Blackstaff Press, Belfast, 1985.
Green, A. J., *Devolution and Public Finance: Stormont from 1921 to 1972*. Studies in Public Finance, no. 48, University of Strathclyde, Glasgow, 1979.
Green, E. R. R., 'The Great Famine', in *The Course of Irish History*, ed. T. W. Moody and F. X. Martin, The Mercia Press, Cork, 1967.
Greer, D. S., 'The impact of the Troubles on the Law and Legal System of Northern Ireland', in *Northern Ireland Living with the Crisis*, ed. by Alan J. Ward. Aldwych Press, London, 1987.
Hamill, Desmond, *Pig in the Middle*. Methuen, London, 1985.
Hamilton, Alexander, Madison, James and Kay, John, *The Federalist*, ed. Max Beloff. Oxford University Press, 1948.
Harbison, J., 'The children of Northern Ireland', *New Society*, 17 April 1980.
Harbison, J. and Harbison, J., *A Society under Stress*. Open Books, London, 1980.
Harkness, David, *Northern Ireland since 1980*. Helicon Press, Dublin, 1983.
Hepburn, A. C., *The Conflict of Nationality in Modern Ireland*. Arnold, London, 1980.
Heslinga, M. W., *The Irish Border as a Cultural Divide*. Van Goram NV, Assen, 1962.
Hewitt, Christopher, 'Catholic grievances, Catholic nationalism and violence during the civil rights period: a reconsideration', *British Journal of Sociology*, 3, no. 3 (1981), 362–80.
Hewitt, John, *The Selected John Hewitt*, ed. Alan Warner. Blackstaff Press, Belfast, 1981, reprinted 1986.
Hezlet, A., *The B-Specials*. Pan, London, 1972.
Hickey, John, *Religion and the Northern Ireland Problem*. Gill and Macmillan, Dublin, 1984.
Horgan, John H., *Parnell to Pearse*. Browne and Nolan, Dublin, 1948.
Hunter, John, 'An analysis of conflict in Northern Ireland', in *Political Co-operation in Divided Societies*, ed. Desmond Rea, Gill and Macmillan, Dublin, 1982.
Hutchinson, Robert, and Shehan, John, 'Ireland: economic problems and policy issues', *Economic Review*, Dublin, March 1985.
Hyde, H. Montgomery, *Carson*. Heinemann, London, 1953.
Insight Team, Sunday Times, *Ulster*. Penguin, London, 1972.
Inter-Church Group on Faith and Politics, *Choose Life*. Belfast, 1986.
Inter-Church Group on Faith and Politics, *Towards an Island that Works*. Belfast and Dublin, 1987.
Irish Episcopal Conference, *Directory on Mixed Marriages*. Veritas, Dublin, 1983.
Isles, K. S., and Cuthbert, N., *An Economic Survey of Northern Ireland*. HMSO, Belfast, 1957.
Jenkins, Roy, *Asquith*. Collins, London, 1964.
Johnston, Edith Mary, *Ireland in the Eighteenth Century*. Gill and Macmillan, Dublin, 1974.

Joint Group on Social Questions, *Violence in Ireland*, A Report to the Churches, Christian Journal, Belfast and Veritas Publications, Dublin, 1976, revised edition, 1977.

Kee, R., *Ireland: a History*. Weidenfeld and Nicolson, London, 1980.

Kendle, John, 'The Round Table Movement and "Home Rule All Round"', *Historical Journal*, (1968) vol. xi, no. 2, pp. 332–353.

Kennedy, Henry, *How Stormont Fell*. Gill and Macmillan, Dublin, 1972.

Kennedy, Kieran A. (ed.), *Ireland in Transition*. Mercier Press, Cork and London, 1986.

Kennedy, Kieran A., Giblin, Thomas and Waugh, Deirdre (eds), *The Economic Development of Ireland in the Twentieth Century*. Routledge, London, 1988.

Kennedy, Liam and Ollerenshaw, Philip (eds), *An Economic History of Ulster, 1820–1939*. Manchester University Press, Manchester, 1985.

Kennedy, Liam, 'The rural economy, 1820–1914' in *An Economic History of Ulster, 1820–1939*, ed. Liam Kennedy and Philip Ollerenshaw. Manchester University Press, Manchester, 1985.

Kennedy, Liam, *Two Ulsters: a Case for Repartition*. Queen's University, Belfast, 1986.

Kenny, Anthony, *The Road to Hillsborough*. Pergamon Press, Oxford, 1986.

Kilbrandon, Lord (Chairman), *Northern Ireland: Report of an Independent Inquiry*, November 1984.

Kirkpatrick, R. W., 'Origins and development of the land war in mid-Ulster 1879–85', in *Ireland under the Union*, ed. F. S. L. Lyons and B. A. J. Hawkins. Oxford University Press, Oxford, 1980.

Lawrence, R. J., *The Government of Northern Ireland*. Oxford University Press, Oxford, 1965.

Lee, Joseph, *The Modernisation of Irish Society, 1848–1918*. Gill and Macmillan, Dublin, 1973.

Lemass, Sean, *One Nation*. Fianna Fail, Dublin, 1959.

Levi, Peter, *The Flutes of Autumn*. Arrow Books, London, 1983.

Leyburn, James E., *The Scotch-Irish*. University of California Press, 1962.

Longford, Earl of, and O'Neill, Thomas P., *Eamon de Valera*. Hutchison, London, 1970.

Loughlin, James, *Gladstone, Home Rule and the Ulster Question*. Gill and Macmillan, Dublin, 1986.

Lowry, Rt Hon. Lord Justice, *Civil Proceedings in a Beleaguered Society*. The Child & Co. Lecture. Inns of Court School of Law, London, 1987.

Lyons, F. S. L., *Culture and Anarchy in Ireland, 1890–1939*. Oxford University Press, Oxford, 1982.

Lyons, F. S. L., *Ireland since the Famine*. Fontana, London, 1973.

McAllister, Ian and Rose, Richard, 'Can political conflict be resolved by social change?: Northern Ireland as a test case', *Journal of Conflict Resolution*, vol. 27, no. 3 (September 1983), pp. 533–57.

McCardle, Dorothy, *The Irish Republic*. Transworld Publishers, London, 1968.

McCarthy, Charles and Bleese, William J., 'Cross-border industrial co-operation: instincts and possibilities', *Administration*, vol. 26, no. 3 (1978).

McCracken, J. L. 'The social structure and social life 1714–60', in *A New History of Ireland*, vol. iv, ed. T. W. Moody and W. E. Vaughan. Oxford University Press, Oxford, 1986.

McCrudden, C., 'The experience of the legal enforcement of the Fair Employment (Northern Ireland) Act', in *Religion, Education and Employment*, ed. R. J. Cormack and R. D. Osborne. Appletree Press, Belfast, 1983.

MacCurtain, Margaret, *Tudor and Stuart Ireland*. Gill and Macmillan, Dublin, 1972.

McDowell, R. B., *Public Opinion and Government Policy in Ireland 1801–1846*. Faber and Faber, London, 1952.

McDowell, R. B. 'The Age of the United Ireishmen – Revolution and the Union, 1794–1800', in *A New History of Ireland*, vol. iv, ed. T. W. Moody and W. E. Vaughan. Oxford University Press, Oxford, 1986.

MacGriel, Father Michael, *Prejudice and Tolerance in Ireland*. Economic and Social Research Institute, Dublin, 1972.

McGrory, Patrick J., *Law and the Constitution: Present Discontents*. Field Day Pamphlet no. 12, Derry, 1986.

Mackintosh, John P., *The Devolution of Power*. Pelican, London, 1968.

MacManus, Francis, *The Years of the Great Test 1926–39*. Mercier, Dublin, 1978.

McMichael, John, *Common Sense*, Ulster Defence Association, 1987.

Macrory, Patrick, *The Siege of Derry*. Hodder and Stoughton, London, 1980.

Magnus, Philip, *Gladstone*. Murray, London, 1954.

Mansergh, Nicholas, *The Government of Northern Ireland*. Allen and Unwin, London, 1936.

Miller, David W., *Church, State and Nation in Ireland 1898–1921*. University of Pittsburgh Press, Pittsburgh, 1973.

Miller, David W., *Queen's Rebels*. Gill and Macmillan, Dublin, 1978.

Moloney, Ed and Pollak, Andy, *Paisley*. Poolbeg Press, Dublin, 1986.

Moody, T. W., *The Ulster Question 1603–1973*. Mercier Press, Dublin, 1974.

Moody, T. W. and Beckett, J. C. (eds). *Ulster since 1800*, 2nd series. British Broadcasting Corporation, London, 1957.

Moody, T. W. and Martin, F. X. (eds), *The Course of Irish History*. Mercier Press, Cork, 1967.

Moxon-Browne, E., *Nation, Class and Creed in Northern Ireland*. Gower, London, 1983.

Mulloy, Eanna, *Dynasties of Coercion*. Field Day Pamphlet no. 10, Derry, 1986.

Murphy, Dervla, *A Place Apart*. Penguin, London, 1978.

Murphy, John A., *Ireland in the Twentieth Century*. Gill and Macmillan, Dublin, 1975.

Murphy, Richard, 'Faction in the Conservative Party and the Home Rule crisis, 1912–14', *History*, 71, no. 232, 1986, pp. 222–32.

Murphy, Richard, 'Walter Long and the making of the Government of Ireland Act 1919–20', *Irish Historical Studies*, XXV, no. 97 (May 1986).

Musgrave, R., 'Approaches to a fiscal theory of political federalism', in *Public Finances, Needs, Sources and Utilisation*. National Bureau of Economic Research, Princeton, NJ, 1961, reprinted in *The Economics of Federalism*, ed. G. Grewal, T. Brennan and R. Mathews, Australian National University, Canberra, 1980.

Neary, P., 'The failure of economic nationalism', in *Ireland: Dependence and Independence*. Crane Bag, Dublin, 1984.

Neeson, Eoin, *The Civil War in Ireland, 1922–23*. Mercier Press, Cork, 1969.

Newark, F. H., 'The law and the constitution', in *Ulster under Home Rule*, ed. T. Wilson, Oxford University Press, Oxford, 1955.

Northern Ireland Consensus Group, *Comments on the Anglo-Irish Agreement*. Belfast, 1985.

Oates, W. E., *Fiscal Federalism*. Harcourt Brace Jovanovich Inc., New York, 1972.

O'Brien, Conor Cruise, *States of Ireland*. Hutchinson, London, 1972.

O'Brien, Conor Cruise, *Neighbours*, The Ewart-Biggs Memorial Lectures. Faber, London, 1980.

O'Clery, Conor, *Phrases Make History Here*. O'Brien Press, Dublin, 1987.

Official Unionist Party and Democratic Unionist Party, *Unionism: A Policy for all the People*. Belfast, 1987.

O'Fiach, T., Address delivered at St John's Monastery, Hamburg, West Germany, 14 September 1987.

O'Grada, Cormac, 'Malthus and the pre-famine economy', in *Economists and the Irish Economy*, ed. Antoin E. Murphy, Irish Academic Press, Dublin, 1984.

O'Halloran, Clare, *Partition and the Limits of Irish Nationalism*. Gill and Macmillan, Dublin, 1987.

Oliver, J. A., 'Ulster to-day and to-morrow', *Political and Economic Planning*, vol. XLIV, Broadsheet 574, London, 1978.

Oliver, John A., 'The evolution of constitutional policy in Northern Ireland over the past fifteen years', in *Political Co-operation in Divided Societies*, ed. Desmond Rea. Gill and Macmillan, Dublin, 1982.

O'Malley, Padraig, *The Uncivil Wars: Ireland Today*. Blackstaff Press, Belfast, 1983.

O'Neill, Terence, *The Autobiography of Terence O'Neill*. Hart-Davis, London, 1972.

O'Rahilly, Thomas F., *Early Irish History and Mythology*. Dublin Institute for Advanced Studies, 1946.

Osborne, R. D. and Cormack, R. J., *Religion, Education and Employment*. The Appletree Press, Belfast, 1983.

Osborne, R. D., Cormack, R. J. and Miller, R. L. (eds), *Education Policy in Northern Ireland*. Policy Research Institute, The Queen's University, Belfast and the University of Ulster, 1987.

O'Tuathaig, G., *Ireland before the Famine 1798–1848*. Gill and Macmillan, Dublin, 1972.

Pakenham, Frank, *Peace by Ordeal*. Jonathan Cape, London, 1935.

Pakenham, Thomas, *The Year of Liberty*. Panther, London, 1972.

Paor, Liam de, *Divided Ulster*. Penguin, London, 1970.

Pearse, Padraic, *Political Writings and Speeches*. Talbot Press, Dublin, 1952.

Pliatsky, Leo, *Getting and Spending*. Basil Blackwell, Oxford, 1982.

Prais, S. J. 'Vocational qualifications of the labour force in Britain and Germany', *National Institute Economic Review*, 1981.

Presbyterian Church in Ireland, *The Northern Ireland Situation*, Church Statements, 1968–85, Belfast, 1985.

Quekett, A. S. *The Constitution of Northern Ireland*, 3 vols. HMSO, Belfast, 1928, 1933, 1946.

Rea, Desmond (ed.), *Political Co-operation in Divided Societies*. Gill and Macmillan, Dublin, 1982.

Rees, Merlyn, *Northern Ireland: a Personal Perspective*. Methuen, London, 1985.

Robinson, Mary T. W., *The Special Criminal Court*, Dublin University Press, Dublin, 1974.

Rose, Richard, *Governing without Consensus: an Irish Perspective*. Faber and Faber, 1971.

Rose, Richard, *Northern Ireland: Time of Choice*. American Enterprise Institute, Washington, DC, 1976.

Rose, Richard, *Is the United Kingdom a State? Northern Ireland as a Test Case*. Centre for the Study of Public Policy, University of Strathclyde, Glasgow, 1983.

Rose, Richard, 'Northern Ireland: the irreducible conflict', in *Conflict and Peace-making in Multi-ethnic Societies*, ed. J. V. Montville and H. Binnerdijk. Foreign Service Institute, Washington, DC, 1988.

Rose, Richard and Garvin, Tom, 'The public policy effects of independence: Ireland as a test case', *European Journal of Political Research*, vol. II (1983), pp. 377–97.

Rose, Richard, McAlister, Ian and Mair, Peter, *Is there a Concurring Majority about Northern Ireland?* University of Strathclyde, Glasgow, 1978.

Ryan, Monsignor Arthur H., *Mirroring Christ's Splendour*. Four Courts Press, Dublin, 1986.

Scottish Council for Development and Industry, *Report on the Scottish Economy*. Edinburgh, 1963.

Shea, Patrick, *Voices and the Sound of Drums*. Blackstaff Press, Belfast, 1981.

Shearman, Hugh, *Not an Inch*. Faber and Faber, London, 1943.

Sheehy, Michael, *Divided we Stand*. Faber and Faber, London, 1960.

Simpson, J. V., 'The finances of the public sector in Northern Ireland', *Journal of the Statistical Society of Ireland*, Dublin, 1980–1.

Simpson, J. V., 'Northern Ireland: the financing of devolution', in *Fiscal Decentralisation*, ed. T. Wilson. Anglo-German Foundation, London, 1984.

Simpson, John, 'Economic development: cause or effect in the Northern Ireland conflict', in Darby, John, *Northern Ireland, the Background to the Conflict*. Appletree Press, Belfast.

Singleton, Dale, 'Housing allocation policy in Northern Ireland', *Housing Review*, 34, no. 1 (Jan.–Feb. 1985).

Smith, Adam, *The Wealth of Nations*. Glasgow edn of the Works of Adam Smith, Oxford University Press, Oxford, 1976, vol. 2.

Smith, David J., *Equality and Inequality in Northern Ireland*. Part 1: *Employment and Unemployment*. Policy Studies Institute, London, 1987.

Smith, David J. and Chambers, Gerry., 'Positions, perceptions and practice', *Fortnight*, Belfast, December 1987.

Smith, Stephen, *Britain's Hidden Economy*. Oxford University Press, Oxford, 1986.

Smyth, Clifford, *Ian Paisley*. Scottish Academic Press, Edinburgh, 1987.

Social Democratic Labour Party (SDLP), *Towards a New Ireland*. Belfast, SDLP, 1972.

Stalker, John, *Stalker*. Harrap, London, 1988.

Stewart, A. T. Q., *The Narrow Ground*. Faber and Faber, London, 1966.

Stewart, A. T. Q., *The Ulster Crisis*. Faber and Faber, London, 1967.

Stewart, A. T. Q., *Edward Carson*. Gill and Macmillan, Dublin, 1981.

Tocqueville, Alexis de, *L'Ancien Régime*. Fontana, London, 1966.

Townshend, Charles, *The British Campaign in Ireland 1919–1921*. Oxford University Press, Oxford, 1975.

Ulster Unionist Council, *The Way Forward*. Belfast, 1984.

Ulster Workers' Council, Strike Bulletins of the Workers Association, 1974.

Unionist Party, *Ulster Must Say No*. Belfast, 1986.

Utley, T. E., *Lessons of Ulster*. Dent, London, 1975.

Vincent, John, *Gladstone and Ireland*. British Academy (Raleigh Lecture), London, 1977.

Wallis, Roy, Bruce, Steve and Taylor, David, *'No Surrender'. Paisleyism and the Politics of Ethnic Identity in Northern Ireland*. The Queen's University, Belfast, 1986.

Walsh, Brendan M., *Why is Unemployment so high in Ireland Today?* Centre for Economic Research, University College, Dublin, 1987.

Watts, David (ed.), *The Constitution of Northern Ireland*. Heinemann, London, 1981.

Wheare, Kenneth C., *Federal Government*. Oxford University Press, Oxford, 1964.

Whitaker, T. K., 'Ireland – land of change'. Presidential Address to the Royal Irish Academy, Dublin, 15 December 1986.

White, Barry, *John Hume*. Blackstaff Press, Belfast, 1984.

Whyte, J. H., *Church and State in Modern Ireland, 1923–79*, second edition, Gill and Macmillan, Dublin, 1980.

Whyte, John, 'Church, state and society 1950–70', in *Ireland 1945–70*, ed. J. J. Lee, Gill and Macmillan, Dublin, 1979.

Whyte, John, 'How much discrimination was there under the Unionist regime?', in *Contemporary Irish Studies*, ed. Tom Gallagher and James O'Connell. Manchester University Press, Manchester, 1983.

Wiener, Ron, *The Rape and Plunder of the Shankill*, 2nd edn. Farset Co-operative Press, Belfast, 1980.

Wilson, Dorothy J. and Wilson, Thomas, *The Political Economy of the Welfare State*, Allen and Unwin, London, 1982.

Wilson, Thomas (ed.), *Ulster under Home Rule*. Oxford University Press, Oxford, 1955.

Wilson, Thomas, *Planning and Growth*. Macmillan, London, 1964.

Wilson, Thomas, 'Ulster and Eire', *Political Quarterly*, July 1939, reprinted in W. A. Robson, ed. *Political Quarterly in the 1930s*, Allen Lane, The Penguin Press, London, 1971.

Wilson, Thomas, 'The Ulster Crisis', *The Round Table*, January 1972.

Wilson, Thomas, 'Regional Government', Written Evidence 6: Northern Ireland, *Report of the Royal Commission on the Constitution 1969–73*. Cmnd 5460, HMSO London, 1973.

Wilson, Thomas, 'Devolution and public finance', *Three Banks Review*, December 1976.

Wilson, Thomas (ed.), *Fiscal Decentralisation*. Anglo-German Foundation, London, 1984.

Wright, Frank, *Northern Ireland Comparative Analysis*. Gill and Macmillan, Dublin, 1987.

Wright, Frank, 'Protestant ideology and politics in Ulster', *European Journal of Sociology*, XIV (1973), 213–80.

Younger, C., *Ireland's Civil War*. Fontana, London, 1970.

OFFICIAL PAPERS

Northern Ireland

An Economic Survey of Northern Ireland (Isles and Cuthbert Report), HMSO Belfast, 1957.

The Belfast Regional Survey and Plan. Cmd 451, HMSO Belfast, 1963.

Economic Development in Northern Ireland. Cmd 479, HMSO Belfast, 1964.

Higher Education in Northern Ireland (Lockwood Report). HMSO Belfast, 1965.

Report of the Committee of Inquiry into Bank Interest Rates. Cmd 499, HMSO Belfast, 1966.

Local Education Authorities and Voluntary Schools. Cmd 513, HMSO Belfast,

Disturbances in Northern Ireland (Cameron Report). Cmd 532, HMSO Belfast, 1969.

Violence and Civil Disturbances in Northern Ireland in 1969 (Scarman Report). Cmd 566, HMSO Belfast, 1969.

Report of the Advisory Committee on Police in Northern Ireland (Hunt Report). Cmd 535, HMSO Belfast, 1969.

Public Education Northern Ireland. HMSO Belfast, 1970.

Development Programme, 1970–75. HMSO Belfast, 1970.

Report of the Review Body on Local Government in Northern Ireland, 1970 (Macrory Report). Cmd 546, HMSO Belfast, 1970.

A Record of Constructive Change. Cmd 558, HMSO Belfast, 1971.

The Future Development of the Parliament and Government of Northern Ireland: a Consultative Document. Cmd 560, HMSO Belfast, 1971.

Review of Economic and Social Development in Northern Ireland. Cmd 564, HMSO Belfast, 1971.

Regional Physical Development Strategy 1975–79. HMSO Belfast, 1975.

Economic and Industrial Strategy for Northern Ireland. Report by Review Team (Quigley Report). HMSO Belfast, 1976.

The Future Structure of Teacher Education in Northern Ireland (Chilver Report). HMSO Belfast, 1980.

Report of an Investigation by the Fair Employment Agency for Northern Ireland into the Non-industrial Northern Ireland Civil Service. Belfast, 1983.

Northern Ireland Housing Executive, *The Belfast Experience.* Belfast, 1984.

Northern Ireland Housing Executive, *Housing Strategy Review, 1988/89–1990/91.* Belfast, 1984.

Northern Ireland Economic Development Office, *Review of Recent Developments in Housing Policy.* Belfast, 1985.

First Report of the Committee on the Government of Northern Ireland of the Northern Ireland Assembly. HMSO Belfast, 1986.

Northern Ireland Civil Service Equal Opportunities Unit. Second Report. HMSO Belfast, 1987

Department of Economic Development, *Building a Stronger Economy: the Pathfinder Process.* Belfast, 1987

Department of Finance and Personnel for Northern Ireland, *Financial Statement 1987–88.* HMSO Belfast, 1987.

Department of Economic Development, *Religious Equality of Opportunity in Employment.* Belfast 1988.

Department of Education for Northern Ireland, *Education in Northern Ireland – Proposals for Reform.* Belfast, March 1988.

Northern Ireland Economic Council, *Public Expenditure Comparisons between Northern Ireland and Great Britain.* Report 18. Belfast, January 1981.

Northern Ireland Economic Council, *Economic Strategy: Industrial Development*. Report 60. Belfast, August 1986.
Northern Ireland Economic Council, *Economic Assessment: April 1987*. Report 64. Belfast, April 1987.
Northern Ireland Economic Council, *Economic Assessment: April 1988*. Report 70. Belfast, April 1988.
Annual Reports of the Chief Constable of Northern Ireland, Belfast.
Annual Reports and Triennial Review of Police Complaints Board, HMSO Belfast.
Annual Reports of the Northern Ireland Commissioner for Complaints, Belfast.
Northern Ireland Annual Abstracts of Statistics, HMSO Belfast.
Ulster Year Book.

United Kingdom

Royal Commission on the Housing of the Working Class. C 1402, HMSO London, 1885.
Report of the Committee on Irish Finance, Cmnd 6153, HMSO London 1912.
Correspondence relating to the Proposals of His Majesty's Government for an Irish Settlement. Cmd 1502, HMSO London, 1921.
Report of the Joint Working Party on the Economy of Northern Ireland (Hall Report). Cmnd 1835, HMSO, London, 1962.
Report of the enquiry into allegations against the security forces of physical brutality in Northern Ireland arising out of events on 9th August 1971 (Compton Report). Cmnd 4823, HMSO, London, 1971.
Report of the Committee of Privy Counsellors appointed to consider authorised procedures for the interrogation of persons suspected of terrorism (Parker Report), Cmnd 4901, March 1972.
Report of the Tribunal appointed to enquire into the events on Sunday, 30th January 1972, which led to loss of life in connection with the Procession in Londonderry on that day (Widgery Report). HMSO, 1972.
Report of the Commission to consider legal procedures to deal with terrorist activities in Northern Ireland (Diplock Report). Cmnd 5185, HMSO London, 1972.
Report of the Royal Commission on the Constitution, 1969–73. Cmnd 5460, HMSO London, 1973.
The Northern Ireland Constitution. Cmnd 5675, HMSO London, 1974.
Northern Ireland: Finance and the Economy: Discussion Paper, Northern Ireland Office, HMSO London, 1974.
Report of the Committee to Consider in the Context of Civil Liberties and Human Rights Measures to Deal with Terrorism (Gardiner Report). Cmnd 5847, HMSO London, 1975.
Our Changing Democracy: Devolution to Scotland and Wales. Cmnd 6348, HMSO London, 1975.
Devolution: Financing the Devolved Services. Cmnd 6890, HMSO London, 1977.
HM Treasury, *Needs Assessment Survey*. HMSO London, 1979.
Report of the Committee of Inquiry into Police Interrogation Procedures in Northern Ireland (Bennett Report). Cmnd 7497, HMSO London, 1979.
The Government of Northern Ireland: A Working Paper for a Conference. Cmnd 7763, HMSO London, 1979.
The Government of Northern Ireland, Proposals for Further Discussion. Cmnd 7950, HMSO London, 1980.
Northern Ireland, A Framework for Devolution. Cmnd 8541, HMSO London, 1982.
Review of the operation of the Northern Ireland (Emergency Provisions) Act (Baker Report). Cmnd 9222, HMSO London, 1984.

Agreement between the Government of the United Kingdom of Great Britain and Northern Ireland and the Government of the Republic of Ireland, 15th November 1985. London.
Fair Employment in Northern Ireland. Cmnd 380, HMSO London, 1988.

Parliamentary proceedings:
  HC Debates.
  House of Lords Debates.
  HC Debates (NI).
  Senate Debates (NI).

Republic of Ireland

Handbook of the Ulster Question, Dublin 1923.
New Ireland Forum, *The Economic Consequences of the Division of Ireland since 1920.* Stationery Office, Dublin, 1983.
New Ireland Forum, *Report of Proceedings of Public Session, 21 September 1983, Dublin Castle.* Stationery Office, Dublin, 1984.
New Ireland Forum, *Report*, Presentations by Sir Charles Carter and Professor Louden Ryan. Stationery Office, Dublin, 1984.
National Income and Expenditure 1985. Central Statistics Office, Dublin, 1986.

Parliamentary proceedings:
  Dail Eireann Debates.
  Seanad Eireann Debates.

Name Index

Subject Index

Alliance Party 177, 178, 195, 270, 302
Anglo-Irish Agreement xv, 193–200, 223, 269–70, 308–9
Anglo-Irish Ascendancy xi, 16–17
Anglo-Irish Intergovernmental Council 187, 222
Anglo-Irish Trade Agreement, 1965 87

Baker Report 240
Bennett Report 239
Black and Tans 48
border *see* partition
Boyne, Battle of the 14

Catholic emancipation 20, 23
Churches
  Anglican Protestant 13, 24, 35, 207
  Catholic Church and Act of Union 20, 22
  Catholic Church and law enforcement 194, 208–9, 213–16
  Catholic relief measures 17
  Church influence in Republic 220, 227–31
  Church membership in NI 204, 207
  ecumenical movement 205–7
  and education 25, 134ff., 205–6, 214
  force and violence distinguished 212–13
  Free Presbyterians 206–7, 209
  joint action in troubles 205, 212
  a 'just rebellion' 215–16
  and Penal Laws 14–17
  and Plantation 13–14
  Presbyterian 13–14, 16, 19, 207, 211–12
  Protestant Churches and Irish unity 207–9
  Vatican II 205–6

and violence xv, 203, 210–16
  see also discrimination, alleged and real; education
Civil Rights Movement xiv, 152–6, 167–8, 287, 301–2
Civil War
  in 17th century 13
  in Irish Free State 62–3
Commissioner for Complaints 119, 130, 155, 302
Conservative Party 25–6, 32, 37, 54, 72, 177–8, 186, 274, 302, 306–7
Council of Ireland xiv, 50, 180–1, 183–4

Democratic Unionist Party 206, 209, 303, 309
detention *see* security policy
devolution
  administrative 24–5, 90
  and fiscal arrangements xiii, 77ff
  legislative xiii–iv, 64ff, 89ff, 163–4, 171–2, 176–8, 186–7, 199, 269–71
  and regional development 87ff
  with power-sharing 176–8
  see also Home Rule
'Direct Rule' xii, 90, 172, 175–7, 273–4, 304
discrimination, alleged and real
  definition of 108
  in employment xii, xiii, 73–4, 107ff
  and industrial location 98–106
  in local government employment 117–18
  in private employment 118–19
  and Protestant work-ethic 108
  in provincial civil service 115–16
  safeguards against 120–3